A Pluralist Theory of Constitutional Justice

A Pluralist Theory of Constitutional Justice

Assessing Liberal Democracy in Times of Rising Populism and Illiberalism

MICHEL ROSENFELD

University Professor of Law and Comparative Democracy and Sydney L. Robins Professor of Human Rights, Benjamin N. Cardozo School of Law, Yeshiva University

Great Clarendon Street, Oxford, OX2 6DP,
United Kingdom

Oxford University Press is a department of the University of Oxford.
It furthers the University's objective of excellence in research, scholarship,
and education by publishing worldwide. Oxford is a registered trade mark of
Oxford University Press in the UK and in certain other countries

© Michel Rosenfeld 2022

The moral rights of the author have been asserted

First Edition published in 2022

Impression: 1

All rights reserved. No part of this publication may be reproduced, stored in
a retrieval system, or transmitted, in any form or by any means, without the
prior permission in writing of Oxford University Press, or as expressly permitted
by law, by licence or under terms agreed with the appropriate reprographics
rights organization. Enquiries concerning reproduction outside the scope of the
above should be sent to the Rights Department, Oxford University Press, at the
address above

You must not circulate this work in any other form
and you must impose this same condition on any acquirer

Public sector information reproduced under Open Government Licence v3.0
(http://www.nationalarchives.gov.uk/doc/open-government-licence/open-government-licence.htm)

Published in the United States of America by Oxford University Press
198 Madison Avenue, New York, NY 10016, United States of America

British Library Cataloguing in Publication Data

Data available

Library of Congress Control Number: 2022938553

ISBN 978–0–19–886268–0

DOI: 10.1093/oso/9780198862680.001.0001

Printed and bound by
CPI Group (UK) Ltd, Croydon, CR0 4YY

Links to third party websites are provided by Oxford in good faith and
for information only. Oxford disclaims any responsibility for the materials
contained in any third party website referenced in this work.

Acknowledgments

This book is the culmination of a long process of endeavoring to integrate two separate strands of scholarship that I have pursued over many years. I had increasingly sensed that there were deeper links between my work in constitutional theory and that in philosophy. This led me to the present project that has centered on the nexus between liberal constitutionalism and distributive justice and that eventually coalesced into the writing of this book. I have benefited throughout from the insights and critical reactions of a large number of interlocutors far too numerous to thank individually. Accordingly, I only single out a handful of individuals who have had a crucial role in bringing the current project to fruition. Marinos Diamantidis of the University of London's Birkbeck School of Law organized and led a most helpful international gathering comprising several interdisciplinary scholars who addressed my project in its embryonic state while I was holding a Leverhulme visiting professorship at his institution. Susanna Mancini, my co-author in projects bearing on the present one, provided me with key insights, comments, and constructive criticisms on several portions of the manuscript. Bernhard Schlink has been an invaluable interlocutor on the main issues addressed in the book over the last couple of decades, both as a co-teacher of comparative constitutionalism and of a seminar on concepts of justice and as a friend who generously shared his profound observations on the relationship between law and justice. Finally, this book owes a great deal to my various encounters with Frank Michelman. These encounters started many years before I met Michelman when, as a law student, I read his work and drew inspiration from his magisterial weaving together of Rawls and legal science. Many years later, I had the fortune to meet and to work with Michelman and to benefit greatly from his advice and constructive critique of some of my work that now emerges as a key bridge to the main thesis advanced in this book.

I wish to thank Elena Cohen for her excellent editorial assistance as well as Kelsey Repka, Cardozo Law JD 2021, and Ameen Khdair, Cardozo Law JD 2022, for their outstanding research help.

On a personal level, I am grateful for the great encouragement and support I received from my wife, Susan, and my children, Maia and Alexis, throughout the writing of this book which for the most part took place within isolated confines in the midst of a pandemic. I also thank Alexis for translating the book's quest into the visual composition that graces its cover.

An earlier version of what is now part of Chapter 2, first appeared in work published in the *Cardozo Law Review* which I thank for its permission to have included in this book.

Contents

List of Abbreviations	xi

Introduction: Liberal Constitutional Democracy, its Illiberal
Challengers, and the Question of Distributive Justice — 1

   I Situating the Nexus between Liberal Constitutionalism and
Distributive Justice in its Historical and Theoretical Context — 4

   II Searching for Liberal Constitutionalism's Distributive Justice
Baseline: The Journey from Rawls's "Constitutional Essentials" to the
Constitution's "Justice Essentials" — 19

   III Organization of the Book — 22

PART I NEW CHALLENGES AND THREATS

1. Disembodied Law, Reinvigorated Religion, and Tribal Politics — 31

   I Imagining an Ideal of a Just Constitution and Laws for Each, All,
and their Multiple Competing Ideologies — 31

   II The Road to Alien and Disembodied Law — 40

     (a) Transnationalization and multiplication of a plurality of legal
regimes that foster layering and segmentation — 44

     (b) Fragmentation and compounding complexity through
administrative regulation, selection of applicable law by the
economically powerful, and the move from public adjudication to
private arbitration — 48

     (c) Asymmetrical uses and evasions of existing legal norms to foster
unprecedented relationships based on domination and control
of the individual's needs and objectives — 50

   III The Redeployment of Religion as a Politic Against Institutional
Secularism — 53

   IV From Adversary to Enemy: The Rise of Tribal Politics — 61

2. Local versus Global, Material Well-Being, States of Stress, and the
Erosion of Justice — 65

   I Introduction — 65

   II The Justice Essentials Confront the Divide between Redistribution
and Recognition — 67

   III The Global Economy, Exacerbation of Economic Inequalities, and the
Justice Essentials — 68

   IV The Minimum of Justice and the Contrast Between First- and
Second-Generation Constitutional Rights — 75

viii CONTENTS

    (a) Philosophy and the correlation between right and duty   75
    (b) Social and economic rights in comparative constitutional law   78
    (c) Second-generation rights versus first-generation rights and their
         respective policy-based and budgetary implications   84
  V Economic Globalization, Transnational Plurality of Legal Regimes,
     and Constitutional Redistribution under Minimum Justice   87
  VI Constitutional Democracies Confront the Stress of Global Terrorism
      and Worldwide Pandemics   89
    (a) Conditions of stress as halfway between ordinary times and times
         of crisis   90
    (b) The stress of global terrorism   94
    (c) Stress and the COVID-19 pandemic   98

PART II REVISITING AND RECONFIGURING THE PHILOSOPHICAL GROUNDING OF LIBERAL CONSTITUTIONALISM'S IDEAL OF JUSTICE

3. Confronting the Gulf between Law and Solidarity: Kelsen
   Encounters Freud   105
     I Introduction   105
    II Kelsen's Kantian Pure Theory of Law and the Minimum of Universal
      Justice According to Law   107
   III Freud's Psychoanalytic Account of the Passage from Individual
      Singularity to Group Identity   113
   IV Kelsen's Turn to Freud to Bolster his Conception of the State as Pure
      Law   122
    V The Broader Implications of the Encounter between Kelsen and
      Freud   124

4. Law *Redux*: Schmitt, CLS, and the Drift to Politics; from Posner Back
   to Marx and the Absorption of Law into Economics   129
     I Introduction   129
    II Schmitt's Secular Theology and its Politics of Division Rallying
      Friends Against Enemies   132
   III Critical Legal Studies (CLS) and Law as Indeterminate and Political
      All the Way Down   140
   IV Posner's Economic Framing of Law to Conform with the Ideology
      of Wealth Maximization   145
    V Rereading Marx on Law as a Tool in the Arsenal of a Materialist
      Political Economy   151

5. Kantian Universalism Reframed for a Post-Totalitarian Age: The
   Legacy of Rawls, Habermas, and Dworkin   160
     I Introduction   160
    II Kant's Categorical Imperative and the Severing of Justice from the
      Good   161

III	Rawls' Hypothetical Social Contract, His Two Principles of Justice, and the "Constitutional Essentials"	167
IV	Habermas' Dialogical Proceduralism, the Dynamic between System and Lifeworld, and the Call for Constitutional Patriotism	174
V	Dworkin's Substantive Political Philosophy and Liberal Egalitarian Constitutional Jurisprudence: A Path to the Justice Essentials?	185

6. Tragic Deconstruction Set Against the Impenetrable Singular and Reconstruction as Spectacle and Administration: From Derrida to Agamben   197

I	Introduction	197
II	Derrida's Deconstruction of the Nexus between Law and Justice: Confronting Irreducible Fissures in the Context of Interpretation and Ethics	199
III	The Nietzschean and Heideggerian Roots of Derrida's Radical Conception of Singularity	202
IV	Derrida's Insurmountable Gap between Law and Justice: A Pure or Merely Relative Tragedy?	210
V	Agamben's Reconstruction: Law's Split into the Glow of Divine Glory and the Minutiae of Administration	212
VI	Assessing the Coupling of Derrida's Deconstruction and Agamben's Reconstruction from the Standpoint of the Justice Essentials	219

PART III BUILDING A COMMONLY SHARED BASIS TOWARD A PLURALIST INCLUSIVIST CONSTITUTION

7. The Dialectics of Comprehensive Pluralism: Approaching the Justice Essentials from the Middle   227

I	Introduction	227
II	Comprehensive Pluralism's Negative and Positive Dialectical Moments and Their Hegelian Origins	229
III	The Normative Case for Comprehensive Pluralism	238
IV	Comprehensive Pluralism's Responses to Critics	245

8. Justice Essentials Minima and Comprehensive Pluralism's Fixed-core Minimum Set Against its Plural Maximum   249

I	The Justice Minima under Comprehensive Pluralism: Linking Justice to Identity, Autonomy, and Solidarity	249
	(a) The bare bones of pluralist justice	249
	(b) Minimal identity as mediation between inward retreat and outward lurch	254
	(c) The combined minimum of autonomy and solidarity within a just constitutional order: care and concern for insiders without demeaning the dignity of outsiders	263

X CONTENTS

II Comprehensive Pluralism's Approach to the Justice Essentials: The
Dialectic between the Fixed-core Minimum and the
Plural Maximum   271
III Challenges and Pathologies Confronting Comprehensive
Pluralism's Quest to Meet the Justice Essentials   282

Conclusion: Projecting the Nexus between Liberal Constitutionalism
and the Justice Essentials into Its Conceivable Futures   287

Bibliography   293
Index   303

List of Abbreviations

AB	Alkotmánybíróság (Hungarian Constitutional Court)
Alberta L. Rev. Soc.	Alberta Law Review Society
BGBI	Bundesgesetzblatt
BVerfG	Bundesverfassungsgericht (German Federal Constitutional Court)
BVerfGE	Entscheidungen des Bundesverfassungsgericht
CC	Corte Constitucional
CEDAW	Convention on the Elimination of All Forms of Discrimination Against Women
CJEU	Court of Justice of the European Union
CLS	Critical Legal Studies
CNN	Cable News Network
Const. Nac.	Constitución Nacional (Argentina)
ECHR	European Convention on Human Rights
ECR	European Court Report
ECtHR	European Court of Human Rights
EHRR	European Human Rights Report
EJIL	European Journal of International Law
ETA	Basque Euskadi Ta Askatasuna (Basque Homeland and Liberty)
EU	European Union
FRG	Fremdrentengesetz
GG	Grundgesetz (German Basic Law)
GU	Gazzetta Ufficiale
ICESCR	International Covenant on Economic, Social and Cultural Rights
I.CON	International Journal of International Law
IMF	International Monetary Fund
Int'l Hum. Rts. L. Rev.	International Human Rights Law Review
IRA	Irish Republican Army
ISIS	Islamic State of Iraq and Syria
LGBTQ	lesbian, gay, bisexual, trans, and queer
NGO	non-governmental organization
NPR	National Public Radio
para.	Paragraph
paras	Paragraphs
PUCL	People's Union for Civil Liberties (India)
RSC	Revised Statutes of Canada
S. Afr. Con. Sec.	South African Constitution Section
SALR	South African Law Reports
SCR	Supreme Court Reports
StGB	Strafgesetzbuch (German Penal Code)

xii LIST OF ABBREVIATIONS

TCE   Treaty Establishing a Constitution for Europe
TIAS   Treaties and Other International Acts Series
UK   United Kingdom
UN   United Nations
US   United States
USC   United States Supreme Court
WTO   World Trade Organization

Introduction

Liberal Constitutional Democracy, its Illiberal Challengers, and the Question of Distributive Justice

Liberal constitutional democracy, which traces back to the Enlightenment and to the French and American late eighteenth-century revolutions, seems to have no more than a purely peripheral intrinsic connection to justice in general, and virtually none to distributive justice. In the broadest terms, the liberal constitution that typically prevails in many contemporary democracies is principally meant to secure four essential pillars: the institution of "checks and balances" through imposition of limitations on the powers of government; adherence to the rule of law; protection of a core of fundamental rights; and assuring certain guarantees necessary for the maintenance of a working democracy (Rosenfeld 2014: 178). Of these, by requiring that everyone be equal before the law and that similar cases be treated consistently, the rule of law does impose a minimum of process-based justice. In addition, insofar as the right to equality is included among the core ones that are afforded constitutional protection, this also assures some minimum of justice which may be largely formal if constitutional equality extends only to rights and procedures without regard to manifestly widely unequal material conditions or consequences. Finally, to the extent that the constitutional guarantee of democracy secures the "one person one vote" principle,[1] it does assure a minimum of representational equality among citizens.

Beyond this minimum, several post-Second World War liberal constitutions comprise certain social and economic rights calling for the provision of some welfare benefits which plainly comport some distributive justice component (Rosenfeld 2021: 764). For example, if a constitution guarantees coverage of everyone's most basic health needs, it is most likely that would require some wealth redistribution which could be achieved through progressive taxation. Accordingly, the constitution in question would incorporate the distributive justice precept "to each according to her most basic health needs." Be that as it may, as many contemporary liberal constitutions, such as that of the United States (US), do not contain any social welfare rights, it is arguable that links between liberal constitutionalism and distributive justice may be best understood as being merely contingent.

---

[1] See, e.g., *Reynolds v. Simms*, 377 US 533 (1964) (holding that voting districts must be of roughly the same size, thus foreclosing some votes in effect counting more than others).

A Pluralist Theory of Constitutional Justice. Michel Rosenfeld, Oxford University Press. © Michel Rosenfeld 2022. DOI: 10.1093/oso/9780198862680.003.0001

2 INTRODUCTION

The impression that liberal constitutionalism is largely cut off from distributive justice concerns seems reinforced by the recently mounted critiques by illiberals, populists, and authoritarians who purport to appropriate the constitutional enterprise in order to stir it towards what they cast as better ends.[2] It is undeniable that liberal constitutional democracies—along with non-liberal and much less democratic world powers such as China—have paved the way to globalization and to its huge acceleration of disparities in wealth. Moreover, in addition to fomenting rapidly increasing material distributive imbalances, globalization coupled with liberal constitutionalism appear to be the culprits in the destabilization of equities and advantages traditionally associated with the attributes of citizenship. Indeed, within the confines of nation-state fitted liberal constitutional units, citizens used to feel treated as full equals with a strong sense of belonging, and a reassuring level of mutual solidarity. But in recent times many such citizens have felt their status eroding as a consequence of globalization's unleashing of vast migrations of capital and labor. As a result, as further specified later in this introduction, a seemingly ever-smaller cluster of persons who control disproportionally vast shares of capital have virtually monopolized the course of their country's economic and political destiny. Concurrently, the great mobility of labor leads to impoverishment of those whose jobs have been exported to locations with much lower labor costs while, at the same time, estranging the native citizens who feel culturally and ideologically threatened by the substantial influx of foreign migrant workers whom they perceive as advancing alien and seemingly hostile religious and cultural ways of life.

As against this, certain kinds of populists, such as Hungary's Viktor Orban, have proclaimed that they stand for the common people against the "cosmopolitan" elites, and have advocated rejection of the "liberal understanding of society" rooted in "ruthless capitalism and selfish individualism."[3] Orban has moreover also wholeheartedly embraced illiberalism and emphasized national pride, Christianity, and family values (Müller 2013: 28)—and with this he has mobilized his supporters not only against the "cosmopolitan" threat within Hungary but also against putative Muslim immigration from without. Orban has insisted that these positions are by no means in conflict with European democracy or constitutional rule, but only the expression of a *Kulturkampf* between his vision and that of the Western European Left (*Id.*)—a position belied in Orban's case due to his abusive use of constitutionalism, now over a decade long (Sajo 2021). Finally, authoritarians of many different stripes have sought to justify their political brand by attacking liberal constitutional democracies as unwieldy, inefficient, and in various respects unjust.[4]

---

[2] See, e.g., Viktor Orban as cited in Jan-Werner Muller, "Moscow's Trojan Horse: in Europe's ideological war, Hungary picks Putinism," *Foreign Affairs*, August 6, 2014, <https://www.foreignaffairs.com/articles/central-europe/2014-08-06/moscows-trojan-horse> viewed April 3, 2022.

[3] *Id.*

[4] See, e.g., Michael Schuman, "China's big new idea: why Xi Jinping won't stop talking about 'common prosperity," *The Atlantic*, December 14, 2021.

Even if all the alternatives suggested by present-day adherents to populism, illiberalism, and authoritarianism were swiftly rejected out of hand, their portrayal of contemporary liberal constitutionalism as going hand in hand with fostering, or at least not resisting, patterns of increasing distributive injustices of various kinds deserves thorough analysis. Actually, pressing questions of distributive justice have also arisen within working liberal constitutional democracies themselves and have often stood in the forefront of public debate. As a dramatic example one can cite recent revelations in the United States to the effect that in the course of the COVID-19 pandemic, the country's billionaires vastly increased their wealth while many formerly employed citizens who lost their livelihood due to the pandemic had to line up for hours to collect food donations.[5] In view of this, the key questions relating to the nexus between the constitution and justice are whether the current seeming increases and exacerbations of distributive injustices are facilitated by liberal constitutional democratic rule or whether they are entirely independent from such rule; and whether liberal constitutionalism can, or ought to be calibrated to promote distributive justice, or at least to thwart or reduce the threats posed by the proliferation of distributive injustices.

One may well think that the incorporation of social welfare rights in several contemporary liberal constitutions provides an at least partial affirmative answer to the second question raised. But, on closer consideration, and as will be more fully discussed in Chapter 2, there are several objections both on philosophical grounds and on those of constitutional theory and practice against the incorporation of social welfare rights within liberal constitutions. According to these objections, social welfare benefits do not fit adequately within the right/remedy framework that has worked well for traditional liberal constitutional rights, such as those that afford protection to liberty, property, privacy, and non-discrimination. Although, as we shall see, these objections are far from conclusive, I propose to launch this book's inquiry from a standpoint of complete neutrality regarding the right answers to the two key questions posed.

With this in mind, I will advance the proposition that going back to its late eighteenth-century origins, liberal constitutionalism has been inherently committed, implicitly or explicitly, to advancing distributive justice objectives. That commitment has often been very hard to discern, however, because liberalism as a *philosophical* and *political* world view has been associated with several mutually contesting divergent theories of distributive justice. Indeed, these theories range from warranting mere formal equality with respect to fundamental rights to exhaustive redistribution of wealth and other benefits and burdens to achieve a highly egalitarian end state. In contrast, *liberal constitutionalism*, which provides

---

[5] See Chuck Collins and Omar Ocampo, "Billionaires made $1tn since Covid-19. They can afford to protect their workers," *The Guardian*, December 9, 2020; Sharon Cohen, "Pandemic pushes newly hungry Americans to crowded food lines," *AP News*, December 7, 2020.

4 INTRODUCTION

its own set of criteria for the structure and functions of constitutions, is consistent not only with philosophical liberalism but also with other world views, such as those advanced by pluralism, republicanism, and certain iterations of communitarianism (Rosenfeld 1998: 217–23).

Because in liberal constitutional democracies distributive justice is an essentially contested concept, any particular constitution seems bound to be considered just by some and unjust by others. Furthermore, as liberal constitutions either garner a broad-based consensus within the relevant polity, or at least can be plausibly cast as deserving of such a consensus, it seems ultimately impossible, and hence unwise, to frame and treat liberal constitutions as if they could aspire to comprehensive distributive justice. Instead, such constitutions should be assessed, and if deficient criticized, according to whether they open the way to meeting a yet to be defined minimum of distributive justice that ought to be constitutionally enshrined.

Before proceeding further, two crucial points deserve mention from the outset. First, borrowing from the political philosopher Nancy Fraser, in the age of globalization, distributive justice issues seem best compartmentalized into three distinct categories: economic *redistribution*, *recognition*, and *representation* (Fraser 2009: 2–6). Transporting these categories to the context of constitutional ordering, redistribution concerns constitutional guarantees relating to material welfare; recognition, both at the individual and collective levels, seems mainly promoted through civil and political rights including individual and group dignity and equality rights; and representation is supposed to be vindicated through constitutional guarantees regarding democracy that require both individual and collective rights to fair political participation and inclusive self-government. Second, with respect to the minimum of distributive justice that a liberal constitution ought to secure, I draw upon Rawls who, departing from justice, links distributive justice and what he calls the "constitutional essentials" (Rawls 2005: 227–30). For my part, I start from the constitution to inquire into the requisite minimum of justice that it ought to secure and that I designate as its "justice essentials."

I Situating the Nexus between Liberal Constitutionalism and Distributive Justice in its Historical and Theoretical Context

If one digs beneath the surface, one can discover that going all the way back to its modern origins in the French and American revolutions, the ideal of liberal constitutionalism has carried within it an essential component of dispensing justice and, above all, distributive justice.[6] As the two revolutions in question were focused

---

[6] Liberal constitutions also typically address issues of procedural justice as evinced by various provisions of the US Bill of Rights. See US Const., amends. V, VI, VII. Also, under certain circumstances, such as those of the post-communist constitutions in Eastern Europe and of the post-apartheid constitution

primarily on overthrow of feudal privilege and social and political dominance, however, their battle cries were centered on liberty, autonomy, democracy, and equal citizenship, thus subsuming or largely hiding their deeply embedded justice dimension. The best iterations of the transition from feudal hierarchy—grounded in status-based distributive inequalities determined at birth—to the ideal of equal citizenship casting every member of the polity as a subject of equal justice are the French 1789 Declaration of the Rights of Man and Citizen and the US 1776 Declaration of Independence with its dictum that "all men are created equal." To be sure, both the French and the American eighteenth-century forays into liberal constitutionalism fell far short from the ideal they invoked: the former most notably for its exclusion of women from equal citizenship (De Gouges 1791), and the latter for its failure to even include an equality provision within its 1787 Constitution given its backing of slavery that would continue until the end of the US Civil War in 1865.[7] Nevertheless, distributive justice is inherent in, and essential to, modern constitutionalism, and the import of this is now perhaps more critical than ever before. Given the baseline of equal citizenship, constitutions must set the broad outlines of allocation of benefits and burdens within the polity—and that along the three axes of redistribution, recognition, and representation.

Within the domain of material socio-economic distributions, conceptions of justice can vary, as already noted, along a wide spectrum, ranging from radical libertarianism to nearly all-encompassing egalitarianism. That said, when looking back at the eighteenth century, it is worth invoking Adam Smith's conception of a free-market economy led by the invisible hand of competition toward the most distributively fair material allocation throughout society consistent with the public good (Smith 1776). Consistent with this, it is easy to envision how constitutions of that period could be regarded as compatible with distributive justice imperatives without having to address explicitly any social welfare issues. Indeed, a free economic market requires maintenance of public order, the protection of liberty and property rights, as well the enforcement of contracts. Accordingly, equal civil and political rights throughout the citizenry could have then been considered constitutionally adequate to foster distributive justice throughout the polity.[8] In short, one can posit that eighteenth-century constitutions did actually guarantee a minimum

in South Africa, it may be desirable to constitutionalize certain compensatory or retributive justice measures.

[7] See US Const. amend. XIII (1865), which abolished slavery and made it unconstitutional. See Richards 1994: 85.

[8] It might be objected that it makes little sense to speak of distributive justice if the economic market itself determines just allocations as opposed to some socio-political redistributive scheme. This objection is easily refuted so long as one realizes that free markets are not "natural" phenomena, but are institutionally framed and backed systems of human interaction based on certain legal institutions and socio-economic norms and practices.

6 INTRODUCTION

of material distributive justice at least implicitly.[9] Moreover, even eighteenth-century constitutions were not completely bereft of social welfare provisions as the 1791 French Constitution mandated that the state should "provide work for the able-bodied poor who may have not been able to obtain it for themselves."[10]

Importantly, the domain of distributive justice associated with the liberal constitutional ideal is not confined to that of material welfare. In addition, constitutions must also dispense the broad outlines of distributively just allocations within the domain of identitarian justice and within that of representational justice. From the identitarian standpoint, distributive justice's task is above all twofold: first, it must carve out the subject class of those entitled to equal citizenship; and second, it must adjudicate between competing or conflicting claims to identarian recognition, self-expression, and path to self-fulfillment. Finally, the third prong of distributive justice associated with the liberal constitutional ideal, representational justice, relates to *who* shall choose representatives, and *what* and for *whom* shall be the principal concern of those who are entrusted with governing. Most generally, all citizens ought to be allocated an equal right to vote. Consistent with this, past deprivations of the vote and other political rights to African-American slaves and women were inherently distributively unjust as they disproportionately favored white men to the detriment of all others in the US polity. Also, in the case of women, for example, the deprivation of the right to vote amounted to an identitarian as well as a representational injustice. Indeed, as the Enlightenment ideal requires that all humans be considered to be equal, thus enshrining the "postulate of equality" (Rosenfeld 1991: 20–1), depriving women, who are in principle equal to men, of the vote requires some explanation or rationalization. Let us assume that the rationalization offered—one advanced in the nineteenth century—is that a woman's social role as wife and mother does not dispose her or inform her sufficiently to be entrusted with the responsibilities of self-government.[11] Based on this, women are deprived of recognition in the political sphere as well as of representation. In other words, issues pertaining to women's identity, status, social role, and aspirations are thus politically taken away from them and either altogether left out or dependent on being filtered through men into the political arena.

What distributive justice requires or what any of its above highlighted three dimensions command are, and have been, highly controverted subjects over which philosophers, judges, lawyers, and politicians have long very much disagreed. Accordingly, to be in a better position to assess what contemporary liberal democratic constitutions could, or should, address regarding relevant questions of

---

[9] Actually, even twentieth-century libertarian political philosophers have argued that any redistributions of wealth departing from those apportioned through the workings of the free market are distributively unjust. See Nozick 1994: 155.

[10] La Constitution Française September 3, 1791, art. 1.

[11] *Bradwell v. Illinois*, 83 US 130 (1872) (Because of their role as wife and mother, women can be prohibited from practicing law.).

distributive justice it is necessary briefly to outline the principal features and trends that confront present-day encounters between such constitutions and pressing issues of distributive justice.

For these purposes, an indispensable historical marker is provided by the collapse of the Soviet empire in the early 1990s. This collapse paved the way to a worldwide push toward liberal constitutional democracy both within nation-states and beyond as transnational and global relationships became increasingly constitutionalized.[12] Some optimists saw this spread of liberal constitutionalism combined with the triumph and nearly complete worldwide expansion of capitalism as the key turning point toward the end of history (Fukuyama 2003). Moreover, this apparent definitive pairing of liberal constitutionalism and capitalism emerged as the culmination of the two major achievements of the twentieth century: the endeavors to construct a world order based on the rule of law and human rights for all built upon the ashes of the unprecedented human devastation wrought by the Second World War and the end of the fierce Cold War struggle between capitalism and communism that had threatened to flare into nuclear mutual annihilation. Notably, the Second World War and the Cold War carved out two distinct historical frameworks set apart by one overarching overall difference. The Second World War featured above all a clash among identities, be they national, ethnic, or racial, with the Nazis proclaiming one race and one nation as superior and as entitled to subordinate or even to exterminate nations and races they designated as inferior. The Cold War, on the other hand, suppressed or subordinated particular identities for the purpose of showcasing the clash between two ideologies with universal designs and aspirations. Both capitalism and communism etched distinct visions of the common good that were equally meant to be suitable for humankind as a whole regardless of national, ethnic, cultural, or religious differences, or more generally, regardless of any identitarian particulars.

The post-Cold War turn to liberal constitutionalism and to the pursuit and institutionalization of global capitalism may be constructively regarded as seeking a balanced and workable integration of identitarian particulars and universal commonalities with salient normative import. The urgency of such integration is underscored both from a retrospective and from a prospective perspective. Retrospectively, it becomes clear that excessive and belligerent identitarian particularism, as evinced by the Nazi experiment, and similarly that systematically repressive universalism, such as that put into place by Soviet communism, have led to devastating consequences. Prospectively, on the other hand, meaningful transition from Soviet communist authoritarianism to liberal constitutionalism required

---

[12] In 2004, all (then) twenty-five member states of the European Union (EU) signed "The Treaty Establishing a Constitution for Europe" (TCE). The TCE failed in 2005, however, due to being rejected in ratifying referenda in France and the Netherlands. Nevertheless, the TCE was adopted in substance in another form as "the Treaty of Lisbon," which was signed in 2007 and entered into force in 2009. See Dorsen 2016; Fassbender 2009.

8 INTRODUCTION

some form of return of the repressed, in this case some recovery of identitarian particulars to provide cohesion to an individual nation-state. Countries behind the Iron Curtain that had been forced to reign in their nationalist aspirations became called upon to shed their Soviet yoke in order to open their institutional and political destiny to liberal constitutionalism. Almost concurrently, as the world's economy accelerated toward globalization, individuals and nation-states needed to project outward and to join in the quest for some normative cohesion subject to universal standards of legitimation as an anchor for, and provider of, a common frame of reference.

As it moved forward from its Enlightenment origins, liberal constitutionalism had to mediate between an *ethnos* with its inescapable particular identitarian imprint and a *demos* with its inevitable universal grounding and reach. The contrast between constitutionalism predominantly reliant on the *ethnos* and that based primarily on the *demos* emerges from a comparison between the traditional German constitutional model and its French counterpart. The German traditional ethnocentric model is premised on the preexistence of a fully developed pre-political ethnically homogeneous nation with a common language, culture, history, and tradition (Preuss 1994: 150). The traditional French model, on the other hand, sets democracy as the basis of, and objective for, constitutional ordering (*Id.*), and envisions a social contract among individuals poised to become the constituted democracy's citizens as carving out the relevant constitutional unit (Rousseau 1947). In theory, the French model is universal in scope and ambition. Accordingly, the original social contract associated with this model seems equally logically suitable to bind together the inhabitants of a single city, like Rousseau's Geneva, those of a single country, like France, or humankind as a whole were it to commit to global constitutional democratic rule. Significantly, the 1789 French Declaration of the Rights of Man and Citizen, which refers to "man" and "citizen" in the abstract and not to "Frenchmen" or "French citizens," reads as universal in scope. Moreover, from its 1789 Revolution to the present, French citizenship and accepted comportment in the public sphere has required extensive purging of identitarian attributes. Pointedly, France was the first country in bestowing full citizenship on Jews in the course of the 1789 Revolution, but it specified that such citizenship extended to the Jew *qua* individual but not *qua* representative of a people or a religion.[13] Similarly, at present French public schools forbid their students from wearing the Islamic veil or any other "ostentatious" religious sign.[14]

In its most sweeping iteration, the purely ethnocentric constitutional model can seemingly completely do away with liberalism and democracy. According to

---

[13] This was most famously expressed by the French revolutionary Clermont-Tonnerre. See Birnbaum 1988: 44–45.

[14] See *Loi n° 2004-228 du 15 mars 2004 encadrant, en application du principe de laïcité, le port de signes ou de tenues manifestant une appartenance religieuse dans les écoles, collèges et lycées publics.*

Carl Schmitt, the foremost proponent of the most radical vision of this model, the German people's constitutional destiny could well be better served by a dictator well cognizant of his people's aims and aspirations than by a democratic government prone to succumbing to calls for accommodating pluralism (Schmitt 1928; Preuss 1994: 155). As Schmitt saw it, all concessions to pluralism posed a threat to the maintenance of ethnocentric integrity. In sharp contrast, the paradigmatic democentric constitutional model conceives each individual in the abstract as a bearer of the capacity to be both a citizen and a private person in a commonly agreed upon democratically run polity that could logically extend to all human beings. Consistent with this, if the traditional democentric French constitutional model had to be deployed within the confines of the late eighteenth-century French nation-state,[15] that was not due to logic but instead to limitations imposed by the prevailing material conditions. Because of the particular eighteenth-century limitations in the realms of communications, organization, and institutional design and operation, it was inconceivable at that time to lay out a polity subject to genuine constitutional rule and democracy on a transnational scale. At present, however, so long as all individuals viewed in the abstract are deemed interchangeable as citizens and as private persons with a capacity for self-fulfillment, there seems to be no ultimate material impediment to a constitutional pact binding together all humans throughout the planet, and thus culminating in liberal constitutional democratic rule on a truly global scale.

The two paradigmatic poles that circumscribe all plausible conceptions of modern constitutional ordering serve, above all, a heuristic function. This is because no actual working liberal constitutional democracy can approximate a purely ethnocentric or a purely democentric model of operation. On the one hand, no contemporary liberal democracy is thoroughly ethnocentrically unified as it seems bound to encompass more than a single ethnic, religious, or cultural group, thus requiring some constitutionally significant accommodation of pluralism. Moreover, even were an occasional contemporary democracy thoroughly ethnically homogeneous, it would still have to be to a constitutionally relevant degree individualistically pluralistic as its citizens would inevitably embrace different ideologies and pursue a variety of competing interests. On the other hand, a purely democentric working constitutional order bereft of any identitarian bonds among the citizenry would be ultimately purely utopian as it would lack the minimum degree of commonality required to conduct a collectively concerted enterprise. Consistent with this, the original viability of the French democentric constitutional model seems in the end better understood not as merely constrained by material conditions, but

---

[15] At the time of the 1789 French Revolution, the French centralized state had been fully established by the absolute monarchy that was about to be overthrown. The French nation, on the other hand, was still in the course of consolidation, and the Revolution would accelerate this process, often through violent means. See Rosenfeld 2010: 157.

10   INTRODUCTION

as actually made possible by the eighteenth century already well-defined French nation-state which supplied it with its essential and indispensable, even if apparently underemphasized, identitarian component.

As simultaneously anchored on an *ethnos* and a *demos*, modern liberal constitutionalism must strive to mediate successfully between the universal, the singular, and the plural. Moreover, as will be emphasized throughout what follows, these three central concepts must be understood in the present context primarily in *relational terms*. Most obviously, the *demos* suitable to liberal constitutionalism must necessarily partake in the universal and in the singular. Indeed, democratic self-government, the rule of law, and the protection of fundamental rights must ultimately be regarded as universal in one of two ways. Either there are some truly universal attributes of democratic self-government, the rule of law, and fundamental constitutional and/or human rights, or the *demos* operating within a particular liberal constitutional polity must figure as universal in relation to all the actors, be they individual or collective, within that polity. On the other hand, liberal constitutional democracy necessarily depends on the singular as embodied in the individual person. It is indeed the individual as an equal who figures as the social contractor who is supposed to lend legitimacy to the prevailing liberal constitutional order, as the citizen who emerges as the indissoluble unit of the requisite scheme of self-government, and as the private person who is the bearer of rights and who can design her own path to self-fulfillment.[16] Moreover, the singular individual may figure in the constitutional constellation in two contrasting ways that can often produce conflict and contradiction. Either the singular person is portrayed as an abstract construct yielding interchangeable individual citizens, voters, property owners, entrepreneurs, workers, consumers, and contract makers, or she is viewed as possessing an irreducible individuality based on a unique history, heritage, experience, and set of challenges and aspirations. In the latter case, singularity is correlated with uniqueness in a profound substantive sense. And this signifies that at its core each person's singularity makes all comparison and all generalization not only inevitably wide of the mark but in some important sense unjust or unfair. In other words, if everyone is irreducibly different from all others in the polity, then any general rule equally applicable to all will inevitably somewhat arbitrarily favor some over others.[17]

For its part, the *ethnos* that must coalesce into a working liberal constitutional order must figure as an amalgam between the singular and the plural. Indeed, every ethnocentric unit—understood broadly as being differentiated along ethnic,

---

[16] Significantly, individualism is essentially a modern Western ideological construct. See Dumont 1977: 4. In the Middle Ages, in contrast, the individual was not recognized as an actor standing on his own but only as a part defined by his specific role within society as a whole understood as an organic unit. See Lukes 1973: 46

[17] This latter proposition is powerfully articulated and defended by Jacques Derrida in his analysis of the relation between law and justice. See Chapter 6 of this book.

religious, linguistic, and/or cultural dimensions—is singular when set against all other such units. Moreover, such ethnocentric singularity must be regarded as essentially pre- or extra-political with a view to preventing it from becoming fully absorbed or dissolved into the *demos*. The singular *ethnos* may be projected as a naturally grounded given, and its purported unity may be conceived along racial or ethnic lines. Preferably and more convincingly, however, consistent with Benedict Anderson's insight, as all social units larger than the family or the tribe must per force mediate relationships among strangers, they are accordingly best understood as seeking to cohere as "imagined communities" (Anderson 1991). This remains equally true for nations as a whole such as, for example, Spain, and for subnational well-defined communal units, such as the Basques or the Catalans within Spain. Furthermore, subnational units may either imagine themselves as being integrated within larger ones without losing their distinct singularity or they may regard the national unit as a threat to their identity and aspire to independence and to transition from a subnational to a national unit. Regardless of the level of integration of all distinct identitarian units within a particular constitutional democracy, the *ethnos* of all contemporary liberal constitutional polities must confront and strive to accommodate the plural. This is because the polities in question will inevitably prove to be multi-ethnic, multi-religious, multi-lingual, multicultural, or inclusive of aboriginal groups that antedate a colonial past.

Just as the singular can attach to individuals and collective units, so too the plural can be found within groups as well as among groups, or even, as already noted, among individuals operating within the same constitutional polity. The plural *among* groups is widely familiar and liberal constitutions can accommodate it to a large extent through freedom of religion provisions, through official recognition of, and support for, different language communities,[18] as well as through constitutional grants of limited self-government to certain minority ethnic or national communities.[19] The plural *within* groups, on the other hand, may be in many cases far less constitutionalized, but it does raise similar issues of recognition and of fairness as those confronting its inter-group counterpart. One assumes that a liberal constitution should grant equal freedom of religion to Catholics and Jews within the relevant polity, but what about feminists or members of the lesbian, gay, bisexual, trans, and queer (LGBTQ) community who identify as Catholics? Should the latter enjoy any institutional support in their quests to have the Catholic Church within their polity effectuate changes from within? Or should their constitutional protections only guarantee a right of exit in case they become too alienated from their country's Catholic mainstream? Furthermore, the boundaries between *inter*-communal and *intra*-communal pluralism can shift and may be frequently

---

[18] See, e.g., Section 23, "Minority Language Educational Rights," of the 1982 Canadian Charter of Rights.

[19] See, e.g., Cullen 1990: 347 (discussing adaptive federalism in Belgium).

difficult to draw. Western Christianity, for instance, may have once carved out a comprehensive intra-communal religious collectivity. However, after the rise of Protestantism and of the wars between Catholics and Protestants that ensued, while both Christian, these two religions certainly regarded and behaved toward one another inter-communally.

What emerges from this preliminary cursory account of its broad outlines is that liberal constitutionalism assembles individuals and groups into a community of communities meant to secure a hierarchy of norms designed to unify the polity by endowing it with legitimacy and integrity through the constitution. To be effective, the said hierarchy of norms must combine a formal logic and coherence— most famously exemplified by Kelsen's Kantian conception of the legal order as a self-contained pyramidal hierarchy topped by the constitution as the *grundnorm* or basic norm[20]—with a substantive backdrop and imprint that aligns with the history, tradition, culture, tensions, and points of contention within the relevant polity, an imprint perhaps best concretized through that polity's "constitutional identity."[21] Consistent with this, the individual as well as the group and the community of communities all partake in the three essential dimensions noted above, namely the universal, the singular, and the plural. As already noted, the individual is conceived alternatively as singular and as (a microcosm of the) universal whereas groups figure at once as both plural and singular (as their own unique features distinguish them from their collective counterparts). Finally, for its part the community of communities must aspire to the universal (in absolute or relative terms)[22] in its quest for the constitutional hierarchy and unity that can hold the polity together while at the same time properly accounting for the singularity of and plurality within that polity to convince the latter's stakeholders of its fairness, legitimacy, and integrity.

The relationship between the individual, groups, and the community of communities in a liberal constitutional setting is dynamic and evolving. This relationship implies a constant striving for a viable harmony which cannot ever be fully realized. All the relevant stakeholders must continuously strive to advance their own position in the constitutional order while at the same time contributing to that order coming closer to its intended harmony. Given the complex makeup of

---

[20] See Chapter 3 of this book for a discussion of Kelsen's theory.

[21] I have developed a theory of how a polity projects its vision of itself as an imaginary community bound together by its constitutional order through the articulation and embrace of a conception of "constitutional identity" which is related but distinct from that polity's self-perception as an imaginary community with a national identity. Rosenfeld 2010.

[22] Either there are universal norms that provide the measure of constitutional legitimacy and fairness regardless of any particulars; or each polity has its particulars—e.g., in terms of specific religions, ethnic, and linguistic groups—and the community of communities must be plausibly legitimate and fair in a way that properly accounts for all its relevant particulars. This distinction between what is universal at all times and places and what is universal in relation to a particular ordered constitutional unit is further elaborated and placed in its proper context throughout the book's inquiry into the nexus between the universal, the singular, and the plural.

contemporary polities, it seems impossible to align every individual, every group, and the whole fully as differences in interests, ideologies, group identity, and clusters of solidarity are prone to fuel tensions, rivalries, and conflicts continuously. In this dynamic, every individual must constantly navigate between the singular, the plural, and the universal whether she happens to be speaking on her own behalf, on that of her group, or on that of her community of communities.

Consider, as an example, the following hypothetical case concerning a German Catholic woman who is a feminist and who supports the European Union (EU). As with all contemporary individuals, she perceives herself as carving out a unique singular trajectory in terms of her past history, relationships, projects, achievements, and aspirations. As an employed woman seeking parity with her male counterparts, she would have to advance arguments that rely in part on propositions that are cast as universal (fairness and justice require equality in pay for men and women engaging in the same job) and in part cast as plural (women as workers should receive special accommodation for circumstances that they may confront but that no man does, such as childbirth). As a Catholic, our protagonist would typically have to manage both inter-communal and intra-communal interactions. Inter-communally, she may take stances when dealing with issues over which Catholic positions may conflict with those of other religions, such as Protestantism, or with those of secularists. Intra-communally, on the other hand, she may take a feminist stance within Catholicism and advocate for the inclusion of women within her Church's clergy. Moreover, typical arguments pertinent in both these inter- and intra-communal contexts are likely to invoke the plural and the universal, and perhaps on occasion the singular. Inter-communally, if our protagonist feels Catholics are at a disadvantage in the German polity, she can appeal to the universal (all religions are entitled to equal treatment) and to the plural (Catholics ought to be entitled to exemptions from laws that though neutral in their provisions disproportionately disadvantage their religion as compared to others). She can also, consistent with the views of Pope Benedict XVI, claim that Catholic conceptions of law and morality ought to apply inter-communally based on the belief that they happen to be universal in nature.[23] Intra-communally, on the other hand, our protagonist can couch her feminist positions in universal terms (equality between women and men ought to be honored in all morally influent contexts) or plural ones (as important constituents within Catholicism, women should be able to feel as included and worthy of leadership as men). She can also, in this intra-communal context, conceivably rely on the singular, by invoking her own biography as a committed Catholic and politically engaged feminist as a potentially potent argument in favor of expanding the inclusiveness of the Catholic community of faith. Furthermore,

[23] In his exchanges with Jurgen Habermas and in other academic settings, Pope Benedict XVI has argued that Catholic faith and reason lead to the same universally valid moral and legal norms. See Cartabia & Simoncini 2015: 3–9.

14   INTRODUCTION

in the process of managing her dual commitment to Catholicism and to feminism, our protagonist will have to aim to reconcile the plural within the singular. Can she find a point of equilibrium between her Catholicism and her feminism within herself? Can she live with a certain degree of inconsistency and dissonance between the religious community and the feminist movement to which she has chosen to belong? Is there a point at which she might feel that continued serious commitment to these two distinct groups might prove too incompatible and force her to choose between them?

As a German citizen, our protagonist will at once seek to identify with, fit within, and contest (in order to make it more inclusive or fairer) the community of communities delimited by Germany's liberal constitutional order as framed by her country's constitution, the German Basic Law. The latter enshrines human dignity as the country's paramount constitutional value,[24] and seeks to reconcile the virtues of the liberal state with those of the social-welfare state (Kommers & Miller 2012: 622–4). Faced with this, our protagonist can seek to reconcile her singularity and the plurality of her group affiliations and differentiations with the legal and political order set forth for Germany by the Basic Law through the mediation of her country's constitutional identity. This identity, which figures as the glue that binds together Germany as an imagined constitutional community (of communities), is dynamic and always subject to further construction, change, and adjustment so as to become more inclusive of all those who find themselves within the rule of the Basic Law. Moreover, whereas the Basic Law is supposed to provide the formal dimension of the universal that binds the German community of communities together, German constitutional identity is meant to project the material substantive dimension that allows all Germans to perceive themselves as forming part of the same constitutional unit. Furthermore, the constitutional identity in question needs to remain dynamic and adaptable. At the outset, post-Second World War Germany mainly comprised Catholics and Protestants. In more recent years, significant numbers of Jews and Muslims have joined the country's constitutional community of communities, and in the case of Muslims initially as foreign guest workers, but more recently as full-fledged German citizens.[25] Accordingly, unlike her grandmother, who had to accommodate for constitutional integration with Protestants and secularists, our protagonist must strive for an iteration of constitutional identity that is inclusive of non-Christian religions.

To the extent that our German protagonist regards herself as an EU citizen and perceives the EU order as essentially a constitutional one, she must imagine the EU as a community of communities and Germany as one of the communities

---

[24] See German Basic Law, art. 1.

[25] The German rules on citizenship were thoroughly revised with the entry into force of the amended Nationality Act (*Staatsangehörigkeitsgesetz*) on January 1, 2000. This new law granted citizenship to children of non-German residents who were born in Germany.

within it. Within this perspective, either the EU is accorded universal attributes and Germany singular ones (in terms of its own national and constitutional identities) and plural ones (as one EU member state among many), or both the EU and Germany are regarded as sharing the same universal attributes as liberal constitutional democratic orders necessarily committed to limitations of governmental powers, the rule of law, protection of fundamental rights, and requisite guarantees of democracy.[26] Also, given the predominantly relational nature of the interface between the universal, the singular, and the plural, as a German citizen within the EU, our protagonist may focus on her singularity and cast the EU as a (relative) universal while at the same time understand the congruence between the German and the EU constitutional ordering as partaking in the same universal norms applicable to all liberal constitutional designs. In speaking to a French counterpart about EU matters, our protagonist may at once experience her singularity as a German, the plurality that binds her to her French interlocutor as fellow EU citizens, and the universality (or the failure to approximate a sufficient universal dimension) of the EU as a constitutional order designed to unify the common designs that bind the Germans to the French and to all others who belong to the remaining EU member states. Finally, the EU itself partakes in singularity, plurality as well as the already alluded to universality, as could become manifest to our German protagonist if she were to compare notes with a US counterpart. Indeed, compared to the United States, which relies more on individualism, self-reliance, and a relatively unbridled capitalism, the EU constitutional order and that of the countries within it share a strong emphasis on promotion of social welfare through the state (von Bogdandy 2005). In short, the EU's constitutional identity (to the extent that it has one)[27] is singular as compared to that of the United States, and these two respective constitutional identities are plural in relation to legal regimes with arguable constitutional dimension that are global in nature, such as that carved by the legally binding resolutions of the UN Security Council.[28]

To sum up, liberal constitutionalism aims for an equilibrium between the singular, the plural and the universal as expressed through a working integration between a coherent *demos* and a unifying *ethnos* capable of sustaining a sufficient level of solidarity throughout the relevant constitutional unit. To be sure, the said equilibrium can never be fully realized, and it seems always subject to further approximation to the ideal of full and stable harmony. But, by the same token, liberal

---

[26] Compare *Internationale Handelsgesellschaft Mbh v. Einfuhr-Und Vorratsstelle Für Getreide Und Futtermittel (Solange I)*, 37 BVerfGE 271 (1974) (German Constitutional Court holding that the EU legal system does not guarantee fundamental rights comparable to those enshrined in German Basic law) to *Re the Application of Wunsche Handelsgesllschaft (Solange II)*,73 BVerfGE 339 (1986) (German Constitutional Court noting that by 1986 the E.U. guaranteed fundamental rights that are comparable to those in force in Germany).

[27] See Grimm 1995: 282 (arguing that the EU lacks a common political identity).

[28] See Öberg 2005: 884 (resolutions of the UN Security Council under Article VII of the UN Charter are legally binding).

16   INTRODUCTION

constitutional democracy cannot be sustained if it falls below a certain minimum threshold, in which case it would become nearly impossible that the relevant constitutional unit could survive intact. Under such circumstances, either liberal constitutionalism could be salvaged through radical changes in the relevant *ethnos* and *demos*, as occurred in the 1993 constitutional dissolution of Czechoslovakia into the Czech Republic and Slovakia,[29] or liberal constitutionalism could be altogether eradicated through the establishment of authoritarian rule that ignores the constitution or replaces it with one tailored to the designs of a dominant constituency and its authoritarian leader who happen to have secured the reigns of state power.[30]

Within the context of the conflict between liberal constitutionalism and authoritarian rule, the relatively recent advent of contemporary illiberal populist constitutionalism looms in many ways as elusive and paradoxical. This is principally because unlike straightforward authoritarianism, populist illiberalism changes the liberal constitution from within, and does so, for the most part, by turning the means provided by the liberal constitution against the latter. Moreover, illiberal constitutional populism erodes the previously achieved equilibrium between *ethnos* and *demos*, but it is not clear whether it precipitates the unraveling of that equilibrium or whether it merely seeks to fill the vacuum after a *de facto* dissolution—albeit a partially or for the most part unacknowledged one—of a previously operable status quo.

As already mentioned in the case of Hungary, and thoroughly exposed in that of Poland, illiberal and populist purported adaptations of constitutionalism and the rule of law appear thus far destined to being abusive and deceptive (Sadurski 2019; Sajo 2021). It seems beyond dispute, however, that both actual liberal and illiberal constitutional democracies can fall significantly short of their professed respective constitutional ideals. But given that the main focus of this book will be on whether it is possible to establish a cogent and persuasive basis of legitimation and justification for contemporary liberal constitutionalism, it seems preferable to concentrate on the plausibility (whether factual or meaningfully counterfactual) of approaching the fundamental requirements associated with the ideal of constitutionalism (whether conceived consistent with liberal or illiberal outlooks) rather than dwelling on actual flaws that stand as obstacles to the advancement of the objectives of constitutionalism within particular individual polities. As noted earlier, Hungary's Orban has advocated Christianity and family values to replace Western European supposedly permissive indulgent ever-expanding bundle of rights much

---

[29]   See *Czechoslovakia's Constitution Act 542*, passed on November 25, which called for the dissolution of Czechoslovakia as of December 31, 1992.

[30]   See, e.g., Emily Rauhala, "Xi cleared to rule indefinitely as China officially scraps term limits," *Washington Post*, March 11, 2018; Declan Walsh, "Egyptian lawmakers back changes that could keep Sisi in power till 2034," *NY Times*, February 14, 2019, <https://www.nytimes.com/2019/02/14/world/middleeast/egypt-sisi.html> viewed April 3, 2022 (proposed constitutional amendments to prolong president's hold on power and tighten his control of the judiciary).

as has a recent US "Commission on Unalienable Rights" set up during the Trump Administration which proposed in 2020 to retreat from rights inflation to recover the values of the nation's founding. According to this Commission, the values involved were principally those of Protestantism, private property rights specially as against social welfare rights, and religious liberty rights[31]—recently interpreted by conservative US Supreme Court Justices as warranting religion based exemptions from generally applicable laws barring discrimination on the basis of sex or sexual orientation.[32] Strictly speaking, these "illiberal" conceptions of rights may be inconsistent with contemporary understandings of liberalism in philosophy and political theory, but not necessarily with the four essential pillars of liberal constitutionalism. Accordingly, and for the sake of argument, both liberal and illiberal constitutional democracies, including populist ones, will be treated as being *prima facie* capable of satisfying the aforementioned four essential pillars. Consistent with this, a key question regarding the difference between liberal and populist or illiberal visions consists in in determining whether the differences between them are reducible to *Kulturkampf* or whether liberal constitutionalism is ultimately downright incompatible with all conceivable iterations of illiberalism or of populism. Before pursuing this line of inquiry any further, however, it is imperative to focus briefly on certain salient factual and normative developments with a view to putting together the best possible framework for a productive analysis.

From a historical perspective, what has best approximated the ideal of liberal constitutionalism has been the mono-ethnic or harmoniously multi-ethnic nation-state. In both cases, the relevant *ethnos* is relatively unproblematically established[33] and the unity of the constitutional community of communities remains solid. In the multi-ethnic context, Switzerland exemplifies success as it harmoniously integrates its French, German, Italian, and Romanche language communities and its Catholic and Protestant religious communities into a loyally adhered to federally unified nation-state functioning as a fully consolidated constitutional unit. In contrast, certain other multi-ethic nation-states, such as Canada and Spain, seem less successful in this respect than Switzerland, as ethnic divisions, such as those manifest in Quebec or Catalonia have on several occasions seriously raised the scepter of secession (Mancini 2012: 481–500). Most recently, however, as indicated

---

[31] US Comm'n of Unalienable Rights, Draft Report of the Commission on Unalienable Rights 8 (July 16, 2020), pp. 21, 31 <https://www.state.gov/wp-content/uploads/2020/07/Draft-Report-of-the-Commission-on-Unalienable-Rights.pdf [https://perma.cc/G67K-265J]> viewed April 3, 2022.

[32] See *Burwell v. Hobby Lobby Stores, Inc.*, 573 US 682 (2014); *Fulton v. Philadelphia*, 593 US ____ (2021).

[33] As the relevant *ethnos* is never incorporated unfiltered and unmediated in the constitutional identity of a liberal constitutional democracy, mono-ethnicity must be constitutionally adapted through a series of mediations. These operate through an interpretive process relying on emphasis and de-emphasis of key features through deployment of a combination of negation, metaphor, and metonymy as essential tools of interpretation. See Rosenfeld 2010: 45–57.

18 INTRODUCTION

earlier, the greatest threat posed to liberal constitutionalism looms is that wrought by globalization.

Globalization, propelled by the accelerated expansion of capitalism throughout the globe, has given rise to huge and momentous material and identitarian changes. The transnational spread of capital combined with the accompanying massive displacements of human labor across nation-states have resulted in serious challenges to the traditional liberal constitutional unit. These challenges, moreover, have come both from within and from without the traditional liberal constitutional unit encompassed within the bounds of the Westphalian nation-state. From within, the flight of capital with its consequent great acceleration of disparities in wealth within the polity combined with the large influx of migrants from very different cultural and religious traditions pose serious threats to both the prevailing *demos* and *ethnos* that had struck a working equilibrium within the established national constitutional order. Indeed, democratically crafted national legislation meant to regulate business appears easy to circumvent through transnational movements of capital to places with more favorable regulation (Rosenfeld 2011: 276). At the same time, the traditional cultural and religious make up of a polity becomes subject to substantial challenges through immigration, such that which brought large numbers of Muslims to several European countries, thus leading to new ethnocentric divisions and tensions.[34] Furthermore, regarding challenges from without the traditional constitutional unit, on the other hand, the trans-nationalization and globalization of economic, social, and political relationships requires some level of regulation and even of constitutionalization on a scale that exceeds that of the nation-state and that at times extends to that of the globe as a whole (Fassbender 2009). As frequently underscored in the context of the EU regarded in its functioning as a legal and constitutional regime in its own right, transnational constitutionalism is prone to being problematic from the standpoint of the *demos* as attested by the famous rallying cry against the EU's "democratic deficit" (Marquand 1979: 64). Also, as again noted in the context of the EU, it seems much more problematic to find a sufficiently shared identity at the level of the *ethnos* in transnational settings than in national ones (Rosenfeld 2014: 184–85).

Globalization and the dislocations that it fosters on the economic and the identitarian fronts have met a stiff resistance that has coalesced into a counterthrust towards balkanization (Rosenfeld 2010: 234–5). The economically displaced and disadvantaged citizen ensconced in the nation-state of his ancestors can easily become convinced that a resurgence of nationalism and of ethnocentric exclusivism may amount to the best antidote against the evils caused by globalization

---

[34] See Shadi Hami, "The major roadblock to Muslim assimilation in Europe," *The Atlantic*, August 18, 2011, <https://www.theatlantic.com/international/archive/2011/08/the-major-roadblock-to-muslim-assimilation-in-europe/243769> viewed April 3, 2022 (arguing that the practice of Islam is incompatible with European secularism and its endeavors to confine religion to the private sphere).

and automation of the economy. Traditional jobs, such as those in manufacturing, are massively exported while the adversely affected country natives see other economic opportunities within their nation's borders lost to ever increasing immigrant populations that confront them with their alien mores and religious traditions. By turning inward to nationalism and ethnic solidarity, those who feel as the losers in the race towards comprehensive globalization can strike at once against their fellow citizen who benefit from the new conditions and against recent immigrants from alien cultures who are often seen as favored in obtaining remaining jobs and ever scarcer social services. By casting the fellow citizens engaged in global capitalism as in some important sense unpatriotic and devoid of solidarity, and by depicting immigrants as unworthy opportunists bent on undermining the country's traditional values, religious harmony, and culture, the nationalists seek to mobilize balkanization to strike a new (or to rekindle what is nostalgically projected as a traditional) equilibrium between *demos* and *ethnos*. From this perspective, moreover, national populist illiberal constitutionalism emerges as the logical antidote against liberal constitutionalism and its seeming increasing pathologies in an era of globalization. These perceived pathologies largely stem, in turn, from liberal democracies' globally oriented elites becoming cast as bent to undermining the democratic integrity of their nation-state, and from rights starved immigrants cast as causing a dilution or degradation of the fundamental rights of the citizenry. Thus, claims for constitutional protection of alien cultural and religious traditions (such as, for example, the ubiquitous wearing of the Islamic veil) have been attacked as prone to threatening the preservation of hard-fought gains in the realm of liberal rights (such as constitutional equality for women) (Dorsen 2016: 1253–5).

II Searching for Liberal Constitutionalism's Distributive Justice Baseline: The Journey from Rawls's "Constitutional Essentials" to the Constitution's "Justice Essentials"

Underlying the conflict between liberal and illiberal conceptions of constitutional rule in the era of globalization is an exacerbation of disagreements about justice and the aura of legitimacy and of integrity that consensus on key elements of justice is apt to sustain. These disagreements extend to all three axes of distributive justice. Moreover, the critiques that either explicitly or implicitly target either traditionally grounded justice deficiencies, the latter's present exacerbations, or the injustices directly linked to globalization, originate both from within liberal constitutional democracies and from without. As already mentioned, proponents of populist and of illiberal constitutions both zero in on the justice related failings of liberal constitutions and claim or vividly hint that they are better equipped to overcome the injustices at stake. For example, from a populist perspective, liberal constitutions compromise and betray the duty to recognize *the* people properly by blurring or

20 INTRODUCTION

falsifying its identitarian mainstays and by diluting or obstructing its rightful representational input. On the other hand, from within liberal constitutional regimes, the plausible critiques are manifold, as already briefly evoked and as will be further elaborated in what follows, and aimed at the various levels of constitutional ordering in place. For example, the nation-state constitution seems increasingly hampered in its aims to secure acceptable levels of material well-being due to the flights of capital and labor linked to globalization. At the same time, in what are at least functionally transnational constitutional orders, several criticisms regarding distributive injustices have been leveled, as evinced by the already alluded to EU much decried "democratic deficit."

Under the ideal of liberal constitutionalism, the constitution must not only dispense distributive justice, but also other forms of justice, such as procedural justice and in certain cases (some modified version of) compensatory justice.[35] As already noted, constitutions are not meant to address all questions of justice or to function as the exclusive fountainhead of a system of comprehensive justice within the polity within which they are enshrined as the highest law of the land. With this in mind, as already announced, I deem it particularly helpful to draw on Rawls' concept of "constitutional essentials" which he derives from his theory of distributive justice (Rawls 2005: 227–30). Just as for Rawls political justice cannot be implemented within a polity without the institutionalization of certain constitutional essentials, the main thesis that will guide the inquiry throughout this book boils down to the proposition that the ideal of liberal constitutionalism necessarily calls for implementation of some "justice essentials," and that individual constitutions can therefore be assessed according to how they fare in terms of these essentials. For his part, Rawls departs from justice and concludes that its realization necessitates institutionalization of a bundle of constitutional norms that he characterizes as essential. I start from the constitution as framed by the ideal of liberal constitutionalism and propose to defend the thesis that the justification and legitimation of any constitution depends on it being capable of dispensing a certain (yet undefined) minimum of (distributive) justice to which I refer as that constitution's "justice essentials." In other words, any constitution that actually complies—or that is readily adaptable to becoming compliant—with both the four essential pillars mentioned at the outset and the justice essentials ought to be deemed as worthy of legitimation and of justification. Within this perspective, therefore, there is no basis for an *a priori* determination of a constitution's normative legitimacy or conformity with the justice essentials based solely on that constitution being *politically* liberal, illiberal, or populist.

---

[35] One example of a constitution that included elements of compensatory justice is the 1978 Spanish Constitution which sought to compensate for Franco's regime of ruthless repression of Basque and Catalan identarian aspirations by creating "autonomous regions" allowing for some measure of Basque and Catalan self-government within the newly minted Spanish constitutional framework. See Rosenfeld 2010: 141.

To elucidate the concept of "justice essentials" further, it is instructive to briefly focus on the particulars of Rawls' "constitutional essentials." Rawls' theory of distributive justice, to which he refers as "justice as fairness" (*Id.*: 9), is a liberal egalitarian one that will be examined in greater depth in Chapter 5. Justice as fairness requires constitutional essentials of two kinds: the first pertains to the general structure of government; and the second to equal basic rights and liberties for all citizens (*Id.*: 227). Moreover, in what is particularly noteworthy from the present perspective, Rawls specifies that the structure of government requirement can be satisfied by a variety of possible arrangements, such as a presidential or a parliamentary system (*Id.*: 228). In contrast, equal rights allow for much less of a margin of variation as freedom of speech, of association, and the right to vote must be protected in much the same manner in any polity bent on conforming with "constitutional essentials" (*Id.*).

The "justice essentials" associated with the ideal of liberal constitutionalism, on the other hand, also involve two essential particulars: a distributive scheme that harmonizes *demos* and *ethnos*, and an overall project of justice that strikes a workable equilibrium between the universal, the singular, and the plural. Also, the first of these particulars is susceptible to being satisfied by a vast number of different configurations. These range from highly democentric constitutions that leave adequate space for ethnocentric pursuits to constitutions built upon the *ethnos* and structuring the *demos* to operate mainly within and among constitutionally enshrined ethnocentric units.[36] The second of these particulars, in contrast, consists in complying with a minimum of justice that is non-negotiable and without which a constitutional arrangement would be bound fail from the perspective of the project carved out by the ideal of liberal constitutionalism. The minimum of justice involved must per force take into serious account the demands of the universal as well as those of the singular and of the plural as these emerge in the relevant constitutional polity. In addition, the minimum in question requires carving out a path toward reconciling and finding a dynamic path aimed at mutual accommodation among the competing demands of the universal, the singular, and the plural in a way that allows for a proper equilibrium among them. In other words, the minimum of justice requires neither disregarding nor belittling the demands of the universal, the singular, or the plural while avoiding disproportionate prevalence of any one of them over the others. Finally, as will be detailed in what follows, constitutions encompassed within the path toward the ideal of constitutionalism may exceed the minimum of justice under consideration but they may not fall short of it.

---

[36] The French model relying on a unified *demos* that saturates the public sphere combined with a private sphere amenable to the accommodation of a plurality of ethnocentric pursuits seems to occupy one end of the spectrum whereas a constitution, such as that of Switzerland which gives ethnocentric priority to its various cantons with guarantees of strong democracy within each of these, comes close to occupying the other end of the spectrum.

III Organization of the Book

In its aim to provide a comprehensive critical assessment of the nexus between the justice essentials and the ideal of liberal constitutionalism, this book is divided into three parts. Part I is entitled "New Challenges and Threats." It consists of two chapters and it examines in greater detail and depth the current conditions wrought by the thrust of globalization and the counterthrust of balkanization briefly alluded to above. Chapter 1, "Disembodied Law, Reinvigorated Religion, and Tribal Politics," details the level of fracture and alienation that have surged as by-products of globalization severely disrupting *demos* and *ethnos* while throwing into disarray previously relied upon ways to seek convergence between the universal, the singular, and the plural. Law increasingly looms as abstract, distant, elusive, and oppressive, as a plurality of transnational legal regimes overlap with domestic ones. This fosters a sense of increasing alienation and inequity as many feel ever more burdened under national and transnational legal regimes over which they have no control while others are powerful enough not only to fashion some laws but also to choose among various regimes so as to maximize their benefits and minimize their burdens under law. As against this, there has been a strong resurgence and repoliticization of religion, with fundamentalism and intolerance on the rise. Moreover, this renewed "religious" fervor has spilled over to other strongly invested identitarian units, such as ethnic or linguistic communities with exclusivist tendencies. Accordingly, politics become increasingly tribal and intransigent, with zero-sum confrontations that leave little room for compromise and genuine cooperation.

Chapter 2, "Local versus Global, Material Well-Being, States of Stress, and the Erosion of Justice," concentrates on the novel and unsettling disruptions to patterns of distributive justice regarding wealth and other material burdens and benefits attributable to globalization and associated developments such as automation resulting in dramatic increases in inequalities based on wealth. The disruptions in question pose vexing new challenges to constitutions and, in particular, national constitutions, relating to their ability of satisfying the justice essentials in the realms of social, political, and economic distributive justice. As already mentioned, in the 1990s after the fall of communism, it was broadly assumed that capitalism would legitimately reign unchallenged, thus warranting a constitutional focus away from questions of wealth and towards questions of identity. More recently, however, questions of wealth have re-emerged and now figure urgently alongside questions of identity and of representation in the quest for constitutional justice. Although identity related debates have dominated the scholarly literature since the 1990s, certain scholars have recently stressed the need to refocus political theory to confront the newly exacerbated wealth disparities and their consequent distributive justice implications. In addition, the twenty-first century has confronted special challenges due to the prevalence of conditions of "stress" that stand halfway between ordinary conditions and states of emergency. Global terrorism and the "war on terror" that ensued, as well as the COVID-19 pandemic and its legal, political, and public health handling, have fostered prolonged and challenging conditions of stress. Such conditions typically test and reset loyalties while tending to compromise civil liberties for purposes of enhancing security or of meeting pressing public health objectives. These conditions of stress are prone to produce shifts in the relationship between the *demos* and the *ethnos*, to pose additional challenges to the justice essentials.

Part II of the book, entitled "Revisiting and Reconfiguring the Philosophical Grounding of Liberal Constitutionalism's Ideal of Justice," provides a rereading and a refocusing of the extant theoretical heritage that has figured prominently as a source of legitimation and vindication of liberal constitutionalism. Although the philosophical heritage in question deals with key aspects of the dynamic between *demos* and *ethnos* and centers on the nexus between the universal, the singular, and the plural, the rereading I propose is specifically grounded in the perspective framed by the interplay between the ideal of liberal constitutionalism and the justice essentials it calls for. Chapter 3, "Confronting the Gulf between Law and Solidarity: Kelsen Encounters Freud," addresses the wide gap that separates abstract law launched from above—as a consistent systemic normative whole most famously developed in Kelsen's positivist Kantian vision—from concrete mainly affective commitment to law-like behavior that springs from below within a given collectivity. On the side of abstract law, emphasis is on the *demos* and the universal; on that of solidarity and communal glue support is drawn from the *ethnos*, the singular, and the plural. The mystery, however, is how there could be any connection between abstract law and concrete bonds of solidarity allowing those under the law in question to accept it as their own. Kelsen himself was puzzled regarding why citizens felt compelled to obey the law and was convinced that fear of sanctions did not supply an adequate answer. This led Kelsen to turn to Freud's theories regarding group psychology in search for some amalgam between an unconscious drive towards group identity and solidarity and a logical acceptance of an orderly and unified polity need for adherence to a constitutional hierarchy. Only such a link could properly account for why those subjected to laws would internalize and validate them as their own. I explore the plausible nexus between Kelsen and Freud further to determine whether, or how far, the conjunction of a formal constitutional order and of an unconscious group drive to law-like conduct may advance the quest for justice through the constitution.

Chapter 4, "Law *Redux*: Schmitt, CLS, and the Drift to Politics; Marx, Posner, and the Absorption into Economics," concentrates on those who, in contrast to Kelsen's conception of law as a self-contained normative order, envision law as ultimately reducible to, or largely absorbed into, politics or economics. Schmitt and the Critical Legal Studies Movement (CLS) envisage law as largely reducible to politics. Schmitt submits law to a political theology resting on the divide between

24   INTRODUCTION

friend and foe whereas CLS characterizes law as infinitely malleable and thus as amenable to serving the interests of the powerful who typically control all the relevant institutions. To the extent that law is politicized and made to serve some against others, the constitution cannot genuinely advance the cause of justice. The thorough politicization of law must be ultimately rejected, but it raises important questions and highlights useful caveats for any attempted reconciliation of the universal, the singular and the plural. Subsuming law to economics, on the other hand, may be equally reductionist as casting it as thoroughly political, but the consequences for justice appear at first to differ. Economics figures importantly in the pursuit of the material component of distributive justice. Posner argues that law should be geared to maximizing wealth which is consistent with a libertarian conception of distributive justice. Marx, on the other hand, casts law as superstructure that figures as secondary to the economy. Although law may appear as independent and fundamental rights as transcending economic interests, Marxist analysis posits them both as exclusively serving the interests of capitalism. To the extent that capitalism is unjust (and Marx himself is notoriously ambiguous on the question of justice), the subordination of law to economics leads to opposite conclusions for Posner and for Marx. For Posner, the subordination in question leads to justice; for Marx to oppression, if not injustice. Even if law could be made reducible to economics and economics tied to *a* conception of justice (among many), any resulting claim to justice would remain contested, thus failing from the standpoint of the plural. Accordingly, to be compatible with justice through the constitution, law must engage with the economy and the political without losing its distinct mediating potential.

Chapter 5, "Kantian Universalism Reframed for a Post-Totalitarian Age: The Legacy of Rawls, Habermas, and Dworkin," revisits the universalist philosophical tradition going back to Kant that provides a categorical justification for the normative order carved out by liberal constitutionalism. The key characteristic of that deontological tradition is that questions of justice can be kept separate from questions of the good, thus opening the way for achieving justice while encompassing a wide plurality of conceptions of the good. I have criticized the deontological claim that justice can be separated from the good in previous work, and my aim in this chapter is to re-examine the contributions of Rawls, Habermas, and Dworkin from the perspective evoked earlier. Within that perspective, the universal must figure as one component in the dynamic that pits it against the singular and the plural. Rawls links the universal to the individual, but largely removes the singular from the latter while virtually completely ignoring the plural. Nevertheless, as already briefly stressed, Rawls provides a key baseline through his conception of "constitutional essentials" which suggests useful insights for purposes of better seizing the potentials and limitations of my conception of justice essentials. Furthermore, Habermas' dialogical ethics and his postulation of consensus-based vindication of universalizable norms opens a path that seems initially more amenable to singularity and plurality than Rawls' theory of justice. Like Rawls, however, Habermas ultimately underplays singularity and plurality. Habermas' dialogical approach and his endeavor to reconcile Kant's universalism and Rousseau's republicanism add a critical dimension that proves useful in assessing the viability of salient claims relating to unity or to solidarity. Finally, Dworkin, who is not a universalist like the other theorists discussed in this chapter, nevertheless advances a position combining liberal constitutionalism with egalitarian justice and presents it as a universally valid one for present-day constitutionalists. Dworkin's position can be described as involving constrained as opposed to unconstrained universalism, and it is of particular interest in as much as it intimates that his theoretical defense of liberal (understood in its moral and political sense) constitutionalism is the best, if not the only one, against the dangers of illiberal constitutionalism. Dworkin ultimately falls short as he does not sufficiently account for the plural, but his arguments must be dealt with before addressing viable alternatives better suited to accommodate the need for pluralism.

Chapter 6, "Tragic Deconstruction Set Against the Impenetrable Singular and Reconstruction as Spectacle and Administration: From Derrida to Agamben," which concludes Part II of the book, provides a critical appraisal of the jurisprudential contributions attributable respectively to Derrida and to Agamben. I argue that Derrida and Agamben can be understood as culminating various theoretical strands that have dominated the field throughout the twentieth century. Derrida, who combines Kantian universalism with Nietzschean–Heideggerian devotion to the irreducibility of the singular, can be regarded as the heir of the CLS movement in the United States. Indeed, Derrida adds a strong ethical component to purely political bent that permeates through most CLS contributions. By using his deconstructive method to stress the indissoluble necessity to pursue justice combined with its insurmountable impossibility, Derrida carves out a tragic path for jurisprudence which traps those subjected to law between an unyielding universal and an impenetrable singular. Morally compelled by the unyielding universal and repeatedly thwarted by the elusive singular, the Derridean quest for justice completely leaves out the plural. Against Derrida's deconstruction, Agamben elaborates a reconstruction that replaces tragedy with a combination between spectacle and acclamation, on the one hand, and administration, on the other. In important ways, Agamben is a successor of Schmitt. At the same time, particularly with respect to his focus on *oikonomia* or administration, Agamben shares much in common with positivism, or more precisely, with the kind of systems-based positivism associated with Luhmann. If justice is central and even obsessive for Derrida, it greatly fades to the point of becoming essentially absent for Agamben, who argues that the glory and acclaim that prevails in a polity where law is necessarily kept separate from administration derives from the mystery of the Christian Holy Trinity. From within the world view promoted by Christianity, the destiny of Christ as the promoter of God the Father's project for the world is by definition just. However, in

26   INTRODUCTION

the context of a contemporary secular polity, Agamben argues that the Christian form and structure remain intact, but the content of the relevant narrative becomes completely open-ended, thus severing any necessary link between justice and glory. Accordingly, consistent with Agamben's theory, it would be as authentic and as plausible to acclaim and glorify in the case of a Churchill as it would be in that of a Mussolini. Furthermore, Agamben 's theory does not seem to accommodate the plural any better than Derrida's although the relative place of the universal, the singular, and the plural in Agamben seems rather muddled and open-ended. In the end, in terms of the book's objective, the pairing of Derrida and Agamben is instructive and suggestive in terms of both the challenges posed by illiberalism and the obstacles to, and possibilities of, overcoming the current impediments to achieving justice through the constitution.

Part III of the book is entitled "Building a Commonly Shared Basis Toward a Pluralist Inclusivist Constitution." The analysis undertaken in Part II leads to the conclusion that neither theories starting from the top, namely from the universal, nor from the bottom, namely from the singular, can satisfactorily carve out a persuasive common ground that ought to garner consensus regarding the justice essentials. In the two chapters of Part III, I seek to demonstrate that starting from the middle, namely from the plural, affords the best means to secure the justice essentials in contemporary contexts in which there are widespread disagreements on the substantive requirements issuing from distributive justice. In Chapter 7, entitled "The Dialectics of Comprehensive Pluralism: Approaching the Justice Essentials from the Middle," I turn to comprehensive pluralism, a theory that is pluralist all the way up and all the way down, and that I have elaborated in previous works (Rosenfeld 1998; 2011). In this chapter, I further explore past insights by inquiring into their implications for a pluralist conception of constitutional justice. Comprehensive pluralism, which is distinguishable from the limited pluralism linked to philosophical liberalism and from the value pluralism articulated by Isaiah Berlin (Berlin 2002: 11–13), relies on a dialectical approach that incorporates some important Hegelian elements (but without any reliance on a course of historical progress leading to any final resolution of major societal conflicts). Comprehensive pluralism emerges in sharp contrast to both philosophical monism and relativism, and because *philosophical liberalism*, as opposed to *liberal constitutionalism*, is monistic in nature, I advance the thesis that comprehensive pluralism is better suited to provide normative legitimation to the latter than is philosophical liberalism. More specifically, because of its dialectical nature, comprehensive pluralism must actually be successively relativistic and monistic: relativistic to dislodge the hegemony of entrenched conceptions of the good that stand in the way of genuine plurality, and monistic to secure the greatest possible inclusion of competing ideologies without risking mere mutual disengagement or a thoroughly relativistic war of all against all. Furthermore, comprehensive pluralism is a teleological theory that rejects the proposition that justice can be properly conceived as

ORGANIZATION OF THE BOOK   27

being independent from the good. For comprehensive pluralism, justice as a good must rely to the greatest extent possible on *accommodation* of competing conceptions of the good—including competing conceptions of distributive justice—even if the later are *inconsistent* with pluralism so long as they do not prove downright *incompatible* with it.

Chapter 8, "Justice Essentials Minima and Comprehensive Pluralism's Fixed Core Minimum Set Against its Plural Maximum," departs from comprehensive pluralism's aim to maximize accommodation of plurality and from its dialectic insight that the such accommodation depends on deployment of a set of fixed normative institutional prescriptions which aggregate as minima from the standpoint of the justice essentials. Regarding justice itself, the search for a pluralistically acceptable minimum depends on a key distinction that must be drawn between factual disagreements and those that relate to what distributive justice ought to be. For example, is a free-market economy or one replete with state intervention better suited to the *advancement* of pluralist maximization with respect to all three facets of constitutional justice? In this context, the pluralist does not seek to maximize plurality but to uncover the best available means to a set goal. In contrast, a normative disagreement between a Nozickian libertarian vision of justice and a radical egalitarian one calls for pluralist *accommodation*. Furthermore, pluralistic minima also arise with respect to matters of identity and of recognition that oscillate between the poles of inward retreat and outward lurch. It is also necessary to address minima relating to autonomy and solidarity to assure a baseline of care and concern among "insiders" within a just constitutional order *while* refraining from demeaning the dignity of "outsiders." These latter minima are prerequisites to justice in recognition and in representation. Next, the chapter tackles the dialectical nexus between a minimum of fixed of core constitutional prescriptions and the maximization of plurality that would be triggered through deployment of a pluralist conception of the justice essentials. Finally, the chapter tackles the series of challenges and pathologies that may currently stand in the way of any straightforward realization of the justice essentials consistent with the vision of comprehensive pluralism.

In spite of inevitable difficulties and of uncertainties about ultimate realization of the justice essentials, the book concludes that the comprehensive pluralist approach offers the best plausible means toward constitutional justice. And this both in terms of optimizing harmonization between *ethnos* and *demos* and of striking the right equilibrium between the universal, the singular, and the plural. Moreover, when evaluated under the criteria of comprehensive pluralism, neither populist nor illiberal appropriations or invocations of the framework of liberal constitutionalism appear to stand any chance of coming close to meeting any of the relevant minima that pave the way to the justice essentials.

PART I
NEW CHALLENGES AND THREATS

New challenges and threats confront liberal constitutionalism due to current conditions wrought by the thrust of globalization and the counterthrust of balkanization. Law increasingly looms as abstract, distant, elusive, and oppressive, as a plurality of transnational legal regimes overlap with domestic ones. There has also been a strong emergence of politicized religion and of increasingly tribal and intransigent politics. Moreover, exacerbation of wealth inequalities pose daunting challenges to constitutional justice in its three dimensions of redistribution, recognition, and representation. Finally, stress deriving from global terrorism and a global pandemic undermine the stability of constitutionally enshrined standards of proportionality.

1

Disembodied Law, Reinvigorated Religion, and Tribal Politics

I Imagining an Ideal of a Just Constitution and Laws for Each, All, and their Multiple Competing Ideologies

To highlight the serious challenges that contemporary liberal constitutions would inevitably confront in any quest to meet the justice essentials, it seems helpful to begin by imagining a counterfactual ideal setting in which the demands of all three relevant facets of distributive justice could be conceivably met. This task requires some constructive speculation regarding how *ethnos* and *demos* could be harmonized while reaching a workable equilibrium among the universal, the singular, and the plural. In the broadest terms, liberal democratic constitutions are supposed somehow to garner a consensus among those they govern as attested by the oft used metaphor of the constitution as a social contract. This supposition seems bound to remain counterfactual as in actuality disagreements about the desirability or legitimacy of any particular constitution are all but inevitable. Moreover, it is even less likely that any actual consensus could materialize with respect to any given constitution meeting the justice essentials, or that questions of justice not within the scope of the latter could be resolved convincingly through democratically embedded majoritarian decision-making. With this in mind, what follows invokes the context of a working contemporary liberal constitutional democracy, and imagines what confluence of conditions, presuppositions, and convictions could counterfactually—but nonetheless instructively, for either furnishing the basis of a constructive critique or an ideal end state carving out a path to greater perfectibility—resolve what we could designate as the paradoxes of consensus and of democracy.

Ideally, a polity's constitution would frame the justice essentials for the relevant citizenry. In addition, the legal and institutional regimes deployed hierarchically below the said constitution would aim at justice beyond the essentials or, at the very least, at expanding the scope and reach of constitutionally mandated justice essentials. Thus, for example, where the constitution prohibits the state from engaging in discrimination based on sex, legislation could extend the breadth and depth of that prohibition by barring sex discrimination in the private employment realm and by confronting historically embedded domination and oppression of women extant within the precincts of private law. Furthermore, the justice essentials enshrined

A Pluralist Theory of Constitutional Justice. Michel Rosenfeld, Oxford University Press. © Michel Rosenfeld 2022.
DOI: 10.1093/oso/9780198862680.003.0002

32 LAW, RELIGION, AND TRIBAL POLITICS

in a constitution would require certain process-based as well as certain substance-based prescriptions.[1] Beyond that, infra-constitutional laws should advance, or at least not hinder, the path to justice by managing an equilibrium, or at least a good faith compromise, among the universal, the singular, and the plural. Habermas posits that law's legitimacy depends on its being at once self-imposed (by all those subject to it) and universalizable (Habermas 1996: 459–60). Derrida, for his part, insists that a just law would be one that at once reconciles the universal and the singular (Derrida 1992: 16–17). In addition, when individuals combine together into groups, whether religious, ethnic, or cultural, just laws should promote, or at least not inhibit, accommodation of such group-based plurality. In short, any law suited to further, or at least not to erode, the constitution's justice essentials ought to be plausibly acceptable to everyone it binds as if it were self-given, as well as justifiable from the standpoint of all involved, and from the various perspectives of the groups that have carved out their own distinct differentiated voice and agenda within a plurally apportioned, commonly shared political arena.

Viewed in terms of the above ideal, all actual laws are bound to fall short. And this for a variety of reasons. Most notably, general laws purporting to be universal in scope will unavoidably fail to meet justice in all singular instances. For example, a law banning all vehicles from a public park from dawn to dusk and prescribing a hefty fine for all violators would certainly be unfair if applied to a driver of an ambulance called into the park to attend a heart attack victim. Moreover, although the particular problem raised by this example can be addressed by supplementing the general proscriptions mandated by the relevant law with exceptions, not all plausible exceptions may be readily reconciled with the law's general objective. Assuming the vehicle ban in question is meant to ensure the safe and quiet enjoyment of the park, should exceptions be granted to children's bicycles, to roller coasters, or to cars carrying disabled people who could not otherwise access and enjoy the park? More generally, as the citizens in large, complex, contemporary polities inevitably embrace a plurality of conceptions of the common good that are bound to result in vigorous dispute over the requisites of justice, disagreements over certain important particular laws will frequently spill over the latter's universal, singular, and plural implications. For example, even assuming a general consensus over the prevailing constitution's justice essentials, a libertarian and an egalitarian would predictably strongly disagree over whether minimum wage laws

---

[1] Conceivably, a constitution could satisfy the justice essentials by relying exclusively on formal and purely procedural rights. For example, arguably the justice essentials could be assured by a constitution that enshrines property, contract, non-discrimination, and formal equal opportunity rights provided such a constitution was inextricably linked to a free and unimpeded market economy. In that case, constitutional rights would be overwhelmingly formal and procedural, but they would be substantively justified by notions of distributive justice purportedly assured by the "invisible hand" that stirs the market to the realization of the public good. Accordingly, in such a case, it would be ultimately the substantive distributions generated by the free market that would enable the formal and procedural guarantees of the relevant constitution to meet the requirements of the corresponding justice essentials.

or laws enshrining and protecting collective bargaining would advance or thwart the path to distributive justice. Similarly, certain committed religious adherents who equate abortion with infanticide would feel morally outraged and deprived of equal dignity and respect when confronted with liberal laws that approximate abortion on demand.

Notwithstanding all these difficulties, laws in a constitutional democracy can go far in significantly, albeit imperfectly, accounting for the universal, the singular, and the plural, thus projecting a broad sense of legitimacy. Many different factors are likely to contribute to this. Some of these are process based, others, substantive. From the standpoint of process, the postulation that in a democracy the law is self-given, if widely accepted as true or persuasive as a hypothetical proposition, can bestow legitimacy on laws. Moreover, a democratic law may be regarded as self-given, either directly or indirectly through invocation of the principle of majority rule.

Constitutions can be defended as self-given on the basis of a consensus among the citizenry. As such, consensus is literally impossible both in terms of the founding generation and in that of all succeeding ones; it can only be hypothesized drawing upon a combination of constitutional logic and constitutional identity. Constitutional logic is informed by the indispensable four pillars of modern liberal democratic constitutions listed at the outset. Constitutional identity, on the other hand, is collectively construed and imagined much like national identity is (Rosenfeld 2010: 29). In addition, the hypothesized consensus in question need not be on the constitution taken as a whole so long as it extends to its common core both in terms of logic and of identity. Thus, for example, there is disagreement in the United States over whether to preserve or abolish the constitutionally mandated Electoral College in presidential elections (Ross 2012; Wegman 2020). The Electoral College gives added voice to small states in the election of the US president, but it has resulted in two recent elections having the loser of the nationwide popular vote actually winning the election (Keyssar 2020: 1). Arguably, neither the current disagreement nor amending the US Constitution to abolish the Electoral College need alter any otherwise firm consensus relating to the US Constitution's fundamental logic or identity.

Regarding infra-constitutional laws, a law can be hypothesized as directly self-given because contesting the legitimacy of such law would amount to a performative—as opposed to a logical—contradiction. It is difficult to imagine, for instance, that a contemporary constitutional democracy could completely do away with laws that seek to afford protection to bodily integrity or to possession of private property. Consistent with this, it may not be strictly speaking illogical to argue that, if asked at time of its adoption, one would not have endorsed a current law prohibiting murder or one affording private property protection to one's essential personal possessions. Nevertheless, it seems fair to impute from the conduct, assumptions, and expectations of any responsible, actively engaged member of the

34 LAW, RELIGION, AND TRIBAL POLITICS

polity that she would have been pragmatically and prudentially behind the adoption of the laws in question had she had a vote in the legislature at the time of their enactment.

Majority rule can provide the next best justification for a law that cannot actually or hypothetically realistically count on consensus. If the justice essentials can be envisioned as secured by consensus, the adoption of majority rule in the enactment of infra-constitutional laws can go a long way in plausibly casting the latter as self-given. This may initially appear paradoxical since in a literal sense those in the legislative minority who opposed the law eventually passed are unlikely to perceive it as "self-given." However, if the focus is shifted from the content of any particular law to parliamentary majority law-making as a principal feature of sovereign democratic self-rule, then, as long as all relevant procedures are fairly adhered to, all laws of parliament may be regarded in an important sense as self-given.

For a person who opposed a law that a legislative majority managed to enact to be able to accept it as self-given, one or more among a few key substantive background conditions must be met. One such condition would be that the law in question boiled down to a preference among alternatives that were in essence indifferent from the standpoint of justice. Whether public school funding increases should be earmarked for improved sporting facilities as against for the strengthening of art and music instruction provides an example of a choice with seemingly scant implications for justice. Proponents of either of these two alternatives would view them as desirable but not essential to satisfying the basic educational needs of the citizenry and may thus reasonably conclude that maintaining the majoritarian process for resolving such choices is far more important than the actual outcome. Accordingly, in this case the process together with its associated outcome may be reasonably conceptualized as being self-given.

The self-given designation may also be plausibly extended to cases involving differences as to what justice requires, provided consensus holds over maintenance of constitutionally prescribed justice essentials. In other words, in this class of cases, neither of the two legislative alternatives up for a vote would pose any threat to justice essentials, but proponents of each of these alternatives would consider that adoption of their alternative would advance overall justice whereas adoption of the rival alternative would not. Suppose, for instance, that the constitution guarantees equal opportunity in education and in employment and that some legislators favor a law that provides remedial training and preferential treatment for those who are competitively lagging because of their socially disadvantaged past. Opponents of that proposed law, however, object that its enactment would undermine equality of opportunity rather than promoting it. In this case, the contested proposed law pits two conflicting conceptions of what justice requires against one another: formal equality of opportunity versus, to use Rawls' terminology, fair equality of opportunity (Rawls 1971: 275). The two camps involved could chose to do battle at the constitutional level if they were convinced that their own conception of equality of opportunity belonged to the constitution's justice essentials. But assuming all agreed that the constitution enshrines the *concept* of equality of opportunity rather than any particular *conception* of it, then they could accept settling their difference in the majoritarian legislative arena. Unlike in the school funding example earlier, in this case the legislative losers would regard the newly adopted law as somewhat unjust but as nonetheless tolerable. And that because the majoritarian process allows the legislative losers to regroup and hope for better luck at some future date and because it leaves open opportunities for them to prevail in similar contests looming on the horizon. Accordingly, in this class of cases, even though the adopted law taken alone may not qualify as self-given from the standpoint of the losing legislative minority, it may still be regarded as indirectly self-given in as much as preservation of the majoritarian legislative process remains the best legitimate means to advance one's own legislative objectives.

Ultimately, whether any law can genuinely be considered as self-given while in accord with the universal, the singular, and the plural depends on a successful blending of logic and identity. Moreover, the identitarian component in this equation must be substantive and apt to blending together the community of communities that frames and sustains the relevant constitutional unit together with all the latter's individuals and groups actually or plausibly entitled to constitutional recognition. Within the typical nation-state, the substantive identitarian component in question will be informed by the country's imagined national and constitutional identities (Rosenfeld 2010: 223–31), its history, culture, political, and social traditions, as well as its most dominant and widespread ideological commitments. For example, the United States seems much more individualistic and free-market-oriented than its Western European counterparts. Accordingly, whereas comprehensive state provided medical insurance for all has been for long a nearly universally welcome policy throughout Western Europe, thus far this policy has been rejected in the United States as many among its numerous opponents cast it as characteristic of socialism and as bound to prove inefficient.[2] Similarly, to cite another example, France and Germany are both secular constitutional democracies, but whereas France strictly prohibits the teaching of religion in its public schools, Germany constitutionally requires it.[3] Notably, however, the strict French prohibition happens to be somewhat relaxed in the Alsace region which has been in the past a part of Germany.[4]

[2] "The fix for American health care can be found in Europe," *The Economist*, August 12, 2017, <https://www.economist.com/united-states/2017/08/10/the-fix-for-american-health-care-can-be-found-in-europe> visited 3 May 2022.

[3] For France, see Breton 2007: 96–9. For Germany, see Basic Law, art. 7, section 3: "[r]religious classes [shall] form ... part of the regular curriculum in state schools, with the exception of secular schools...."

[4] Steven Erlanger, "Church-state tie opens door for Mosque," *NY Times*, October 7, 2008, <https://www.nytimes.com/2008/10/07/world/europe/07iht-alsace.1.16744303.html> visited 3 May 2022.

36 LAW, RELIGION, AND TRIBAL POLITICS

Laws that are in harmony with a distinct identitarian component of a particular polity plausibly qualify as both self-given and universally justifiable within the relevant overall community. Whether or not he voted for a law that bars religion in the public sphere, a Frenchman can regard this law as his own based on his strong support for French *laïcité* and consider it to be equally celebrated by all his compatriots to the extent that he regards *laïcité* as an essential and non-negotiable component of France's national and constitutional identity (Gunn 2004: 428–30). Even acknowledging the almost inevitable fact of lack of unanimity—not everyone in France endorses *laïcité* (Daly 2012)—the combination of a strong identitarian bond and of the fact of democracy go a long way in boosting both the legitimacy and the justice of majoritarian laws that further the relevant commonly shared identitarian component. Thus, constitutionally enshrined *laïcité* can be construed as framing an important part of the justice essentials within the French legal order. Indeed, *laïcité* universalizes the separation between Reason and Faith, reserving the public sphere for the former while keeping open the private sphere for the latter. Moreover, *laïcité* promotes equality among all individuals in France: as equal citizens without regard to religious differences in the public sphere and as equally free in their capacity as private actors to practice or not to practice a religion of their choice in the private sphere. Finally, *laïcité* may also be viewed as consistent with (but not as actively promoting) the maintenance of pluralism, religious and otherwise, by affording constitutional protection to freedom of association, of religion, and of speech (*Id.*), and hence protecting the formation and functioning of religious and other civil society collective entities within the confines of the private sphere.

Even a cursory comparison between French *laïcité* and German constitutionally enshrined secularism reveals that a just and legitimate ordering of the relationship between religion and the state for the polity as a whole, individual citizens and diverse religious and non-religious communities in Germany could not rely on the French model. The perceptions, problems, and potentially just solutions are bound to be different in the German context where the public sphere was traditionally regarded as apportioned between Catholics and Protestants and where questions of justice in the realm of public education have centered on achieving greater inclusiveness by accommodating the non-religious as well as Jewish and Muslim minorities (Koenig 2015: 52–3). More generally, it is by sharing a particular and distinct socio-political and legal-constitutional tradition that diverse polities view their respective identitarian convictions and struggles as their own. Accordingly, laws addressing and purporting to advance these shared identitarian concerns can be quite persuasively envisioned as self-given for the polity as a whole. Additionally, whereas shared identity factors and majoritarian law-making seem bound to be mutually reinforcing in the casting of laws as self-given and for the good of all, a shared identitarian heritage can in some cases stand by itself as the source of legitimacy that validates certain laws as the product of all those who end up with an obligation to obey them.

IMAGINING AN IDEAL OF A JUST CONSTITUTION 37

Perhaps the most acute example of a conception of a constitutional order as self-given without necessity for any recourse to democratic rule is Carl Schmitt's. As already noted, in his ethnocentric theory focused on pre-Second World War Germany, Schmitt envisions the constitution and the state as having to give expression to the pre-political character and culture of a nation that is built upon the identity of an ethnically defined people (Schmitt 1928; Preuss 1994: 153–5). Because Schmitt assumes that the relevant people is ethnically homogeneous, thus obviating the need for any pluralist accommodation, dictatorship can be cast, consistent with his theory, as the functional equivalent of democracy to the extent that, to put it in Preuss's terms, "the dictator successfully claims to incarnate the identity of the people" (Preuss 1994: 155).

Schmitt's anti-pluralist, ethnocentric constitutional vision is obviously unsuitable for any present-day multi-ethnic or individually pluralistic polity. Nevertheless, even in a multi-ethnic setting with ample room for pluralism, there may well be distinct aspects of national and constitutional identity that are so widely ingrained within the citizenry as to justify characterizing laws that give them expression as being self-given and universalizable in relation to the relevant community of communities that binds the polity together. More generally, particular constitutional and legal regimes can be deemed to be for the most part just and legitimate if, viewed as a whole, they conform to both the procedural and the substantive requisites discussed earlier in this chapter. Not every law or constitutional provision need individually satisfy these criteria, but to borrow Rawls's term, the "basic structure" (Rawls 1971: 9) that holds together the prevailing legal and constitutional order would have to do so. In other words, if the constitutional provisions and laws consistent with them that qualify as essential for purposes of stabilizing the relevant polity under a well-functioning rule of law regime satisfy the above detailed criteria, then the corresponding legal and constitutional basic structure may be deemed to be essentially just and legitimate.

To complete the key features of this best-case scenario for concluding that a legal-constitutional regime deployed in a complex contemporary polity may qualify as essentially just and legitimate, it is necessary briefly to address a seemingly paradoxical feature typical of well-functioning constitutional democracies. Such democracies for the most part have an essential anti-majoritarian feature, namely the judicial enforcement of fundamental individual rights leading in several cases to the striking down of highly popular laws supported by nearly all legislators and a vast majority of the citizenry (Bickel 1963). In some such cases, there may be a near consensus behind the law that a handful of citizens find objectionable, with the latter pitting the constitution against the relevant law, and the constitutional adjudicator either upholding or striking down the contested law (Rosenfeld 2001: 1314). For example, a law may prohibit spreading views that almost all within the polity find highly offensive and repulsive and yet the constitutional adjudicator may invalidate that law as infringing the free speech rights of the few who insist on offending and shocking their fellow citizens. On first impression, it appears that the highly popular law that is struck down by the constitutional adjudicator is self-given whereas the constitutional adjudicator's invalidation seems not only anti-majoritarian but also tantamount to selective eradication of the self-givenness of law. On the other hand, from the standpoint of the right holder who has been judicially relieved from what she has experienced as the oppressive other-givenness of the constitutionally invalidated law, the anti-majoritarian process and result seem bound to figure as just and legitimate. Moreover, as constitutional rights and/or their judicial interpretation expand, the perceived conflict between the citizen as rights holder and the citizen as self-legislator may well prompt an erosion of confidence in the justice and legitimacy of the prevailing approach to the rule of law.

Leaving aside for now claims that we have entered into an age of "juristocracy" in which judges have acquired far too much power (Hirschl 2004), it is possible to address the paradox associated with the apparent contemporary conflict between rights holders and self-legislators. To be sure, strong animosity between legislative majorities and minority rights holders who trigger judicial invalidation of popular laws may cause major erosion of a polity's sense that its legal system is self-given or universally justifiable to all those under its sway. Nevertheless, under conditions approaching those of an ideal setting, the dynamic surrounding anti-majoritarian constitutional adjudication may well produce conflict and tension but no animosity and no perceived threat to the integrity of democracy or to the strong working unity of the whole. This is because of one or the combination of the following two factors.

First, the whole split between legislative majority and minority rights holder may be cast as a dynamic expression of the unity of the polity provided it is approached from the perspective of the whole as opposed to those of its constituent parts. Indeed, both the constitution and legislative majoritarianism are to be regarded as self-given and legitimate for the whole, with the constitution figuring as more profoundly so in as much as it is supposed to be more unanimously, solidly, and enduringly self-given as the guarantor of justice essentials. In other words, in an ideal setting there is deep agreement on the constitutional and justice essentials and much less significant disagreement on the actual particular clash pitting popular legislation against an individual's fundamental rights. Thus, those who oppose what they consider the noxious views of certain of their fellow citizens would nonetheless be fully supportive of free speech rights and would insist on full protection for those of their views that others may deem offensive. More generally, the self-legislator and the constitutional author converging within every individual citizen would recognize upon reflection the priority of constitutional rights over policies advanced through laws and would accept the need to curb any initial interest-based preference for a legislative agenda eventually to lend support to initially disliked judicial anti-majoritarian vindication of constitutional rights. Alternatively, a citizen may disagree with the particulars of a judicial interpretation of constitutional rights that go against her strongly held views of the scope and limits of the right at stake and yet, in an ideal setting with broad consensus on process and on constitutional identity, that citizen may nevertheless still fully support the constitutional adjudicator's legitimacy and affirm her stake in the legal system as a whole.

Second, in any setting approaching the relevant ideal, the conflict between the self-legislator and the anti-majoritarian judicial vindication of individual constitutional rights is likely to figure as a dynamic means to further and adjust combined issues of process and constitutional identity in order to secure a proper equilibrium between the universal, the individual, and the plural within the ambit of the prevailing constitutional order. Indeed, the very conflict between majoritarian policies and individual rights claims as mediated by constitutional adjudication both signals, and allows for the resolution of, disruptions in the proper alignment among the universal, the individual, and the plural within the constitutional polity. To illustrate this, take the criminalization of Holocaust denial which was upheld as constitutional by the German Constitutional Court. The German Basic Law grants individual free speech rights which must be subject to some limitations, as are all such rights—at a minimum, no citizen can be allowed to use his freedom of speech right to deprive another citizen of hers. In the German case, free speech is subjected to specific limitations[5] as well as to those arising under the overriding constitutional commitment to the principle of human dignity.[6] With this in mind, the German prohibition against Holocaust denial not only represents an instance of majoritarian self-legislation but also a key component of the country's constitutional identity built upon a radical rejection of all the evils wrought by the Third Reich. As against that, an individual Holocaust denier can claim that he should be equally entitled as is every other individual in Germany to express his own views and opinions. As abhorrent as Holocaust denial may be, a simple judicial denial of protection regarding its utterance would seemingly unduly skew the German Basic Law in favor of the universal (and possibly the plural assuming the legislative majority and other important civic and political groups favor criminalization) against the individual. On further thought, however, as noted by the German Constitutional Court, Holocaust denial poses a great threat to the sense of inclusion and of dignity of the post-Second World War Jewish community living in Germany.[7] Accordingly, in this case, given the paramount importance of the memory of the Holocaust to contemporary Germany's national and constitutional identity (the universal component) and to its Jewish community (the plural component), limiting the scope of the free speech rights of the Holocaust denier quite reasonably promotes the requisite equilibrium among the three

---

[5] See German Basic Law, No. 92-308 DC art. 5.
[6] *Id.*, art. 1.
[7] 90 BVerfGE 241, 251.

40 LAW, RELIGION, AND TRIBAL POLITICS

pillars of constitutional justice.[8] In contrast, in the context of the United States, with no Nazi past and in light of differences in ideology and in constitutional identity, constitutional adjudication has struck the requisite equilibrium elsewhere by extending free speech protection to Holocaust denial (Rosenfeld 2012). In sum, constitutional strife pitting the individual, the plural, or the universal against one another falls within the essence of pursuit of the needed equilibrium called for by constitutional justice. From the standpoint of the ideal setting, the crucial requirement is that all actors in conflicts among legislative majorities and individual rights holders both accept their resolution, regard the latter as in the service of adhering to the proper equilibrium mentioned earlier, and continue their strong adherence to the polity's community of communities, no matter the actual particular judicial decision in their constitutional case.

II The Road to Alien and Disembodied Law

The farthest a constitutional order strays from the above sketched ideal, the more likely it becomes that part or all of the citizenry will become alienated from the status quo. Some or most will be feeling that laws have become more imposed than self-given, that the equilibrium between the universal, the individual, and the plural is unraveling, and that interpretation and application of the constitution is gradually moving away from the relevant justice essentials requirements. Ideal conditions are never achieved and existing equilibriums generating sufficient solidarity and fair confidence in acceptable approximation to the constitution's justice essentials are for the most part fragile. Internal erosion or even sudden irruption can certainly cause serious damage and in some cases dangers of irreparable rupture. For example, Spain's 1978 Constitution, negotiated after decades of authoritarian dictatorship, managed to unify the country into a thriving constitutional democracy (Rosenfeld 2010: 127–46). In more recent years, however, due to changed political circumstances and to deeply contested constitutional adjudication,[9] political upheaval and constitutional discord over the identitarian dimension of justice essentials—the Catalans call for a much greater degree of political autonomy than Spain's central government or its Constitutional Court have been willing to recognize—Spain's constitutional order has come under serious threat (Kiewiet 2018). At this writing, it seems possible that the order in question may be eventually restored, or reconfigured, or even conceivably dissolved as a consequence of some future secession initiative by Catalunya.

---

[8] Arguably, Holocaust denial in Germany may cast its proponents outside the country's constitutional community of communities. Significantly, the speaker in the German case was David Irving, a British citizen intent on addressing a German audience.

[9] Spanish Constitutional Court Judgment, (2010) No. 31/2010 (June 28)

The situation in Spain or that in Canada, with periodic initiatives aiming at the secession of Quebec,[10] involve *internal* fluctuations, ebbs and flows, or crises within the precincts of a working constitutional order in relation to which the community of communities could again sufficiently cohere to sustain the legitimacy and common quest toward justice of the polity at stake. In contrast to the internal dynamics mentioned earlier, there are *external* factors that may threaten or erode the viability or the integrity of a working legal and constitutional system otherwise capable of properly attending to the relevant justice essentials. An obvious potential such external disruptor is a transnational legal regime with widely perceived unjust domestic effects. Thus, for example, if a pro-business E.U. regulation were to force abandonment of regulations protective of workers' rights in an E.U. member state, this may well be regarded by a significant portion of the latter's citizenry as not only the imposition of an injustice from without but also an erosion of their country's democracy which undermines the traditional majoritarian recourses to seek redress.

Empirically, it may often be difficult to differentiate internal from external factors or to disentangle their respective effects. For example, mass migration together with transnational flow of capital are two of the key pillars of globalization and heavily factor in external factors raising challenges for national legal systems. Thus, in many highly predominantly Christian European constitutional democracies immigration in very significant numbers by Muslims has raised various issues including legal and constitutional ones. In its initial phases, this immigration may be seen as posing external challenges to existing legal arrangements. But at some subsequent point, such as when German Muslims seek their new country's public school religious education to include the teaching of Islam (Berglund 2015: 16–19) or when French Muslims seek official tolerance for students wearing the Islamic veil in their country's public schools (*Id.*: 39–42), the "external" becomes mixed with, or converted into the "internal." From a conceptual standpoint, however, it is useful to maintain a clear distinction between internal and external factors. Thus, German constitutional identitarian justice before the influx and nationalization of large numbers of Muslims was largely constructed around the apportionment of the religious landscape between Catholics and Protestants (Korioth & Augsberg 2015: 320). Consistent with that, conceptually from the standpoint of the German legal/constitutional system, the new challenges posed by the influx of Muslims and by their acquisition of citizenship are best viewed as posing an external challenge to the prevailing legal/constitutional ebbing and flowing status quo. With this in mind, the following discussion will concentrate on major changes and challenges that may be conceptually understood as stemming from external factors affecting the inner constitutional equilibrium of the relevant constitutional polity.

---

[10] *Reference re Secession of Quebec*, [1998] 2 SCR 217.

42 LAW, RELIGION, AND TRIBAL POLITICS

Before further examining the principal external factors that pose novel and serious threats to established and reasonably well-functioning legal/constitutional orders, it bears emphasizing that the conceptually "external" ought not be equated with what originates beyond the relevant polity's geographic boundaries. Indeed, in this regard certain contemporary developments, such as in effect delegating certain areas of legislation and of administrative rule-making to powerful concerned corporate interests (Metzger 2003:1400–10), or allowing for systematic relegation of a vast percentage of commercial and consumer disputes to private arbitration (Schill 2015: 112–14), are preferably regarded as essentially "external" factors that impact the justice and legitimacy of the prevailing legal/constitutional system from the "outside." In other words, just as transnational legal norms interpreted by a multinational array of judges sitting on international courts often seem largely to escape key democratic and constitutional controls functioning within affected nation-states, so also, in significant measure, do delegations of traditional public functions to private actors. Conversely, moreover, in the course of increasing thrusts toward globalization, legal developments beyond state boundaries may be increasingly best be regarded as conceptually "internal." For example, rights protected by the European Convention on Human Rights (ECHR) as interpreted by the European Court of Human Rights (ECtHR) sitting in Strasbourg, may be regarded as the functional equivalent of constitutional rights. Consistent with this, these European rights may either become absorbed within the domestic constitutional order of affected countries through national judicial or legislative incorporation or reconciliation,[11] or through invocation by such countries' citizens against their own public authorities before the ECtHR as they would before their country's constitutional adjudicator in cases involving their national constitutional rights.[12]

As will be detailed later in this chapter, it is useful to rely on the conceptual contrast between the internal and the external and to emphasize how the latter predominates in fostering contemporary perceptions of law as alien and disembodied. That said, even at the conceptual level, some important operating factors that play a significant role in the process of alienation and disembodiment under consideration may be as plausibly regarded as internal or as external. Take, for instance, the proliferation of administrative regulation that is both inevitable and essential within contemporary constitutional democracies. On the one hand, the advent of the administrative state may be regarded as the culmination of a process of internal development—the 1787 US Constitution did not foresee the advent of the administrative state, but it has in more recent times incorporated the latter, relying

---

[11] See, e.g., *Ghaidan v. Godin-Mendoza* [2004] UKHL 30 (where the UK Supreme Court applied principles of legal analysis from ECtHR to answer questions about rights for same-sex couples in the United Kingdom); see also Human Rights Act, 1998, c. 42 (UK).

[12] See, e.g., *Markin v. Russia*, App. No. 30078/06, EU.Ct.H.R. 2010 (where Markin sought to enforce his right to paternity leave under rules of the Russian military and art. 38(1) of the Russian Constitution).

on standards articulated in the context of constitutional adjudication (Metzger 2017: 42–6, 51). On the other hand, the proliferation of increasingly complex and technical administrative regulation covering an ever-larger domain is easily regarded as undemocratic, difficult to follow, and virtually incomprehensible to the average citizen much as are specialized transnational legal norms, such as those issued by the World Trade Organization (WTO) (Joseph 2011: 56–90). Accordingly, contemporary national administrative regulation may be reasonably considered as external in contrast to much state-originated ordinary private and public law. In the end, whether administrative regulation and policies are better regarded as internal or external depends on whether one views them primarily as the product of scientific and technical expertise or as inevitably as the products of contested politics (Shane 2016: 146–58). Thus, for example, if there is broad consensus on minimizing air and water pollution and the corresponding administrative responsibility to advance these objectives is left in the hands of scientific and technical personnel that are widely regarded as politically neutral, then the proliferation of the administrative state may be reasonably considered as involving an internal evolution that ought not threaten confidence in the polity's law as essentially self-given. Conversely, if expert pollution policy and administration are understood as inextricably political then they may well loom as neither self-given nor plausibly majoritarian as ordinary citizens would for the most part be unable to untangle the politics from the expertise wielded in the course of massive deployments of power by the state's administrative apparatus.

Keeping these preliminaries in mind, the contemporary path to alienation from, and disembodiment of, law that fosters much of the expanding distancing from the ideal of constitutional justice detailed earlier is framed by a series of external developments. The principal, among the latter, include: (a) trans-nationalization and multiplication of a plurality of legal regimes that foster layering and segmentation (Rosenfeld 2008); (b) fragmentation and increasingly compounding complexity of powerful special interests-driven legal and administrative regulation coupled with privatization of the body of applicable law through selective handpicking of favorable laws from the vast repository found in diverse legal regimes and through relegation of disputes under the tailored and self-chosen laws applicable in private arbitration (Pistor 2019); and (c) asymmetrical uses of legal norms to impose and evade legal obligations simultaneously for purposes of cementing unprecedented forms of domination and control over the individual's needs and objectives (Zuboff 2019).

Furthermore, before exploring these developments, it is worth briefly addressing in what sense these may be understood as fostering alienation from law and projecting the latter as being to an increasing degree disembodied. Greater alienation from law is likely to occur along two main coordinates: the ever-expanding remoteness of the law-maker (e.g., the faceless EU or WTO rule-maker), and significant shifts from laws plausibly understood as being made in the general interest to

44 LAW, RELIGION, AND TRIBAL POLITICS

laws tailored to suit the aims of powerful special interests (e.g., from transactions governed by general contract and tort laws to gaining access to social media accounts subject to acceptance of lengthy technical fine print conditions resulting in the consumer unwittingly losing virtually all rights to privacy) (Zuboff 2019: 48–50). On the other hand, the "disembodiment" of law as conceived in the present context should be understood in a metaphorical sense. The point is not that the law loses its body but instead that the body in question becomes either invisible or mired in such an array of entangled and often incomprehensible details that it is nearly impossible to fathom it as any discernible embodiment. Traditional criminal law as encapsulated in a series of proscriptions and a set of judicial interpretations expanding on the latter easily figures as a distinct body of law with well-defined contours. In contrast, complex contemporary operations subjected to a broad number of often conflicting legal regimes issuing from various national, transnational, and global international orders can become so dense and elusive that, as one commentator puts it, we confront a "global disorder of normative orders" (Walker 2008: 373).

(a) Transnationalization and multiplication of a plurality of legal regimes that foster layering and segmentation

As legal regulation becomes more transnational and as legal regimes become increasingly plural, the unity and hierarchy that binds together the constitutional order of the Westphalian polity gives way to a growing encroachment by a plurality of legal regimes that become implanted through a process that combines layering and segmentation.[13] A prime example of layering is provided by the legal regime that the EU imposes on its member states. The EU laws and directives are more comprehensive and intrusive upon the legal order within the EU member states than are US federal laws upon the legal orders of the various states in that country. Yet unlike in the US case where the US Constitution as interpreted by the US Supreme Court guarantees unity within the country's multipronged legal system, there is no comparable hierarchy and unity within the EU. That is because several of the EU member state constitutional courts have held that in case of conflict their national constitution prevails over any incompatible EU law.[14] Due to this lack of unity, EU law amounts to a separate *layer* of legal norms that is added to the national one that functions in each of the EU member states. Although *de facto* legal unity has thus far been largely preserved within the EU, this is only because constitutional judges who have asserted the hierarchical superiority of their own

---

[13] The following discussion draws on the analysis and sources found in Rosenfeld 2008.

[14] See, e.g., *Lisbon Treaty Case*, Federal Constitutional Court (Germany) Judgment of June 30, 2009 2 BvE 2/08, 2 BvE 5/08, 2 BvR 1010/08, 2 BvR 1022/08, 2 BvR 1259/08, 2 BvR 182/09.

national constitution have nonetheless managed to interpret the challenged EU law before them as not being contrary to their domestic constitution.[15]

As a general matter, layering is prone to increasing alienation from law both from a process based and an identitarian standpoint. The EU well publicized "democratic deficit" certainly erodes any sense of self-givenness and perhaps even more so since the EU has become empowered to enact legal norms without the unanimous approval of all its member states.[16] Moreover, it stands to reason that the plurality of national and constitutional identities spread throughout the EU's vast territory encompasses many more dissonances and conflicting positions than its counterpart within any single EU member state. Finally, both the dilution of self-givenness and the dissipation of identarian poles of convergence seem bound to accelerate as superimposed layers of legal regulation multiply. Thus, for example, the EU's highest court, the Court of Justice of the European Union (CJEU), has asserted that binding UN antiterror regulation with the force of law is unenforceable within the EU if it violates the latter's mandated protection of fundamental rights.[17] Notably, the threefold layering involved in this example leads not only to one conflict between the UN and the EU but also to another between the EU and some of its member states to the extent that the latter's domestic legal system require conformity with UN legally binding regulation (Vara 2011).

Segmentation is instituted by transnational legal regimes that cover one among the many areas of regulation that typically coexist in nation-states (Rosenfeld 2008). Examples of segmented legal regimes include international or regional human rights covenants or conventions, such as the European or the Inter-American, and international regulation of trade such as that provided by the WTO. The regime put in place by the WTO regulates free trade throughout the globe but virtually no other legal relations that ordinarily affect trading companies. Accordingly, whereas on the national level all the just mentioned legal relations coexist and weave together, at the transnational segmented level, such as that carved out by the WTO, trade is largely severed from all other relevant areas of law.

From the standpoint of alienation from, and the disembodiment of law, segmentation somewhat differs from layering, but ultimately the two converge to multiply challenges to self-givenness and to identitarian congruence. Segmentation can at once enhance the self-givenness and identitarian solidarity of those encompassed within its legal reach and exacerbate the alienation experienced by those left out whom it nonetheless affects. Thus, in the case of the WTO, the corporate interests

---

[15] In some cases, like the French Constitutional Council's Maastricht Treaty decision, the E.U. law was found to violate the French Constitution, but the conflict turned out to be relatively inconsequential as it proved easy to amend the French Constitution to obviate any inconsistency. Conseil constitutionnel (CC)(Constitutional Court) decision No. 92-308 DC, April 9, 1992.

[16] Only a qualified majority is required for about 80 per cent of E.U. legislation, including on proposals on immigration, asylum, and agricultural services (Craig 2010: 37).

[17] Case C–402/05 P and C–415/05, *P. Kadi and Al Barakaat International Foundation v. Council and Commission* [2008] E.C.R. I–6351.

that partake in the international free trade regime typically share much in common and, most likely, more than each of them does within the nation-state in which it originated.[18] Indeed, within the confines of the nation-state, corporate actors engaging in international trade must confront labor, environmental, consumer, and even ideological anti-free trade antagonists with widely disparate visions and agendas. Accordingly, segmentation is capable of fostering greater solidarity within its delimited sphere of regulation than does layering. At the same time, segmentation seems prone to lead to greater alienation beyond its confines than does layering. Although layers may be superimposed on one another with deficits in hierarchy and unity, they remain suited to accommodation of a full array of ordinarily diverging interests. This is well exemplified in the present-day EU legal regime which encompasses most of the subject matters dealt with in the national regimes of its member states.

For all their differences, transnational segmentation and layering converge in paving the road to increased alienation from law. They both combine in multiplying the remoteness, and in many cases the opacity of the actual originators, which become exacerbated as the plurality of legal regimes yields an increasing array of legal regulation. Remote laws are much more difficult to rationalize as self-given. Moreover, segmentation governed by faceless regulators in favor of special interests, such as those of internationally trading corporations subject to the WTO, may undermine both self-givenness and identitarian convergence within the nation-state. While confined within the legal bounds of the nation state, large corporations must confront and compromise with other constituencies, such as organized labor and consumer protection groups. To the extent that such corporations can evade constraints under national law through adhesion to segmented transnational legal regulation, however, they may loom as unjustifiably increasingly privileged within their own original national setting. And as a consequence, those within the polity with opposing interests may well feel increasingly disenfranchised and unjustly disfavored or cast aside.

For all their shortcomings regarding self-givenness and identitarian congruence, transnational layering and segmentation still harbor within them a potential for advancing law's legitimacy. This is conceivable under certain favorable circumstances that depend on the materialization of key future institutional and political developments. At the level of the nation-state, federalism bears a strong structural and functional resemblance to transnational layering, notwithstanding the key difference between them, as federalism fits within the bounds of constitutional hierarchy and unity whereas currently transnational layering does not. In pluralist polities, federalism seems often poised to afford a better means of integrating the

---

[18] Although there are certainly disagreements within the W.T.O. constituencies, see Stewart and Ratton 2011, the points of convergence among the free trading cohort are bound to be far stronger than any poles of divergence.

universal, the individual, and the plural, thus optimizing the sense of self-givenness and of identitarian solidarity. For example, in a multi-ethnic polity, federalism could grant each ethnic group a federated unit of self-government combined with a national federal governmental sphere to rule over country-wide common matters, such as environmental policy and foreign affairs. In addition, the federalism in question could add a purely local level of governance allowing each municipal unit to control its own fate regarding its day-to-day concerns and projects. Moreover, federalism may not only enhance law's legitimacy through vertical divisions of power but also through redistributions to de-escalate conflicts among the citizenry. Thus, in an ethnic-based federation, minorities within an ethnic majority-ruled federated entity may feel better protected at the federal level than at the federated one. This is exemplified by the concerns of the native Canadians living in Quebec when that province was seriously considering secession (Buchanan 2003). Analogously, transnational layering, such as that prevailing in the EU, while seemingly increasingly alienating may nonetheless be imagined as a vector of integration assuming certain institutional adjustments and the development of stronger identitarian bonds across member state borders.

Segmentation, on the other hand, may be a unifying force within and beyond national boundaries much in the same way as it can be alienating within these same precincts. One segmented legal domain that has thus far fomented both increased solidarity and increased alienation is that of human rights (Rosenfeld 2010: 261–8). In substantive terms, contemporary human rights are embodied in transnational covenants and conventions as well in national constitutions. Solidarity has cemented around a broad array of human rights protectors and promoters, including judges, ombudsmen, advocates, activists, non-governmental organizations (NGOs), and these operate at both the national and transnational levels. Notably, human rights vindication can sometimes be obtained in a transnational venue, such as the ECtHR, for individuals who have failed to secure the requisite protection within their own country.[19] At the same time, however, the transnational human rights regime has been cast as culturally biased and imperialistic, as exemplified by the controversy surrounding the claim that such rights bear strong Western ideological imprints, thus undermining "Asian values" (Ingiyimbere 2020). Moreover, even within the Western tradition, there are notorious instances of alienation from transnational human rights regimes. Thus, certain common law jurisdictions such as the United Kingdom and the United States have touted their own civil liberties traditions as superior to international human rights conventions they have refused to join fully or wholeheartedly.[20]

---

[19] See, e.g., *Opuz v. Turkey*, App. No. 33401/02 (EU.Ct.H.R. June 9, 2009), <http://www.echr.coe.int/eng> visited 3 May 2022.

[20] See, e.g., Stephen Clear, "UK Human Rights Act is at risk of repeal—here's why it should be protected," *The Conversation*, February 12, 2019 (proponents of the United Kingdom withdrawing from the ECHR argue for a return to "a more British," "less European" understanding of human rights); *Report of the Commission on Unalienable Rights* (United States), <https://www.state.gov/wp-content/uploads/

48 LAW, RELIGION, AND TRIBAL POLITICS

In sum, although transnational layering and segmentation can foster both solidarity and alienation, under current conditions marked by increases in illiberalism, right-wing populism, Brexit, and growing Euro-skepticism within the EU, alienation is on the increase and seems to far outpace solidarity.

(b) Fragmentation and compounding complexity through administrative regulation, selection of applicable law by the economically powerful, and the move from public adjudication to private arbitration

As noted earlier, the ever-expanding reach and complexity of the realm of administrative regulation within contemporary constitutional democracies can be portrayed in two contrasting ways. The first casts the administrative state as predominantly delegating technical and scientific management to experts, thus largely remaining beyond the political fray. As against this, the second view regards the administrative state as for the most part catering to the self-interests of the powerful through politically and ideologically driven co-option of the know-how of scientists and technocrats (Metzger 2017). Under the first of these views, the administrative state and its bureaucracy, whether fulfilling welfare, public housing, public health, or central bank functions, is apt to fitting well within the dictates of constitutionalism and to operating consistently with the justice essentials incorporated into the relevant constitution. Under the second view, however, the administrative apparatus may become predominantly a tool to shield powerful private interests from democratic control and accountability, thus contravening central precepts of constitutional democracy and weighing against furthering the latter's justice essentials. Thus,

> administrative law has sometimes served as a check on populist or democratic demands by organized and powerful interest groups a way to challenge policy .... Public law provisions that are justified as a check on overarching state power can also be a means of entrenching existing private interests. (Rose-Ackerman & Lindseth 2010: 3)

Moreover, consistent with this, not only can the administrative regime be garnered to enable private actors to evade democratic controls but it can also be structured

---

2020/08/Report-of-the-Commission-on-Unalienable-Rights.pdf> visited April 3, 2022 (underlining the "distinctive American contributions to the human rights project" and singling out private property and religious liberty rights as paramount).

so that elected officials may avoid accountability for their decisions.[21] For example, elected legislators can enact broad legislation designed to promote clean air and clean water[22] and leave it to administrative agencies and their bureaucracies to set and enforce technically complex air and water pollution standards. Often enough, the latter turn out to be more attuned to the private interests of powerful regulated industries, such as chemical plants or automobile manufacturers, than to the public health interests of the citizenry at large.

Complex and opaque regulation favoring powerful private interests provides strong fuel to populism and to its anti-elite and anti-expert stance. Accordingly, it speaks in the name of the left-out "ordinary" citizens whose votes are counted in democratic elections, but whose interests become increasingly ignored or defeated in legislation orchestrated by powerful lobbies and in administrative regulatory regimes shielding those they are supposed to restrain in pursuit of the public good. Under such circumstances, fewer and fewer citizens regard laws as self-given, and more and more of them become alienated from the self-images of the polity projected by the expert and elite classes.

This tendency toward skewing law in favor of powerful private interests is compounded by the increasing prospects, in an era of globalization, for transnational corporate enterprises to choose among a variety of different existing legal regimes[23] or to fashion a private one suited to their own purposes. Indeed, as capital and labor span across the globe, multinational corporations can select among manifold legal jurisdictions the one that suits them the best, and in some cases, with the assistance of a panoply of transnational specialized law firms, to craft a private contract-based legal framework precisely suited to their own business purposes (Pistor 2019). At the same time, these multinational corporations can meet their labor needs in jurisdictions wages are the lowest and workers' protections the weakest (*Id.*: 221). These opportunities and their crucial legal underpinnings facilitate enormous accumulations of wealth and produce ever-increasing inequalities (*Id.*: 1–2). Whereas global capitalism cannot prosper without law and without the means to resolve disputes under the legal terms that corporate multinationals impose or agree to, the latter's extraordinary ability to choose or to dictate the law applicable to their wide-ranging activities obviously contributes to perceptions of law as becoming ever more removed from the citizenry and as at once appearing more oppressive and more opaque.

---

[21] See, e.g., *Bowsher v. Synar*, 478 US 714 (1986) (US Congress attempt to have Comptroller General determine program funding cuts to balance the budget, which might shield elected representatives from responsibility in the eyes of their constituents, held unconstitutional as in violation of separation of powers).

[22] See the US Clean Air Act, 42 USC §§ 7401–7671q.

[23] "Global capitalism ... is built around two domestic legal systems, the laws of England and those of New York State ...." (Pistor 2019: 132).

50 LAW, RELIGION, AND TRIBAL POLITICS

In addition to the ever-greater opportunities to choose the law under which they operate, large corporate enterprises have also increasingly managed to have the disputes in which they become embroiled settled by arbitration rather than by adjudication in public courts (*Id.*: 181–2). One of the main advantages of this recourse to arbitration is that the arbitrators chosen by the parties involved are drawn from the business community and hence much less likely to being attuned, as a civil judge would, to other interests affected by a particular business dispute, such as those of consumers. Notably in this respect, after the US financial crisis in 2008, the US Congress enacted legislation prohibiting banks from submitting consumer loan disputes to arbitration. This legislation, however, has since been repealed (*Id.*: 182). In short, whereas law and legal experts have figured front and center in the global expansion of corporate power, the law at stake has been increasingly subordinated to the needs of a narrow class of capitalist entrepreneurs and its interpretation mainly left in the hands of business-oriented arbitrators unlikely to give any weighty consideration to any of the non-business interests bound to be significantly affected by their decisions.

(c) Asymmetrical uses and evasions of existing legal norms to foster unprecedented relationships based on domination and control of the individual's needs and objectives

The recent development and rapid expansion of the Internet and of social media augured a vast potential for an unprecedented expansion and democratization of information, communication, forging of social bonds across the globe, and an almost inexhaustible range of possibilities for better and more rapidly meeting the needs and aspirations of ever larger portions of humanity. In the last few years, however, optimism about these new media has become significantly tempered as they have been enlisted in the spread of "fake news," hate speech, disinformation to manipulate electoral campaigns, as well as to exacerbate disparities in power and wealth (Zuboff 2019: 507–11). Although all the new media and all the above-noted problems they pose have important legal dimensions and raise difficult questions of regulation, I shall focus exclusively on a single particularly momentous development that involves new approaches to law and leads to what appear to be yet unseen new forms of alienation and disembodiment. This new development consists in the implantation of a new era of "surveillance capitalism" (*Id.*: 8–12). Major multinational corporate enterprises, such as Google, Apple, and Facebook, have acquired extraordinary amounts of wealth and power while providing virtually indispensable services to a vast portion of humanity. This unique combination of wealth and indispensability has enabled these enterprises to achieve two feats with broad impact on the realm of law that sets them qualitatively apart from their predecessors in the prior era of managerial capitalism (*Id.*: 495–504). The first of these feats is the ability of these enterprises to condition their services to consumers on more onerous and much more intrusive legal concessions than those extracted by the typical fine-print consumer contracts of the previous generation. The second feat, in turn, is the capacity of these enterprises to draw on their seemingly unending potential for accumulation of ever greater wealth in order to violate laws that stand in their path to the appropriation of information belonging to others in their pursuit of new frontiers of economic dominance.

Surveillance capitalism is built upon amassing a huge and ever-expanding "information surplus" and exploiting it for profit, without, for the most part, the knowledge or meaningful consent of those from whom the information in question is extracted. For example, to have a thermostat wired through the Internet working properly so as to avoid frozen pipes when one is away from home requires entering into several intricate fine-print agreements allowing for disclosure of sensitive household and personal information to be shared with third parties for predictive behavioral analysis and further commercial exploitation (*Id.*: 7). More generally, Internet companies such as Google, smartphone providers such as Apple, and social media platforms such as Facebook, exhaustively collect and commercially exploit detailed intimate information about individuals, their whereabouts, their interactions, and their environment. In essence,

> [s]urveillance capitalists know everything about *us,* whereas their operations are designed to be unknowable to *us* ... They accumulate vast domains of knowledge *from us* but not *for us.* They predict our futures for the sake of others' gain, not ours. [In] surveillance capitalism ... ownership of the new means of behavioral modification eclipses ownership of the means of production as the fountainhead of capitalist wealth .... (*Id.*: 11. Emphasis in original)

The difference between an unfair consumer fine-print contract and a contract to extract an information surplus from a consumer relying on Internet wiring services is qualitatively remarkable, though both these types of contracts may be qualified as highly one-sided and unfair. In the former type of contract, the consumer obtains what he wishes, a television or an automobile, under unfavorable contractual conditions, such as installment payments with the seller's right of repossession of the sold item for failure to pay any single installment even if the purchased good is almost fully paid for. In the latter contract, on the other hand, the seller extracts intrusive surplus information in disregard of the buyer's innermost privacy, which bears no direct link to the particular transaction between the parties, and which is systematically kept secret from the buying individual. Moreover, the systematic pursuit of information surplus that stands at the forefront of surveillance capitalism is not only launched to make it possible to turn every behavioral inclination into a source of profit but also to reshape human behavior unbeknown to all those targeted in order to further expand the range of attainable profits (*Id.*: 8). To the extent that surveillance capitalism proves successful, it threatens the very singularity of every individual, the latter's judgement as an agent of democracy, and the maintenance of a workable proportion among the one, the many, and the whole. Previous generations may have battled false consciousness and false needs, but these pale when compared to the threat of humans being systematically spied upon regarding their perceived needs, fears, and aspirations without meaningful awareness of how they are being manipulated so as to be redirected from within.[24]

As noted earlier, the second important feat that surveillance capitalism manages to achieve in the context of law consists in having recourse to downright violations of law when it deems the latter necessary for completion of one of its comprehensive objectives. To be sure, leading surveillance capitalists use all the tools available to multinational corporate enterprises in order to shape law-making, select laws, choose among jurisdictions, and exploit the advantages of private arbitration. But when none of that suffices, the surveillant capitalist can deliberately violate the law and easily pay the ensuing damages or fines as these will usually amount to no more than a marginal increase in costs for a project that is sure to yield enormous profits (*Id.*: 144–8). A stark example of this is provided by Google's project, Google Street View, the worldwide street mapping operation it launched in 2007 (*Id.*: 141). In the course of this project Google collected illegitimately 600 billion bytes of personal data and was in violation of the laws of at least nine countries (*Id.*: 144). After several years of litigation and regulatory proceedings throughout the globe, Google preserved its overall project virtually intact. Moreover, in those instances in which Google's position was legally indefensible, it ignored responding to legal process for as long as possible and eventually settled for very little, such as the US$ 7 million fine it paid in an action brought by attorneys general of thirty-eight US states (*Id.*: 146–7), or the €145,000 fine paid for massive illicit intrusions in Germany (*Id.*: 149).

In sum, when we add layering and segmentation, selection, and privatization of law by powerful corporate interests, and the legal extraction of surplus information and strategic law violations of surveillance capitalism, it becomes obvious why law might seem increasingly alienating and its contours opaque and without perceptible delimitation. Under such circumstances, claims that law is self-given and that it reflects identitarian congruence sound hollow. As mentioned earlier, layering and segmentation may become more or less alienating and identity congruent depending, in large part, on institutional factors. In the context of law selection and as well as in that of the legal practices of surveillance capitalists, in contrast, law plays an important role, but its particular modalities are overwhelmingly determined by the sheer disproportionate economic power of its corporate mentors.

---

[24] "Surveillance capitalism knows and shapes human behavior toward others' ends. Instead of armaments and armies, it works its will through the automated medium of an increasingly ubiquitous computational architecture of 'smart' networked devices...." (Zuboff 2019: 8).

Consistent with that, in these latter two circumstances questions of law become largely subordinate to questions of distributive justice relating to social and economic welfare—which will be broached in Chapter 2.[25]

III The Redeployment of Religion as a Politic Against Institutional Secularism

One of the key aims of the Enlightenment was the depoliticization of religion through the deployment of institutional secularism as a key pillar of modern constitutionalism (Rosenfeld 2020: 22). Based on a decoupling of the realm of Reason from that of Faith, religion was meant to be expelled from the public sphere while at the same time being afforded special protection within the private sphere. Prior to the Enlightenment, the prevalent practice in the Western world was for the state officially to embrace the polity's majority religion, as encapsulated in the famous dictum *cujus regio eius religio.* As a consequence of this, the state and the official religion ruled the realm and most often did so to the detriment of minority religions. This promoted official religious intolerance resulting in several cases in wars of religion (Rosenfeld 2014: 100–8). As against this, the Enlightenment thrust toward the depoliticization of religion paved the way to a pluralistic accommodation of various religions and non-religious ideologies. From a constitutional standpoint, the separation between the state and religion seems best achieved through the adoption of institutional secularism (Mancini & Rosenfeld 2021: 494–5). As an ideal, institutional secularism requires the state to exhibit complete agnosticism regarding religion. This can be accomplished by combining an areligious public sphere with constitutional guarantees of freedom *of* and *from* religion in the private sphere. Furthermore, *institutional* secularism is conceptually distinct from *ideological* secularism, which is a conception of the good grounded in an immanent world view that rejects all transcendence from an epistemological, ontological, moral, and political point of view (Taylor 2007: 18–20). In other words, institutional secularism is designed to foster accommodation, tolerance, and pluralism within constitutional units whereas ideological secularism is one conception of the good among many in typical contemporary constitutional democracies.

The institutional secularist ideal can at best be approximated. Two principal constitutional iterations of institutional secularism are found respectively in

---

[25] In this context, it is noteworthy that for all its downsides, the information surplus generated by surveillance capitalism has also great potential for promotion of the public good. For example, Google and Apple have proposed to team up to put special software in smartphones to trace those infected with the coronavirus and thus significantly slowing the spread of a pandemic. Jack Nicas & Daisuke Wakabayashi, "Tech giants to team up in tracing the infected," *NY Times*, April 12, 2020, at B1. Needless to add, in case projects of this kind were eventually to progress, legal measures would have to be deployed in order to minimize abuses of personal privacy.

54   LAW, RELIGION, AND TRIBAL POLITICS

France and the United States. French *laïcité*, enshrined in Article 1 of that country's 1958 Constitution, aims to expel all religion from the public sphere in order to render the latter a thoroughly areligious space, thus becoming a prime example of a militant secularist model of regulation of the relationship between religion the state (Mancini & Rosenfeld 2014: xxiii). As against this, the United States has adopted an agnostic secularist model framed by the two religion clauses of the First Amendment to its Constitution. These clauses are the Establishment Clause, which prohibits the state from adopting any religion as the official one, and the Free Exercise Clause, which mandates that the state afford protection to the "free exercise of religion." Unlike France, the United States does not require systematic expulsion of religion from the public sphere, but it prohibits the state from endorsing or privileging any particular religion to the detriment of other religions (Rosenfeld 2014: 85–7).[26] Moreover, even certain countries with an official religion, such as the United Kingdom, need not contradict the institutional secularist ideal. This is provided that the state link to the official religion be ceremonial rather than substantive and that ample room be left for genuine religious pluralism (Mancini & Rosenfeld 2014: xxiii–xxiv). Although all actual constitutional adaptations of institutional secularism are bound to remain far from ideal in various ways, what is crucial for our purposes is that all these adaptations remain compatible with the two principal aspirations associated with the said ideal. These aspirations are commitment to religious pluralism (understood as inclusive of non-religious conceptions of the good) and to the related principle that in the affairs of the state and in public policy, no religion shall be considered or treated as the possessor of *the* truth. Accordingly, each religion is entitled to comport itself as the sole possessor of the truth within its communal life carried out in the private sphere whereas no religion is entitled to insist within the public sphere on institutionalization of its own truth so long as the latter is contested by proponents of other religions or of non-religious perspectives.

Pursuit of these two aspirations and of ever-closer approximation to the institutional secularism ideal emerge as highly propitious from the standpoint of achieving a fair equilibrium among the universal, the singular, and the plural within modern Enlightenment-based constitutional units. Indeed, by expelling religious divisiveness from the public sphere, institutional secularism can emphasize what unites the polity within the constitutional community of communities while at the same time forcefully setting aside what divides the citizenry. In this setting, the universal ought to be what rises above religious (and other ideological) divisions. The singular, in turn, is embodied in the constitutional rights-bearing individual who

---

[26] There is disagreement among US judges and scholars over whether the Establishment Clause mandates preserving a "wall of separation" between state and religion or whether it allows for state preference of religion over non-religion so long as the state does not pick favorites among religions (Chermerinsky & McDonald 2019).

can blend her role as a self-governing citizen in the public sphere with her religious or non-religious project of self-determination and self-fulfillment in the private sphere. Finally, through combined exercise of freedom of speech, of religion, and of association rights, individuals can engage in common religious or non-religious ways of life, thus furthering a plurality of conceptions of the good within the precincts of their polity's private sphere.

The ideal of institutional secularism has come under heavy attack in the latter part of the twentieth century both on account of the "disenchantment of reason" (Rosenfeld 2011: 211–66) and of the "repoliticization" of religion (Casanova 1994). The disenchantment in question is basically two-pronged. On the one hand, reason's potential as the means towards the common good in an age of democracy, science, and technology has been undermined by the emergence and prevalence of "instrumental reason" (Rosenfeld 2011: 274–80). The latter narrows the reach of reason to the deployment of efficient means toward specifically chosen ends, and enables the rich and powerful to mold their society so as to maximize realization of their own interests. Whereas the instrumentalization of reason does not directly impact institutional secularism, it does facilitate exacerbations of material welfare injustices within the polity. On the other hand, the second prong of the disenchantment of reason stems from an epistemological postmodern critique of reason as unique or superior to passion, faith, or ideology in the realms of human interaction affected by law, morals, and politics (*Id.*: 11). In other words, when it comes to determining ends, aspirations, and the good, reason is ultimately not qualitatively more reliable than faith, passion, or ideologically grounded values. Consistent with this, the very foundations of the divide between Faith and Reason come into question thus posing a serious challenge to institutional secularism.

The second attack on institutional secularism is linked to the "repoliticization" of religion in various parts of the world. This new phenomenon has been complex and variegated. In some cases, such as in that of Iran, a secular regime has been replaced by a theocratic one (Chehabi 2001); in others, such as that concerning Protestant fundamentalists in the United States, religious fervor has motivated strong political organization and deployment with notable policy successes but without thus far altering the basic tenets of the prevailing constitutional order (Williams 2020: 287–92). The repoliticization of religion has taken different forms, ranging from radically progressive to radically conservative ones. One can think of the political praxis of Latin American liberation theologians, who integrated Catholic teaching and Marxism to advocate for social justice and the liberation of oppressed people (Araujo 1994–95: 65). In many recent cases, however, one of the most salient and far-reaching consequences of the repoliticization of religion is its starkly antipluralist thrust, which is perhaps best exemplified by contemporary instances of religious nationalism and of religious populism (Mancini & Rosenfeld 2021). In both these cases, what is crucial is not whether there is a significant or widespread commitment to religious belief or dogma but instead the use of religion

56 LAW, RELIGION, AND TRIBAL POLITICS

as the basis for forging identitarian bonds that are strongly exclusionary of those cast as the "other" (Mancini & Rosenfeld 2014: xxi).

The ideal of institutional secularism, which is difficult to approximate even under the most favorable circumstances, becomes increasingly problematic as the modern welfare state encroaches on what traditionally pertained to the private sphere. A primary example is provided by education. So long as education remains exclusively within the private sphere, parents should have no trouble integrating the religion of their choice within the schooling of their children. Once the state becomes the principal educator through its public school system, however, both inclusion of religion within the curriculum and its exclusion from it are apt to raise serious doubts about institutional secularism's potential for neutrality. One striking example of attack on institutional secularism's aspiration to neutrality is provided in lawsuits brought by US fundamentalist Protestant parents against their children's public schools alleging violations of the Establishment Clause.[27] The parents claimed that the assigned reading in their children's literature class of a text which characterized a tsunami as resulting from the mysterious forces of nature amounted to an unconstitutional state imposition of the religion of "secular humanism." In the fundamentalist parents' view, God is the cause behind phenomena and therefore the implication that nature acts by itself amounts to a teaching by a religion that contradicts the truth of the transcendent Christian God. In other words, the school may be pretending to comply with institutional secularism as it is embodied in the US Establishment Clause, but it is in fact imposing the religion of "secular humanism" which coincides with ideological secularism and which contradicts fundamentalist Protestant theology. Although the courts rejected the parents' arguments and found no violations of the Establishment Clause, conceptually, in these cases, the distinction between institutional and ideological secularism seems to depend on an interpretive nuance. If the reference to the force of nature in the relevant literary text is taken as being agnostic on the question of whether or not God is behind every natural phenomenon, then the teaching at stake would seem fully consistent with institutional secularism. On the other hand, if the reference in question is understood as implying a negation of divine intervention in natural phenomena, then the text advances an ideological secular perspective. Apparently, for the suing parents, the mere omission of an attribution of divine agency amounted to a denial of a cardinal Christian truth.

Although the blurring of the boundaries between the public and private spheres certainly increases the burdens on institutional secularism, what poses by far the greatest threat to the latter's legitimacy and viability is the major systemic re-entry of religion within the political sphere of many different countries throughout the world, starting in the 1980s. This new development consists in

---

[27] See *Smith v. Board of Comm'rs of Mobile County*, 827 F.2d. 684 (11th Cir. 1987); *Grove v. Mead School District*, 753 F. 2d 1528 (9th Cir. 1983).

the "deprivatization" of religion (Casanova 1994: 4) and involves two interrelated processes: the "repoliticization of the private religious and moral sphere," and the "renormativization of the public economic and political spheres" (*Id.*: 5–6). As already noted, in some cases, such as that of Iran, the repoliticization in question has led to the installment of a theocracy where religious law is meant to rule.[28] Theocracies, even constitutional ones like that in Iran,[29] and regimes dominated by fundamentalist religion[30] subsume all governance and rights to religious precepts, institutions, and authorities, hence amounting to a negation of all that modern liberal democratic constitutionalism stands for. Contemporary theocratic regimes bear no further discussion in the present context as they loom as inherently unsuited to meet the minimum identitarian requirements of the justice essentials. Accordingly, the focus should be on repoliticized religion that seeks to change the constitution, politics, law, or the interpretation of fundamental rights, but that does not come close turning into a theocracy.

Repoliticized religion may take several different forms. This includes the one propagated by the type of fundamentalist Protestantism politically active in the United States referred to earlier, to the extent that it operates and seeks changes within the existing constitutional order. Viewed from a moral, political, and constitutional standpoint, US Protestant fundamentalism does not openly seek to overthrow or replace the constitutional or political order within the United States. Instead, it endeavors to fight for laws and to advocate for constitutional interpretations that accord with its religious creeds and its understanding of biblically prescribed morality (Harding 2000: 202). Thus, for example, Protestant fundamentalists have used laws in ways that undermine women's equality,[31] and fought for laws and constitutional decisions against rights to abortion,[32] and against the rights

---

[28] The Preamble to the 1979 Iranian Constitution states in part: "In the view of Islam, government ... represents the fulfillment of the political ideal of a people who bear a common faith and common outlook, taking an organized form in order to initiate the process of intellectual and ideological evolution towards the final goal, i.e., movement towards Allah. Our nation, in the course of its revolutionary developments, has cleansed itself of the dust and impurities that accumulated during the past and purged itself of foreign ideological influences, returning to authentic intellectual standpoints and world-view of Islam. It now intends to establish an ideal and model society on the basis of Islamic norms. The mission of the Constitution is ... to create conditions conducive to the development of man in accordance with the noble and universal values of Islam."

[29] Article 12 of the Iranian Constitution provides, in relevant part, "[t]he official religion of Iran is Islam and the Twelver Ja'fari school, and this principle will remain eternally immutable." In spite of the all-encompassing place of Islam in Iran's public sphere, Article 13 of its Constitution does afford protection to a small number of religious minorities: "Zoroastrian, Jewish, and Christian Iranians are the only recognized religious minorities, who, within the limits of the law, are free to perform their religious rites and ceremonies, and to act according to their own canon in matters of personal affairs and religious education."

[30] Religious fundamentalists consider their religion as the repository of absolute truth and insist that the state be ruled exclusively pursuant to the dictates of the true religion. Habermas: 224.

[31] See, e.g., *Burwell v. Hobby Lobby Stores, Inc.*, 573 US 682 (2014).

[32] Chris McGreal, "The 50-year fight by radical evangelicals that could end US abortion rights," *The Guardian*, March 4, 2020, <https://www.theguardian.com/world/2020/mar/04/us-abortion-rights-evangelical-campaign>, visited April 3, 2022.

58 LAW, RELIGION, AND TRIBAL POLITICS

of sexual minorities.[33] More generally, Protestant fundamentalists have attacked both institutional and ideological secularism which, as already mentioned, they have characterized as the "religion" of "secular humanism."

Another brand of repoliticized religion, championed in the name of Catholicism by former Pope Benedict XVI, relies on the assumption that faith coincides with the dictates of universal reason which are embodied in natural law, and that accordingly its normative prescriptions can be equally derived from faith or from reason (Cartabia & Simoncini 2015: 3–9).[34] In this light, the "right" use of reason in legal arguments leads to the same conclusions as theological reasoning (Lemaitre 2012: 493–511). Moreover, consistent with this, in sharp contrast to Catholic-sanctioned universally valid law and morality, ideological secularism amounts to a "dictatorship of relativism."[35] This perceived relativism is supposed to a multitude of evils that conspire to deprive human life of all meaning and to reduce human beings to depraved hedonism or to mere calculating mutual exploitation.[36]

Repoliticized religion can also be enlisted to erode institutions by conspicuously re-entering the public sphere as inextricably linked to the culture of the polity. Examples of religion figuring as culture include requiring the display of the crucifix in public school classrooms in constitutionally secular Italy,[37] and inclusion of the Christian creche in a holiday municipal grounds display in the United States.[38] The culturalization of religion need not be on its face hostile to ideological secularism. The premise, however, is that states must recognize the culture emanating from the nation's dominant religion not just as one among many such religion-based cultural by-products, but rather as a key element of civic cohesion that cements identitarian bonds of national solidarity. This grants the historically dominant national religion a preferential treatment that may be incompatible with the justice essentials. For example, insistence on saturating the public space with Christian cultural symbols may well exacerbate the marginalization of non-Christian cultures, thus lowering the protection of religious freedom (Mancini 2014). In some cases, religion can become essential in the very definition of peoplehood. This is the case in Israel where Judaism, the religion of a single people, has become the national religion, as the country's Declaration of Independence proclaimed it to be

---

[33] See, e.g., *Masterpiece Cakeshop, Ltd. v. Colo. Civil Rights Comm'n*, 138 S. Ct. 1719 (2018).

[34] The former Pope's view that Catholic faith and reason coincide in affirming universally valid morality and law is not widely shared in the legal academy. See, e.g., Christopher McCrudden's pointing to "major tensions" between the Catholic Church and several secular human rights positions, including those on abortion (McCrudden 2015: 164–5).

[35] See Homily of Cardinal Joseph Ratzinger, Saint Peter's Basilica, April 18, 2005, for the Mass "*Pro Eligendo Romano Pontifice*," in "L'Osservatore Romano," April 19, 2005, available at <http://www.vati can.va/gpII/documents/homily-pro-eligendo-pontifice_20050418_en.html>, visited April 3, 2022.

[36] See, e.g., John Paul II, *Evangelium vitae* (March 1995), paras 22 & 23, available at <http://www. vatican.va/holy_father/john_paul_ii/encyclicals/documents/hf_jp-ii_enc_25031995_evangeliumvitae _en.html>, visited April 3, 2022.

[37] *Lautsi and Others v. Italy* App. no. 30814/06 ECtHR, GC (2011).

[38] See, e.g., *Lynch v. Donnelly*, 465 US 668 (1984).

a "Jewish and democratic" state. In 2018, the Israeli Parliament went further and adopted a controversial bill designating Israel as a Jewish state even though 20 per cent of the country's citizens are not Jewish.[39] Significantly, what "Jewish" means to Israeli Jews is a hotly disputed matter. Ultra-Orthodox Jews want the country ruled according to religious law, the *halacha*, whereas secular Israeli Jews are likely to acknowledge the biblical origin of the connection between Jews and the land of Israel, celebrate in a more nationalistic and cultural than religious way certain religious holidays, such as Passover marking the exit of the Jews from slavery in Ancient Egypt, but otherwise aspire to enjoy the way of life and the rights typical of Western liberal constitutional democracies.[40]

The repoliticization of religion can take many forms, involve different kinds of religion, and make use of the religion at stake in different ways. These range from imposing select religious prescriptions through law and public morality to the use of religion for purely identitarian purposes as a vehicle of cultural inclusion and/or exclusion in relation to the polity's political and public spheres. In all cases undermining, or posing major challenges to the ideal of institutional secularism, the repoliticization of religion seems poised to provoke setbacks affecting all three among the universal, the singular, and the plural. If a contested religion or religious culture is incorporated in the constitutional community of communities, those feeling left out are likely to contest, or become alienated from the latter's claim to universality. Similarly, a minority religion adherent or irreligious individual confronted with majority religion symbols and teachings in state schools and other public sphere institutions is likely to feel pressured within the ambit of her singular pursuits. Institutionally, these official impositions are likely to strike her as official curtailments of her rights to freedom of and from religion—keeping in mind that freedom *from* religion is as necessary for the religious person who does not embrace the official state religion as it is for the non-religious. Finally, whereas the repoliticization of religion is not necessarily at odds with maintenance of the plural, it does appear incompatible with adhering to the plural consistent with the justice essentials. Indeed, if a country's constitution, laws, institutions, and official culture are harmonized to suit the needs and aspirations of its Christian majority, that country's Jewish, Muslim, and Buddhist minorities may well feel neglected, subordinated, or antagonized. For example, how is a Jewish student attending public school and his parents to feel about display of the Crucifix in the classroom—albeit in the guise that it is there merely as a national cultural symbol[41]—given that

---

[39] David M. Halbfinger & Isabel Kershner, "Israeli law declares the country 'nation-state of the Jewish people," *NY Times*, July 19, 2018, <https://www.nytimes.com/2018/07/19/world/middleeast/israel-law-jews-arabic.html>, visited April 3, 2022.

[40] See Kelsey Jo Starr & David Masci, "In Israel, 'Jews are united by homeland but divided into very different groups," *Pew Research Center*, March 8, 2016, <https://www.pewresearch.org/fact-tank/2016/03/08/in-israel-jews-are-united-by-homeland-but-divided-into-very-different-groups>, visited April 3, 2022.

[41] See, e.g., *Lautsi v. Italy*, no. 30814/06, Judgment of March 18, 2011.

60 LAW, RELIGION, AND TRIBAL POLITICS

Judaism negates the divinity of Jesus and that Jews have been until recently accused by Christians of responsibility in the killing of Jesus?

The question of how one might promote the justice essentials while confronting the challenges posed by the repolitization of religion will be deferred until Part III of this book. At this juncture, however, one important conceptual observation needs to be briefly addressed. As already noted, the maintenance of institutional secularism seems well suited to the promotion of the justice essentials. But does the postmodern dethroning of reason combined with the repolitization of religion completely remove the institutional secularism ideal from its pedestal? Is then striving to achieve the justice essentials doomed to failure?

Although institutional secularism aligns with the justice essentials, it is by no means indispensable for purposes of maintaining pluralism or for systematically excluding the contested truth of any religion from institutionalization by the state or within the public sphere. As long as one adopts a pluralist *ethos*,[42] one can abandon instrumental pluralism wherever two crucial provisos are satisfied. The first of these is the recognition of ideological secularism as a conception of the good that is *prima facie* equally entitled to constitutional accommodation as are all its religious counterparts. Such accommodation amounts to a necessary but not a sufficient condition to achieve the justice essentials after discarding institutional secularism. Indeed, in a polity with a large majority adhering to a fundamentalist religion uniformly hostile to science, a small ideologically secularist cohort may be conceivably minimally accommodated. In such a setting, however, the kind of widespread freedom of scientific inquiry and experimentation prevalent in the context of institutional secularism would in all likelihood be sorely lacking. With this in mind, the second proviso is contextual in nature. Ideological pluralism can substitute for its ideological counterpart in ways consistent with the achievement of the justice essentials in settings such as those that typically prevail in most major contemporary constitutional democracies. The settings in question are highly pluralistic and comprise a wide range of conceptions of the good that extends from fundamentalist religion to ideological secularism. Among those settings, the best suited for purposes of the justice essentials would be those that comprise a small percentage of religious fundamentalists, and more significant numbers of ideological secularists, proponents of liberal religions, such as several denominations of Protestantism that include women and sexual minorities among their clergy, and Reform Judaism, as well as proponents of strong religions such as Catholicism and Orthodox Judaism (Rosenfeld 2014: 80–1). To be sure, in such typical contemporary constitutional democracies, such as the United States, there may be a combination of religious fundamentalists and proponents of strong religion that seek to prohibit the teaching of evolution theory or to impose the teaching of

---

[42] For a thorough account of the conception of normative pluralism that I have articulated and defended, namely "comprehensive pluralism," see Chapter 7 of this book.

creationism alongside evolution theory in public school science classes (*Id.*: 87). Nevertheless, most of those who oppose freedom of scientific inquiry on religious grounds in the United States tend to commit a performative contradiction. It is certainly logically consistent with certain interpretations of Judaism and Christianity to seek prohibition of the teaching of evolution theory. But, inasmuch as those who reject evolution on religious grounds also make regular use of the products of free scientific inquiry, in fields such as medicine—whether for religious reasons[43] or otherwise—the persons involved are behaving in a way that clashes with their publicly proclaimed religious normative commitments. In short, to the extent that performative contradictions can be factored into the pluralistic calculus, in many of the relevant contextual settings under consideration ideological pluralism may be substituted, at least in principle, for institutional secularism in the pursuit of the justice essentials.

IV From Adversary to Enemy: The Rise of Tribal Politics

The dynamic of the justice essentials in a constitutional democracy entails both a downward flow from the constitution to politics and infra-constitutional laws and an upward flow from the latter back to the constitution. The constitution provides substantive and procedural guidance that enable politics and law to maintain the justice essentials or expand upon the minimum that the latter prescribes. Politics and law within the appropriate constitutional constraints, on the other hand, can also contribute preserve surpass the minimum called for by the justice essentials. As discussed in section I of this chapter, democratically enacted law can bear the imprint of the justice essentials or build upon the latter in areas reserved for infra-constitutional resolution. At the same time, in matters left indeterminate by the justice essentials, democratic law-making can insure against injustice by issuing from a political process that gives each citizen an equal voice. To return to an example already discussed, if additional public funding is available to enhance either the sports offerings or the art offerings of schools and the citizenry is divided, submitting the issue to the will of the majority may well represent the optimal means to guarantee that affected citizen is given an equal voice in the relevant decision-making process.

In a working democracy, politics is supposed to afford individuals and groups the means to channel their interests and aspirations into policy. For their part, political parties ought to focus on formulating agendas and goals yielding diverse policy packages that would ideally add up so as to provide outlets for the full gamut of political aims issuing from all individuals and groups that have a legitimate stake

---

[43] Orthodox Judaism, for example, requires use of all available medical means to save or prolong life (Robinson 2001: 200).

in the relevant polity. Furthermore, the political process should aspire to yield consensus or compromise, and whenever that proves impossible, to settle differences by following the will of the majority. Consensus is best suited to reconcile the requirements of the universal with those of the singular and those of the plural. Compromise accounts for all three of these and provides a temporary equilibrium that may not equally suit all three but leaves the door open for further adjustments. Finally, majority rule consistent with the minimum required by the justice essentials takes the universal, the singular, and the plural seriously into account, but satisfies none of them. To the extent that political majorities shift rather than favor the same larger political cohort against all others, over time all citizens are supposed to emerge as occasional political winners and occasional political losers.

For politics to remain consistent with plausible reconciliation of the universal, the singular, and the plural, political agendas and political discourse must aim to articulate visions providing roadmaps to the reconciliation at stake. The political visions in question may be in contradiction with one another, embraced by some while rejected by others, but still coherent in terms of their specific aims for reconciliation. For example, a liberal libertarian political party may be at odds with a social democrat one, but both may eye the requisite road to reconciliation. For the libertarian party, society, the individual, and civil society groups, such as religious or cultural organizations, are thought likely to fare better with greater private initiative and less government intervention. For the social democrat party, in contrast, society's well-being, individual thriving, and religious and cultural groups will all fare much better with ample government intervention and vigorous initiatives to achieve significant measures of wealth redistribution. In spite of these differences, however, the two political parties at stake emerge as broadly sharing the same goals and the same ideal of reconciliation while strongly disagreeing with respect to the best means toward advancing their ultimate ends. Because of the sum of what they share and what sets them apart, the two political parties in question are most likely to interface with one another as adversaries rather than as enemies. Moreover, whenever one of these parties is in power and the other in the opposition, the latter would much more likely be regarded by all as the "loyal opposition" rather than as an enemy bent on destroying the polity as a whole or any of its constituent stakeholders.

Political representatives in the majority and those in the loyal opposition typically share a common commitment to the community of communities enshrined by their polity's constitution. Such common commitment is bound to break down, however, whenever political adversaries turn into enemies (Levitsky & Ziblatt 2018: 21–4). Populism, as already mentioned, is characterized by setting some of the people as the whole and the remainder of the citizenry as enemies of "the" people. Populism may set up the common citizen against the elites, the members of one ethnic or religious group against all others, or even partisans of one political persuasion and of its charismatic leader against all those who do not share the same bonds of allegiance. Thus, for example, in deploying his populist vision of US nationalism and tying it to the Republican Party, Donald Trump has attacked as the country's internal enemies those who took exception to his views or his agenda. These attacks have included calling most of the US press the "enemies of the people,"[44] and the Democratic Party "un-American."[45] Other populist leaders, such Hungary's Orban and Italy's Salvini have appealed to their country's Christian heritage to bolster their xenophobic anti-Muslim stances directed against immigrants and would be refugees as well as against domestic elites branded as atheistic and cosmopolitan.[46]

When political opponents in a democracy are delegitimized and cast as enemies, not only is democracy itself in danger of slipping away but justice essentials become entirely beyond reach. Casting opponents as enemies has been identified as one of the main signs of a transition from democracy to authoritarianism (Levitsky & Ziblatt 2018: 21). As enemies are not part of the legitimate political whole, populist, nationalist, or any other denigration of part of the citizenry and of political representatives of that part of the citizenry irreparably contravenes what practically figures as the universal, the singular, and the plural. If only part of the people counts as the whole, the partial becomes cast by force as the universal (for the concerned polity), hence locking in injustice for all those treated as internal enemies. Furthermore, it follows from this that the singularity of those cast as internal enemies will become systematically disregarded and that pluralism will be completely or largely eliminated.

In the last analysis, all three threats posed by the alienation from and disembodiment of law, the repoliticization of religion, and the tribalization of politics, become major threats to liberal constitutionalism and to the achievement of the justice essentials. Moreover, in many cases, all three of these threats operate in conjunction to erect even more formidable obstacles in the pursuit of the constitutional ideal and its associated justice essentials requirements. Indeed, economic globalization and its legal consequences often give rise to a counter movement of balkanization that invokes religion as a powerful unifier and divider associated with tribalized politics veering toward authoritarianism. Whether it be Hungary's

---

[44] Brett Samuels, "Trump ramps up his rhetoric on media, calls press 'the enemy of the people,'" *The Hill*, April 5, 2019, <https://thehill.com/homenews/administration/437610-trump-calls-press-the-enemy-of-the-people>, visited April 3, 2022.

[45] Jessica Taylor, "Trump: Democrats 'Un-American,' 'treasonous' during State of the Union," *National Public Radio*, February 5, 2018, <https://www.npr.org/2018/02/05/583447413/trump-democr ats-un-american-treasonous-during-state-of-the-union>, visited April 3, 2022.

[46] See Ishaan Tharoor, "Hungary's Orban invokes Ottoman invasion to justify keeping refugees out," *The Washington Post*, September 4, 2015; <https://www.globalist.it/politics/2020/01/04/salvini-alla-guerra-santa-sto-con-trump-perche-difende-i-valori-cristiani-2051196.html>, visited April 3, 2022. Notably, the most influential Catholic press in Italy has systematically denounced Salvini's instrumental use of religion. See, e.g., Davide Re, "Salvini brandisce il rosario durante il comizio e ribadisce: porti chiusi," *L'Avvenire* (May 18, 2019), <https://www.avvenire.it/attualita/pagine/salvini-a-milano>, visited April 3, 2022.

Orban railing against the EU while benefiting from the latter's economic subsidies and criticizing Western Europe by invoking allegiance to Christian values (Müller 2013: 18), or Trump pursuing tax and deregulatory policies favoring his country's global capitalist magnates while placating Christian evangelicals in his constant assaults against those he portrays as his internal and external enemies,[47] the clash of apparent opposites results in a standstill where tensions exacerbate the threats to constitutional democracy rather than opening new paths towards their resolution. The standstill in question clearly gives rise to formidable identitarian obstacles standing in the way of the justice essentials. But also, as will be detailed in the next chapter, the dynamic standstill between the forces of globalization and the counterforces of exclusionary retrenchment poses a major threat regarding the achievement of the requisite minimum of material justice called for by the justice essentials.

---

[47] Jeff Sharlet, Trump's brand of biblical capitalism makes him stronger than you think, *Vanity Fair*, August 26, 2020, <https://www.vanityfair.com/news/2020/08/trumps-brand-of-biblical-capitalism-may-make-him-unbeatable>, visited April 3, 2022.

2

Local versus Global, Material Well-Being, States of Stress, and the Erosion of Justice

I Introduction

Within the ambit of the Westphalian framework, nation-state constitutions could comfortably handle both the material and the identitarian requirements of the constitutionally prescribed justice essentials. To be sure, what these justice essentials may actually require at a particular moment in history is inevitably contestable. It also stands to reason that distributive issues were bound to vary significantly from the pre-industrial period of the late eighteenth-century American and French constitutions through the nineteenth- and early twentieth-century industrial period and through the post-Second World War Cold War period that pitted countries devoted to capitalism against those that had embraced communism. Whereas the economy has had a transnational dimension going all the way back to antiquity (Kearney 1995: 549–51), the modern political, legal, and constitutional order has remained for the most part within the precincts of the nation-state until the middle of the twentieth century. One should not overlook that the trajectory of liberal constitutionalism encompassed in Westphalian units has had glaring deficiencies, such as slavery, colonialism, and the exclusion of women and others from basic civil and political rights. Nevertheless, there have been no logical or inherent institutional impediments for these deficiencies to be overcome within the Westphalian order through removal of existing barriers to access to, and expansion of, existing fundamental rights.

As already noted, upon the fall of the Soviet Union capitalism became perceived as triumphant in the quest for optimizing material well-being on a worldwide scale (Fukuyama 2003). Globalization's rapid expansion and the increased migration of capital and labor across national boundaries drove distributive justice concerns primarily towards identitarian issues. Some of the most salient legal, constitutional, social, and political problems associated with globalization were examined in Chapter 1. These seemingly dwarfed material social and economic justice preoccupations on two principal grounds. First, globalization has led to an impressive increase in overall worldwide material well-being as billions of people were extricated from hunger and extreme poverty (Goklany 2007: 59–64); and second, with communist ideology largely discredited, material wealth and income differences did not loom as *inherently* unjust. And that held whether one adopted a neoliberal

A Pluralist Theory of Constitutional Justice. Michel Rosenfeld, Oxford University Press. © Michel Rosenfeld 2022.
DOI: 10.1093/oso/9780198862680.003.0003

capitalist perspective relying on global free markets to maximize wealth extending to the largest possible swath of humanity; or a liberal egalitarian one, such as that enshrined in Rawls' "difference principle," according to which differences in wealth were justified to the extent that they improved the material well-being of those who were economically worst off (Rawls 1971: 302).

Globalization, however, has dramatically exacerbated differences in income and wealth. Whereas inequalities in wealth had somewhat decreased in advanced capitalist economies during the 1950–1970 period (Piketty 2013: 51), in 2010 the top 0.1 per cent held 20 per cent of the world's wealth, the top 1 per cent held 50 per cent, and the top 10 per cent held 80–90 per cent (*Id.*: 698). These exorbitant differences in wealth have gone hand in hand with dramatic increases in power for a small cadre of national and international elites that dominate the economic, political, and international relations spheres. These elites have recently often become characterized by proponents of populism as internal and/or external "enemies" that pose an existential threat to the "people."[1] Accordingly, the global capitalist elites may in principle figure as sources of identitarian injustice in as much as they may be regarded as the producers of material injustice. Indeed, the global capitalist elite exports jobs, imports cheaper labor, fosters internal displacements and cultural upheavals, and thus greatly foments identitarian threats and perceived identity-based injustices. Political philosophers disagree over whether the consequences of increasing wealth disparities should be primarily dealt with as instances of material economic distributive injustice or as a subset of identitarian distributive injustice as vastly disproportionate wealth disparities threaten the dignity and self-worth of those left behind (Fraser & Honneth 2003). Be that as it may, there are at least two salient material justice issues that arise as a consequence of the exacerbation of income and wealth differences in a globalized capitalist economy. First, are the economic losses of those displaced or dispossessed by globalization tantamount to the imposition of a material injustice inuring to the benefit of those who are disproportionately enriching themselves? And second, are the huge disproportionate increases in wealth in themselves sufficient to generate an unacceptable material distributive injustice (assuming that pre-existing 1970s differences in wealth were not inherently unjust)?

These two questions only concern us in so far as they relate to the justice essentials of a well working constitutional democracy. In other words, given the effects of globalization, must income and wealth redistribution be prescribed *within* the constitution as contrasted to being entrusted to infra-constitutional public policy? And, if so, which such redistributions might suffice to uphold the justice essentials? Finally, even assuming consensus on the requisite redistributions, how can constitutions and the relevant constitutional regimes they implant be adapted to secure

---

[1] C-66/18, *Commission v. Hungary (Higher Education)*, 2020 available online at <http://curia.europa.eu/juris/liste.jsf?num=C-66/18>, visited April 3, 2022.

the requisite redistributive objectives? Moreover, in relation to this last question two separate concerns arise. First, economically redistributive objectives can be addressed constitutionally through enshrinement of social and economic rights, such as rights to a minimum of welfare, shelter, and health protection, but such rights known as "second-generation" rights seemingly pose certain difficulties that do not appear to afflict "first-generation" civil and political rights. And second, as increased wealth disparities have a major transnational dimension, it is by no means clear whether adaptations of nation-state constitutions may sufficiently address the requirements of the justice essentials or whether transnational or international constitutional, administrative, and/or treaty based legal orderings can supplement or replace the said nation-state constitutions for the purposes at hand.

With this in mind, I will first briefly address the need for a separate economically redistributive track in order to deal with justice essentials requirements in the era of globalization. Second, I will explore in broad contours the reasons why, absent economic redistribution, the justice essentials cannot be met in contemporary constitutional democracies. Third, I will focus on how familiar objections to social and economic constitutional rights fare from within the perspective of the justice essentials. And fourth, building on some of the discussion in Chapter 1, I will examine how the transnationalization and pluralization of legal regimes pose challenging obstacles to securing the justice essentials as they relate to economic redistribution.

Finally, two recent phenomena inextricably linked to globalization, global terrorism and the COVID-19 pandemic, give rise to what I have described as "conditions of stress" (Rosenfeld 2006: 2084–102). These conditions, which stand halfway between ordinary conditions and emergency ones, have both marked material and identitarian implications. As will be detailed in the last part of this chapter, these conditions of stress produce disproportionate shifts in constitutional rule that can pose daunting challenges to approximating the justice essentials.

II The Justice Essentials Confront the Divide between Redistribution and Recognition

Vastly increasing inequalities in wealth propelled by globalization raise new issues of distributive injustice. Is there a point at which these increasing inequalities become unjust? And if so, how might these injustices be best addressed? In as much as welfare state entitlements can secure sufficient material well-being for the citizenry, then arguably mere increases in economic inequalities due to globalization need not result in economic distributive injustices of their own. Thus, for example, if a worker in a manufacturing industry loses his job to cheaper labor in a foreign country, he may nevertheless not be *economically* adversely affected if his country provides unemployment benefits commensurate with his pre-termination salary.

On the other hand, any long-term unemployment or underemployment is quite likely to affect a person's sense of dignity and of self-worth adversely. In this scenario, globalization may increase identitarian injustices rather than material ones and economic dislocations that result from globalization may well be better assessed from an identitarian than from a materialistic perspective.

From a comprehensive perspective, there is a close relationship between all three facets of distributive justice. If women earn less than men doing the same work, are systematically subjected to institutionally embedded sexist attitudes, and are denied the right to vote, they are clearly victims of injustice under all three facets of distributive justice. Nevertheless, from the standpoint of constitutional redress, the income disparity seems best addressed as an economic redistribution issue which may be tackled alone or in conjunction with the other alluded to injustices. Furthermore, there may be cases where more than one injustice is involved, but where it would be constitutionally preferable to emphasize one of them above all others. For example, suppose that there is a dramatic health insurance disparity and that members of a racial minority, as opposed to the less well-off generally, highly disproportionately lack health insurance in a particular country. this latter scenario, there is both an economic and an identitarian inequity. Nevertheless, from a constitutional perspective, it seems better to focus primarily on the recognition-based injustice and pursue a racial discrimination claim under a constitutional equality provision. And this, for moral, constitutional, and tactical reasons. Morally, racial discrimination is universally condemned in liberal constitutional democracies and its prohibition is uniformly constitutionally enshrined. In contrast, "to each according to her needs" seems to be the preferred criterion of justice when it comes to preservation of health, but there is no consensus on this, and proponents of "to each according to his means" cannot be merely discarded as being absolutely wrong or immoral. Also, as a constitutional matter, a first-generation racial discrimination claim is, as further discussed later in this chapter, categorically more firmly entrenched than a second-generation social and economic right claim. Finally, given this categorical difference and the likely greater consensus against racism versus compensating for economic disparities in the health care domain, it could well be easier to win a racial discrimination case than one concerning an economic inequity.

III The Global Economy, Exacerbation of Economic Inequalities, and the Justice Essentials

The constitutional implications of globalization's great increase in economic disparities may not be immediately apparent as the requirements of the justice essentials vary depending on the overall wealth of the relevant polity under consideration. Although systematic examination the nexus between the justice essentials, overall wealth, and economic inequalities will be deferred until Part III of this book, for now I will focus on what may seem beyond reasonable dispute regarding the minimum of justice demands of the constitution.

Economists disagree as to whether the enormous increases in inequalities in wealth in the era of globalization eventually lead to a stifling of overall economic growth or whether neoliberal free-market policies provide the best means towards the maximization of wealth.[2] Proponents of the former view emphasize that extreme inequalities threaten society, democracy, and the market itself.[3] Furthermore, even some free-market economists have acknowledged that although there would be a trade-off, it would be difficult to argue against some sacrifice in efficiency in exchange for more equity, fairness, and compassion.[4] On either of these two competing economic theories, the prevailing inequalities amply support the conclusion that those in poverty and without any health care protection in the wealthiest countries in the world are being deprived of the minimum of justice from the standpoint of all three among economic redistribution, recognition, and representation.

Whereas it seems beyond dispute that the most basic needs of the most disadvantaged ought to be constitutionally guaranteed, it may be more difficult to determine how far the wealthiest countries of the world should go in constitutionalizing social welfare interests to meet the demands of minimum justice. Consistent with current constitutional norms applied in various jurisdictions as exemplified later in this chapter, the proper scope of protected social welfare interests is to be assessed pursuant to standards of reason and of proportionality. With this in mind, it is useful briefly to address two salient dimensions of the political economy of the wealthiest nations as well as certain relevant considerations weighing on distributive justice due to greatly expanding inequalities coupled with considerable increases in overall wealth.

These two dimensions underscore the order of magnitude of state expenditures and the nature and size of inequalities in wealth distribution in globalized economy. Moreover, the U.S.'s recent experience alongside these two dimensions is highly instructive and all the more striking because of that country's complete lack of constitutionally protected social and economic rights. It makes sense to single out the US for purposes of illustrating how these conditions fare in advanced economies.

---

[2] See Katie Lederer, "Equality? That's what's good for growth," *NY Times*, August 30, 2020, Sunday Business p. 1, 5 (comparing economist Heather Boushey who argues that addressing inequalities can lead to economic growth to economist Casey Mulligan who argues that increases in equity cause decreases in market efficiency).

[3] *Id.* See also, Boushey 2019: xiv.

[4] See Casey Mulligan cited in Lederer, at note 5.

70 LOCAL VERSUS GLOBAL

The US Tax Cuts and Jobs Act of 2017[5] cost more than US$1.5 trillion and bene-fited corporations and the wealthiest Americans in a highly disproportionate way (Cohen & Viswanathan 2020: 7). The top 1 per cent of the population were pro-jected to receive up to 83 per cent of its benefits within a decade.[6] At the same time, corporations received a major tax rate reduction from 35 per cent to 21 per cent with the stated purpose of expanding and providing more and better paying jobs (Cohen & Viswanathan 2020: 1). After the first two years of the said tax re-duction, however, a large proportion of corporations used their tax savings to pay dividends or to repurchase their shares rather than to increase their work force. In addition, the 2017 law reduced the estate tax which already greatly benefitted the very wealthy at an approximate cost of $80 billion over a decade, leaving only 0.1 per cent of all estates subject to federal taxes.[7] Finally, in line with the current global economy, 35 per cent of US corporate equities are owned by foreign investors and thus the 2017 law is forecast to result in a $700 billion cost to the US Treasury for the benefit of overseas interests.[8]

Since the coronavirus pandemic seriously impacted the U.S. economy starting in March 2020, a unified US Congress adopted relief bills to reinvigorate a de-pleted economy, compensate for massive new unemployment, and to address the pandemic, which cost around $3 trillion.[9] More recently, the US House of Representatives passed the Heroes Act with a cost of $3.4 trillion to address a large number of problems arising from the pandemic which failed to gain traction in the US Senate, but which resulted in enactment of a $900 billion package by the end of 2020.[10] To this was added in 2021 the American Rescue Plan Act which included $1.9 trillion in stimulus expenditures.[11]

Although these trillion-dollar projects have raised concerns about the size of the US debt,[12] they have been adopted in some cases with near Congressional

---

[5] Act to provide for reconciliation pursuant to titles II and V of the concurrent resolution on the budget for fiscal year 2018, Pub. L. 115–97, 131 Stat. 2054 (2017).

[6] "Distributional analysis of the Conference Agreement for the Tax Cuts and Jobs Act," *Tax Policy Center*, December 18, 2017, <https://www.taxpolicycenter.org/publications/distributional-analysis-conference-agreement-tax-cuts-and-jobs-act/full>, visited April 3, 2022.

[7] Howard Gleckman, "Only 1,700 estates would owe estate tax in 2018 under the TCJA," *Tax Policy Center*, December 6, 2017, <https://www.taxpolicycenter.org/taxvox/only-1700-estates-would-owe-est ate-tax-2018-under-tcja>, visited April 3, 2022.

[8] See Paul Krugman, "Trump's $700 billion gift to wealthy foreigners," *N.Y. Times*, October 26, 2017, <https://www.nytimes.com/2017/10/26/opinion/trump-taxes-wealthy-foreigners.html>, visited April 3, 2022.

[9] 15 USC § 9001 (LexisNexis, Lexis Advance through Public Law 116–58, approved August 14, 2020); Konnoth 2020: 200.

[10] Emily Cochrane, "House passes $3 trillion aid bill over Republican opposition," *NY Times*, May 15, 2020, <https://www.nytimes.com/2020/05/15/us/politics/house-simulus-vote.html?searchResultPosit ion=2>, visited April 3, 2022; Seung Min Kim et al., "Trump signs stimulus and government spending bill into law, averting shutdown," *The Washington Post*, December 27, 2020, <https://www.washingtonp ost.com/us-policy/2020/12/27/trump-stimulus-shutdown-congress>, visited April 3, 2022.

[11] Public Law No: 117-2 (03/11/2021) American Rescue Plan Act of 2021.

[12] See, e.g., Richard Kogan & Paul N. Van de Water, "Rising federal debt should not shortchange response to COVID-19 crisis," *Center on Budget and Policy Priorities*, September 9, 2020, <https:// www.cbpp.org/research/federal-budget/rising-federal-debt-should-not-shortchange-respo

unanimity.[13] Reductions in taxes are distinguishable from government spending in that they leave money in the pockets of private actors by collecting less from them. But that distinction is of little consequence for present purposes, particularly since the 2017 tax law has not led to a significant expansion of the economy or of increases in tax revenues.[14] What is crucial from the standpoint of minimum of justice considerations is that the US Government can afford choosing among policy-making alternatives that carry a price tag in an order of magnitude in the trillions of dollars.

Turning to the question of increases in US wealth inequalities in the era of globalization, a recent Rand Corporation working paper concludes that from 1975 till 2018 the top 1 per cent in the United States has taken nearly $50 trillion from the country's bottom 90 per cent.[15] From 1945 till 1974, differences in wealth within the US economy were both stable and more equitable than in more recent years. The $50 trillion figure represents the sums the bottom 90 per cent would have earned between 1975 and 2020 had the conditions prevalent in the preceding period remained stable throughout. Moreover these $50 trillion were not only "lost" to the bottom 90 per cent but transferred from them to the top 1 per cent.

To compound all this, the above inequalities are allocated unequally among those disadvantaged by them. Thus, lower wage earners and their families, who are disproportionately people of color, suffer far more from chronic diseases and have been far worse affected by COVID-19.[16] Moreover, these disparities have been compounded by the rising costs necessary to maintain a dignified middle-class

---

nse-to-covid-19-crisis>; Jeff Stein, "U.S. government debt will nearly equal the size of the entire economy for first time since World War II, CBO finds," *The Washington Post*, September 2, 2020, <https://www.washingtonpost.com/us-policy/2020/09/02/government-debt-economy-coronavirus/>, visited April 3, 2022.

[13] See, e.g., Congressional voting records for the CARES Act: Roll Call Vote 116th Congress—2nd Session, us Senate, <https://www.senate.gov/legislative/LIS/roll_call_lists/roll_call_vote_cfm.cfm?congress=116&session=2&vote=00080>, visited September 22, 2020 (where the bill was passed with a vote of 96–0, with four not voting).

[14] William G. Gale, "A fixable mistake: the tax cuts and jobs acts," *Brookings Institution*, September 25, 2019, <https://www.brookings.edu/blog/up-front/2019/09/25/a-fixable-mistake-the-tax-cuts-and-jobs-act/>, visited April 3, 2022.

[15] See Carter C. Price & Kathryn A. Edwards, "Trends in income from 1975 to 2018" 12 (Rand Corp., Working Paper No. WR-A516-1, 2020), <https://www.rand.org/pubs/working_papers/WRA516-1.html>, visited April 3, 2022.

[16] Nick Hanauer & David M. Rolf, "The top 1% of Americans have taken $50 trillion from the bottom 90%—and that's made the U.S. less secure," *Time*, September 14, 2020 at 9:30 a.m. EDT, <https://time.com/5888024/50-trillion-income-inequality-america/>, visited April 3, 2022; Molly Kinder & Martha Ross, "Reopening America: low-wage workers have suffered badly from COVID-19 so policymakers should focus on equity," *Brookings Institution*, June 23, 2020, <https://www.brookings.edu/research/reopening-america-low-wage-workers-have-suffered-badly-from-covid-19-so-policymakers-should-focus-on-equity/#:~:text=of%20the%20pandemic.-,Social%20distancing%20measures%20taken%20in%20response%20to%20COVID%2D19%20resulted,concentrated%20among%20lower%2Dw age%20workers.&text=But%20their%20pay%20could%20be,the%20beginning%20of%20the%20p andemic>, visited April 3, 2022.

life.[17] A 2018 two working person household earned around the same as a one working person household would have had the rate of inequality remained stationary.[18] Accordingly, large numbers of people currently struggle to meet their housing, health care, education, childcare, and transportation costs.[19]

Some have attributed the dramatic increase in inequalities in the United States to phenomena such as globalization and automation that are beyond the country's control and that force it to adapt to remain competitive in a world economy where capital and labor can no longer be effectively managed within national boundaries (Lee 1999; Autor, Katz, & Kearney 2008). Others disagree and maintain that the current US predicament is closely tied to national policy decisions made since 1975 and that therefore the $50 trillion transfer to the top 1 per cent is a matter of choice rather than of economic necessity.[20] Whether or not globalization is principally responsible for the current level of economic inequalities in the United States, the sheer size of the 2017 tax cuts and of the COVID-19 legislation just discussed prove that the United States has the capacity to engage in massive internal economic redistribution while remaining competitive in the global arena. More generally, to the extent that globalization contributes to increasing inequalities within nation-states, national constitutional social and economic rights may well require reinforcement by infusing full legal force on transnational and international equivalents. Further exploration of plausible combinations of national and international social welfare rights will be undertaken in section IV below. What does require further inquiry at this point, however, is the question regarding the requirements of minimum constitutionally guaranteed distributive justice in countries that approximate the level of wealth and of wealth inequalities currently manifest in the United States.

As already mentioned, philosophical theories of distributive justice range from the libertarian one limiting equal distribution to formal rights to egalitarian ones which counsel massive economic redistribution to minimize material inequalities for purposes of satisfying the social welfare needs of all. Instructively from a minimum justice perspective, Robert Nozick, one of the foremost twentieth-century libertarian political philosophers, argued just before the onset of the current increasingly unegalitarian trajectory that the private property regime generated by the free market economy could not be subjected to any redistribution that would comport with justice, whether through taxation or otherwise (Nozick 1974). Consistent with this, Nozick claimed that no state assuming more extended powers than those necessary to carry out a minimal night watchman function could be

---

[17] "Under Pressure: The Squeezed Middle Class," *Organization for Economic Co-operation and Development* 16 (2019), <https://www.oecd.org/els/soc/OECD-middle-class-2019-main-findings.pdf>, visited April 3, 2022.

[18] See Price & Edwards, note 25, at 32–9.

[19] See Hanauer & Rolf, note 16.

[20] See Price & Edwards, note 15, at 3.

deemed legitimate (*Id.*: 123–5). In other words, according to Nozick's libertarian vision, the market economy is an independent self-regulating system and the sole legitimate role for the state is to protect that system from external disruption or interference. From this it follows that there is no distributive justice-based support for any state-backed social welfare rights.

Not only the massive inegalitarian surge since the 1970s but also the vast institutional changes that have occurred since then clearly underscore the unsuitability of a libertarian approach to a determination of what ought currently to amount to a minimum of justice from a constitutional perspective. Indeed, as discussed in Chapter 1, globalization has greatly multiplied the plurality of national, transnational, and international legal regimes that bear on economic, social, and political relationships within and across national borders. In particular, the combination of the plurality of legal regimes and the great mobility of capital and labor has at once given great flexibility to transnational corporations and vastly reduced the bargaining power of workers across many industries and service-providing enterprises. As we have seen, transnational corporations not only can seek to relocate in fiscal heavens with more favorable corporate laws but also, in a large number of cases, they can largely avoid the law of their places of business in favor of a largely self-serving private contractual regime that avoids official judicial oversight by subjecting disputes to business-friendly private arbitrators. From the standpoint of labor, on the other hand, job security becomes more precarious as a consequence of various factors, including automation and the availability of cheaper labor in less developed countries. Inequalities in wealth have greatly increased throughout countries with advanced economies, with even greater disparities in the United States than in Western Europe (Alvaredo et al. 2018: 73).

Whatever role may be reserved transnational and international institutions, it behooves the nation-state authorities to assume the duty to meet the needs encompassed within the minimum of justice as much as possible. And, based on the economic situation in countries approximating the United States, it seems amply justified to provide a constitutional guarantee extending to the vast cluster of social welfare rights that are included in the United Nations International Covenant on Economic Social and Cultural Rights (ICESCR) to citizens in the countries with the most advanced economies. These ICESCR rights include: the right to earn a living through dignified work and through provision of appropriate technical and vocational training;[21] fair wages allowing for a decent life for the wage earner and her family as well as safe and healthy working conditions;[22] the right to form and join labor unions and the right to strike within reasonable limits;[23] the right to social security and social insurance;[24] adequate food, housing, and continuous

---

[21] ICESCR, art. 6.
[22] *Id.* at art. 7.
[23] *Id.* at art. 8.
[24] *Id.* at art. 9.

improvement of living conditions;[25] the right to receive the medical services required to preserve one's health, the prevention and control of epidemics, and the control of environment and occupational hazards;[26] and the right to education, including higher education and free primary education.[27] Moreover, in the wealthiest countries the minimum of social welfare rights should go even farther than those guaranteed by the ICESCR. For example, given the vast array of opportunities reserved for those with higher education the state should subsidize university education for those who could otherwise ill afford it. Finally, rights such as the ICESCR ones mentioned are currently in large part protected either constitutionally or through infra-constitutional legislation in economically advanced Western democracies, including in the United States. Wherever relevant, however, constitutionalization remains preferable to avoid unwarranted majoritarian led reductions in benefits which would contravene the justice essentials.

Failure to meet the minimum sketched earlier would certainly fail to approximate the distributive justice minimums in the world's wealthiest countries and would do so in all three of economic redistribution, recognition, and representation. Moreover, it does so at all three levels of the universal, the singular, and the plural. This can be illustrated by focusing on the single case of the right to health care services which is guaranteed to all through state administered socialized medicine in a large number of Western democracies, but denied as of this writing to around 26 million persons in the United States.[28] From a broad distributive justice perspective, medical needs could be variously subjected to two already mentioned broad principles of substantive justice: "to each according to her means" or "to each according to his needs."[29] Although there is no universal consensus regarding which of these principles should govern health care issues, a strong preference can be expressed in favor of adopting a criterion of needs rather than of means in any country such as the United States where discretionary governmental expenditure in the trillions of dollars has repeatedly been made in recent years. Basic medical care is essential for the material well-being of every individual, and it should not be denied because it requires a measure of economic redistribution that involves a relatively small sacrifice from those who find themselves in the country's higher wealth brackets. Basic medical care is also paramount to maintain one's dignity and sense of well-being. And finally, lack of basic medical care because of poverty also caries representational implications in as much as it tends to exacerbate disparities between the medically uninsured poor and their better-off counterparts

---

[25] *Id.* at art. 11.

[26] *Id.* at art. 12.

[27] *Id.* at art. 13.

[28] Jeanna Smialek, Sarah Kliff, & Alan Rappeport, "U.S. poverty hit a record low before the pandemic recession," *NY Times*, September 15, 2020, <https://www.nytimes.com/2020/09/15/business/economy/poverty-record-low-prior-to-pandemic.html>, visited April 3, 2022.

[29] For a listing of these and other criteria of distributive justice, see Perelman 1980:1–24.

within the confines of the political sphere. Furthermore, these distributive injustices are bound to have repercussions at all three levels of the constitutional polity. At the universal level, which is that of the relevant constitutional community taken as a whole, it appears unseemly that some of those who ought to count as parties to the basic constitutional social pact are deprived of some of the most basic material and dignitarian attributes in a setting bathed in enormous streams of wealth. At the level of the singular, 26 million individuals in the United States are glaringly deprived of one of the mainstays of the minimum of justice that ought to be constitutionally assured. And in addition, at the level of the plural, to the extent that the lack of medical insurance afflicts certain racial and ethnic minorities much more than those not within those disadvantaged groups, it adds group-regarding inequities to individual-regarding ones.

IV The Minimum of Justice and the Contrast Between First- and Second-Generation Constitutional Rights

Social and economic rights, often closely tracking those featured in the ICESCR, have been typically included in post-Second World War constitutions but have been steeped in controversy both from the standpoint of theory and from that of practical application. This controversy centers on whether such rights can ultimately be counted as genuine ones. From a philosophical standpoint, some have argued that such rights automatically fail the strict correlation test between right and duty that the very concept of right requires (Feinberg & Naverson 1970: 243). From a more pragmatic legal perspective, on the other hand, many argue that second-generation rights are, unlike their first-generation counterparts, unenforceable and, more pointedly, judicially unmanageable (Hunt 1993: 154). I first briefly consider the theoretical issue and then through a comparative constitutional analysis evaluate the legal/constitutional, as opposed to political, viability of social and economic rights.

(a) Philosophy and the correlation between right and duty

The philosopher Maurice Cranston has called for a strict correlation between right and duty and he accordingly argued against second generation human rights (Cranston 1973). Pursuant to this view, a party has a right to something if what she is entitled to corresponds fully to what another party has the duty to provide her. Strict correlation emerges clearly in the realm of legal contracts. A contracts with B to buy a specific painting at a mutually agreed price. A then pays B but B refuses to hand over the painting, whereupon A sues B, and the judge in the case issues an order of specific performance compelling B to deliver the painting to A. This

76 LOCAL VERSUS GLOBAL

paradigmatic contractual case can be, for the most part, substantially replicated in the context of first-generation constitutional or human rights, so long as the latter remain purely negative rights. Thus, for instance, the US First Amendment forbids laws abridging the free exercise of religion.[30] Accordingly, my constitutional right to pray to whomever I choose and in whichever manner I prefer strictly correlates with the governmental duty to abstain from legislating or otherwise intervening so as to hinder my freedom to pray as I choose. In contrast, a second-generation right to decent shelter to which thousands of indigents are deemed entitled cannot be satisfied without government action over time and thus defies strict one-to-one correlation between right and duty.[31] And consistent with conceptual adherence to strict correlation, the second-generation right in question is best envisioned as a justified aspiration calling for a public policy commitment to provide adequate housing for the poor over a reasonable period of time.

At the theoretical level, there are many considerations suggesting that it is preferable to adopt a broader, more relational and more contextual conception of the nexus between right and duty than that espoused by proponents of strict correlation.[32] Moreover, upon discarding strict correlation as overly restrictive, the main question is where to set the minimally acceptable nexus between right and duty on the spectrum spanning from no remedy (which is equivalent to no enforceable duty) to strict correlation. At a minimum, for some claim to amount to genuine legal right, it must trigger some obligation on the part of the corresponding duty holder such that the latter is legally compelled either to abstain from acting or to do so in a way that is designed to address the legitimate demands brought forth by the right holder significantly. To what extent must the duty holder be compelled to act or forgo action in order to satisfy the obligation to the right holder in a "significantly" sufficient manner? If one accounts for pertinent contextual factors, there is a strong argument for adopting a proportionality-based criterion combined with reasonableness as a minimum requirement. Thus, for example, in the above-mentioned reference to the right to pray, it is both reasonable and proportionate for a complete government forbearance resulting in a strict correlation between constitutional right and duty. In contrast, in the situation regarding adequate shelter for indigent citizens, it would be proportionate to have the government meet all the right holders' claims over time through a promptly initiated systematic building project urgently pursued to complete the task as soon as reasonably feasible. Also, for purposes of adhering to this building project, the government would be obliged to limit its budgetary discretion and to postpone or set aside certain priorities to which it might have otherwise given precedence. On the other hand, it would be reasonable, and hence not in violation of the government's duty, to provide

---

[30] US Const., amend I.
[31] See *Government of South Africa v. Grootboom*, 2001 (1) SALR 46 (CC).
[32] ·See, e.g., Da Silva 2020; Perry 2009.

adequate shelter, for the latter temporarily to delay completion of the building project to attend to a major unforeseen emergency such as a natural disaster or a deadly epidemic. Furthermore, assuming individual rights to adequate shelter owed to several thousands of individuals and a three-year construction project, the mere fact that some of these individuals would be housed within a few months and certain others would have to wait up to three years would not negate in any way any of the rights or violate any of the duties involved; that is, unless the order set for the allocation of housing units were disproportionate or unreasonable. To clarify this further with another example, assuming that a right to government-provided health care included both necessary and elective medical treatment, prioritizing the former and occasionally postponing the latter due to justified limitations in available resources would be both proportionate and reasonable, whereas the contrary would be neither.

Except where perfect correlation between right and duty is practically feasible, the duty holder must prioritize efforts towards satisfying the corresponding right. In the face of conflicting rights seeking vindication all at once and other compelling societal needs competing within the ambit of limited resources, the amount of actual effort that a duty holder must expend at any given time to satisfy a corresponding right holder's entitlement ought to be proportionate and reasonable. Also, constitutional rights have priority over infra-constitutional ones and over majoritarian policies. Accordingly, significantly addressing a claim to entitlement pursuant to a constitutional right requires meeting a distinctly higher threshold than in the case of an infra-constitutional right.

In sum, from a theoretical perspective, the more flexible and nuanced contextual approach to the nexus between right and duty seems clearly preferable to the strict correlation theory. If failing strict correlation implies that no genuine right is involved then any constitutional right to adequate housing or health care would at best be the equivalent of a mere policy-based preference that may be ignored or revoked through a mere majoritarian process.[33] If, on the other hand, a constitutional right creates some tangible entitlement and a corresponding significant obligation not subject to majoritarian overriding, then the more flexible theoretical approach seems far better suited to account for the nature and scope of entitlements and corresponding obligations promulgated by the vast majority of contemporary constitutions.

---

[33] If a constitution treats a right to health care as merely aspirational, such as a constitutional declaration in a preamble to the effect that it commits to allow for the "pursuit of happiness," then it does not institute any right at all. If, on the other hand, the constitution is understood to prescribe adoption of laws relating to health care but leaves the content of such laws entirely up to the discretion of the legislature, that would be tantamount to the absence of any *constitutional* rights on the subject.

78   LOCAL VERSUS GLOBAL

(b) Social and economic rights in comparative constitutional law

Even if one deemed them perfectly sound in theory, second-generation rights would still pose daunting practical challenges when tackled from within the bounds of human rights or constitutional law. These challenges relate to all three of the right holder's legal entitlement, the duty holder's corresponding legal obligation, and the legal enforcer's—in most cases a court—decision-making criteria and remedial toolbox. Significantly, the ICESCR, which has been ratified by 171 countries[34] and adopted in many of them as law or referred to in constitutional adjudication, includes a set of rights that do not provide as clearly circumscribed an entitlement as the right to pray under the US Constitution, to which reference was previously made. What is an adequate standard of living or of housing? What medical services should be guaranteed to all the sick? What should be an acceptable minimum of social security? Furthermore, assuming overcoming the indeterminacies affecting the entitlements of rights holders, how could the government obligations as duty holder be specified? Supposing an agreement on what constitutes adequate housing and an ascertainment that 100,000 individuals lack such housing, how should one specify how long to give the government to satisfy all rights holders, or how the government should proceed in cases of conflicting priorities and budgetary shortfalls? Finally, does the judge deciding a housing rights dispute have adequate standards of adjudication or adequate remedies distinguishable from overtaking a seemingly purely legislative task involving a budgetary decision and prescription of a government housing building project over a set number of years?

Unlike first-generation rights that are nearly universally judicially enforceable, constitutionally enshrined social and economic rights can be divided into three different categories. In roughly in one-third of the cases, the constitution makes these rights aspirational only; in another third, justiciable; and in yet another third, some such rights are justiciable and others aspirational (Jung, Hirschl, & Rosevear 2014). In cases involving a purely aspirational understanding of social and economic rights, these seem ultimately to boil down to moral exhortations to legislators to address certain basic material needs without creating or implying any significant legal right or obligation. In contrast, when rights that are aspirational require legislators to enact legal provisions to secure certain material essentials,

---

[34] Formally, the ICESCR creates treaty based international law as distinguished from constitutional law. However, in substance the content of some of the human rights created by the ICESCR is virtually identical to that of certain social and economic rights adopted by various nation-state constitutions. Some countries, such as Argentina, have actually incorporated the ICESCR into their constitution. See Art. 25, Constitución Nacional (Const. Nac.) (Argentina). The United States has signed, but not ratified the ICESCR. *Status of Ratification Interactive Database*, U.N. Human Rights Office of the High Commissioner, <https://indicators.ohchr.org/>. In any case, for purposes of the present general discussion relating to content, in contrast to reference to a particular national constitution, human rights and constitutional rights will be used interchangeably.

but do not allow for individual claims under the rights themselves (as opposed to existing legislation made pursuant to these rights) to be judicially enforceable, then there is some guaranteed benefit for the citizenry and a duty under the constitution imposed on the state (*Id.*: 1081–2). In some situations, aspirational rights may indirectly provide some justiciable individual constitutional rights. This has happened, as further addressed later in the chapter, in certain cases where repeal of existing legislation advancing a social welfare objective enshrined in the constitution has been successfully challenged as being unconstitutional. In addition, aspirational social welfare rights that do not themselves provide individual rights may in certain cases indirectly do so through other constitutional rights, such as that to equality. For example, the Latvian Constitutional Court held that a child care benefit limited to non-working parents violated the equality rights of working parents.[35] Finally, Germany's constitution, the Basic Law, does not provide for social and economic rights, but these have been integrated to a significant degree in the catalogue of the country's justiciable rights. This has been due not only indirectly through the right to equality but also through the overall interpretative gloss provided by the Basic Law as a whole which sets Germany as a democratic, rule-of-law (*Rechtsstaat*), and a social welfare state (*Sozialstaat*).[36]

In all but the purely aspirational cases, there may be sufficient elements of entitlements and corresponding obligations to fit within the broad outlines of the relational and contextual conceptual correlation between rights and duties embraced above. More importantly for our purposes, however, a full handle on the scope of benefits and drawbacks associated with constitutionalized social and economic rights requires evaluation of actual judicial disposition of cases arising in jurisdictions where such rights have been treated as justiciable. Accordingly, I proceed to discuss exemplary cases from relevant constitutional jurisdictions.

The following cases can be roughly divided into three different categories. The first of these comes closest to the paradigmatic first-generation negative right as it matches an individual right and a government duty and allows for a direct judicial remedy enabling the right holder to obtain her claimed entitlement. Thus, for example, if everyone is constitutionally entitled to a minimum of subsistence then a failure by government to provide that minimum to a particular individual could be fully remedied by a judicial decree commanding the government to comply with its duty. The second category also matches an individual right and a government duty but is only amenable to a class-wide judicial remedy allowing some individuals to receive a prompt remedy while forcing others to stand in line over an extended period of time. The above-mentioned example relating to decent housing right belonging to 100,000 indigent citizens and requiring a three-year government

---

[35] See *Latvian Constitutional Court Judgment of Sept. 1, 2005*, reprinted in Dorsen 2016: 1455.
[36] See Grundgesetz (GG) (Basic Law) art. 20 § 1, translation at http://www.gesetze-im-internet.de/englisch_gg/index.html..

construction project illustrates this second category. Finally, the third category is one that gives some indirect vindication to a social welfare right through invocation of another constitutional right. The right to equality plays an important role in this respect and calls for addressing a key distinction. Many equality claims have nothing to do with social welfare entitlements as all wrongful exclusions from the class of recipients of a government benefit give rise to a constitutional equality claim. Thus, for instance, if government subsidizes free public golf courses and tennis courts but prohibits their use to an ethnic minority, members of the latter would have a clear constitutional equality grievance that in no way implicates any social welfare entitlement. On the other hand, if the same ethnic minority were deprived of basic subsistence benefits enjoyed by all other needy citizens, then their equality grievance would plainly relate to their basic social welfare interests.

A most forceful and direct vindication of an individual's constitutional social welfare right emerges in a key decision regarding health services by the Colombian Constitutional Court. In this 2008 decision,[37] the Court held that an individual is entitled to a judicial remedy ordering the state to provide specific previously refused or unavailable health services "that are indispensable to maintain one's health when one's life, personal integrity or dignity is seriously threatened."[38] In reaching that conclusion, the Court emphasized that the right to health services has a negative as well as a more pervasive positive dimension.[39] On the one hand, the state must refrain from acting in ways that endanger the health of the citizenry while, on the other, the state needs to undertake programmatic and administrative action to satisfy the individual health care rights that are constitutionally protected. Remarkably, the Court stressed that although the positive dimension of the right generally affords the state significant discretion, that is not the case in the more urgent instances where an immediate remedy is appropriate even if that requires the state to mobilize additional resources.[40]

Unlike its Colombian counterpart, the South African Constitutional Court has considered the eventuality of unanticipated additional governmental expenditures as a key consideration in denying direct individual remedies in cases involving constitutionally protected health care rights. Thus, in the *Soobramoney* case,[41] the Court held that the individual right to access health care under Section 27 of the country's Constitution did not entitle a terminally ill patient to be provided life prolonging renal dialysis. Nevertheless, the Court did recognize an enforceable individual right to emergency medical services when suffering a crisis calling for

---

[37] Corte Constitucional (C.C.) (Constitutional Court), Sala Segunda de Revisión, July 31, 2007, MP:MJC Espinosa, Sentencia T-760/08 (Colom), summarized English translation at <https://www.escr-net.org/sites/default/files/English_summary_T-760.pdf>.

[38] *Id.* at para. 4.4.1.

[39] *Id.* at para. 3.3.2.

[40] *Id.* at paras 3.32 & 3.36.

[41] *Soobramoney v. Minister of Health (Kwazulu-Natal)*, 1998 (1) SALR 765 (C.C.).

immediate medical treatment.[42] Although this involves a very restricted direct individual right, it still imposes a positive governmental duty with associated costs.[43]

Minimum welfare and pension rights have also at times been judicially vindicated through direct remedies for aggrieved individuals. In the "Right to Food" case,[44] the Supreme Court of India issued an order requiring government implementation of a program to provide meals at schools. The Colombian Constitutional Court carved out an implicit right of survival requiring individual remedies regarding entitlements to basic subsistence needs and minimum pension benefits.[45] The Estonian Supreme Court specified that the constitutional right to subsistence benefits is subject to legislative implementation except when assistance falls below a minimum level, at which point the courts have a duty to intervene.[46]

Somewhat different, but still for the main functionally equivalent, are cases involving the reduction or elimination of legislatively established benefits in accordance with constitutionally established social welfare rights. Thus, the constitutional tribunals in Poland and Hungary invalidated reductions in the levels of government benefits relating to social welfare and pension entitlements.[47] The 1995 Hungarian Constitutional Court decision is particularly notorious as it pitted preserving settled levels of social welfare benefits against urgent and weighty budgetary pressure bearing on the future health of the Hungarian economy. The reduction of benefits imposed by the Hungarian government and later judicially invalidated was undertaken at the behest of would-be foreign investors who agreed to reinvigorate the then ailing Hungarian economy subject to a prior commitment to significant fiscal restraint.[48] The Portuguese Constitutional Court also held in various cases that genuine budgetary considerations did not necessarily justify reductions in public employees' salaries or pensions (Dorsen 2016: 1486–8). In one of these cases decided in 2014 when Portugal was facing an economic crisis and depended on loans from the EU and the International Monetary Fund (IMF) which required certain structural changes, the Court nevertheless ruled against reductions in certain benefits as the amounts that would have been saved were too insignificant to affect the crisis (*Id.*: 1488).

---

[42] *Id.* at para. 20.

[43] See *id.* The Court characterizes the right to emergency medical services as a "negative" one because it draws on available resources, such as existing ambulances and hospitals. To the extent that the right in question is extended to those who cannot pay for the costs involved, however, individual vindication of the right requires some level of "positive" government action and expenditure.

[44] *People's Union for Civil Liberties v. Union of India and Others (PUCL)*, Writ Petition (Civil) No. 196 of 2001 (India) (November 28, 2001 interim order).

[45] Corte Constitucional (CC) (Constitutional Court), June 24, 1992, Sentencia T-426/92 (Colom).

[46] Riigikohus (Supreme Court of Estonia), Constitutional Review Chamber of the Supreme Court, January 21, 2004, Constitutional Judgment 3-4-1-7-03.

[47] See Judgment K 14/91 of February 11, 1992, 1992(I) Orzecznictwo Tryb. Konst. (Constitutional Tribunal) 93 (Poland); Alkotmánybíróság (AB) (Constitutional Court) June 30, 1995, MK 56/1995. No. 43/1995 (Hungary).

[48] I am following the account of the circumstances surrounding this case provided in Tushnet 2008: 235–7.

82 LOCAL VERSUS GLOBAL

The lesson to be drawn from these Polish, Hungarian, and Portuguese cases is that by preventing reductions in benefits in spite of serious budgetary implications, courts imposed substantive limitations on government economic policy objectives. These instances of social welfare rights judicial enforcement that trumped legitimate government fiscal and budgetary concerns seem amply justified pursuant to the minimum a standard within each of the relevant constitutional settings involved.

A prime example of the second category of cases involving a judicial imposition of a social welfare obligation on government that does not result in an immediate satisfaction of an individual plaintiff's constitutional entitlement is *Grootboom* decided by the South African Constitutional Court.[49] Section 26(1) of the South African Constitution grants a right of access to adequate housing. In interpreting this provision, the Court made it clear that government has the responsibility to set up and administer programs designed to vindicate social welfare rights within the scope of its budgetary capabilities.[50] So long as a government program is reasonable, the courts are not supposed to intervene. In *Grootboom*, however, the Court found the contested government program adequate for purposes of medium- and long-term housing needs, but unreasonable in its failure meaningfully to provide for "people in desperate need."[51] Accordingly, the Court ordered the government to modify its existing program in order to meet the needs of those, who like the plaintiff, Mrs Grootboom, were in the direst conditions.[52] The upshot was that the government was ordered to build adequate housing for those in desperate need within a reasonable time frame and all those within that category were supposed to be individually accommodated by the end of the building period. Mrs. Grootboom was thus not entitled to immediate satisfaction of her constitutional right but was slated to be adequately housed sometime between the completion of the first units meant for those in desperate need and the full realization of the Court-ordered program.[53]

Another example of a court-mandated government program, this time in the area of health care rights, is provided by *Prakash Mani Sharma v. Government of Nepal*.[54] The Nepal Supreme Court found that existing government programs failed to prevent or address the serious problem of uterus prolapse, which led to premature death for a majority of the country's women. This was in violation of

---

[49] See *Grootboom*, 2001 (1) SALR 46 (CC).

[50] See S. Afr. Con. Sec. 27(2)(1996).

[51] See *Grootboom*, 2001 (1) SALR 46 at paras 14, 20, 43, 64, and 99 (CC).

[52] *Id.* at para. 99.

[53] In point of fact, it appears that Mrs Grootboom was never provided with the housing she was entitled to at some point as four years after the Court's decision she had seemingly "disappeared." See Tushnet 2008: 244.

[54] Supreme Court of Nepal (Writ N. 064-WS-0230 of year 2060). Decided in 2066 BS (2009).

these women's constitutional right to life, which includes a right to health care.[55] The existing government programs and resources were woefully inadequate as the women lacked access to health facilities, proper equipment, and medical professionals, and were relegated to unsafe abortions and great poverty.[56] In view of this, the Court ordered the legislature to enact appropriate legislation within a reasonable time, and the executive branch of government to set up facilities and to provide free treatment and consultations for the aggrieved women. Thus, although the judicially ordered legislation and executive programs and resources would require gradual realization within a reasonable period of time, the goal was eventually to afford all women with the health care necessary to surmount the problems associated with uterus prolapse.

Cases within the third category, namely indirect vindication of social welfare rights through recourse to other constitutional rights, must satisfy two conditions: first, they must come to a significant extent within the scope of a non-social and economic right, such as equality or dignity; and second, the judicial enforcement of the latter right ought substantially to advance constitutionally recognized social welfare interests. As noted earlier, many vindications of constitutional equality claims have no social welfare rights implications. Similarly, many dignity claims, such as the assertion that Holocaust denial amounts to an affront against the constitutionally protected dignity of Holocaust survivors in Germany,[57] do not bear any non-purely contingent link to social welfare interests.

The German Constitutional Court has held in several cases that the minimum of subsistence for children is constitutionally guaranteed as a matter of basic dignity. In the *Children Allowance* case,[58] the Court concluded that the state was obliged to provide for the burdens of child care either through tax deductions or through state subsidies. In the *Minimum Livelihood* case,[59] the Court specified that income tax law must allow safeguarding the minimum conditions of livelihood consistent with respect for human dignity. Furthermore, drawing on the right to equality, the Italian Constitutional Court held that emergency medical treatment could not be withheld from those who could not afford the fees associated with it,[60] and, in another case, that experimental cancer treatment provided to certain terminally ill patients could not be denied to similarly situated others.[61] Finally, the Polish

---

[55] The Court also found a violation of art. 12 of the Convention on the Elimination of All Forms of Discrimination Against Women (CEDAW) which provides that reproductive health is considered part of the human rights of women. *Id.* at paras 17–18.

[56] *Id.* at para. 1.

[57] Strafgesetzbuch (StGB) (Penal Code), November 13, 1998, Bundesgesetzblatt (BGBI). I at 3322, last amended by Gesetz, October 10, 2013, BGBI. I at 3799 art. 6(18), § 130 Fremdrentengesetz (FRG); *Holocaust Denial Case*, Bundesverfassungsgericht (BVerfG) (Federal Constitutional Court) April 13, 1994, 90 Entscheidungen des Bundesverfassungsgericht (BVerfGE) 241 (F.R.G.).

[58] BVerfG November 23, 1976, 43; BVerfGE 108 (F.R.G).

[59] BVerfG May 29, 1990, 82; BVerfGE 60 (F.R.G).

[60] Corte Cost., July 17, 1998, n. 267, Gazzetta Ufficiale (GU) n. 29, 1998 (Italy) (hereinafter *Italian Cancer Treatment Case*).

[61] Corte Cost., May 26, 1998, n. 185, Giur. it. 1998 (Italy).

84 LOCAL VERSUS GLOBAL

Constitutional Tribunal held eviction of pregnant women, minors, and disabled persons to be in violation of the right to dignity and indicated that families in difficult material and social circumstances had the right to special assistance by public authorities.[62] Along similar lines, the Hungarian Constitutional Court held that although there is no constitutional right to housing, the right to life requires state provided housing where a person's life would otherwise be endangered.[63]

(c) Second-generation rights versus first-generation rights and their respective policy-based and budgetary implications

Unlike purely negative first-generation rights which may only necessitate the state to refrain from any action, second-generation rights require some state action. From the right holder's standpoint, in justiciable cases either an immediate remedy is available (e.g., an order to provide emergency medical treatment at no cost to those unable to pay) or a deferred remedy over a foreseeable period of time (e.g., planned state-financed construction of housing units or court-ordered adoption of suitable legislation within a judicially set deadline). Whereas immediate remedies are preferable to deferred ones, the latter can significantly contribute to the entitlements of the concerned right holders. Accordingly, social welfare rights holders seem clearly better off with justiciable guarantees than with having to depend on the vicissitudes of majoritarian policies.

From the state duty standpoint, on the other hand, second-generation rights present two difficulties that are not inherent to first-generation rights. First, enforcement constrains legislative discretion which in some cases is virtually eliminated due to judicially ordered specific law-making obligations. And second, satisfying constitutionally protected social welfare entitlements almost invariably entail budgetary implications requiring either a shifting of, or an increase in, government expenditures.

Constraints on legislative discretion, whether due to negative prohibitions in the case of first-generation rights or of affirmative obligations to enact social welfare laws that would not otherwise see the light of day, are inevitable in any constitutional system that endeavors to afford meaningful protection to anti-majoritarian rights. From the pure perspective of the pursuit of majoritarian political initiatives, it may well be equally frustrating to endure a judicial strike down of a popular law that discriminates against a widely reviled religious minority as it would be to accept a judicially mandated legislation that imposes an obligation to provide cost-free essential health care services to the neediest citizens. Accordingly, the

---

[62] Judgment K 11/00 of April 4, 2001, 2001 (3) Orzecznictwo Tryb. Konst. (Constitutional Tribunal) 54 (Poland).

[63] AB November 7, 2000, ABH 2000/329. No. 42/2000 (Hungary).

difficulties relating to the constraints on legislative discretion due to social welfare rights seem better considered as raising questions of degree rather than of kind. In the broadest terms, one can object to enforceable social and economic rights both because they expand the realm of legislative constraints and because they apparently do so to a much greater extent than do civil and political rights. The first of these objections is, upon further thought, not intrinsically tied to social and economic rights. Some commentators have been critical about what they regard as an unwarranted inflation of fundamental rights (Glendon 1993), whereas others have favored the expansion of such rights.[64] In essence, therefore, the objection in question is one levelled by those with restrictive conceptions of anti-majoritarian rights against those with more expansionist views of such rights. Moreover, whether or not social welfare rights require more extensive legislative constraints than other rights hardly seems paramount in the present context. It may be much more upsetting to a larger majority of a particular citizenry to have a court strike down a very intensely favored anti-abortion law than having a court instructing public authorities to institute a free lunch program in public schools. In short, the conflict between restrictive and expansive conceptions of rights is theoretically separable from the categories of rights that it may relate to.

The difficulties posed by the budgetary implications of judicial enforcement of social welfare rights, in contrast, pose a more vexing problem that may seem less onerous in the context of first-generation rights. Also, judicially decreed added government expenditures are likely to be relatively much more burdensome in poor than in rich countries. Nevertheless, increased expenditures in all the above cases dealing with the direst needs of the most disadvantaged members of the citizenry are plainly called for by the minimum justice standard. Indeed, for any country not so poor as to as to render distributive justice concerns superfluous (Hume 1907: 15–38), state satisfaction of the most basic needs of the most disadvantaged ought definitely to be constitutionally mandated. Moreover, this is justified both from the standpoint of economic redistribution and from that of recognition.

Comparison of first- and second-generation rights in terms of their implementation in actual historical settings reveals that meaningful protection of first-generation rights often depend on positive state action. For example, if one's right to own private property were only protected by a complete lack of action by the state, this could more often than not result in frustration of the benefits to which the right holder is expected to be entitled. Without police protection, trespassers and thieves could invade a private residence with impunity. At the same time, without courts to settle property disputes, the rights of buyers, sellers, and inheritors of private

---

[64] Compare Justice Kennedy's majority opinion in *Obergefell v. Hodges*, 576 US 644 (2015) (same-sex marriage is protected by the Fourteenth Amendment's Due Process Clause) and Chief Justice Roberts' dissent (the legalization of same-sex marriage should be left to legislators).

86 LOCAL VERSUS GLOBAL

property would remain unbearably fragile and insecure. Moreover, even as traditionally a negative right as that to freedom of speech can at times be conditioned on positive state action for its realization. This occurs in the heckler's veto cases under the US Constitution's First Amendment.[65] These cases involve unpopular but constitutionally protected speech in front of a hostile audience that may become threatening to the speaker. Under such circumstances, protection of both free speech and public peace are better achieved wherever possible through police control of the hostile crowd than through removal of the provocative speaker.

A further inquiry into implementation of first-generation rights also reveals that they sometimes require staggered state fulfillment of entitlements over time, judicial orders commanding adoption of particular legislation, and judicial overriding of budgetary limitations or imposition of remedies requiring redirection or increases in public expenditures. A prime example of a staggered remedy is that provided by the judicially ordered, constitutionally mandated racial desegregation of public schools arising after the U.S. Supreme Court landmark decision in *Brown v. Board of Education*.[66] If the Court had limited itself to invalidating state laws mandating racial segregation in public schools, then it would have afforded a purely negative remedy consisting in the removal of legal barriers to racial integration. The Court, however, interpreted the US Constitution's Equal Protection Clause as requiring implementation of a right to a racially integrated public-school education. This imposed on the states found to have violated the Constitution a duty to affirmatively intervene "with all deliberate speed" to achieve an actually racially integrated system of public education.[67] But because of massive white resistance to racial integration, little progress had been achieved in well over a decade, which prompted the Court to decide in favor of greater judicial intervention which lasted several decades, stressing that the federal courts' "equitable powers to remedy past wrongs is broad."[68]

Finally, judicial orders to legislatures mandating adoption within a limited time frame of laws designed to satisfy entitlements associated with fundamental rights have long been issued both in the context of first-generation rights as in that of second-generation ones. Thus, for example, if a law grants higher pension benefits to men than to women, a court could simply invalidate such law as violating constitutional equality between the sexes and leave it up to the legislature to either do nothing, add to the pensions of women, or lower those of men, so long as parity between the sexes is realized. In the alternative, however, as is frequently done by the German Constitutional Court (Zeidler 2016: 504–7), a court could order adoption of a specific legislation that follows judicially laid down instructions.

---

[65] See, e.g., *Terminiello v. Chicago*, 337 US 1 (1949).
[66] 347 US 483 (1954).
[67] See *Brown v. Board of Education* (Brown II), 349 US 294 (1955).
[68] *Swann v. Charlotte-Mecklenburg Board of Education*, 402 US 1 (1971).

In our example, the court could give the legislature six months to raise the level of women's pensions to that of men. In this particular example, the court would command legislation and impose an additional financial burden on the state. In other cases, such as that in which the South African Constitutional Court found the unavailability of same-sex marriage under law unconstitutional,[69] the judicial remedy consisted in ordering the legislature to include same-sex marriage in an amendment to its existing marriage law. And obviously, this latter remedy does not require any state assumption of additional expenditures.

In spite of traditionally articulated conceptual and practical differences, this comparison between first-generation and second-generation rights reveals much more of a continuum rather than any unbridgeable gap. Both from the respective perspectives of rights holders and of duty-bound state actors, social welfare rights can find adequate vindication through easy adaptation and expansion of judicial tools and practices developed in the context of first-generation rights adjudication. Also, it is evident that a minimum of justice under the justice essentials calls for constitutional guarantees that make the state responsible for satisfaction of the most basic needs of those in the most precarious predicament. What needs to be investigated further at this point is whether, and to what extent, the minimum of justice under consideration may have to be apportioned among national constitutions and transnational legal regimes depending on disparities in wealth among particular constitutional units.

V Economic Globalization, Transnational Plurality of Legal Regimes, and Constitutional Redistribution under Minimum Justice

To render the global economy fairer and more accountable and to reduce the harms of its most salient externalities, such as climate change, would require stringing together a series of legal and administrative measures securing coordination between national, transnational, and international actors and sources of law. Environmental threats are for the most part global in scope and thus effectively combatting them depends heavily on worldwide cooperation.[70] Corporate accountability and fair dealing as well as amelioration and equalization of labor conditions, on the other hand, can benefit incrementally through subjection to a plurality of national and extranational layered and segmented legal regimes that intersect without necessarily becoming fully integrated into a single, harmonious,

---

[69] *Minister of Home Affairs and Another v Fourie and Another; Lesbian and Gay Equality Project and Others v. Minister of Home Affairs and Others*, 2006 (1) SA 524 (CC) (South Africa).

[70] Paris Agreement to the United Nations Framework Convention on Climate Change, December 12, 2015, Treaties and Other International Acts Series (TIAS) No. 16-1104.

88 LOCAL VERSUS GLOBAL

hierarchically blended system.[71] Accordingly, independently of whether transnational or international measures should actually bear some of the burden of providing for the social welfare needs that minimum justice requires for every living human being, it behooves the nation-state authorities to assume the duty to meet the needs of minimum justice as much as possible. Indeed, failure to meet the minimum sketched earlier would violate the distributive justice requirements imposed by the minimum of justice as it pertains to all three of economic redistribution, recognition, and representation. And it would do so at all three levels of the universal, the singular, and the plural as was illustrated earlier through focus on the case in favor of the right to essential health care services which is guaranteed to all through state-administered socialized medicine in a large number of Western democracies.

Entrenched protection of fundamental social welfare entitlements should be enshrined in nation-state constitutions. Because of transnational and international inequities and imbalances due to globalization, however, national protections ought to be supplemented by transnational ones. To the extent that some countries may not be able to secure an adequate level of well-being for all within their borders, transnational economic redistribution ought ideally to become legally mandated with the goal of eventually satisfying the justice essentials on a worldwide basis. Moreover, even where a nation-state constitution may secure the minimum, actual and potential mass flights of capital and deterioration of labor opportunities and conditions counsel in favor of supplementation through deployment of transnational economic, legal, and institutional regimes. This could be accomplished through layered legal regimes, such as that deployed by the E.U., or through segmented ones, such as the ICESCR. In the latter case, the challenge remains, to a large extent, one of enforceability. For example, the European Convention on Human Rights (ECHR) does not comprise social and economic rights and the European Court of Human Rights (ECt HR) has only given them minimal indirect recognition (Viljanen 2003: 254–8). More generally, there is no current co-ordination between national, transnational, and international socio-legal, institutional, and political actors which works well enough to effectuate adjustments to, and limitations on, the systemic spread of the globalized economy and its trajectory towards seemingly ever-increasing inequalities. Illiberal populism, exclusivist nationalism, trade wars, retrenchment within the bounds of the nation-states, and mounting hostility towards cosmopolitan elites have all been enlisted in campaigns against the economic and identitarian inequities fostered by globalization (Frieden 2019: 181). Thus far, however, these campaigns appear to have had little success in slowing down, let alone reducing, the spread of inequality fueled by the engine of

---

[71] See Rosenfeld 2008: 415–55 (contrasting layered regulations, such as those that superimpose E.U. laws on those of national member states without achieving a fully federalized system, with segmented ones, such as those of the World Trade Organization (WTO), an international treaty-based regime aimed at imposing a common legal regime on worldwide trade).

globalization. Accordingly, the challenge to properly tackle globalization's inequities endures and it is unclear whether the liberal constitutional ideal and its deployment beyond the nation-state offer the best means toward progress in the quest for the justice essentials.

In sum, under current conditions, a large measure of economic redistribution is necessary for purposes of achieving the justice essentials called for by the liberal constitutional ideal. In the most economically advanced countries, the national constitution suffices for purposes of guaranteeing the minimum of justice and most probably the full panoply of entitlements necessary to meet the demands of the justice essentials. Many other countries can undoubtedly also secure the minimum of justice. Nevertheless, the requisite redistribution which must be secured to extend the reach of the justice essentials to all polities requires a transnational legal, political, and institutional system of cooperation that is by no means currently within reach. Some of the institutional apparatus for such a system may already be in place as the transnational legal and institutional regimes and modalities discussed in Chapter 1 may be suitably adapted. What remains to be seen, however, is whether there might be a viable path to further institutional development and consolidation of the will to channel economic globalization towards the kind of redistributive policies that could ensure the justice essentials for all.

VI Constitutional Democracies Confront the Stress of Global Terrorism and Worldwide Pandemics

Globalization has recast both terrorism and pandemics in ways that magnify their confrontation in contemporary constitutional democracies, in general, and the justice essentials, in particular. To be sure, both terrorism and pandemics have long preceded the present era of globalization. Nevertheless, global terrorists fostering panic, death, and destruction in faraway lands, such as Al Qaeda attackers who destroyed the twin towers in New York on 9/11/2001, seem to differ widely from their nationalist counterparts, such as the Irish Republican Army (IRA) in Northern Ireland or the Euskadi Ta Askatasuna (Basque Homeland and Liberty, ETA) Basque separatists in Spain. Similarly, the COVID-19 pandemic that rapidly spread to all corners of the world in 2020 has had institutional and political consequences that previous transnational pandemics lacked. For example, the COVID-19 pandemic led EU countries within the Schengen zone, which had long maintained open internal borders, to close their borders to those coming from neighboring Schengen countries.[72] More generally, global terrorism and

---

[72] Martina Stevis-Gridneff, "Coronavirus nightmare could be the end for Europe's borderless dream," *NY Times*, February 28, 2020, <https://www.nytimes.com/2020/02/26/world/europe/coronavirus-european-union.html?searchResultPosition=2>, visited April 3, 2022.

90   LOCAL VERSUS GLOBAL

COVID-19, as a pandemic raging through a globalized economy and puncturing a socially and politically intertwined human landscape, have both exacerbated some of the difficulties confronting the quest for justice essentials thus far, and created some thorny additional challenges to mediation among the universal, the singular, and the plural. Above all, global terrorism and the COVID-19 pandemic have driven constitutional democracies towards conditions of stress which stand halfway between ordinary conditions and conditions of crisis or of emergency. In what follows, I first concentrate on what constitute conditions of stress[73] and how global terrorism and the COVID-19 pandemic subject polities to life under stress. Next, I focus on how conditions of stress exacerbate previously addressed material, identitarian, and representational justice quandaries and how they pose new problems of their own.

(a) Conditions of stress as halfway between ordinary times and times of crisis

Under ordinary conditions, liberal constitutional democracies maintain sufficient congruence between the universal, the singular, and the plural and sufficient approximation to the justice essentials to foster a working consensus that it seems preferable for almost everyone concerned to operate within the institutional status quo than to opt for a radically different alternative, such as revolution, civil war, or secession. In ordinary times, adherence to the community of communities of the constitutional unit remains relatively firm. This is because frustrations due to failures to reach a proper equilibrium between the universal, the singular, and the plural seem reasonably open to rectification through the mainstays of an existing constitutional order within the ambit of the justice essentials and through the workings of a solidly institutionalized and widely accessible realm of majoritarian politics.

Times of crisis, in contrast, occur when the common identity of the community of communities or the very life of the polity are in imminent peril. The cause of the peril may be external, as in the case of a foreign war, or internal, as in the case of a civil war or a violent thrust toward secession. Moreover, emergencies may also be triggered by natural causes as opposed to direct human agency as exemplified by devastating earthquakes or hurricanes. In times of crisis, there may be a rallying towards unity, with common emphasis on the universal at the expense of the singular and the plural. To unify in one's country's fight to forestall a foreign occupation, the citizenry may well temporally set aside religious or ethnic differences as well as readily accept substantial curtailment of individual rights. In contrast, in a

---

[73] The following discussion relies on, and further elaborates the analysis undertaken in Rosenfeld 2006 and Rosenfeld 2008.

civil war, the community of communities would be most likely to verge towards a split or a reconfiguration. A split upon a collapse of the universal and the singular into the plural would be likely to occur in a civil war pitting hostile religious or ethnic groups against one another. A reconfiguration, on the other hand, is likely to take place—as it did in the course of the US Civil War—as part of the whole violently secedes from the rest and the latter confronts redesigning the contours of *its* universal, singular, and plural while determined to carry on under existential and identitarian threat. In this connection, it is telling that during the US Civil War, the Union regarded itself as the preserver of the US nation and of its constitution while fighting against the southern states who saw themselves as waging a war of secession in order to form a new separate political unit (Downs 2019: 23–5). Furthermore, natural disasters tend to have a dynamic of their own, at times fostering extraordinary bonds of solidarity whereas at others resulting in existential crisis, despair, and resentment for significant segments of the population. Many major earthquakes resulting in massive destruction of buildings and high loss of life foster particularly strong bonds of solidarity not only on a national but also on a transnational scale. In many memorable instances, several foreign countries sent rescuers to help saving lives in the afflicted area and at times virtually the whole world was wired together on live television while anxiously awaiting the rescue of children trapped within a collapsed building (McAlister 2012). In contrast, certain other natural disasters, such as the 2017 Hurricane Maria in Puerto Rico, which resulted in a very large number of deaths and massive disruptions relating to essential needs and services, generated divisions, resentment, and recriminations (García-López 2018: 101–2). The Puerto Rican population and their representatives felt like second-class citizens because the victims of similar disasters in Florida and Texas had been much better treated by the US federal government *(Id.*: 107). At the same time, President Trump largely blamed Puerto Ricans for their handling of the hurricane and displayed a striking lack of empathy or solidarity towards the island's victims (*Id.*).

Typically, emergency conditions prevail during sharply delimited temporary acute crises characterized by sudden, extraordinary existential threats accompanied by loss of life, widespread destruction and/or institutional turmoil that threatens the very fabric of the constitutional order within the affected polity. The crises at stake foster a dynamic that veers between a strengthening of highly intensified bonds of solidarity and an exacerbation of hostility, vilification, and exclusion of those who are cast as responsible for the unbearable new state of turmoil. Moreover, in cases of and civil war, intensified solidarity and exacerbated vilification feed directly on one another, thus tearing apart any pre-existing harmony or compromise between the universal, the singular, and the plural.

Many contemporary liberal constitutions provide for extraordinary emergency powers invocable in times of crisis (Dorsen 2016: 1578). These emergency powers typically provide the head of government with extremely broad executive powers

92 LOCAL VERSUS GLOBAL

and allow for significant limitations of civil liberties for the duration of the triggering crisis (*Id.*). Although these emergency powers have been at times abused by political leaders with authoritarian tendencies (*Id.*), when properly used for a limited time they can make for a justified sacrifice of individual and group interests in order to secure the survival and well-being of the polity as a whole.

Times of stress span the spectrum between ordinary times and times of crisis. In times of stress, there is less extensive and less successful accommodation and integration of politically relevant competing conceptions of the good than in ordinary times. The community of communities, the individual, and relevant groups are less likely than in ordinary times to consider institutional processes of conflict resolution to be just or fair. The identity or unity of the common self that is supposed to bind together the citizenry is not disintegrating, but it is destabilized and under various pressures. Whereas a conventional war is likely to cause a crisis, terrorism and the "war on terror" seem more prone to generate stress. Indeed, unlike a military invasion, terrorist acts are likely to be sporadic and widespread, causing more psychological than physical harm. Having terrorists hidden within the polity's population is undoubtedly unnerving and can easily lead to overreactions, undue suppression of fundamental rights, or exacerbation of ethnic or racial prejudice such that certain minorities and the conceptions of the good they endorse may become increasingly unhinged. For example, terrorist acts by individuals coming from distant foreign lands, such as the Al Qaeda attacks on 9/11, or by one's neighbors, such as the ISIS (Islamic State of Iraq and Syria) attacks in Paris on November 2015, have aroused intense anti-Muslim sentiments (Britton 2015). This has led to mounting hostility against peaceful, law-abiding Muslim minorities living in countries that have been attacked or that fear that they will be (*Id.*).

At some point, erosion of accommodation of certain minorities and of their conceptions of the good may place increasing strain on the working unity of the polity's citizenry. In short, both the threat posed by the terrorist and the dangers posed by overreaction may fray the common glue that binds the polity together. Thus, the dangers looming on the horizon in times of stress may not be very different in nature than their counterparts present in times of crisis. Nevertheless, in times of stress, these dangers are markedly less imminent and less intense. That the "war on terror" unleashed after 9/11[74] gives rise to conditions of stress rather than of crisis is well captured in the following passage from Law Lord Hoffman's opinion in a UK case involving pre-emptive detention of certain foreign nationals suspected of terrorist affiliation:

---

[74] Significantly, in the immediate aftermath of the 9/11 attacks, US President Bush characterized the latter as international crimes and asserted that those responsible would be eventually arrested and tried for murder (Rosenfeld 2006). Soon thereafter, however, Bush announced that the attacks warranted the launching of a "war on terror," which was meant as a worldwide campaign against global terrorists and which by October 2001 resulted in an actual foreign war against Al Qaeda operatives and their sponsors the Taliban who were then the rulers in Afghanistan (*Id.*: 2117).

[The United Kingdom] is a nation that has been tested in adversity, which has survived physical destruction and catastrophic loss of life. I do not underestimate the ability of fanatical groups of terrorists to kill and destroy, but they do not threaten the life of the nation. Whether we would survive Hitler hung in the balance, but there is no doubt that we shall survive Al-Qaeda. The Spanish people have not said that what happened in Madrid [where in 2004 Al Qaeda detonated explosives in several trains causing 191 deaths], hideous crime as it was, threatened the life of their nation. Their legendary pride would not allow it. Terrorist violence, serious as it is, does not threaten our institutions of government or our existence as a civil community.[75]

In ordinary times a workable equilibrium between liberty, equality, and security presumably can be steadily maintained. In times of crisis, on the other hand, existential or identitarian survival warrants a temporary restriction of liberty and equality to optimize security. Under conditions of stress, however, it is not obvious whether liberty and equality ought to be strengthened or somewhat restricted. The reason for this is that conditions of stress prevail within a continuum that extends from the boundaries of ordinary conditions to those of emergency conditions. Logically, it would seem that the closer particular stress conditions may be to ordinary ones, the more the ordinary constitutional equilibrium ought to be for the most part maintained. Similarly, the closer conditions of stress are to crossing the line into a crisis, the more they may call for something very akin to emergency powers. Paradoxically, however, upon further thought, conditions of stress may in some cases call for *reinforcement* rather than for restriction of the civil, political, and democratic rights that prevail in ordinary times (Rosenfeld 2010a: 271–2), whereas in other cases it may justify the opposite. Indeed, if the persistent fear and unease caused by real and imagined threats posed by global terrorists lead to extensive discrimination against a particular minority, such as Muslims, and to legislation awarding sweeping security powers to government that allow for vast restrictions on the exercise of civil liberties, as exemplified by US enactment of the Patriot Act[76] shortly after 9/11, then reinforcement of constitutional liberty, equality, and democracy rights may well serve the polity better than any other alternative (Rosenfeld 2010a: 266–8). In contrast, in a prolonged, stressful, health-related situation, such as that produced by the COVID-19 pandemic, certain restrictions of the rights to assemble and to travel may be fully justified in order to reduce deaths, to avoid overwhelming available hospital facilities, and to avoid saddling medical personnel with unbearable working conditions (Lang 2021). With this in mind, I now briefly consider the conditions of stress and their impact

---

[75] *A(FC) et al.* v. *Secretary of State for the Home Department* [2004] UKHL56 (House of Lords) at para. 96 (Lord Hoffman, concurring).
[76] Beydoun 2016: 115–16.

94   LOCAL VERSUS GLOBAL

on the justice essentials respectively deriving from global terrorism and from the COVID-19 pandemic.

(b) The stress of global terrorism

The initial impact of the attacks on 9/11, 2001, which in rapid succession led to the destruction of the World Trade Center in New York, deadly damage to the Pentagon in Washington DC, and the crash of a plane I Pennsylvania that was meant to hit the White House or the Capitol, was as devastating as it was unexpected. It was easy to imagine on the day of the attacks and a few days thereafter that similar attacks against US civilians and essential governmental facilities might well trigger a state of emergency. After a few weeks without further attacks, however, the national mood became much more one of stress rather than of crisis. The daily routine of New Yorkers was slowly restored, except for those affected by a personal loss, but a sense of unease persisted. This was due, in part, to fear and vulnerability regarding possible future attacks and, in part, to difficulty in making any sense of why a group of Middle Eastern religious fundamentalists would engage in a suicide mission killing thousands of victims living an ocean away for no palpable political reason. Thus, New Yorkers returned to their pre-9/11 habits and regularly used public transportation, but displayed various degrees of anxiety about unexpected bombings or chemical attacks underground as had happened in the Tokyo subway a few years earlier,[77] or even about the detonation of a radioactive "dirty" bomb in one of the densest parts of town.[78] Moreover, the stress associated with these persistent fears were nurtured by periodical police warnings of increased danger of terrorist threats.[79] On the other hand, the seeming impossibility of ascribing any meaning to the 9/11 attacks was shared by political figures, such as US President George W. Bush (Simko 2015), as well by philosophers such as Jacques Derrida (Borradori 2003: 86–137). Indeed, whereas nationalist terrorism, such as that of ETA in Spain or of the IRA in Northern Ireland, is politically comprehensible—no matter how morally reprehensible—global terrorism is in all appearance not. In a nationalist context, the goal is regional self-government or secession, and the use of terrorist means an option in a struggle marked by a stark asymmetry of forces.

---

[77] Sewell Chan, "Easing anxiety on mass transit," *NY Times*, July 17, 2005, <https://www.nytimes.com/2005/07/17/weekinreview/easing-anxiety-on-mass-transit.html?searchResultPosition=4>, visited April 3, 2022.

[78] In 2002 Jose Padilla was arrested at the airport in Chicago on suspicion that he was plotting to detonate a "dirty" bomb. Abby Goodnough, "Jose Padilla convicted on all counts in terror trial," *NY Times*, August 16, 2007, <https://www.nytimes.com/2007/08/16/us/16cnd-padilla.html>, visited April 3, 2022.

[79] See, e.g., David E. Rosenbaum & David Johnson, "A nation challenged: the alert; Ashcroft warns of terror attacks soon against U.S.," *NY Times*, October 30, 2001, <https://www.nytimes.com/2001/10/30/us/a-nation-challenged-the-alert-ashcroft-warns-of-terror-attacks-soon-against-us.html?searchResultPosition=6>, visited April 3, 2022.

Global terror, in contrast, looms as at once nihilist and prompted by a misguided aim at apolitical transcendence. The 9/11 attacks could in no way give the terrorists a foothold in the United States and their suicide emerges as incomprehensible except within what strikes most people as an abhorrent metaphysical perspective.

Global terrorism's profoundly disorienting and seemingly meaningless intrusion from afar appropriates the quotidian tools of those it attacks—such as the passenger planes used on 9/11 or the delivery truck that killed eighty-six and injured more than 400 individuals in Nice on Bastille Day 2016[80]—and turns them against its victims. These attacks are sporadic, but they embed the most heinous foreign "other" within and prompt a constant reminder that the routine trappings of the polity's everyday life can suddenly and without any warning be transformed into opportune weapons of death and destruction. As evinced by enactment of the Patriot Act (2016: 115–16), the launch of Bush's "war of terror," and the US invasions of Afghanistan and Iraq in the aftermath of 9/11, US presidential power, police presence, and government surveillance were greatly enhanced in the pursuit of security at the expense of liberty and equality. In Derrida's analysis, the reaction to the global terrorist's violence deprived of all meaning, which lead to the war *on* terror, drove the United States towards an "autoimmune" condition whereby democratic rule turned against itself in the name of its own self-preservation (Borradori 2003: 20–1).

From the standpoint of liberal constitutionalism and of the justice essentials, the state of stress foisted by global terrorism is haunted by a ceaseless and persistent specter of disproportion (Garapon & Rosenfeld 2016). Whereas emergencies may call for drastic measures, these can usually be assessed pursuant to a manageable criterion of proportionality. Thus, for example, what sacrifices in civil liberties, and for how long, might be necessary or prudent in the face of a foreign invasion or a devastating earthquake seem readily susceptible of evaluation under a proportionality standard. In contrast, as the global terrorist threat is open-ended, potentially endless, sporadic, and its possible locations and instrumentalities as varied as unpredictable, it is nearly impossible to tailor a proportionate response to it. The United States overreacted to 9/11, as made manifest in several judicial decisions issued beginning three years after the 9/11 attack itself.[81] But, more generally, what should the security goal be and how much freedom and equality ought to be sacrificed to attain it? Zero attacks and no deaths at a drastic cost to liberty and massive discrimination against a particular minority, such as the 6 million Muslims peacefully living in the United States, because the bulk of the global terrorist attacks in that country were carried out by foreign Muslims, domestic Muslims, or converts

---

[80] Alissa J. Rubin & Aurelien Breeden, "France remembers the Nice attack: 'We will never find the words,'" *NY Times*, July 14, 2017, <https://www.nytimes.com/2017/07/14/world/europe/nice-attack-france-bastille-day.html>, visited April 3, 2022.

[81] See, e.g., *Hamdi v. Rumsfeld*, 542 US 507 (2004); *Rasul v. Bush*, 542 US 466 (2004).

96   LOCAL VERSUS GLOBAL

to Islam? Or should freedom and equality be left alone as global terrorism, even if it killed a few thousand people per year, would not create any existential threat to the United States or the United Kingdom a comparable to those posed in the past by Nazi Germany or the Soviet Union? Finally, precisely because the stress due to global terrorism tends to lead to an overemphasis on security and to an intensification of prejudice against certain minorities, should not freedom and equality rights be reinforced rather than constrained while struggling against global terror?

There is no proportionate handling of global terrorism because no concession, accommodation, or compromise is possible. From within his own transcendent religious fundamentalist perspective, the global terrorist regards the Western polity he targets as representing absolute evil and his own suicide bombing as an absolutely justified moral and religious imperative completely cut off from any political calculations. Notably, the seemingly inevitable overreaction to such terrorism does adversely impact distributive justice in all three of its constitutionally relevant dimensions. On the level of material redistribution, the costs of the war on terror are extensive, to the tune of around $5.4 trillion (Zakaria 2020: 9), in terms both of increased security at home—one need only refer to the massive increased security apparatus set up at airports after 9/11—and of expanded military and policing endeavors at home and abroad. On the identitarian recognition front, on the other hand, there are multiple destabilizing threats. The most obvious one relates to surges in hostility and discrimination against certain minorities. In addition, one's identity and relations to others are prone to becoming destabilized by increased surveillance, body frisking, and other such affronts to individual dignity, and the effects of the autoimmune pathologies referred to earlier on the people's political and constitutional identity. Finally, the disproportionate shift of power to the chief executive, such as the virtually unlimited delegation of surveillance and war-making powers ceded by the Patriot Act to President Bush after 9/11, dilutes the requisite representational accountability to the citizenry.

The 9/11 attacks symbolize an assault from afar by a terrifying and incomprehensible other, lingering in disguise in the land of its victims and striking from within. Later attacks, like those in London in July 2015, Paris in November 2015, or San Bernardino in California at a December 2015 Christmas party, in contrast, were perpetrated by citizens of the country attacked. As such, these latter attacks were perpetrated by the victims' neighbors who had grown up within the same political and cultural milieu, but who had become radicalized, turning their Muslim roots into the brand of Islamist fundamentalism propagated by the likes of Al Qaeda and ISIS Even perhaps a more striking blurring of the boundaries between internal and external as well as between self and other has arisen in cases in which fully secularized individuals who grew up in households steeped in Christian tradition became converts to the extreme version of Islam espoused by suicide bombers.[82] In short,

---

[82] Two prominent examples of this are John Walker Lindh and Adam Gadahn (Pearlman). Both men were raised in the United States, with Lindh being baptized Catholic, and Gadhan raised in a religious

in the increasingly globalized and interconnected contemporary sphere of inter-action, the most heinous and threatening ideologies from afar can sneak into our midst and attack us at any moment while at the same time some among our most familiar neighbors can tear away under our eyes, reject everything that seems to hold our polity together, and embrace our farthest foreign enemies to sow fear and destruction at our doorstep.

Whether confronted by radical incomprehensible violence from afar or by vio-lent absolute rejection from within, the justice essentials of the constitutional polity are threatened in all its universal, singular, and plural dimensions. The stress fueled by the global terror threat provokes tension within the national political unit as a whole as well as in the space between the latter and the larger transnational stage to which it is linked by economics, law, and politics. The autoimmune condition afflicting the national constitutional unit upsets the pre-existing equilibrium while obscuring any reliable sense of proportion. This affliction perturbing the consti-tutional unit in its universal dimension also directly impacts every citizen in her singular capacity. Individual fear, unease, and uncertainty make a person's life as a private actor and as a citizen stressful, and this all the more so given the random and sporadic occurrence of actual attacks and the impossibility to envisage any foreseeable endpoint to terrorist activity. Finally, and most obviously, the stressful unease provoked by global terror readily increases or exacerbates discrimination and exclusions of certain groups within the polity, as has been the case with respect to Muslims in many of the Western countries where global terrorist attacks have occurred.

On further analysis, global terrorist suicidal attacks are not strictly speaking devoid of any meaning. Unlike for Derrida, for whom these attacks communi-cate no meaning, for Habermas they are instances of "distorted communication" (Borradori 2003: 19–20). Globalization has magnified dislocations and wealth dis-parities to the advantage of Western powers at the expense of certain non-Western parts of the world. Consistent with Habermas's analysis, global terrorists manifest their anger and frustration without achieving any improvement in their situation. However, if all parties engaged in genuine dialogue, both antagonists in the war on

---

Protestant household (Frank Lindh, "America's 'Detainee 001'—the persecution of John Walker Lindh," *The Guardian*, July 10, 2011, <https://www.theguardian.com/world/2011/jul/10/john-walker-lindh-american-taliban-father>, visited April 3, 2022; Raffi Khatchadourian, "Azzam the American," *The New Yorker*, January 14, 2007, <https://www.newyorker.com/magazine/2007/01/22/azzam-the-ameri can>, visited April 3, 2022). Lindh was released from federal prison in 2019, after serving seventeen years for several terrorism-related charges (Carol Rosenberg, "John Walker Lindh, known as the 'American Taliban,' is set to leave federal prison this week," *NY Times*, May 21, 2019, <https://www.nyti mes.com/2019/05/21/us/politics/american-taliban-john-walker-lindh.html>, visited April 3, 2022). Gadhan, who was considered the "leading American voice" in Al Qaeda, was killed in a drone strike in 2015 (Eric Schimtt, "Adam Gadhan was propagandist for Al Qaeda who sold terror in English," *NY Times*, April 23, 2015, <https://www.nytimes.com/2015/04/24/world/middleeast/adam-gadahn-propa gandist-for-al-qaeda-who-sold-terror-in-english.html>, visited April 3, 2022.

terror could benefit in the long run by more equitably channeling globalization toward greater economic parity among all parties affected by it.

Habermas is right that global terrorist acts are not meaningless, but unpersuasive in his suggestion that a fair and genuine economic dialogue may open a path toward reconciliation. This is because the global terrorist's resentment is not only economic but also identitarian. The global terrorist message to the Western powers is something along the lines as follows. "You have exploited us economically and sought to destroy our culture and way of life. We cannot stop you, but can disrupt you in ways that are economically costly and socially and politically painful. And because we are prepared to die, you can neither effectively fight us nor browbeat us in negotiations." Accordingly, the problem is not that the suicide bomber's nihilistic act is meaningless but that its consequences and effective proportionate responses to it remain intractable. In other words, the dangers of global terrorism sustain conditions of stress, and the constant danger of under- or over-reacting magnify these conditions and persistently threaten adherence to the justice essentials.

(c) Stress and the COVID-19 pandemic

Unlike global terrorism which pits humans against one another, the COVID-19 pandemic is a destructive natural phenomenon that inflicts death, disease, incapacity, and destruction much in the way that natural disasters such as earthquakes or hurricanes do. In places, such as Bergamo, Italy, or New York City in the spring of 2020, where hospitals were overwhelmed and the victims so numerous that their bodies could not be buried in a timely fashion, the pandemic had all the trappings of an emergency.[83] But as the pandemic spread throughout 2020 and into 2021, with some surges and a few peaks and valleys, this settled into conditions of stress. This stress was fueled by a combination of disruptions, exacerbations, retreats, and inabilities to maintain workable standards of proportionality.

The disruptions were manifold. They included lockdowns, restrictions on travel, high unemployment, and the most acute economic downturn since the Great Depression of the 1930s (Zakaria 2020: 10). Moreover, these disruptions led to a combination of an enduring sense of isolation, fear, and purposelessness in large segments of society (*Id.*). Exacerbations due to the pandemic were particularly dramatic as they pertained to the great disparities in wealth within and among countries, deficiencies in public health regimes, and widening inequities between

---

[83] See, e.g., Jason Horowitz & Emma Bubola, "Italy's coronavirus victims face death alone, with funerals postponed," *NY Times*, May 19, 2020, <https://www.nytimes.com/2020/03/16/world/europe/italy-coronavirus-funerals.html>, visited April 3, 2022; Alan Feuer & William K. Rashbaum, "'We ran out of space': bodies pile up as N.Y. struggles to bury its dead," *NY Times*, May 20, 2020, <https://www.nytimes.com/2020/04/30/nyregion/coronavirus-nyc-funeral-home-morgue-bodies.html>, visited April 3, 2022.

majority groups and racial and ethnic minorities. Wealth disparities were greatly magnified during the pandemic as white-collar workers could adapt to working remotely whereas their blue-collar counterparts were either laid off or forced to work in close quarters that made them much more susceptible to infection with the virus (*Id.*: 161). In addition, poor countries lacked the means to mitigate the burdens imposed by the pandemic that their wealthier counterparts had available. This was strikingly highlighted during the launch of the COVID-19 vaccines in 2021 when almost all the supply of the most effectives ones were secured by the wealthiest among the world's nations (Dyer 2020). Ironically, this tendency to hoard vaccines for rich countries may prove self-defeating. Indeed, failure to eradicate the pandemic worldwide may well result in greater economic losses for the most advanced economies as globalization is poised to prevent disentanglement between leading economies and the rest.[84]

There are many reasons why the United States, with about 4 per cent of the world's population, recorded about 20 per cent of COVID-19 fatalities by the end of 2020. One of the glaring contributors to the US's dismal handling of the pandemic is its subpar public health system, which suffers from lack of unity and of sufficient resources while harboring wide regional discrepancies (Lal et al. 2021). In this respect, the US's experience has been in stark contrast with Canada's universal health care system. Moreover, the US's health care deficiencies have also exacerbated racial and ethnic inequities. Thus, African-Americans and persons of Hispanic origin have had a much higher rate of disease and of death due to COVID-19.[85] Also, because of Trump's incessant reference to COVID-19 as the "China virus" in attempts to deflect attention from his policy inadequacies, the pandemic occasioned increased discrimination against Asian-Americans.[86]

The retreats related to the pandemic are numerous and they range from curtailment of medical services for emergencies unrelated to COVID-19 to the closing of borders between countries and even among regions within the same country.[87] Thus, because of the overwhelming of hospital emergency and intensive care units during upsurges of the pandemic, there were decreases in treatment for other

---

[84] *See* Peter S. Goodman, "If poor countries go unvaccinated, a study says, rich ones will pay," *NY Times*, January 25, 2021, <https://www.nytimes.com/2021/01/23/business/coronavirus-vaccines-global-economy.html>, visited April 3, 2022.

[85] Richard A. Oppel Jr., Robert Gebeloff et al., "The fullest look yet at the racial inequality of coronavirus," *NY Times*, July 5, 2020, <https://www.nytimes.com/interactive/2020/07/05/us/coronavirus-latinos-african-americans-cdc-data.html>, visited April 3, 2022.

[86] Sam Cabral, "Covid 'hate crimes' against Asian Americans on rise," *BBC News*, March 1, 2021, <https://www.bbc.com/news/world-us-canada-56218684>, visited April 3, 2022.

[87] See, e.g., Reed Abelson, "Hospitals struggle to restart lucrative elective care after coronavirus shutdowns," *NY Times*, updated May 21, 2020, <https://www.nytimes.com/2020/05/09/health/hospitals-coronavirus-reopening.html?searchResultPosition=2>, visited April 3, 2022; Ian Millhiser, "Governors are starting to tighten their borders. The implications are staggering," *Vox*, March 28, 2020, <https://www.vox.com/2020/3/28/21196934/greg-abbott-texas-closed-borders-travel-ban-constitution-trump>, visited April 3, 2022.

serious and life-threatening conditions (Birkmeyer et al. 2020). On the other hand, as already noted, countries with open borders, such as E.U. member states within the Schengen zone, closed them in an effort to stem the spread of the virus (Zakaria 2020: 238–9). Along with efforts to nationalize the production and distribution of COVID-19 vaccines, this seemed to signal a pulling back from globalization. However, as the pandemic persisted and as various strains of the virus kept migrating transnationally, it became apparent that the pandemic resulted in adjustments to the deployment of globalization rather than in any significant reversal or change of course (*Id.*: 167–86).

Except for the increases in fear, isolation, and sense of purposelessness, the consequences of the pandemic can be for the most part subsumed within the categories of material redistribution and identitarian recognition phenomena discussed up to this point. In some cases, the pandemic accentuated existing deficiencies or inequities; in others, it greatly increased existing disparities or created additional ones of its own. For example, given the high number of people severely ill with the virus, and given its highly contagious nature, many people with other life-threatening health conditions, such as cancer or heart disease, went untreated or undertreated as hospitals were overwhelmed with COVID-19 patients (Birkmeyer et al. 2020).

The situation is quite different, however, with respect to the last of the pandemic consequences listed earlier, namely the erosions in the workings of the standard of proportionality. Indeed, when measured in terms of the multiplication of disproportionate responses that it gives rise to, the reactions to the pandemic share much in common with the reactions to global terrorism. Although there are notable differences between these two reactions, they both similarly contribute to the fostering of conditions of stress. Moreover, reactions to the pandemic contribute to conditions of stress through regression in the handling of the standard of proportionality in two different ways. First, much like the war on terror has resulted in nation-states having trouble finding an equilibrium between freedom and security, the fight against the virus results in difficulty finding the proper balance between restraining and vanquishing the disease and safeguarding the dignity and economic well-being of the citizenry. And second, the pandemic has magnified the political and societal rift, launched by certain brands of populism and certain religious or quasi-religious perspectives, which pits science and the rule of experts against the "common" person and the latter's charismatic political or religious leaders.

The first of these challenges to achieving a workable measure of proportionality is illustrated by the disparate national reactions to the pandemic and by the varying results achieved by different countries. Although it was by no means transparent in its handling of the virus, China eventually achieved dramatic results in containing the pandemic, but did so through authoritarian and repressive means while at the same time further consolidating its overall authoritarian trajectory (Zakaria 2020: 32–3). Populist democracies, such as the United States under Trump and

Brazil under Bolsonaro, had dismal responses and much higher percentages of casualties than other democracies such as Canada, Germany, South Korea, and Australia (*Id*: 35). More generally, regardless of the particular political regime in place, finding a proper balance between lockdowns to limit the spread of the virus, on the one hand, while curtailing certain economic activities and restricting individual liberties on the other, proved quite elusive.

The second challenge to implementing proportional responses to the pandemic arises in the context of the culture wars that are highlighted and intensified within the confines of populist rule. This challenge builds on the typical populist tendency to pit the ordinary person against the experts but, in the case of fighting the pandemic, with more dire consequences than in most other settings. The resulting imbalances from this kind of tendency are perhaps best illustrated by the struggle within the United States between Trump and his followers against the scientists and public health experts. This struggle led to the politicization of the wearing of masks and of other mitigating policies and practices—including, most importantly, resistance to effective vaccines based on social media disinformation and misinformation[88]—thus contributing to the country's dismal failure in its handling of the virus leading it to the highest mortality rate among all industrialized countries.[89] Trump's followers' rejection of science and their defiant resistance against the wearing of masks or becoming vaccinated were not only highly political but also imbued with a quasi-religious fervor. Moreover, beyond all politics, some religious groups, like some ultra-orthodox Hasidic communities, both in Israel and the United States, defied the law and congregated in large numbers, frequently without wearing masks.[90] Was this defiance predicated on the belief in special divine protection? Or was it based on the belief that congregating for religious purposes commanded priority over protection against the virus? In any event, once quasi-religious or religious objections lead to resistance to the best that science has to offer, and because defiant behavior is likely to afflict many outside the resisting group as well as many inside, it becomes apparent that there is a lack of a common basis upon which proportionate polity-wide responses to the pandemic could be grounded.

In the end, what the different conditions of stress sustained respectively by the war on terror and responses to the COVID-19 pandemic share in common is their propensity to block the plausible paths to proportionate solutions to these major challenges that confront contemporary societies. Both reactions to global

---

[88] See Anagha Srikanth, "12 prominent people opposed to vaccines are responsible for two thirds of anti-vaccine content on line," *The Hill*, March 24, 2021.

[89] Jonathan Rothwell & Christos Makridis, "Politics is wrecking America's pandemic response," *Brookings Institution*, September 17, 2020, <https://www.brookings.edu/blog/up-front/2020/09/17/politics-is-wrecking-americas-pandemic-response>, visited April 3, 2022.

[90] David E. Rosenberg, "The government can't save ultra-orthodox Jews from COVID-19. Religious leaders can," *Foreign Affairs*, October 12, 2020, <https://foreignpolicy.com/2020/10/12/the-government-cant-save-ultra-orthodox-jews-from-covid-19-religious-leaders-can>, visited April 3, 2022.

terrorism and to COVID-19 have exacerbated the kind of tribal politics referred to in Chapter 1. As all distributive justice determinations depend on maintaining a workable handle on proportional reasoning and action, the two kinds of conditions of stress examined earlier thus pose vexing challenges to the articulation and deployment of the justice essentials. It is important to explore how these latter challenges figure in relation to the other challenges addressed throughout the preceding discussion. Further consideration of this subject will be deferred until Part III, however, as it is first necessary to shed further light on key theoretical issues raised by the quest for balance in relation to the interplay between the universal, the singular, and the plural.

PART II

REVISITING AND RECONFIGURING THE PHILOSOPHICAL GROUNDING OF LIBERAL CONSTITUTIONALISM'S IDEAL OF JUSTICE

Part II of the book provides a rereading and a refocusing of the extant theoretical heritage that has figured prominently as a source of legitimation and vindication of liberal constitutionalism. Although the philosophical heritage in question deals with key aspects of the dynamic between demos and ethnos and centers on the nexus between the universal, the singular, and the plural, the rereading I propose is specifically grounded in the perspective framed by the interplay between the ideal of liberal constitutionalism and the justice essentials it calls for. The wide gap that separates abstract law launched from above from concrete mainly affective commitment to law-like behavior that springs from below is approached through the encounter between Kelsen and Freud. Next, the implications for justice of attempted absorption of law into politics or economics are explored through a rereading of Schmitt, CLS, Marx and Posner. The attractions of the Kantian tradition of separating justice from the good suggests achieving constitutional justice by anchoring it in the universal as exemplified by contemporary thinkers such as Rawls, Habermas and Dworkin. Finally, alternatives to the ultimately wanting departure from the universal, by greater focus on the singular and on spectacle and administration as a means to divert from the tensions between the universal, the singular, and the plural are suggested through juxtaposition of Derrida and Agamben.

3
Confronting the Gulf between Law and Solidarity

Kelsen Encounters Freud

I Introduction

As detailed in Part I, the ideal of liberal constitutionalism and its justice essentials requires some blending of *ethnos* and *demos* and proportionate mutual integration of the universal, the singular, and the plural. Achievement of both the required blending and integration depend on the law of the constitution and on law pursuant to the constitution. The *ethnos* provides the basis for the solidarity that glues a community together, but is insufficient for purposes of assuring the unity and functioning of contemporary constitutional units that are typically multi-ethnic, multicultural, religiously and ideologically diverse, and individually pluralistic. On the other hand, the *demos* is grounded on principles and processes but is also insufficient in that there can be no workable democratic unit without a nucleus of common identifications, problems, concerns, mutual recognition, and divisions along alternative political perspectives. Furthermore, the key dynamic between the universal, the singular, and the plural that circumscribes the search for a just and proportionate accommodation of the varied relevant confrontations between the self and the other, be they individual or collective, internal or external, has thus far been considered in purely relational terms. The constitutional unit has been posited as the relevant universal, the individual citizen in her public and private capacity as the expression of the singular, and plausibly politically relevant groups as the subjects of the plural. The latter relational approach, however, leaves several important questions unanswered. Is there a workable conception of the universal that is both relevant to constitutionalism and persuasively equally applicable to all human beings? And, if not, is designating what holds together the community of communities of the relevant constitutional unit as the universal ultimately unsatisfactory as it is susceptible to significant instability and to inevitable waves of momentous changes? Does the singularity of the individual create an insurmountable barrier between every self and every other? Or is every individual singular in ways that share much in common with the attributes of singularity of other individuals, thus making all of them sufficiently comparable to facilitate proportionate reconciliation of the singular with the universal and the plural? Also, whereas it is clear

A Pluralist Theory of Constitutional Justice. Michel Rosenfeld, Oxford University Press. © Michel Rosenfeld 2022.
DOI: 10.1093/oso/9780198862680.003.0004

that not all groupings ought to count as a collective unit with constitutional significance, is it possible to determine systematically which groups should be included in the quest for the justice essentials? Finally, as groups stand halfway between the individual and the community of the whole, is it possible to articulate a conceptually persuasive criterion for purposes of distinguishing between when a group should stand on its own as opposed to being dissolved into a voluntary association of its individual members or incorporated into the collectivity of the constitutional unit as a whole?

To provide cogent and systematic answers to these questions it is necessary to place liberal constitutionalism and its justice essentials in broader theoretical perspective. In Chapter 1, I provided an impressionistic account of a counterfactual ideal based on the constitution as law and law pursuant to the constitution that could lead to a legal regime that may be justified as both self-given and universalizable within the confines of the relevant polity. However, even for those generous enough to accord that ideal every benefit of the doubt, as I have discussed, there remain serious unsolved threats. These are posed by the contemporary alienation and disembodiment of law, by religion-based clamoring for exemptions from certain laws or for enactment of metaphysically called for laws strenuously objected to by those who do not share the religious convictions of the law's proponents, by the threatened breakdown of politics when partisans turn from adversaries to enemies, and by powerful legal actors who can either escape domestic legal regulation or create a private law regime of their own choosing. Moreover, as laid out in Chapter 2, the great disparities of wealth linked to the globalized economy and the pervasive conditions of stress brought about by phenomena such as the spread of global terrorism or of a deadly global pandemic pose difficult challenges to maintenance of a proportionate constitutional order.

For the constitution as law and for law pursuant to the constitution to qualify in a conceptually coherent and persuasive way as both self-given and universalizable involves meeting at once a recognition-based identitarian requirement and a process-based systemic one subject to rational justification open to all concerned. From a purely logical standpoint, there could conceivably be a complete overlap between identitarian solidarity and system-wide rational accord. In actuality, however, contemporary legal systems can only muster partial and uneven identitarian solidarity coupled with limited and to varying degrees unsatisfactory systemic rationality. In order to explore these challenges and to assess whether they can be overcome, mitigated, or circumvented, this chapter concentrates on the encounter between Kelsen, the legal theorist who elaborated the most comprehensive account of the normative systematicity of law *qua* law, and Freud, who shed light on the depths of the recognition and identitarian struggles and journeys of both individuals and groups. Kelsen mastered the systemic rationality of law as a self-contained normative realm. For all the systematicity and coherence he had discovered in law, however, Kelsen could not account, within the ambit of his pure theory of law, for why those subjected to it would voluntarily accept and internalize its precepts. In other words, Kelsen had brought to light the systematicity of law from above, but happened to turn to Freud for clues on how law might find concrete affective anchoring emanating from below.

After examining the interface between Kelsen and Freud in this chapter, the remaining chapters in Part II will focus on theories that broaden and deepen our understanding of how law placed in the broader normative context inhabited by morals, ethics, politics, and economics may be susceptible of proportionately mediating between the universal, the singular, and the plural so as to advance the quest for the justice essentials. As will become manifest, none of theories broached in the last three chapters of Part II provide a fully satisfactory backing of, or justification for, the justice essentials. Nevertheless, taken together these theories point to key caveats and provide salient insights that may be usefully incorporated into building blocks of an alternative theory, namely that of comprehensive pluralism, that I will argue in Part III provides the best available theoretical grounding for the justice essentials.

II Kelsen's Kantian Pure Theory of Law and the Minimum of Universal Justice According to Law

The juxtaposition between Kelsen and Freud which, as we will see later in this chapter, Kelsen himself sought after having met Freud is of particular interest for present purposes because it squarely brings to the fore the confrontation between *ethnos* and *demos*, and how that confrontation circumscribes the field of possible interaction among the universal, the singular, and the plural. Kelsen's systematic theory of law emphasizing form and process aligns, albeit perhaps only at the margins, with *demos* whereas Freud's concentration on the relationship between individual- and group-based affective links of identification and differentiation grounded in manifestations of emotional attachment, fear, guilt, remorse, solidarity, repulsion, and hypnotic fixation looms as highly congruent with *ethnos*. Kelsen sought to account exhaustively for what law is, but remained puzzled regarding why those meant to obey it might adhere to it or embrace it as their own. Consequently, Kelsen looked into Freud's theory of group psychology to inquire whether it could be of help in resolving his quandary. Notably, as will be explained shortly, Kelsen's inquiry into Freud led him to the conclusion that law *qua* law stood even more apart from the realm of emotions than originally indicated. Nevertheless, for our purposes, as we shall see, the conjunction of Kelsen and Freud does open the door to possible confluences between the systemic and the affective connotations of law.

The logic of Kelsen's theory of law bears a strong affinity to that of Kant's moral theory based on the categorical imperative (Kant 1969: 53–4). As will be further discussed in Chapter 5, based on the premise that all individuals are free, equal, and autonomous, Kant conceives of morality as deriving from the categorical imperative which requires that each person treat every other person as an end in him/herself and not as means. The categorical imperative makes Kantian morals universal, all encompassing, and completely self-contained. Kantian morals apply to all humans at all times and systematically delimit what constitutes moral conduct as against all else. Analogously, Kelsen's pure theory of law "only describes the law and attempts to eliminate from [its] object everything that is not strictly law" (Kelsen 1967: 1). For Kelsen, law is a distinct normative order that governs intersubjective relations between humans and that is logically and systemically entirely separable from other normative orders, such as those carved out by morals or religion (*Id.*: 62–3). In Kelsen's positivistic legal theory, law institutes a coercive normative system that prohibits and permits certain human behavior and that imposes sanctions for violations of legal obligations. Moreover, what distinguishes law from other coercive intersubjective relationships, such as those prevalent in a neighborhood overtaken by a gang of robbers (*Id.*: 44), is its formal institutional structure. For a system of coercive ordering to amount to law, there must be a combination of a basic norm (*Grundnorm*) (*Id.*: 8) that determines who and how individual laws can be made, applied, and interpreted in cases of conflicts regarding what the law commands, forbids, or authorizes. The basic norm which corresponds to the constitution (Kelsen 1945: 115) sets at a minimum *who* (e.g., the parliament) and *how* (e.g., by majoritarian process) can enact valid laws, *who* (e.g., the executive branch and the administrative bureaucracy) can execute and enforce the law, and *who* (e.g., judges) can interpret and apply the law in individual cases. In short, the constitution as the basic norm figures as the top of an integrated pyramid and whichever norms and norm-related actions can be fitted within the confines of the said pyramid qualify as law while those that cannot be so fitted are categorically excluded from the normative realm of law as systematically distinct to those of morals, politics, or religion. Thus, it may be that a parliamentary law against murder corresponds in content to the biblical prohibition enshrined in the Ten Commandments; and it may even be that the parliamentarians enact the law in question because of their religious faith in the Bible; nonetheless, it is exclusively because of the parliamentarian enactment that the ensuing normative prohibition counts as a law and is inscribed within the coercive order circumscribed by the legal system.

As a self-contained distinct normative system, law as conceived by Kelsen can be portrayed as delimiting its own "language game," to borrow Wittgenstein's celebrated expression (Wittgenstein 1968: 5). Thus, for example, certain identical arguments may can be made within the language game of law and within that of philosophy or of religion, but that does not blur the boundaries between these different fields. A particular religion may prescribe that life starts at conception and that all abortions are tantamount to murder, and that view may be turned into a legal argument in a case where a court must decide whether an unwritten abortion right ought to be read into a constitutional privacy or equality between the sexes right. The argument in question would not be within the confines of the language game of law, however, in a jurisdiction that explicitly protects a woman's right to have an abortion within its constitution. Similarly, there are philosophical arguments in favor of affirmative action benefiting racial minorities or women on distributive or compensatory justice grounds (Rosenfeld 1991: Ch. 10). These same arguments may be put forth before a judge who must decide whether a constitutional provision banning discrimination based on race and sex permits or forbids preferential treatment in the context of past discrimination. In contrast, the same arguments would be superfluous in a constitutional setting such as Canada's in which the constitution explicitly permits affirmative action,[1] and completely out of place in a constitutional setting that explicitly outlaws affirmative action.[2]

Kelsen rejects any systemic conflation of the realms of law and morals, and hence opposes all natural law theories, on the grounds that modern societies do not agree on morals (Kelsen 1967: 66–7). If law coincided with morals and justice, then the three could be conflated. But because there are disagreements within and among societies concerning what ought to count as moral or just, law as a normative system must remain formally separated from morals and justice. Nazi and Soviet laws may have been highly immoral and unjust, but they were nonetheless laws so long as they could be understood as the product of a coherent legal system hierarchically dependent on what may be plausibly postulated as an operative basic norm. In short, in Kelsen's view whether a law is just or moral is a contingent matter depending on one's theory of justice and one's vision of morals.

Strictly speaking, consistent with Kelsen's positivism, merely having a constitution and a system of laws deriving from such a constitution does not in and of itself guarantee or advance any minimum of justice. In Kantian terms, Kelsen's categorical imperative is compressed into the conjunction of a basic norm whatever its content with conforming positive laws whatever their content. Moreover, although his methodology is Kantian, Kelsen criticizes Kant's embrace of natural law which Kelsen explains in terms of Kant's adoption of the prevalent Christian worldview of the times (Kelsen 1945: 445). From the standpoint of the current inquiry, however, even accepting Kelsen's categorical imperative for law as leaving justice completely aside, one can postulate as a hypothetical imperative consistent with Kelsen's positivism that contemporary constitutional democracies do impose a minimum of formal justice that is by no means completely insignificant in relation to the justice essentials. In other words, all contemporary liberal democracies have constitutions

---

[1] See Section 15(2) of the 1982 Canadian Constitution.

[2] See, e.g., California Proposition 209 (1996) banning affirmative action in that state. Michigan amended its constitution to impose a similar ban in 2006. The Michigan ban was upheld by the US Supreme Court in *Schuette v. Coalition to Defend Affirmative Action*, 572 US 291 (2014).

that provide for some kind of division of powers among the legislative, executive, and judicial branches of government and adherence to some plausible iteration of the rule of law.

This hypothetical imperative is silent on two of the four constitutional prerequisites associated with liberal constitutions, namely the protection of fundamental rights and some specific guaranties regarding maintenance of an appropriate level of democracy. This is because whereas all the constitutional systems within the purview of the hypothetical imperative in question prescribe some kind of division of powers, set procedures for law-making, and relatively consistent and reliable application of law, they lack consensus on which rights should be deemed fundamental or how typically standard rights, such as freedom of speech or equality, ought to be interpreted. In addition, although all the liberal constitutions associated with our hypothetical imperative comport some elements of democracy, these may widely vary from minimal and largely nominal ones to thorough and pervasive ones.

Focusing on the division between law-making and judicial interpretation and application of law, the hypothetical imperative under consideration yields something approaching the positivist *Rechtsstaat* that emerged in the aftermath of the 1848 failed revolution in Germany (Rosenfeld 2001: 1324–5). Although "*Rechtsstaat*" is usually translated as "rule of law," the positivist *Rechtsstaat* in question here is better understood as "state rule through law" (*Id.*: 1319). Although the positivist *Rechtsstaat* had no component of democracy, it did assure parliamentary law-making and the law being made public before becoming effective, thus informing all those subject to it of their rights and obligations thereunder. Also, the positivist *Rechtsstaat* entrusted the disposition of all individual cases involving legal disputes to the judicial branch of government.

These features of the positivistic *Rechtsstaat* which are also present in contemporary liberal democratic constitutions do assure a minimum of distributive justice at both the universal and the individual levels. At the universal level, laws are to be predictable and consistent. This should allow those subject to law both to know in advance of undertaking any course of action what is legally permitted and prohibited and to count on equality before and under the law. Predictability and stabilization of expectations does provide some small degree of material distributive justice which becomes palpable when compared to submission to the arbitrary will of an absolute monarch or totalitarian dictator—even if the latter operate within what Kelsen would count as a legal system in which the basic norm grants them absolute legislative prerogative and supreme judicial authority. In addition, universally implemented legal consistency does grant some modicum of recognition-based justice. On the other hand, at the individual level, entitlement to have one's case heard and decided by a judge when involved in a legal dispute does afford each individual in her singular capacity a limited slice of recognition-based justice. This is in contrast with the kind of recognition given by law's predictability and consistency which looms as much more abstract and as directly tied to the relevant legal/constitutional unit as a consistent whole. Notably, neither the universal nor the individual aspects of the justice at stake here have anything to do with the substance of law or with the democratic level of support that the latter may garner. Accordingly, the minimum of justice involved here is certainly consistent with great substantive injustice as, for example, it would not foreclose massive sex or race discrimination imposed by law. Therefore, to avoid confusion between this minimum Kelsenian positivistic notion of justice and the earlier discussed minimum of justice considered in relation to the justice essentials, I shall refer to the former as the "bare minimum of justice."

The bare minimum in question certainly seems preferable to a Hobbesian state of nature pitting all against all or even to all legal regimes bereft of predictability, consistency, or the rudiments of formal justice when it comes to individual cases. Moreover, what this Kelsenian bare minimum of justice under the operative hypothetical imperative may lack in depth, it can more than make up in breath. Indeed, on the one hand, Kelsen maintains that international law and national law can be harmonized and unified into a single system deriving from a common basic norm, which is either that of national law extending to international law or that of international law subsuming national law (Kelsen 1967: 339). Consistent with this, the plurality of legal regimes variously operating at the national, regional transnational, and worldwide international levels typically operative within our globalized environment can be integrated into a harmonized legal order with its own universally implanted language game. Also, on the other hand, Kelsen conceives not only of law as produced by the state but also of the state itself as being within the realm of law through and through and thus as being seamlessly interwoven within the same language game (*Id.*: 286–7). With the state as law and producing, enforcing, and applying law, the bare minimum of justice pervades throughout the polity in all its dealings with state and law.

Though systemically coherent, casting the state as law, as Kelsen himself acknowledges, runs counter to the traditional view (*Id.*: 284–5). Historically, the state has been personalized and ascribed an individual or a collective will transcending the law. As King Louis XIV, the French seventeenth-century absolute monarch, famously proclaimed "*l'État c'est moi.*" More recently, in modern democratic settings in which the people are deemed to be the sovereign, the state embodies their will as *mediated* through their representatives. As Kelsen notes, as traditionally conceived, the state has three component elements: its people, its territory, and its "so called power" (*Id.*: 287). Nevertheless, in Kelsen's view these three elements can only be cogently determined within the language game of law, that is their legitimacy can only be understood within the "spheres of validity of a legal order" (*Id.*). For our purposes, consistent with Kelsen's analysis, regardless of the peculiarities of those who are aggregated into a people, of the distinct nature of the territory involved, or of the nature of the powers exercised in the name of the state, the latter's *legitimate* bounds and powers can only be ascertained by reference to law. In short, to be coherent and legitimate the state must be viewed exclusively in its dimension as law throughout; for example, a polity's constitution imbues the state with legal existence and circumscribes its legal powers and limitations in terms of legally defined citizens comprised within a legally determined territory. Finally, by conflating state and law within a single unified legal normative order, one can extend the bare minimum of justice associated with Kelsenian positivism to all that pertains to state and law.

To garner universal validity, the Kelsenian state and law must be abstracted to the point of becoming independent of all substance. Similarly, the Kelsenian constitution as basic norm must be postulated above all determinate *ethnos* or *demos*—or, in the case of our added hypothetical imperative, of all but an abstract minimum of *demos*. In other words, unless the state and law are abstracted beyond *ethnos* and a barebones *demos*, controverted conceptions of the latter—which are inevitably inscribed in actual states and existing law—will be bound to negate the purity of the law *qua* law, thus undermining the bare minimum of justice. Taking the state and law to such a high level of abstraction, however, poses a vexing problem that Kelsen fully acknowledges (Kelsen 1945: 24). Indeed, although the law associated with the bare minimum of justice is in a shallow sense universalizable, it does not in any significant sense appear self-given. And it is not self-given both in relation to authorship and to congruence with one's own identity. A person may be inclined to internalize a law and to adhere to it voluntarily genuinely because she considers herself or those whom she identifies with as the authors of the law in question or because she identifies with the content of that law as being congruent with her religion, morals, or culture.

Kelsen rejects the notion that individuals obey the law only out of fear of sanctions. As he observes:

> We do not know exactly what motives induce men to comply with the rules of law … In all probability … the motives of lawful behavior are by no means the fear of legal sanctions or even the belief in the binding force of the legal rules. (*Id.*)

Kelsen grants that a person may have ample motivation to adhere to a law that coincides with that person's religious or moral convictions or that advances what that person sees as a worthy benefit (*Id.*). Such motivation would be completely insufficient to contribute to a sense of validity within the relevant legal community as a whole, however, as modern polities are religiously and morally pluralistic whereas given laws typically benefit some while burdening some others. In view of this, Kelsen concludes that there are no satisfactory explanations to account for the "psychic compulsion" to remain faithfully law abiding (*Id.*). In order to obtain further insights into the aforesaid psychic mystery, Kelsen turned to Freud, whom he had personally met in 1922 (Balibar 2011: 384). Following that meeting, Kelsen engaged in an exploration of Freud's insights into individual and group psychology and into their potential for further advancing his own theory of law and of the state (Kelsen 1924).

III Freud's Psychoanalytic Account of the Passage from Individual Singularity to Group Identity

Freud did not react in writing to Kelsen's extensive discussion of his *Group Psychology and the Analysis of the Ego*, first published in 1921, except for a short footnote added to the second edition of that work in 1923 (Freud 1959: 25, n. 4). Before tackling Kelsen's analysis of Freud and the conclusions he draws from it relating to his own theory of the state, it is useful from the standpoint of the main lines of inquiry pursued throughout this book to concentrate briefly on how Freud carves a path from the psychology of the singular individual to group psychology and to the psychological bases for adherence to law. As noted earlier, Freud proceeds to law from below. He starts from projections of the individual's *libido* to the needs to constrain and redirect the latter in the context of larger intersubjective settings. That, in turn, fosters a transition from individual to group psychology which is linked to a need to be subjected to law in large measure due to guilt. Against Kelsen's starting point based on law as a universal, Freud grounds his analysis in *homo psychologicus* who enters this world in his irreducible singularity and who is eventually driven to internalize law as he learns through frustration of his libidinal desires that he requires the mediation of others to reach any semblance of psychic equilibrium. Upon first impression, conjoining Kelsen's approach from above to Freud's search from below opens the way for fruitful combination of enlightening iterations of both the universal and the singular, and for juxtaposition of a universal that transcends all content with a singular that is pure substance. Assuming this line of inquiry could prove productive, its only apparent initial shortfall would be in regard to the plural. On closer inspection, however, as will be discussed later in this chapter, combining Kelsenian universality with Freudian singularity proves much more complex and less straightforward than one might initially think.

Before delving further into Freud's thought and into its contribution to our understanding of why people internalize their adherence to law, it is necessary to specify the approach to Freud and the aspects of his theory that will be emphasized in what follows. Indeed, in a work centered on the justice essentials of the constitution, some explanation seems required in relation to some of the elements of Freud's theory that bear on the relevant discussion, such as the Oedipus complex or the primitive horde's ritual murder of the father to replace his rule by that of his male progeny united as brothers, which are subject to criticism as being systematically sexist (Horney 1973; Pateman 1980: 20; Benjamin 1986). With this in mind, in what follows the focus shall remain on three mainstays of Freud's opus: his laying out of the psychological life of the individual in terms of the dynamic between the

114 CONFRONTING GULF BETWEEN LAW AND SOLIDARITY

id, the ego, and the superego; his reliance on the hypothesis that ontogeny recapitulates phylogeny, namely that the development of the individual replicates the historical evolution of the species (Freud 1950: 167);[3] and his theory of interpretation articulated in the context of dreams (Freud 1965) and driven by the discursive trilogy of repression, condensation, and displacement (labeled by Freud's subsequent interpreters as negation, metaphor, and metonymy) (Rosenfeld 2010: 45–65). Furthermore, based on my previous work drawing on Freud's theory of interpretation to elaborate a theory of constitutional identity (*Id.*), what follows is designed to shed some further light on the justice essentials' call for an appropriate blend between the relevant polity's constitutional *ethnos* and constitutional *demos* in the larger context of the dynamic between Freud and Kelsen.

What is essential for present purposes in the familiar tale surrounding Freud's conception of every singular individual as being held together by a dynamic that integrates an id, ego, and superego (Freud 1960) is that it provides a roadmap of the psychological journey that every single uniquely situated individual undertakes as she evolves from a completely self-enclosed unconscious being to a dependent family member and eventually to a member of a larger society. At first, the infant desires things that are not within her but does not draw any distinction between the desiring subject and the desired object (*Id.*: 19). At that stage, the universe looms as wholly within and wholly unique. As the infant's quest for attention and for objects is frustrated, however, she realizes that she is dependent on her parents for both attention and for access to desired objects. At this point, Freud introduces the Oedipus complex (*Id.*: 22). For our purposes, suffice it to extract from the Oedipal conflict, the discovery of dependence on others, jealousy, and frustration, which requires adjustment through repression of desires that are unwelcome and repelled by parental figures. This leads to sublimation of frustrated desires cast as inappropriate by redirecting them towards more permissible objects. In this context, every individual's id is a world of unconscious desires, drives, and processes that elude consciousness or that are repressed as manifestations of the pleasure principle. The latter clashes with the reality principle which is activated through the same individual's ego and which functions as a locus of common sense and reason (*Id.*: 15). Whereas the ego seeks to control the impulses of the stronger id, and Freud likens their struggle to that of a horseback rider who seeks to assure obedience by a much stronger animal *Id.*), the ego's efforts at mastery are bound to fall short or to lead to new problems, such as melancholia or narcissism (*Id.* 18–20). Because of this, Freud postulates that the ego needs to be supplemented by an "ego ideal" or "superego" which becomes embedded within the ego, and which can be mustered in handling what is generated within the id (*Id.*: 18). Drawing on the

---

[3] This hypothesis, which originated in zoology, has now been thoroughly discredited (see Gould 1977), but that does not affect for present purposes its extension by analogy to the fields of psychological or sociological development.

Oedipus complex, Freud posits the superego as a vehicle for handling the son who at once wishes to be like his father who has sexual relations with his mother while enduring his father's stern prohibition against treating his mother as a libidinal object (*Id.*: 24–5). Moving away from the specificity of the Oedipus triangle, what is essential in terms of Freud's invocation of the superego is the realization that the use of the ego's common sense and reason is insufficient to control repressed drives launched from the id. The superego's function is to juxtapose a version of the untamed drive with the latter's strong prohibition—first through a parental figure and later through religion, morals, and law—to reinforce the ego's handling of the id. Moreover, the superego is internalized but not made fully explicit to the ego. For the child, the stern gaze of the parental figure triggers a feeling of guilt for not having fully mastered a repressed drive stemming from the id that lurks in disguise within the bounds of the ego's consciousness. In short, Freud's superego is above all guilt inducing and it first reinforces the viability of family life and eventually that of the broader society which becomes indispensable for adults to manage the competing demands of the pleasure and realty principles as individualized within each of them.

As each individual's history of desires, libidinal and sublimated, family relations as well as societal encounters and challenges is unique, one may think that the singularity of *homo psychologicus* turns every individual into a hermetically closed monad. That, in turn, would seemingly preclude any meaningful linking of the singular to the universal or the plural. And if that were true, every individual may have some attachment to law through guilt, but law would have no plausible link to justice as there could be no mediation between law's generality and the impenetrable particularity of every singular individual. Freud's theory does not lead to this impasse, however, due to his postulation that ontogeny recapitulates phylogeny. Indeed, to the extent that the individual's psychological development recapitulates the history of the species, there are points in common that allow for connections between the singular, the plural, and the universal.

In Freud's account, the place of the Oedipus complex within ontogeny corresponds to that within phylogeny of the murder within the "primal horde" (Freud 1950: 175) of the father by his sons and of the replacement of fatherly rule by that of his sons in brotherly union (Freud 1960: 27). Paternal absolute power chased away and thoroughly frustrated the sons. Individually, none of the sons could muster the courage to confront his father, but acting all together they managed to do so, and ended up murdering him. After killing him, each of the brothers ate a part of the father's corpse. Moreover, this act of cannibalism was meant to have a dual symbolic purpose: first, by incorporating a part of their father, each of his sons assumed the latter's mantle of leadership; and second, because they all partook in the body of their father, none could claim superiority over his brothers, thus assuring joint equal fraternal rule (Freud 1950: 175–6). This empowering original killing, however, also led to remorse and guilt (*Id.* 177–8). Accordingly, as Freud puts it, this memorable crime became "the beginning of so many things—of social organization, of moral restrictions and of religion" (*Id.*: 176). In other words, elimination of the father not only surmounts a daunting obstacle but also gives rise to a haunting void. With the all-powerful father present, the sons' repressed desires could be held in place by fear. With the father gone, that fear disappears, and remorse and guilt set in as otherwise fraternal equality may promptly devolve into a fratricidal conflict to emerge as the father's lone replacement. Idealization of the father and eventually his deification can turn remorse and guilt into positive instruments in the quest for social peace. Guilt, as already mentioned, is associated with the superego and, as Freud sees it, social identification is cemented upon the realization that each individual possesses "the same ego ideal" or superego (Freud 1960: 27).

Metaphorically, and stripped of its particulars, Freud's account suggests three relevant considerations that are of import to the present inquiry. These relate respectively to self-government, to socialization to advance commonly shared psychological needs, and to internalizing an adequate measure of normative self-restraint—including through law—to maintain social cohesion. The passage from tyrannical parental rule to associational co-equal sibling self-rule is analogous to the transition, within the constitutional realm, of the locus of sovereignty from a divinely appointed monarch to the people as a unified whole. This latter transition has often been achieved through revolution as it was in eighteenth-century France where the old order was shattered through a regicide. Furthermore, closely associated conceptually with the assumption of sovereignty by the people is the idea of a social contract along the lines proposed by philosophers such as Locke and Rousseau. What is most salient about the social contract narrative is that it portrays the resulting allocation of societal and governmental benefits and burdens as self-given and as presumably fair as no individual contractor would have a reason to agree to contractual terms deemed unfair. Notably for our purposes, and particularly in view of Freud's account of the power struggles within the primal horde as a purely masculine matter, there have been strong feminist critiques of invocations of the social contract construct to legitimate self-government (Pateman 1980: 22–6; 1988). The thrust of this feminist critique is that the social contract idea, while neutral in the abstract, actually bolsters a fraternal accord that leaves out women and relegates them to a subservient position. In order to have the leisure to self-rule in the public sphere, men must manage to confine women to the home and the private sphere where they remain politically non-existent or subservient. Keeping this critique in mind, as the social contract construct is counterfactual in nature, it seems adaptable metaphorically to projecting inclusion of women and all other traditionally left out constituencies at the bargaining table to work out a requisite allocation that would be fair to all. Factually, no such bargain may ever be concluded, but counterfactually it nevertheless remains imaginable. Accordingly, Freud's phylogenic account of the transition from tyranny to self-rule has some metaphoric resonance in terms of the current quest to combine self-government, self-given law, and universalizable fairness extending to the people as a whole.

From the socialization standpoint, Freud's ontogenetic and phylogenetic narratives point to a psychological quest launched from within the singular individual, extending to the family, and spilling over into larger extra-familial social groupings. Within the individual, this journey is manifested in the dynamic between the id, the ego, and the superego. The ego becomes distinct within the family as specified by Lacan who, building on Freud, famously proclaimed that the child first perceives her distinct identity as a name in the discourse of her parents (Lacan 1966: 298–300). For its part, the superego bears the imprint of societally implanted normative precepts. Beyond their place of origin, the id, ego, and superego are engaged in a constant dynamic that plays out within the individual as well in the latter's familial and broader societal encounters. Importantly, from the present inquiry's perspective, the dynamic in question yields an amalgamation of *sui generis* unique singularities circulating within familial and social frameworks that generate common patterns allowing for certain comparisons. Whereas the precise interaction between id, ego, and superego within a particular individual may remain irreducible, all individuals must deal with similar patterns of parental and societal issues. From a Freudian psychoanalytical perspective, ontogenetic and phylogenetic commonalities allow for comparisons between successful adaptations and pathological disruptions, such as those manifest in cases of obsessional neurosis. From our own perspective, on the other hand, the fact that singularity may be in some respects irreducible does not preclude room for some significant measure of universality or of plurality. What remains unclear for now is whether and how a Freudian amalgam of singularity, plurality, and universality as radiated in the dynamic between the id, the ego, and the superego might shed any light on the justice essentials.

The last of the three important insights derived from Freud's account described earlier concerns the need for greater and greater self-restraint as one is prompted to move beyond the family ontogenetically and from rule by the father figure to rule by fraternal association phylogenetically. Fear of parents or of tyrannical monarchs can be maintained by the constant presence or anticipation of direct threats. When moving away from rebelling against one's parents or killing a tyrant in the course of a revolution, remorse may be out of place, but guilt is more likely to increase than to fade. Indeed, self-government requires self-sacrifices (Rousseau 1947) and the thrusts of the id or of conscious self-fulfillment may prompt urges to commit transgressions. Because one still wishes to transgress in spite of having overcome fearful dependence, this fuels and even increases a sense of guilt and prompts one to turn to outward sources to bolster self-restraint, such as religion, morals, and law. From this, it would appear that at least psychologically guilt requires greater internalization of, and adherence to, law in times of democracy and self-rule than in authoritarian settings.

In summary, in the context of any kind of constitutional democracy, to Kelsen's bare minimum of justice we can add Freud's psychological insight that strong adherence to law is promoted through guilt fueled by the superego in an ontogenetically adult and phylogenetically socially advanced setting in which fear and remorse recede in the thrust to preserve social harmony. Before broaching Kelsen's inquiry into Freud to determine whether it opens the way to something over and above the minimum provided by law *qua* law and adherence to law due to guilt, it is useful briefly to examine key aspects of Freud's views on social psychology which are at the center of Kelsen's engagement with Freud.

Remarkably, both Freud and Kelsen regard the individual as primordial and the group, to the extent that it may be anything beyond a mere aggregation of individuals, as problematic. Specifically, what draws Kelsen to Freud is the following question: "How do the separate individuals forming a state, or their individual activities, combine into a super-individual whole?" (Kelsen 1924: 1). The answer to that question, as Kelsen stresses, is supposed to reveal the actual nature of the state (*Id.*). For his part, Freud starts, as already indicated, from the psychology of the individual as encompassed in the dynamic between the id, the ego, and the superego. Moreover, what is key in Freud's understanding of group psychology is the role of *libido* (Freud 1959: 29), which is a paramount instinct that drives the individual to love, sexual desire, orientation to coveted objects, friendship, and devotion to concrete undertakings as well as to abstract ideas (*Id.*). In short, as the individual's libidinal urges cannot be self-fulfilled or adequately taken care of within the confines of the family, she must turn to larger social units to seek satisfaction. Given that libido provides the unifying thread that leads from individual to group psychology, the overriding question confronting Freud's account is whether his conception of group psychology is distinct in nature from its individual counterpart or whether it predominantly amounts to the spread of the mainstays of individual psychology over a vastly enlarged terrain.

The key link to the distinction between individual and group psychology within Freud's theory is the migration of the superego from the individual to the group (*Id.*: 78–9). Upon the onset of conflict and frustration within the family, the individual turns to the superego to mediate the tensions between the ego and the id. As neither satisfaction nor control of libidinal urges can be sufficiently realized within the family, however, the individual projects his ego ideal from the superego *within* to a collective unit that transcends the family. Whereas the family functions through interactions among the individuals who belong to it, the group is driven by the common ego ideal that binds all its members together. Phylogenetically for Freud, group psychology originates within the above-mentioned primal horde (*Id.*: 69).[4] The first groupwide event is thus the murder of the father and the passage

---

[4] When viewed in terms of both ontogeny and phylogeny, however, Freud concludes that individual psychology and group psychology were originally contemporaneous (Freud 1959: 71).

FREUD'S ACCOUNT OF GROUP IDENTITY   119

to the collective unit in which brotherly rule is assured by a common sharing and internalization of the father ideal. The father himself is gone, but through him a shared normative group ego ideal governs the common life of his sons.

After this initial thrust into group psychology, the requisite collective ego ideal is provided, according to Freud, by totemism (*Id.*). The totemic animal replaces the father and gives rise at once to a taboo within the group that sanctifies it and to group solidarity among those who share bonds of kinship. These bonds must be ritually renewed through periodic sacrifices of the totemic animal followed by consumption of its flesh at meals shared by all members of the kin group (Freud 1950: 168–9). Furthermore, totemism is, according to Freud, at the origin of all group-based ego ideals. As Freud puts it, "the development of totemism ... comprises in itself the beginnings of religion, morality and social organization" (Freud 1959: 69).

Leaving aside the specifics of primal hordes and totemism, once the ego ideal is projected onto religion, morality, and law it would appear that group psychology provides the basis for a collective bond. That bond built upon common identification (*Id.*: 50) points to solidarity through converging libidinal sublimation and to mutual self-restraint through guilt mustered in the combat against persisting irruptions originating within the id. Just as the individual within the family must rely on the superego to manage the tensions between libidinal urges and the thrust of admonitory parental authority, the individual within a group must rally around a common ego ideal instantiated in a divine figure, a commonly embraced moral code, or commonly shared working legal regime. Presumably, this leads to a combination of identification, group solidarity, and pervasive guilt spread among all group members which can be mustered to internalize, and to become emotionally invested in, rule by law. But does this have any further implications for justice beyond that symbolized by the removal of the tyrannical leader who wielded absolute power over his entire kin?

Upon further inquiry into the particulars of Freud's conception of group psychology, it becomes plain that the answer to the latter question is in the negative. In addition, Freud specifies that the migration of the ego ideal from the individual to the group involves a regression (*Id.*: 62) and that organized groups are only likely to endure over time under the leadership of an individual who stands above the rest (*Id.*: 69–70). In other words, as will be briefly detailed shortly, either a collective mindset leads to a step backwards from individual self-control or the collective unit must depend for its continued viability on an individual leader who stands alone above the rest. And because of this, in the end because every ordered group stands under the sway of a hierarchically superior and separate individual, group psychology looms ultimately as a derivate from its individual counterpart.

Freud distinguishes between what he terms "common" groups and "organized and artificial" ones (*Id.*: 62–3). The former groups are characterized by emotional group attachments out of weakness, lack of intellectual ability, and failures to restrain impulsive drives that amount to regression to "earlier stages" such as those involving "savages or children" (*Id.*: 62). In short, in this context group psychology appears to dull reason and to foster anarchic mutually encouraged excesses. If anything, this approaches pre-legal horde-like conduct. In contrast, in organized and artificial groups law, like order, seems to prevail as a consequence of submission to a leader who remains above the group. Notably, Freud refers to two highly hierarchical groups, the army and the Catholic Church, as prototypes of the latter kind of groups (*Id.*: 32–9). In the army, it is the commander-in-chief who is above all others and who garners loyalty among all those under her by projecting equal love for all her troops (*Id.*: 33–4). Freud insists that this equal love is an illusion, but one that sustains solidarity among all soldiers who feel equally valued by their leader whom they devotedly follow (*Id.*). In the case of the Church, on the other hand, the separation between the leader and the followers is even more radical as Freud alludes to Christ's equal love of all believers whom he binds together in communal solidarity as "brothers in Christ" (*Id.*: 33).

What best underscores the importance of strict hierarchy within Freud's conception of group psychology is his invocation of hypnosis to characterize the relationship of members of a group to their leader who figures as the embodiment each of his followers' ego ideal (*Id.*: 58–9). As Freud emphasizes, "the hypnotist is the sole object ... [of] attention ... The hypnotic relation is the unlimited devotion of someone in love" (*Id.*). Consistent with this, organized group functioning boils down to total individual submission to an individual leader to whom one has surrendered one's ego ideal coupled with solidarity toward all those other individuals who have done the same. Moreover, the resulting horizontal relationship among group members in this scenario is primarily twofold: a common mutual recognition of an equal incapacity successfully to manage an ego ideal individually; and an identitarian bonding due to the equal total devotion to the same gloriously personified ego ideal.

If one transposes Freud's vision of group psychology to the realm of political theory, one notices a stark resemblance to Hobbes' theory of the social contract which comprises a contract of association among free and equal individuals followed by a contract of submission entrusting government to an all-powerful Leviathan (Hobbes 1978: 189–90; Rosenfeld 1985: 849–50). For Hobbes, submission to a virtually absolute leader[5] is warranted to overcome the war of all against all in the state of nature. For Freud, hypnotic devotion to a father-like or God-like leader to whom one has entrusted one's ego ideal is called for to the extent that one cannot properly handle the tensions between the id, the ego, and the superego standing alone or within the bounds of one's family. In a Hobbesian setting, the social contract leads to rule by law, but it remains virtually indifferent to justice

---

[5] The Leviathan is not an absolute ruler because the social contractors grant him all powers but one, namely that over their lives (Hobbes 1973).

by leaving the fashioning of law entirely in the hands of the Leviathan—with the exception of prohibiting the imposition of the death penalty. Would it be the same in a Freudian setting in which the personified ego ideal incorporates rule by law?

Freud asserts that enduring groups are made up of equals under the leadership of a single superior person (FREUD 1959: 68). As society evolves from totemism and idol worship to a more abstract transcendent deity, and to submission to morals and law, it may seem that commitment to rule by law would acquire a much-expanded role within the confines of the ego ideal. Although what binds equals within groups together are identitarian bonds built upon similarly sublimated libidinal drives, these are regarded by Freud as mainly accepted passively and as largely exclusionary. As Freud sees it, with "little originality" or "personal courage," every individual "is ruled by those attitudes of the group mind ... such ... as racial characteristics, class prejudices, public opinion, etc." (*Id.*: 63). It is obvious that as an institutional group an army closely matches solidarity within with hostility, if not downright lethal designs, against enemies without. More surprisingly, Freud finds a similarly exclusionary attitude within the Catholic Church. Christ's message of love and inclusion is universal in scope and addressed to humanity as a whole. Nevertheless, Freud insists that Christianity as well as other religions couple love toward believers with "cruelty and intolerance" towards non-believers (*Id.*: 39).

Because the projected ego ideals that sustain group solidarity also prove exclusionary, Freudian rule by law seems no more apt to advancing justice than its Hobbesian counterpart. Not only does guilt-based law abidingness remain detached from justice in Freud's vision but he also conceives justice itself as being psychologically motivated by envy (*Id.*: 67). Indeed, social justice for Freud seems to boil down to wanting others to deny themselves what I am called to deny myself or conversely to make sure that others are denied the thing that I willingly may consider depriving myself of. Tellingly, Freud refers to King Solomon's notorious biblical judgment as follows: "If one woman's child is dead, the other shall not have a live one either" (*Id.*). Ironically, by focusing on the envy of the dead child's mother, Freud seemingly sets aside the true import of Solomonic justice, which is to find a way to assure the return of the surviving child to his own natural mother with whom he rightfully belongs.

Freud's group psychology may offer a plausible account for the internalization of law through the workings of collectively reinforced guilt. That, however, does not bridge the gap between the universal, the singular, and the plural, and thus fails to open any viable path from law to justice. Furthermore, on closer inspection, Freudian internalization of law through guilt seems wanting in the context of any polity that harbors a multiplicity of groups with differing ego ideals. For example, why should a believer within a minority religion internalize the law imposed by believers in the majority religion who embrace an ego ideal hostile to all religions other than their own? As will be further discussed, in spite of these limitations, some useful lessons may be drawn from Freud's group psychology for purposes of further elucidating the justice essentials within the constitutional context. But before pursuing this any further, it is now time to take a closer look at Kelsen's encounter with Freud's group psychology.

IV Kelsen's Turn to Freud to Bolster his Conception of the State as Pure Law

As mentioned earlier, what prompts Kelsen's interest in Freud's group psychology is the quandary over how a group of individuals divided over competing ideologies, interests, and pursuits could unify and cohere within a state constituted as a super-individual whole. Given this preoccupation, it is not hard to understand why Kelsen would be drawn to Freud's group psychology. Indeed, within Kelsen's theory, the nexus between the state and law is crucial (Kelsen 1924: 4) particularly because within the Westphalian context prevailing between the two world wars, the law that had legitimate normative authority over any particular individual was that of his or her own state. Indeed, German law did not bind French citizens in their dealings within their own country. And therefore, why French citizens would internalize their adherence to the law issuing from their own state and enforced by the latter looms as normatively tied to the interrelation between the French state and French law. The attraction of Freud's group psychology to shed light on the nexus between the state and law thus becomes obvious. The combination of horizonal solidarity among members of an organized group and the vertical devotion to the ego ideal embodied within that group's leader—once transposed from the primeval horde to the advanced settings in which depersonalized abstract ideals predominate—suggest a seemingly fruitful hypothesis concerning internalization and legitimation of the laws of one's own state. Just as in an advanced group setting, under Freud's theory, the membership can share commitment to the same religious or moral ideals, so too they may well embrace the associated legal norms put forth by the state.

There arises, however, one immediate objection against reliance on Freud's account of group psychology to explain the legitimacy of the contemporary state's leadership. As already noted, Freud's group solidarity and submission to leadership is exclusionary in nature and therefore in a multi-religious state, believers within one religion are prone to being hostile towards the leadership and membership of the remaining religions within the polity. Accordingly, would not a religiously, morally, culturally, and politically split citizenry be equally divided over the laws issuing from their state? Whereas the answer to this question may well be in the affirmative, it does not necessarily have to be so. Indeed, arguably in as much as modern states lack group homogeneity, the state and law must transcend diverse religious, political, and cultural groups, and superimpose a more abstract all-encompassing ego ideal embodied within the state and the law while coexisting with the somewhat more deeply ingrained and less abstract prevailing religious and cultural ego ideals. Thus, for example, at the end of the European wars of religion, states and laws—as evinced by the 1598 French Edict of Nantes[6]—institutionalized religious tolerance without thereby dislodging the competing ego ideals respectively embraced by the two previously warring religions. In short, within the phylogenic journey envisaged by Freudian group psychology it seems perfectly logical to consider it possible that the evolution from incarnation of the ego ideal within a single living individual to a transcendent deity and more abstract ideals could be followed by an era wherein an all-encompassing normative unity between law and the state would make possible peaceful coexistence among otherwise competing ego ideals.

Kelsen himself not only does not entertain this last possibility but he also ends up altogether rejecting Freud's group psychology as capable of providing a plausible solution to his quandary about the state (Kelsen 1924). In spite of this conclusion, Kelsen's engagement with Freud does lead him to a key though negative insight: psychology cannot account for the unity of the state or the normative bindingness of law (*Id.*: 33–4). Specifically, Kelsen rejects the very notion of a Freudian group psychology as he finds an internal contradiction in Freud's transition from individual psychology to its group counterpart. As I noted earlier in this chapter, Freud's account of the psychology of the group looms at best as identifying a derivate of individual psychology. Kelsen goes even further and argues that Freud's passage from individual to group ideology is based on "a conceptual error" (*Id.*: 35). In the primal horde setting, as Kelsen understands it, each individual identifies individual to individual with the feared and admired leader and with all similarly situated individual followers of the same leader. In organized groups, in general, and in states, in particular, however, cohesion is not attributable to identification as Kelsen believes that the latter requires person-to-person interaction (*Id.*: 3). Accordingly, within the ambit of the state, as Kelsen stresses, one deals with a large number of strangers, most of whom one is not even aware of, and with whom one has had no interaction (*Id.*). In sum, as Kelsen's sees it, consistent with Freud's psychoanalytic theory, in groups two kinds of individual relations—mutual individual recognition and individual submission to the leader—predominate but they cannot be combined into any separate or distinct group generated psychological phenomenon.

The useful negative lesson Kelsen draws from his encounter with Freud is that neither individual nor group psychology can account for the unity of the state or the binding nature of law. However, even without Freudian group psychology, it remains quite plausible that individuals would turn to vertical adhesion to a seemingly hierarchically predominant abstracted ego ideal such as a transcendent

---

[6] This Edict was proclaimed by King Henry IV on April 13, 1598. <https://www.britannica.com/event/Edict-of-Nantes>, visited April 3, 2022.

god or the state as personified in a monarch or some collective ruling body with a personality and will of its own. Kelsen does not reject this possibility, but he draws a further negative conclusion from it. He equates personalizing the state to introducing God as ruling over the law of nature (*Id.*: 37). But, as Kelsen insists, just as the reference to God is superfluous in the context of scientifically apprehending the laws of nature, similarly personifying the state only obscures how the state actually relates to the law. Accordingly, Kelsen's initial quandary relating to the state turns out, after his inquiry into Freud, into a false problem. In the end, "[t]he state as a code of human conduct is precisely identical with the compelling code which is understood as the law or legal code" (*Id.*: 35). In other words, it may be that one personalizes the state or follows the law out of religious or moral conviction, but that does not change the systemic unity and coherence of the state and law as a *sui generis* normative order that pervades through and through. Just as for Kant the moral universe perched on the categorical imperative is universal and completely self-contained, for Kelsen state and law carve out a normative order of their own which can only remain well-functioning and meaningful so long as it is understood as self-enclosed and self-referential.

V The Broader Implications of the Encounter between Kelsen and Freud

Kelsen's conception of law from above and Freud providing a basis for solidarity to law from below never come close to meeting. Nevertheless, the preceding account of the interrelation between Kelsen and Freud does provide a useful baseline for purposes of framing the theoretical quest for a systematic and coherent account of the nexus between the constitution and the justice essentials. Kelsen's systematic account of the self-enclosed unity between state and law extends to all law, not just the constitution, and requires some minimum constitution—for example, a basic norm that sets some person or institution as the law maker. Because of the formal and reciprocal nature of the relationship between state and law for Kelsen, transnational actors, such as the UN, the EU, the World Trade Organization (WTO), or the Council of Europe as law-maker of the European Convention on Human Rights, can either assume a state like role or become incorporated by extension within more traditional states rooted within the Westphalian framework.[7] Moreover, no viable contemporary polity can truly function without instantiation of the unity between state and law. In other words, law and the language game of law provide a necessary component of the ordering required by contemporary polities. Notably, as we have seen in Chapter 1, even transnational corporations that

---

[7] This follows from Kelsen's views on the integration of national and international law already briefly discussed earlier in this chapter.

manage to avoid certain of their own country's laws need to subject their activities to combinations of state and law capable of giving them legal assurances against certain risks and legal clout in the pursuit of certain objectives. Law and the state are thus necessary, but they have no categorical implication for justice. For Kelsen, law and justice have no intrinsic relation, but for present purposes, as indicated earlier, constitutional democracies give rise to a hypothetical imperative that results in a bare minimum of justice that falls far short of any minimum required by the justice essentials. In view of all this, Kelsen's account plus the hypothetical imperative provide the bare minimum of justice that can be referred to as "justice according to law." The latter provides a baseline that confirms that justice under law or the constitution as well as the justice essentials must be found somewhere other than in law *qua* law. In short, the justice essentials depend on what can be termed as "justice beyond law." Moreover, what will be explored in the remaining chapters of Part II is whether it is possible to find a suitable version of justice beyond law—or a combination of the latter with justice according to law—that strikes a proper balance between the universal, the singular, and the plural.

Turning to Freud, two salient points emerge that suggest helpful analogies in the search for a suitable combination between *ethnos* and *demos* as required by the justice essentials. These points are respectively that the id, the ego, and the superego are in a constant dynamic punctured by conflicts leading to ongoing attempts at resolution, and that the dynamic between the three must simultaneously play out at all three levels of the singular, the plural, and the universal. Moreover, as pointed out earlier, Freud's theory of interpretation developed in his *Interpretation of Dreams*, and not in play in his interaction with Kelsen, also provides valuable tools in the search for a proportionate nexus between *ethnos* and *demos*. Indeed, nation-states harboring political relationships among strangers must construct national identities which, as already mentioned, emerge interpretively as imagined communities. And so too constitutionally ordered polities must have recourse to a commonly imagined constitutional identity. I shall now briefly indicate how the combination of these three distinct contributions to psychology made by Freud can shed light by analogy in the context of the intersection between law, justice, and the constitution.

Beyond any Freudian particulars, the divide between an id or unconscious, an ego based on reason and purposiveness, and a superego as a locus of normative constraints and ideals provides a useful explanatory framework in the context of both nationalism and constitutionalism. The nation-state, as already noted, is a joint enterprise among strangers who form an identitarian bond around nationalism which projects a commonly shared vision as an imagined community. Modern nineteenth-century nationalism was steeped in secularism at a time when religion was waning as the overriding unifying force within organized polities (Smith 1981). To bring about secular nationalism—and more recently religious nationalism (Mancini & Rosenfeld 2021: 479–82)—a polity's past with interweaved unconscious, preconscious, and conscious elements had to be processed through repression, idealization, and clusters of special emphasis and de-emphasis into a blend of characteristics and aspirations that could bridge past, present, and future into a unifying imagined narrative with nationwide appeal. Thus, for example, the prior politically and institutionally dominant religion had to be either somewhat repressed, reframed to de-emphasize its historical dominance, or transformed into a cultural rather than transcendent religious common heritage for purposes of rallying a people around a unifying nationalist imaginary. Similarly, constitutional identity must also rely on construction of an imaginary that at once breaks and preserves through reformulation key aspects of the relevant polity's past. Thus, for example, the abolition of slavery and the introduction for the first time of a constitutional equality right at the end of the US Civil War amounted to a veritable constitutional revolution (Richards 1994). This revolution required an extensive reformulation of the country's constitutional identity which was fraught with difficulties due to insufficient repression of suddenly incompatible past attitudes and traditions. These inconsistencies are well illustrated in the much-decried US Supreme Court 1896 decision in *Plessy v. Ferguson*.[8] Although it is currently obvious that state-legislated racial segregation is wholly incompatible with constitutional equality among all races, the Court in *Plessy* found a way to reconcile equality with segregation by limiting constitutional equality to civil and political rights and explicitly declaring it inapplicable to social rights. This distinction can only be understood in terms of insufficient repression—or a return of the repressed—of then seemingly repudiated past nationally and constitutionally engrained attitudes, habits, and values.

In the course of the preceding discussion of Freud's group psychology, I noted that there is no logical impediment to extending the notion of the ego ideal beyond the individual, the family, and the homogeneous group that self-identifies in an exclusionary manner. Both national and constitutional identity can be regarded as apt rallying points for the deployment of important ego ideal projections rising above parochial schisms within the polity. This is particularly relevant in the pursuit of the justice essentials by opening a path to a suitable ego ideal leading to normative convergence at the level of the polity as a whole. Indeed, an ego ideal permeating through the polity as a whole in its capacity as a national and constitutional imagined community may lead to equilibration between Freudian-like individual and parochial group aspirational identities and a constitutionally circumscribed universally aspiring counterpart. Thus, for example, in a polity marked by sharp ethnic tensions, the constitution may seek to diffuse the latter at the level of community of the whole by proscribing ethnic-based political parties.[9]

---

[8] 163 US 537 (1896).

[9] See, e.g., Constitution of Bulgaria, art. 11(1) ("Political parties may not be founded on ethnic, racial, or religious grounds").

Leaving aside for now the case of global constitutionalism, all other constitutional regimes, whether national or transnational, are per force exclusive and at least to some extent exclusionary. US nationalism and constitutional identity are certainly quite different from that of its counterparts in Europe, Asia, or Africa. Similarly, EU member states rally around their social welfare commitments while remaining critical of what they view as the US's extreme individualism and unbridled capitalism. In short, in view of the just mentioned unifying potential provided by national and constitutional identity, recourse to a notion of the ego ideal inspired by its Freudian counterpart may prove useful in trying to disentangle the dynamics and tensions among the singular, the plural, and the universal in the context of functioning contemporary constitutional units. And that, in turn, ought to facilitate assessments pursuant to criteria set by the justice essentials.

As already underscored, both Kelsen and Freud prioritize the individual over the group. From the standpoint of constitutional justice, however, there is no need to privilege any among the singular individual, the plurality of constitutionally relevant groups, or the (universal) unit framed by the community of communities encompassed within a single constitutional unit, over any of the others. Indeed, with respect to any question bearing on the justice of the constitution, the individual, various relevant groups, and the group of the whole must all be equally considered to arrive at a proper balance between *ethnos* and *demos* and to generate proportionate allocations of benefits and burdens among the universal, the singular, and the plural.

Finally, as noted earlier and as I detailed in previous work (Rosenfeld 2010), building, transforming, and maintaining any given constitutional identity entail interpretive undertakings that are analogous to those that Freud articulated in his engagement with the dynamic between the id, the ego, and the superego while psychoanalyzing dreams. The three most salient interpretive devices concerned include, as already mentioned, negation, metaphor, and metonymy. All three of these bear upon key identitarian issues, or in other words, upon determinations along axes of identification and of differentiation. Quite obviously, a constitution crafted after a revolution must rely upon some instances of negation to distance those who are supposed to embrace it from no longer acceptable features of the prerevolutionary self-image of the polity. Metaphoric reasoning, on the other hand, can be used to string together various contended constitutional propositions into more abstractly assembled strands of common identification. Thus, for example, the US Supreme Court has relied on eighteenth-century exaltation of heterosexual marriage as essential for purposes of legitimate procreation and of preservation of traditional family life in order to justify constitutionalizing the right to same-sex marriage in the twenty-first century.[10] In order to accomplish this, the Court had

---

[10] *Obergefell v. Hodges*, 576 US 644 (2015).

to abstract traditional marriage away from its historical setting in order to find a continuous fundamental right for every person to join together with a single other person of her choice to form a special life lasting bond that is paramount and that should not be denied on the basis of sexual orientation (*Id.*: Ch. 3). Unlike metaphoric thinking, its metonymic counterpart relies on differentiation and displacement. An example in the psychoanalytic context is that of developing a hatred of canes to at once express and hide to consciousness an inadmissible hatred of a close relative who happens to use a cane. In the US constitutional setting, the landmark *Griswold* case[11] provides a prime example of metonymic reasoning in that it strikes down as unconstitutional a prohibition to use contraceptives on the basis of a traditional entrenchment of marital privacy. Because eighteenth-century Christian-based marital privacy by no means extended to a right to contraception, it is only by displacing traditional marriage through focus on a single one of its modern attributes—the choice to decide whether or not link sex to procreation—that the Court was able to project an image of constitutional continuity and consistency. Moreover, this metonymic approach was furthered when a few years after *Griswold* the Court found a law that barred the use of contraceptives in non-marital sex unconstitutional.[12] In this latter case, marriage itself is dissolved into the individual right of any person to decide whether or not to link sex and procreation in any consensual non-marital sexual relationship.

In conclusion, the three just-discussed aspects of Freud's theory offer valuable means to investigate important aspects of identification and solidarity relating what amounts to a constitutionally relevant *ethnos* and its relation to a corresponding constitutionally adaptable *demos*. Just as Kelsen's law *qua* law taken by itself has no particular implication for justice beyond law, so too Freudian-based identification and solidarity do not by themselves advance the quest for justice through proper calibrations of *ethnos* with *demos*. Indeed, as the US example in the age of slavery or that of South Africa in its apartheid era demonstrate, it is quite possible to have a working constitutional order which garners weighty clusters of identification and solidarity while remaining thoroughly and systematically unjust. In the end, Kelsen's law and Freud's account of what binds the individual to others provide a useful baseline in the quest for the justice essentials. With this in mind, it is now time to explore theoretical contributions that may shed important light on how to achieve justice beyond law and requisite strands of identification and common loyalty susceptible of advancing justice instead of stacking against it or remaining completely indifferent to it.

---

[11] *Griswold v. Connecticut*, 381 US 479 (1965).
[12] *Eisenstadt v. Baird*, 405 US 438 (1972).

4

Law *Redux*

Schmitt, CLS, and the Drift to Politics; from Posner Back to Marx and the Absorption of Law into Economics

I Introduction

Since justice according to law proves widely insufficient in the pursuit of the justice essentials, it seems propitious to turn elsewhere for appropriate criteria of justice beyond law which could either supplement or subsume the bare minimum of justice built upon Kelsen's positivistic approach. Moreover, politics and economics loom as particularly promising fields for the purpose at hand. Indeed, these fields are at once separate from law and closely intertwined with the latter throughout all contemporary societies. Upon initial impression, it seems obvious that economics is of great import in relation to material distributive justice issues. By measuring the economic implications of laws, one can presumably subject these to a criterion of justice beyond law that may shed crucial light on the quest for the justice essentials. In sharp contrast, politics appears initially ill-suited to inform any cohesive criterion of justice beyond law that may help in sorting out just from unjust laws. This is because, even if we set aside the most critical appraisals of contemporary politics as centered on the narrow interests of politicians and of their powerful and moneyed backers, politics in working democracies are for the most part partisan in nature, with the citizenry divided among numerous rival political parties with competing ideologies and agendas. Accordingly, even granting that political party politics may satisfy the singular and plural aspirations of justice, it is difficult to imagine how such politics might contribute in any way to advancing the universal requirements of justice. In short, both constitutions and laws are inevitably political in nature as they embody respectively the political vision of the constituents or the policy interests of the relevant legislative majorities. The politics inscribed in constitutions and laws may be just or unjust but that seems due to some criterion of justice beyond politics as opposed to any justice according to politics counterpart.

Upon closer examination, however, referring back to Aristotle's famous characterization of human beings as political animals (Aristotle 1946: I.2 1253a), politics can be regarded ideally as being guided by the quest for, and pursuit of, the common good of the entire citizenry within the relevant political unit. If politics can be invested with an Aristotelian mission to realize the common good and to stir the citizen to virtuous action, then it can certainly yield justice as well as

---

A Pluralist Theory of Constitutional Justice. Michel Rosenfeld, Oxford University Press. © Michel Rosenfeld 2022.
DOI: 10.1093/oso/9780198862680.003.0005

providing the means to sort out justice from injustice within the bounds of the polity. Similarly, from a civic republican perspective based on Rousseau's proclamation that the self-governing citizenry must put into effect the "general will" (Rousseau 1947: 26), politics would also provide the requisite criterion to distinguish between just and unjust republics. Indeed, Rousseau's general will, which is neither the will of all nor the will of the majority (*Id.*), requires every person as a self-governing citizen to sacrifice personal private interests to the extent necessary to advance the good of the polity taken as a whole (*Id.*). Although the contents of Rousseau's general will remain somewhat obscure, at least in the abstract, normative adherence to the latter could be plausibly associated with satisfying distributive justice in all its three relevant dimensions.

In the broadest terms, therefore, politics or economics or a combination of the two could furnish the elements of justice beyond law that would pave the way to the justice essentials. Presumably, the justice beyond law in question would provide both tools of critique oriented to those constitutional orders that fall far short of the justice essentials and criteria of perfectibility allowing for better ordering constitutional regimes towards justice. Even in the best of cases, just politics and just economics could not do away with law but would instead inform the substantive content of laws or rely on compatible legal norms that satisfy the bare minimum of justice. Thus, for example, if a free market economy were deemed essential in the quest for the justice essentials, property and contract law would be more or less just depending on whether they facilitated or hindered the smooth workings of the market. At the same time, within the free market perspective some laws would advance the quest of justice regardless of their content. This would be the case of a law specifying that the seller of goods must insure the buyer while in transit before delivery to the buyer unless otherwise specifically provided for in the contract of sale. Assuming that two commercial enterprises of equal bargaining power are involved, insurance of goods in transit enhances market efficiency and having a rule is both legally and economically efficient as it avoids both economic losses and increased chances of legal disputes. The legal rule itself is indifferent as to content in the sense that it would equally serve its purpose whether the buyer or the seller were responsible for the insurance at stake. That is because the parties can contract around the rule with either a provision that the buyer assumes responsibility for the insurance or that the sales price of the goods is adjusted in view of the seller's legally assumed insurance costs.

Notwithstanding the logical possibility that politics and economics may be the source of the justice beyond law that would couple with justice according to law in order to forge ahead toward the justice essentials, the theories linking law to politics or economics that will be addressed in the course of this chapter all militate against the said possibility. Moreover, in the last analysis, these theories not only dispel the notion that politics or economics may provide convincing justice beyond law criteria but they also largely stand for the more radical and contrary proposition that politics and economics are poised to undermine the integrity of law by in various ways puncturing the mainstays of justice according to law. This, as will be discussed next, is clearly manifest in Carl Schmitt's theory of the political according to which rule by law is inevitably periodically interrupted by politics characterized by warring confrontations between friends and enemies. Also, as one contemporary commentator has noted, Schmitt can be regarded as the (unacknowledged) precursor of two movements originating in the United States within the legal academy that will also be examined below, namely CLS on the left and law and economics on the right (Strong 2005: xix). According to Critical Legal Studies (CLS), law is inherently indeterminate and can thus be dissolved into divisive politics. According to law and economics, on the other hand, law should be made, interpreted, or reinterpreted to further the goal of wealth maximization, thus subsuming law under a conception of distributive justice. But, as already noted, the conception of justice involved is a highly contested one that seems particularly unpersuasive in the current era of ever-increasing wealth disparities. Finally, Marx's dialectical materialism casts law as downright subservient to the economy. The struggle between the capitalists and the proletariat, which Marx considers the paramount dialectical mover of his times, is overwhelmingly centered in the economic domain. Accordingly, for Marx the economy figures as the "base" in contrast to law which forms part of the economic dependent "superstructure" (Marx 1859; 1846). Specifically, as Marx sees it, nineteenth-century law is formulated (in formally neutral but materially biased terms) and appropriated by the bourgeois class to bolster its economic interests in its confrontation against the dialectically opposed and revolutionary anti-capitalist economic interests of the working class (Marx & Engels 1979: 84–93).[1] Marx's is a political economy, and as Schmitt observes, it comports its own friend versus enemy dynamic which is class based as distinguished from traditional nation-state-based ones (Schmitt 2007: 37, 74).

What this initial sketch of the role of politics and economics in the justice aspirations for law reveals is highly paradoxical. On the one hand, it is irrefutable that politics and economics have a significant impact on whether constitutions or laws advance or thwart justice. On the other hand, all the authors to be considered in greater detail in what follows in various ways assert or intimate that politics and economics thwart law's pretense or ability to produce justice. What this paradox may mean in terms of the pursuit of the justice essentials and what potential there may be for politics and economics ultimately to derail law from viable paths toward justice urgently call for further elucidation. This in turn requires taking a closer look at each of the above-mentioned theories that set politics or economics against law.

---

[1] Many of the writings of Marx and Engels on law are assembled in Cain & Hunt 1979. For convenience, I refer to that source which contains references to the specific works of Marx and Engels from which the relevant passages are drawn.

II Schmitt's Secular Theology and its Politics of Division Rallying Friends Against Enemies

Schmitt, a contemporary of Kelsen, attacks the latter's conception of law and state as a hermetically self-enclosed normative system (Schmitt 2005: 18–22) and asserts that law cannot avoid penetration and periodic overriding by politics. What makes this inevitable, according to Schmitt, is that in times of crisis it is the top political officer within the polity that fully assumes the powers of sovereignty (*Id.*: 4). This is accomplished by deciding when to declare a state of emergency and by following that with a determination of "what constitutes the public interest or interest of the state, public safety and order" and of how and for how long to manage the emergency (*Id.*: 5). In short, for Schmitt both the declaration and the management of any existential conflict or crisis within the polity requires extraordinary powers that cannot be encapsuled in law and that therefore require politics overriding law for the requisite duration.

If emergency powers must transcend law—and Kelsen argues to the contrary (Kelsen 1945: 175)—and if they can be and have been subject to abuse (Dorsen 2016: 1593–5), it seems plain that they may pose a threat to constitutional rule and to associated justice essentials concerns. That in itself, however, need not pose a serious ongoing threat to constitutional democracy so long as a fairly broad consensus can be maintained within the polity over what ought to be considered an existential crisis. Accordingly, in the context of Schmitt, the main problem is not that politics may have to override law in grave crises but instead that in his particular conception, politics comprises a theological dimension and overwhelmingly concentrates on conflicts that all too often harbor dire existential implications.

To improve our understanding of the broader theoretical implications of Schmitt's theological elevation of politics above law as against Kelsenian hermetic legal positivism, it is useful to refer briefly to Luhmann's more systemic and more dynamic legal positivistic approach. Luhmann's theory shares with Kelsen's positivism the conviction that the validity of legal norms is not dependent on extra-legal norms. Unlike its Kelsenian formalistic counterpart, however, Luhmann's theory relies on systemic self-referential structural elements that are self-contained in their functioning. Specifically, Luhmann's theory draws on the self-referential and self-enclosed systemic approach framed by autopoiesis (Luhmann 1992) and posits law as a normatively closed subsystem of the social system that creates and reproduces elements through communications (Luhmann 1990: 3). In other words, legal autopoiesis is supposed to result in a legal system that remains operationally severed both from extralegal norms and from arbitrary subjectivity by relying on self-referential circularity as the foundation of law. Placed in its broader context, as society becomes more complex, it requires greater social differentiation and the legal autopoietic system, which Luhmann characterizes as environmentally and cognitively open but normatively closed, serves to stabilize expectations (Luhmann 1987: 27).

Luhmann's autopoietic theory tackles law at such a high level of abstraction that it is difficult to get a manageable handle on it. Accordingly, his conception of the systematicity of law can be perhaps better grasped by reference to the analogy he draws between autopoietic economics and autopoietic law (Luhmann 1990: 230–1). The key to the autopoietic economy is the process of monetarization. In broad terms, the economic system is open to needs, products, services, etc., but closed in that it converts all economic transactions into the system of monetary exchanges. In the context of a market economy, everything that comes within the purview of the market must be quantified by being ascribed a monetary value.

What is important to retain from Luhmann's theory, for our purposes, is that a complex contemporary society cannot do without an economy that systematically spreads monetarization or without a legal system that systematically provides for stabilization of expectations—in the sense that one can enter into a contract requiring future performance by another party and inevitably face *factual* uncertainty concerning that performance, but not *legal* uncertainty as the law provides either for performance or for a remedy in case of a failure of performance. For Luhmann, as for Kelsen, there is no inherent connection between law and justice, or, more precisely, between justice according to law and justice beyond law. Law as a self-referential normatively closed autopoietic system is all inclusive within its bounds and it can encompass anything within its environment pursuant to its criteria for sorting out all human interaction according to whether it is legally permissible or legally impermissible. Again, the analogy to the economy is helpful. In a free market, all can be monetarized, from the value of goods to that of human organs for transplant, and to that of a lost arm or of a deceased relative in a tort case where judgments routinely monetarize losses due to injury or to loss of next of kin. A market for human organs may be deemed immoral as would be a law authorizing the employment of nine-year-old children. For Luhmann, however, these questions of morality would have nothing to do with either economics or law. That is because in his autopoietic framework morals, economics, and law are separate, normatively closed societal subsystems that may share cognitive and environmental elements but not normative values or criteria.

Within Luhmann's systemic legal dynamics all decisions relating to triggering a state of emergency at a time of crisis could be unequivocally determined as being either legally permissible or legally impermissible. Accordingly, if we add the systemic dynamic discrepancy between Schmitt's claim that politics interrupts law and Luhmann's insistence on normative closure to the formal dispute between Schmitt and Kelsen, we get a better sense of the magnitude of Schmitt's challenge and of its consequential potential for disruption. Moreover, Schmitt's personal trajectory as a committed supporter of Hitler's Nazi regime (Strong 2005: vii–x) place his friend/enemy dynamic in a historic context that makes it difficult to disentangle

134 LAW REDUX

his political theology from his Nazi politics (*Id.*: xxx–xxxi). Is the friend/enemy dynamic a means to legitimate totalitarianism and Nazi racial ideology? If so, then Schmitt's theory could be relatively easily dismissed from the standpoint of constitutional democracy and of the pursuit of justice essentials. As we shall see, however, Schmitt's theory cannot be reduced in all fairness to an apology for Nazi ideology. Indeed, Schmitt's conception of the friend/enemy dynamic is by no means limited to racial or ethnocentric based conflicts[2] as it also encompasses cultural, national, and religious divides and even class struggle along Marxist lines (Schmitt 2007: 37–8). What is crucial for our purposes, is that Schmitt, who after the Second World War has had numerous followers both on the right and on the left, is a critic of liberalism and of pluralism. And it is principally because of this that he poses a significant challenge to liberal constitutionalism and to its aspirations towards the justice essentials.

The three mainstays of Schmitt's theory that require further attention at this point are: his political theology; his politics centered on exacerbating the animosities between friends and enemies; and his existential disdain for liberal efforts to deflate political conflicts through adherence to law and through concentration on technology. Regarding political theology, Schmitt asserts that modern concepts of the state are for the most part secularized theological concepts for both historical and systemic reasons (Schmitt 2005: 36). Moreover, Schmitt insists that "the exception in jurisprudence," whereby the state's head of government suspends the law in an emergency, "is analogous to the miracle in theology" (*Id.*). Historically, as Schmitt recounts, God was the law-giver and ruler through his designates on earth, but in more recent times he has been substituted by the monarch, the dictator, or the democratically chosen president or prime minister. What politics requires is decisions, and in times of crisis, calling for exceptions from the ordinarily applicable legal regime, these requisite decisions are of utmost existential import, and they must be uncontestably final. The religious miracle defies the laws of nature and bestows a great divine favor on its human beneficiaries, such as the manna from heaven which is said to have provided nourishment to the children of Israel who sojourned in the desert on their way to the promised land. Analogously, a country's secular leader is called upon to muster extraordinary resources above the possibilities afforded within the constraints of the existing legal regime. Religious political theology is best exemplified by the Catholic Church, which from its internal perspective stands for the one and only true religion, and which is headed by a pope who can render final and infallible decisions in matters of religious import (*Id.*: 55). Dictators or presidents having invoked the exception are in an equivalent position to that of the pope, with the difference that their final decisions concern

---

[2] Strictly speaking, friend and enemy have no actual content for Schmitt, they are just oppositional positions: "The political enemy ... is ... the other, the stranger; and it is sufficient for his nature that he is ... existentially something different and alien" (Schmitt, 2007: 27).

secular matters such as a nationalism considered from within as worth dying for, their people's non-negotiable cultural integrity, or the defense of capitalism at the risk of nuclear war against communism during the Cold War. In sum, consistent with Schmitt's understanding, the content over which an existential crisis occurs is basically indifferent so long as it can be addressed swiftly and with finality by a leader who is closely identified with the concerns, values, and aspirations that unify those whom she represents.

For Schmitt, politics is entirely contained within the friend versus enemy dynamic. As he sees it, just as morality is about the dynamic between good and evil, esthetics as that between the beautiful and the ugly, economics as that between the profitable and the unprofitable, so too politics "can be reduced" to "that between friend and enemy" (Schmitt 2007: 26). The friend versus enemy confrontation, according to Schmitt, does not depend on questions of justice, morality, or economics but only on the enemy figuring as "the other, the stranger" who existentially poses threats to one's way of life. Accordingly, this other "must be repulsed or fought in order to preserve one's own form of existence" (*Id.*: 27). Throughout history, who counts as a friend or an enemy changes. During the sixteenth-century wars of religion between Catholics and Protestants in Europe, the enemy was religious (Schmitt 2007: 89). Later, with the onset of the Westphalian nation-state operating within *the jus publicum Europaeum*, with which Schmitt most closely identified, the relevant dynamic was predominantly among sovereign *nations* that did or could pose existential threats that may result in war (Schmitt 2007: 26, 46 ff.). Thus, for example, France and Germany were at war with one another three times between 1870 and 1945, with the Alsace-Lorraine region ceded to Germany in 1871, returned to France in 1919, receded to Germany in 1940, and once again returned to France in 1945 (Parry & Girard 2003). In all those wars, the entire friend-versus-enemy dynamic was projected outward beyond each of the warring nations' borders with internal countrywide divisions along religious, ideological, social, and policy lines remaining non-political in Schmitt's sense of the term.

From the present perspective, so long as the friend/enemy axis remains at the level of interactions among sovereign states, it need not pose any insurmountable challenge to the integrity of constitutional orders tailored for nation-state units. As Schmitt notes, religious, economic, and cultural differences within a country pose no threat to dealings with other countries unless they intensify to the point of interfering with, or distorting, the existentially necessary dealings with those foreign countries that pose an actual or potential threat of war (Schmitt 2007: 39). In other words, so long as Schmittian politics are confined to foreign affairs, presumably the universal (within the nation-state unit), the singular and the plural can by and large be accommodated within the purview of the justice essentials. That is, however, with one major exception. Even if we leave aside that contemporary wars frequently demand momentous internal sacrifices and policy changes, what if there is no unanimous consensus regarding war and peace politics within a nation-state

136 LAW REDUX

that is a constitutional democracy? Schmitt's theory may be fairly persuasive in cases where one country is under attack and survival becomes literally an existential matter for the citizenry as a whole as was the case in the United Kingdom under continuous and intense bombardment by the Nazis in the early part of the Second World War. But what about wars that a country chooses to engage in, such as the US war in Vietnam in the 1960s or in Iraq in the 2000s, that some Americans felt were existentially necessary and others wasteful and highly counterproductive?

This last question raises a broader one concerning whether Schmittian politics are altogether compatible with democracy. Schmitt himself answers this latter question in the affirmative as he sharply distinguishes democracy from liberalism while making the latter the villain from the standpoint of politics (Schmitt 2007: 69–70). As a practical matter, Schmitt admits of pluralism so long as it does not overflow into politics. An individual can belong to different associations, organizations within civil society, religious communities, labor unions, etc., so long as these do not interfere with or curtail the exercise of sovereign power. However, once they do, and divisive politics erupt *within* the sovereign nation, then the latter is bound for Schmitt to head toward civil war (*Id.*: 40–3).

Schmitt insists that pluralism is flatly incompatible with politics (*Id.*: 44–5). Accordingly, the only kind of democracy that seems genuinely capable of achieving legitimacy within the bounds of Schmittian politics is democratic populism. Democratic populism is built on the friend/enemy model, with the "people" being defined as including part of the polity's citizenry against both internal and external "enemies" (Muller 2016: 10–11; Mancini & Rosenfeld 2021: 491). If those who count as *the* people are the polity's common citizens who constitute a majority of the voters and who confront their country's elite as their internal enemies and certain foreign nations as their external enemies, then these common citizens can democratically elect a leader who shares their political outlook. In addition, fittingly from a Schmittian standpoint, populism tends to sacralize politics by casting the people's charismatic leader as the secular equivalent of a pastor or savior who is meant to guide her flock to triumph over all enemies, internal and external (*Id.*).

Populism both on the right and on the left is illiberal in nature.[3] Nevertheless, to the extent that it is democratic and that the right to vote is equally accorded to common citizens and to members of the elite, constitutional populism might plausibly be compatible with some version of the justice essentials. If internal "enemies" are granted all rights and only disempowered because outvoted and stripped of unfair advantages previously obtained through their disproportionate influence, then as long as the democratically elected populist regime mainly redresses various distributive inequities that previous elitist governments exacerbated, illiberal constitutional populist democracy need not be declared out of bounds from a justice

---

[3] For a comparison between populism on the right and on the left, see Tushnet 2018: 639.

essentials standpoint. Of course, this assumes the populist "war" against internal "enemies" is but a peaceful struggle aiming at shifts in power and not at killing the enemy to achieve victory as is the typical objective in classical wars between sovereign nations. Be that as it may, to obtain a fuller handle on Schmitt's insistence that politics inevitably punctures law, it is now time briefly to examine his attack on liberalism.

Schmitt's condemnation of liberalism and its associated individualism is by no means limited to a rejection of the latter's insistence on keeping law above politics. Instead, Schmitt accuses liberalism of engaging in a much more radical project consisting in minimizing the state and in eliminating politics (Schmitt 2007: 70). Liberalism aims at doing away with politics, according to Schmitt, by turning to ethics and economics and thus circumventing the paramount political dynamic between war and peace. This is achieved through focus on competition (as opposed to enmity) in economics and on discussion (as opposed to decision) in the realms of ethics and of (what in non-Schmittian terms is ordinarily understood as) politics (*Id.*: 71–2). In other words, the liberal individual focuses on property and liberty rights in ways that allow for cowardly avoiding risking one's life in any political call to go to war against those who should properly be considered mortal enemies (*Id.*). And within this liberal perspective, the political is avoided—though, as Schmitt notes, speaking from his own perspective, what liberalism promotes as non-political is still political (*Id.*: 70)—and refuge is sought through compartmentalization into a plurality of seemingly apolitical self-contained fields, such as the economy and technology as well as into numerous associational organizations, such as the church, labor unions, literary clubs, chambers of commerce, etc. Moreover, this liberal associational pluralism is pernicious, in Schmitt's view, to the extent that it amounts to a politics of avoidance. In short, for Schmitt, so long as friend/enemy politics remain paramount, mere apolitical associational pluralism is tolerable. Otherwise, pluralism is unacceptable and must be vigorously fought against.

Liberalism is particularly nefarious because of what Schmitt regards as its disingenuous aspirations towards humanist universalism. As Schmitt underscores, liberalism's misleading pairing with universalism dates back to the bourgeois-led third estate seeking, in the course of the French Revolution, at once to do away with feudal privilege and to ward off the demands and blunt the ambitions of those in the lower classes (Schmitt 2005: 56–60). Used as a sword against feudal privilege, bourgeois appeal to universalism may well seem persuasive. When used as a shield against the powerless and the propertyless at the bottom of the social ladder, however, the appeal to universalism and to its indissolubly linked exaltation of individual rights to freedom and to private property may on the surface appear inclusive while at bottom aimed at cementing exclusion. Indeed, being offered a right to freedom when one lacks the means to exercise it and a right to enjoy the benefits of private property possession when one is propertyless hardly smacks as a ticket

138   LAW REDUX

of admission into some universal communal association fostering equal worth and equal dignity.

Schmitt is very critical of liberalism's thrust toward universalism because of its attempted overcoming of the friend/enemy dynamic. Liberalism may do so in the name of borderless economic competition and of transnational spread of human rights, but all this serves the purposes of (above all US) modern economic imperialism (Schmitt 2006: 292–4). As it seeks to spread its economic domination worldwide, imperialism purports to speak in the name of humanity as a whole, but this displaces rather than abolishes the friend/enemy struggle. As Schmitt sees it, those who resist the burdens of imperialism are cast as the enemies of humanity (Schmitt 2007: 79) and subjected to worse violence than the ones involved in historical wars between sovereign states adhering to the *jus publicum Europaeum* (Schmitt 2006: Part III).

Besides his insistence on the impossibility of law avoiding disruption by politics, Schmitt's stance suggests one intriguing possibility and poses two thorny challenges regarding constitutional democracy's quest to satisfy the justice essentials. The possibility in question is the already mentioned recourse to illiberal populist democracy with a charismatic leader who fully internalizes the *ethnos* of his people both when she oversees rule by law and when she invokes and operates under the exception. As already noted in the introduction, Schmitt's ethnocentric conception of constitutionalism allows for dictatorship so long as the leader of the polity embodies the identity and aspirations of her entirely homogeneous people. Indeed, once pluralism in politics is set aside, one may assume a functional equivalence between a dictator and an elected leader who are equally attuned to their people's political needs. To be sure, the possibility of an essentially just illiberal populist constitutional democracy seems exceedingly modest. On the one hand, such possibility depends on the presence of actual factual conditions that are difficult to imagine in contemporary polities whereas on the other hand, as already mentioned, the historical record relating to present day illiberal populist democracies is hardly encouraging. Nevertheless, what reference to Schmitt's theory suggests is that the prospect of an essentially just illiberal populist constitutional democracy cannot be categorically dismissed *ex ante*.

The two challenges that Schmitt's theory poses to constitutional democracy achieving the justice essentials are the exclusion of any meaningful pluralism within the constitutional order or as a significant feature within a working constitutional identity construct; and the foreclosure of most, if not all, transnational or global constitutional ordering on account of the impossibility of transcending the friend/enemy dynamic. These two challenges are obviously related and the question they pose in the context of the present undertaking is whether and to what extent they must be taken seriously even if one does not buy into Schmitt's theory as a whole.

Schmitt's anti-pluralism must be rejected both on factual and on normative grounds. Factually, most all contemporary polities are highly pluralistic as a matter of fact and prone to becoming more so as a consequence of increased migration due to globalization. In addition, the pluralism in question cannot realistically or equitably be confined to an associational level with no political or constitutional consequences. Even France, the country that historically stood out the most for trying to subordinate *ethnos* to *demos*, is currently besieged by controversies over proper recognition of its large Muslim minority[4] and over greater openness to multicultural perspectives as evinced by recent attacks on manifestations of identity politics on the grounds that they represent the import of disruptive American trends within the French academy.[5] Because of this, as already noted, normatively pluralism must be adequately factored within the precincts of the constitution to avoid systemic identitarian recognition-based distributive injustices.

Schmitt's anti-pluralism should and can be rejected as many existing constitutions actually do; such as, for example, the Canadian one which accords a privileged place to the pursuit of multiculturalism.[6] Nevertheless, Schmitt's stance should be kept in mind as a caveat. Indeed, maintaining a constitutionally equitable degree of pluralism requires flexibility and sacrifices. When the status quo seems too radically or too rapidly disrupted, as many have felt in the course of the expansion of globalization, then anti-pluralist sentiment can be stirred up as a means to ward off or to mitigate unwelcome change. This certainly accounts for recent turns to exclusionary nationalism and illiberal populism. Disruption and dislocation of significant portions of the citizenry foster hostility towards expansion of pluralistic inclusion of new ways of life, such as those of Muslim immigrants in Western Europe. Rapidly changing circumstances to the disadvantage of many also rekindle ancient enmities among groups that had reached a truce or accommodation under constitutionally more favorable circumstances. In light of all this, the Schmittian caveat can be put to good use when recalibrating the balance between *ethnos* and *demos* and when expanding or limiting identitarian recognition to maximize pluralist accommodation without disproportionate inclusion or exclusion of competing group-based conceptions of the good.

The Schmittian insistence that the friend/enemy conflict cannot be ultimately avoided and that any attempts at doing so will actually make things worse should also be granted some cautionary value even if it must be rejected as constituting the dominant mover of all politics. What is most surprising about Schmitt's friend/enemy dynamic is the existential importance and intensity he attributes to it. As

---

[4] See Karina Piser, "A new plan to create an 'Islam of France'," *The Atlantic*, March 29, 2018.

[5] See Norimitsu Onishi, "Will American ideas tear France apart? Some of its leaders think so," *NY Times*, October 11, 2021.

[6] *See* Canadian Charter of Rights and Freedoms, § 27, Part I of the Constitution Act, 1982 which provides: "This Charter shall be interpreted in a manner consistent with the preservation and enhancement of the multicultural heritage of Canadians."

140   LAW *REDUX*

some commentators have observed, Schmitt draws on Hobbes' war of all against all, but whereas Hobbes confines this predicament to the state of nature Schmitt extends it to all politics within organized societies (Strauss 2007: 105–6). Also, whereas Hobbes envisions individual against individual violence in the state of nature, Schmitt contemplates group-based violence among sovereign nations or other organized groupings made up of friends against their counterparts standing against them as enemies. For Schmitt, a worthy existence depends on the willingness to die to preserve what one shares with friends against the threats of violence posed by enemies (Schmitt 2007: 26–9). Although Schmitt lived during a period that saw two world wars followed by a cold war which risked escalating into a nuclear conflagration, it is difficult to understand his *positive association* of warring against one's enemies with existential self-fulfillment and vindication.

III Critical Legal Studies (CLS) and Law as Indeterminate and Political All the Way Down

CLS brought together a diverse group of legal scholars, ranging from nearly orthodox Marxists to existentialists and even, in the eyes of some, nihilists (Singer 1984). CLS started in the United States in the 1970s and later spread to other countries (Goodrich 1992), but pretty much faded in the United States by the end of the 1980s (Tushnet 1991). What united this otherwise disparate group of legal scholars is their combined efforts throughout virtually all fields of private and public law to "thrash" and "debunk" (Kelman 1984) law's pretentions to objectivity, determinacy, and neutrality, and to apolitical reliance on systematically transparent rules (Singer 1984). CLS regarded the law of their time as serving the interests of capitalism and of those it had thrust into positions of power. Accordingly, CLS's perspective is well-anticipated in the following observation by Schmitt (whom CLS virtually completely ignored): "[concerning positive law] the rule of law means nothing else than the legitimization of a specific *status quo*, the preservation of which interests particularly those whose political power or economic advantage would stabilize itself in this law" (Schmitt 2007: 66).

For present purposes, two principal CLS claims require further inquiry: that lawmakers and the laws they produce are ideological; and that judges are political and can vindicate their partisan outlook as the laws they interpret are per force indeterminate and thus open to diverse and even contradictory interpretations (Unger 1976: 66, 69, 129). Moreover, and this is key for CLS proponents, both the ideology of the legislator and the politics of the judge are sought to be largely masked so as to misleadingly convey respectively a professed neutrality of rights and laws that are universally applicable within the polity and an air of apolitical impartiality in the practice of judicial interpretation. Finally, to place these claims in their proper historical context, CLS proponents assumed that those on the right within the

American political spectrum were for the most part in power while those on the left—either as anti-capitalists or embracing the causes of those left behind by the capitalist system—were by and large powerless. Notably, after a period of great expansion of social welfare policies from the Roosevelt Administration in the 1930s to the Johnson Administration in the 1960s, the 1970s and especially the 1980s under the Reagan Administration became a new era marked by an ideologically and policy-driven vivid retrenchment from the largesse of the social welfare state.

One of the main features of the conception of the rule of law grounded in the Enlightenment, as clearly articulated by Kant, is that a law must be universal in form and thus at least in theory possibly self-given in order to be legitimate (Kant 1991: 79). As Kant specifies, a law that differentiated between a hereditary ruling class and the rest of society could not possibly be acquiesced to as being just by all (*Id.*). In contrast, a generally imposed tax to pay for an unpopular war would be legitimate as it would be logically possible for all to agree to it even if many in fact virulently objected to the war it meant to finance (*Id.*). Obviously, Kant's criterion for satisfying the requisites of the rule of law is quite weak as it amounts essentially to a right to formal equality before the law (Rosenfeld 2001: 1321). Consistent with Kant's easily met requirement of legitimacy, constitutional rights as well as the bulk or ordinary laws in contemporary constitutional democracies qualify as universal in form and appearance. Contract law applies equally to employers and employees and to the rich and the poor. Similarly, free speech rights are equally available to media moguls, to those who can purchase political advertisements to influence elections, and to the impecunious student or welfare recipient.

Kant is clear that the purely formal requirements that he relies on are silent concerning the substance of laws and concerning whether these laws may be materially just or unjust. In contrast to Kant, who views the formal universality of laws positively, CLS does so negatively. This is because CLS regards the formal universality of laws as providing a deceptive façade allowing those in power to conceal the substantively unjust nature of laws that favor them. Accordingly, CLS launches what amounts to a two-pronged attack against law as a language game in contrast to positivists such as Kelsen and Luhmann who view it as both necessary and societally beneficial. On the one hand, CLS's critique leads to the proposition that the language game of law is fully translatable into that of politics. On the other hand, the language game of law must nevertheless be propped up as distinct and not simply merged into that of politics. This is for the benefit of the powerful who can achieve their aims better by disguising their politics in the rhetoric of seemingly neutral and universal laws and rights.

That legislators are ideological in democracies divided along different conceptions of the public good and along competing political philosophies seems obvious and, taken by itself, uncontroversial. Moreover, both constitution makers and drafters of ordinary laws are undoubtedly of different ideological and political stripes even among all those who adhere to the essential precepts that underly

142 LAW REDUX

liberal constitutionalism. As already discussed, constitutional identities vary, as do conceptions of whether and to what extent constitutions should guarantee social welfare needs as detailed in Chapter 2. In light of this, CLS's attack on the ideology of US legislators is better understood as presupposing that the latter are committed to wrong and objectionable ideological positions and that they deceptively seek to blunt objections to their legislative work product by concealing its true nature. In this context, CLS's aim is to provide a critique that exposes the ideological biases involved and that stresses how self-serving they prove to be for the powerful while remaining harmful to others. Notably, this critique is an overwhelming negative one that exposes what CLS sees as wrong, but that offers little on how to replace or to reconstruct what has been debunked.

CLS's most notorious contribution is its critique of legal doctrine as malleable and contradictory and of law as indeterminate, thus allowing judges to interpret it in political ways that favor the powerful with whom they for the most part identify with. CLS's greatest impact on the legal academy stemmed from its various particular critiques of distinct fields in both private and public law. Thus, for example, a leading CLS scholar has argued that contemporary US contract doctrine has been defined by juxtaposing a vision based on freedom of contract and market values with a countervision drawing on communitarian values and fairness (Unger 1983: 616–33). This manifestly allows judges a great measure of discretion as they can draw from a broad and contradictory set of normative sources to reach the most politically palatable result from the standpoint of those with whose ideology they most identify with. Similarly, referring to US constitutional law, another leading CLS scholar claimed that constitutional theory is "impossible" because "no available approach to constitutional law can effectively restrain both legislators and judges" (Tushnet 1988: 313). Because of this, in the end, "[c]ritique is all there is" (*Id.*: 318). In other words, in this CLS perspective, all constitutional law is nothing but politics and all that can be done is to critique that body of law by exposing its political biases. Whereas constitutional law may be more controversial and open-ended than certain private law subjects, CLS does not draw any meaningful distinction between differences in judicial philosophy, which can be encompassed within the language game of law, and political and ideological differences, which pertain to the realm of ordinary politics (Rosenfeld 2019). Constitutional judges may disagree over whether they should adopt an "originalist" position as many US judges do or a "tree of life" approach as Canadian judges do. These two judicial approaches may well lead to different results in similar cases, but consistent applications of either of these will most likely not align over time with any particular ordinary politics ideological stance (*Id.*). Principled judges may therefore not control the ordinary politics consequences of their decisions if judicial philosophies restrain judicial interpretation. For example, if a judge with integrity construes all rights narrowly, she will have to adhere to that approach whether she is adjudicating the rights of employers or those of employees. CLS's position, however, is that whether we focus on judicial philosophy or legal doctrine, matters turn out to be so indeterminate and so contradictory that ordinary politics can end up trumping all else.

One may seriously question whether all law is as indeterminate and subject to political manipulation as CLS contends. On first impression, common law systems seem much more open-ended than their civil law counterparts as the former rely to an important extent on judge made law based on precedents whereas the latter rely above all on statutory codes. The common law judiciary thus proceeds mainly through a process of induction whereas civil law judges are supposed to rely on deduction in their application of a code to specific facts. Nevertheless, whatever differences may prevail in private law, in constitutional law the two systems converge as questions regarding the right to dignity under the German Basic Law appear as open-ended as substantive due process questions under the US Constitution. Accordingly, the question becomes whether all open-ended constitutional law questions can ultimately be fully reduced, as CLS maintains, to mere politics.

Even if we disregard language game differences, there is one non-trivial difference between law and politics that cannot be reasonably overlooked. At the very least, law is tantamount to frozen politics. For example, it has long been debated in the United States whether it is better to mandate a minimum wage by law or to leave wages to market forces. Also, among minimum wage proponents there have been disagreements about the level at which it ought to be set, with some arguing for a lower figure and others for higher ones. The politics behind these minimum wage disputes are varied. Both certain proponents and opponents of the minimum wage base their arguments on the grounds that they seek to promote wealth maximization through the market. Some other proponents advance social welfare and fairness concerns that they maintain ought to override wealth maximization objectives. In spite of all these political differences, supposing a law were adopted setting a national $15 minimum wage, the political debate on the subject would be in effect suspended and employers and judges would have to abide by the $15 figure. To be sure, the $15 figure adopted by the legislature's majority is political, but once converted into law, further political debate within the realm of lawful conduct, law enforcement, and adjudication ought to remain frozen until the law in question is repealed, amended, or superseded. In sum, although the language game of politics may inevitably inform the language game of law, and although judicial discretion may be prevalent in many cases, the $15 law would bind judges in a large number of cases, even if in not all of them—for example, would the $15 minimum apply to the case of asking one's cousin to build bookshelves over an eight-hour period based upon an offer to take him out for a meal that ends up costing $90?

What precipitated the decline of CLS in the United States is a twofold sequel issuing from its own trajectory. On the one hand, once a great body of purely negative critiques of existing laws in most specialized fields was released, the CLS perspective

144   LAW REDUX

and conclusions were either accepted or rejected[7] without leaving room for much else. Also, on the other hand, by a dialectical twist, some of the CLS-influenced critical scholars found that laws could make a positive difference in spite of indeterminacy and top down politicization. This dawned upon proponents of both Critical Race Theory and Feminist Critical Legal Theory. In essence, the insight made by proponents of these two theories, who were in many ways close to CLS, was that the evolution of civil rights in the United States had made both women and African-Americans better off than they would have been otherwise (Williams 1987; Crenshaw 1989). In other words, politically biased as mid-twentieth-century US civil rights might have been, and notwithstanding the remaining outstanding grave injustices endured by women and African-Americans, evolving civil rights enforcement did lead to an improvement in their respective fates. Moreover, the key theoretical implication that follows from this insight is that critique all the way down is insufficient. Instead, whereas critique in the name of those systematically oppressed by the law is essential, it must be supplemented by a positive project of fighting for laws and rights that may contribute to the amelioration of the plight of women and of racial minorities.

Critique paired with a positive agenda, whether realistic or utopian, will be further explored in Chapter 6 of this book in the course of the discussion of Derrida's deconstructive account of the nexus between law and justice. For now, suffice it to emphasize that CLS's critique, like Schmitt's theory, while ultimately wanting, offers several useful insights. In an important sense, law must be understood as political all the way through, but that does not eliminate the distinction between law and politics as distinct language games. Furthermore, whereas it is true that law is often indeterminate—and even more so in the case of constitutional law— the implications that CLS draws from that appear to a significant extent unwarranted. First, if the indeterminacy in question is due to differences in judicial philosophy concerning constitutional interpretation, they may well be resolved within the language game of law without recourse to ordinary politics. Second, if CLS, contrary to Luhmann's claim of no normative interpenetration, convincingly demonstrates that indeterminacy allows politics to sway adjudication, this does not exclude morals or conceptions of justice from doing the same. Thus, in certain oppressive regimes, such as the one that prevailed in South Africa during the apartheid era, certain judges made use of the indeterminacies of certain common law principles in a quest to somewhat mitigate the harshness of the prevailing racial injustices.[8] More generally, in the context of general and open-ended constitutional rights, such as those to dignity or equality, judges can deal with indeterminacies within the language game of law consistent with the precepts of recognition-based

---

[7] For a critique and refutation of CLS' principal claims, see Fiss 1986.

[8] "While the judiciary was certainly not free from blame for the role it played under apartheid, this was no reason to denigrate 'its very substantial contribution' to society during a contentious

or redistribution-based justice. Finally, viewed in terms of the workings of the language game of law within specific historical and institutional contexts, legal indeterminacy can only legitimately give rise to bounded judicial choices as contrasted with free-flowing ones (Rosenfeld 1998: 27). For example, in the late nineteenth-century US judicial interpretation of constitutional equality, state-ordered racial segregation[9] and state-prohibited women practicing law[10] were deemed unequivocally constitutionally permissible. Today, both of these interpretations have been repudiated and racial segregation as well as state-mandated exclusion of women from professions are firmly condemned as unconstitutional under the very same equality provisions. Moreover, whereas no-one can assure that American equality jurisprudence will not regress back to its origins 200 years from now, it is clear that no self-respecting contemporary lawyer or judge would entertain arguments based on these discredited nineteenth-century precedents. In short, history and context leave open certain paths of interpretation while closing others for the foreseeable future.

IV Posner's Economic Framing of Law to Conform with the Ideology of Wealth Maximization

Posner and Marx are not only two ideologically polar opposites but they also respectively embrace very different positions concerning the workings or optimal nexus between law and economics. Whereas Marx focuses on the inherent contradictions of capitalism paving the way to communism, Posner champions a neo-classical free-market economy singularly oriented toward wealth maximization. In addition, for Marx, bourgeois law and rights seem neutral but serve the capitalists' interests against those of the proletariat (thus in a certain way anticipating Schmitt's contention that liberalism seeks to displace and subvert the friend/enemy dynamic), but for Posner law and economics ideally go hand in hand and the language game of law should aspire completely to mirror that of economics. For both Marx and Posner, law is, or ought to be, subordinate to economics, but for Posner, as we shall see, economically validated law figures as a definite value-added positive. Posner, as already mentioned, links wealth maximization and distributive justice. Marx, as will be discussed, is himself quite ambiguous on the question of justice in relation to capitalism. From an external standpoint, however, it seems plain that one who shares Marx's account of capitalist exploitation might well conclude that

---

and troubled era in South Africa" (Statement by High Court judges to Truth and Reconciliation Commission); <https://www.justice.gov.za/trc/media/1997/9710/s971024g.htm>, visited April 3, 2022.

[9] See *Plessy v. Ferguson* 163 US 537 (1896).
[10] See *Bradwell v. State of Illinois*, 83 US 130 (1873).

146 LAW REDUX

capitalism is inherently unjust. From our perspective, what this underscores and calls for further inquiry after taking a closer look at Posner and Marx is that subordination of law to economics does imply commitments to particular conceptions of distributive justice. And to the extent that these conceptions happen to be highly contestable, they appear to pose a daunting challenge to achieving a broadly based constitutionally suitable articulation of the justice essentials.

The law and economics movement centering on the economic analysis of law was launched in the United States in the 1960s and came into full theoretical fruition in the 1970s (Horwitz 1981: 905 ff.). Richard Posner became the movement's central figure with the publication of his *Economic Analysis of Law in 1973*. In his own, far from modest assessment several years later, Posner asserted that:

> [t]he most ambitious and probably the most influential effort in recent years to elaborate an overarching concept of justice that will both explain judicial decision making and place it on an objective basis is that of scholars working in the interdisciplinary field of law and economics .... (Posner 1990: 353)

Although there are certainly differences among the numerous proponents of law and economics, exclusive focus on Posner is warranted as he concentrates on the three crucial claims that are at the foreground of the entire scope of the movement. First, Posner advances the factual claim that economics is an objective, positive science and that subjecting laws to economic analysis will assure that the laws in question are efficient (Posner 1990: 353). Second, Posner assumes that individuals are instrumentally rational and self-interested (*Id.*: 367), and that therefore laws that address non-market subjects, such as punishment for violent behavior, can also be factually rendered most efficient by being made to conform to an economic approach involving the calibration of incentives and disincentives (Posner 1995: 416). And third, Posner advances the normative proposition that laws ought to promote or facilitate wealth maximization—not as an end in itself, but because "wealth maximization may be the most direct route to a variety of moral ends" (Posner 1990: 382). Although Posner's normative stance is close to the libertarian one embraced by Nozick and by his fellow law and economics proponent, Richard Epstein (Epstein 1995: Ch. 1), it differs somewhat from the latter. Indeed, Posner does not posit wealth maximization and therefore the free-market economy as an end itself but as a means to best enable individuals to pursue their preferred normative pursuits.

Leaving to one side Posner's contestable treatment of economics as an objective positive science distinct from other social sciences, and assuming for the sake of argument that, within the economy, individuals are consistently instrumentally rational and steadfastly self-interested, let us attempt to distill the essentials of the nexus between law and economics consistent with his theory. Above all, we must keep in mind Posner's assertion that if law is efficient and fine-tuned to assure wealth maximization it is bound to be (distributively) just. Consequently, if law satisfies the requisite economic test, then justice according to law will supposedly assure economic justice. Furthermore, wealth maximization plays an equivalent role for Posner as maximization of utilities does for utilitarians (Posner 1990: 357, 390–1) though the two are not equivalent. Indeed, in some cases the pursuit of wealth maximization may well reduce the overall level of happiness within the polity, such as when a major economic gain for the few resulting in a net gain in wealth for the polity as a whole is combined with a large number of the less well-off becoming food insecure, which as already noted happened in the United States in the midst of the COVID-19 pandemic. Nevertheless, Posner, who like the utilitarians is a consequentialist, embraces a conception of justice that affords an expansive potential for individual self-fulfillment. Finally, the law of the constitution, if molded to be efficient and wealth maximizing would secure a Posnerian version of the justice essentials. As will be briefly considered shortly, Posner himself has given an account of how the US Constitution may be understood to best approximate the quest for economic justice as he sees it (Posner 1987).

That there ought to be a close tie between law and economics in a capitalist democracy is obvious and taken by itself fairly uncontroversial. The more controverted question is how much of law should be molded by economic criteria, and to the extent that economic views may be plural, by which among competing economic descriptive or prescriptive criteria ought laws be molded, modified, or repealed. Even in the case of a completely unrestrained free-market economy operating within a Nozickian minimal watchman state, private property, contract, and criminal laws would be required and the most efficient among these—those that best sustain the market economy without interfering with it—preferred. Other laws meant to preserve the integrity of the market, such as anti-monopoly laws, should also be constantly reviewed for efficiency and judicially interpreted accordingly. Thus, if an anti-monopoly law actually results in greater anticompetitive economic concentration rather than promoting greater competition, it ought to be modified to serve its intended purpose better. In general, when law is meant to directly affect the functioning of the economy there ought to be a high degree of correlation between the language game of law and that of economics.

Posner goes farther, however, and advocates that all common law judicial lawmaking conform to an economic efficiency standard. Laws that are necessary for a free market to function can be regarded as facilitative whereas laws that are meant to make up for obstacles impacting the proper functioning of markets can be characterized as regulative. Where there are no transaction costs, market functioning can be viewed, from a law and economics standpoint, as fair and efficient. In developed contemporary markets though there are large numbers of transaction costs primarily due to the asymmetrical availability and cost of information. For example, it would make a difference for a person looking for a drug to relieve headaches in a pharmacy to know whether such a drug can give rise to serious side effects. Because

148 LAW REDUX

the drug manufacturer possesses such information and the would-be drug purchaser does not and faces difficulty or prohibitive costs in obtaining it, the economic efficiency of the market involved requires imposing a legal obligation on the drug manufacturer to provide the relevant side effect information on the drug's label.

Posner has asserted that the judge-made common law of torts is efficient (Landes & Posner 1987). More generally, Posner insists that:

> [m]any of the law's doctrines, procedures, and institutions can usefully be viewed as responses to the problem of transaction costs, being designed either to reduce those costs, or, if they are incorrigibly prohibitive, to bring about the allocation of resources that would exist if they were zero. The law tries to make the market work and, failing that, tries to mimic the market. (Posner 1995: 416)

Accordingly, where there are no transaction costs, the law would be ultimately indifferent. This was the case in the earlier example involving the cost of insurance in a contract for goods where buyer and seller can adjust their contract terms regardless of where the law places the obligation to insure the goods while in transit. On the other hand, where there are transaction costs, such as in the example involving a headache medicine, the manufacturer should be obliged to provide the side effects information either by an enacted law or a common-law judicial decision. Finally, as an example of a prohibitive transaction cost issue, such as the long-term side effect risks of a vaccine needed to mitigate a deadly pandemic, the government could solve the problem by assuming responsibility for all future long-term damages. In that situation, the vaccine manufacturer and the vaccine user could contract as if there were no (prohibitive) transaction costs.

Even leaving aside the wealth maximization criterion of justice advanced by Posner, the efficiency standard he advocates is itself problematic as illustrated by the following example. Suppose a factory generates water pollution that compromises the water supply to residences within a certain distance of the factory. Suppose further that this problem could be solved through installation of water filtration devices. The factory could install the necessary devices within its premises for a total cost of $200,000 whereas each of the ten homeowners affected could purchase devices that would secure their water supply for $15,000 each. Under these facts, the law should impose the burden of protection against water pollution on the individual homeowners rather than on the factory. Is that, however, fair? What if the factory has an annual $1,000,000 in profits and the average homeowner's annual salary is $60,000? Under these circumstances, it clearly seems, under a wide range of criteria of justice, that the efficient legal ruling would be distributively unjust.

Treating somewhat arbitrarily this last example as one that only concerns economic justice in the realm of material redistribution, it becomes apparent that Posner's efficiency standard is even more problematic in non-market contexts. Let us illustrate this by reference to criminal law. Whereas instrumental reason may well play a decisive vote in relation to economic crimes, it is unlikely to do anything comparable in other crimes, such as those of passion. Thus, a producer of canned food may be deterred from mislabeling ingredients to increase profits by 10 per cent if the law subjects him to fines that would result in a 25 per cent loss of profits and if that law were vigorously enforced and his chances of being caught high. On the other hand, it seems highly unlikely that one who is about to kill a spouse in an immense burst of jealousy upon learning about the latter's affair with the neighbor could be dissuaded depending on the severity of the punishment. Moreover, even if the economic analogy were not flawed, application of the economic paradigm to non-economic crimes would grossly reduce human interaction to fit within a bare-bones image of *homo economicus*. Take the case of the death penalty that Posner supports provided it leads to greater deterrence than life imprisonment (Posner 1987: 38). This approach completely leaves out the dignitarian and recognition-based justice issues raised by the death penalty. Indeed, one may reasonably regard the state executing any one of its citizens as an affront against the human dignity of the citizenry as a whole and as a distributively unacceptable cruel and disproportionate punishment. And consistent with this latter normative approach, Posner's deterrence argument would lose most, if not all, of its persuasive force.

Posner's specific account of the US Constitution as an "economic document" (*Id.*) is instructive from the standpoint of the justice essentials. As Posner himself reminds us, he is not the first to have done so and he refers to Beard's early twentieth-century account of the document produced by the US Founding Fathers in 1787. The latter, in Beard's view, were not primarily motivated by any particular political philosophy but by the economic aim to concentrate wealth in the hands of the agrarian and business elites to the detriment of all other classes within the country (Beard 1913). Although Beard's view of the U.S. Constitution in economic class struggle terms had long been controversial, Posner dismisses it summarily as discredited (Posner 1987: 4). Without delving into any controversy regarding Beard's historical account, if the latter were right, then the 1787 US Constitution could be condemned as patently unjust from a wide variety of perspectives. Indeed, a constitution aimed at entrenching wealth redistribution from the less well off to the best off would run diametrically counter to an acceptable minimum of justice for most liberals and for all social welfare egalitarians.

Posner himself tackles the US Constitution from the standpoint of economic efficiency and wealth maximization and finds its bundle of structural separations of power and fundamental rights as judicially elaborated through the years to amount to a mixed bag (Posner 1987). Absent amending the US Constitution, Posner is resigned to accept its entrenched features even though they may place obstacles to achieving wealth maximization (*Id.*: 21–2). At the same time, Posner is heartened by the breath of many constitutional rights, such as those to "due process" or "equal protection," as they afford judges broad latitude allowing for interpretations that are most congruent with wealth maximization (*Id.*: 30ff.).

150 LAW REDUX

If wealth maximization coincided with the justice essentials, then Posner's analysis of the US Constitution would serve a most important complementary dual purpose. One of these would be a critical one designed to unearth the aspects of a constitution that stand as obstacles to the achievement of the justice essentials and, in the case of Posner, wealth maximization. The second purpose, in turn, would be geared to perfectibility with a view to clearing the path to the justice essentials. In Posner's case, this second purpose can be accomplished in the case of the US Constitution through a combination of constitutional amendments and of judicial interpretations aimed at wealth maximization (*Id.*).

In sum, although Posner's prescription that law ought to be subsumed to economics must be rejected, his approach provides both positive and negative lessons that ought to be heeded in the pursuit of the justice essentials. The positive lesson is that, in part, both the law and the constitution must be harmonized with economics. This is clear, as already noted, in the case of anti-monopoly law, and proves obvious in certain constitutional areas, such as the scope of protection of private property or the delimitation of social welfare rights. The negative lessons, on the other hand, are manifold. First, the economy is either altogether irrelevant or at best peripheral with respect to certain legal and constitutional matters. To his credit, Posner recognized this in his later work where he noted that it does not make sense to rely on a wealth-maximizing standard in dealing with a constitutional right to abortion. And this, according to Posner, because there is no way to determine in any economically coherent way the "cost" of an abortion to the aborted fetus (Posner 1995: 22). Second, even if amenable to an economic approach in the broad sense, as in the case of the death penalty mentioned earlier, non-economic factors, such as dignitarian ones, may be pre-emptive or much weightier. Third, even where a law or the constitution addresses a straightforward economic issue, questions of recognition-based and representation-based distributive justice may have to be factored in thereby preempting any "pure" economic solution. Thus, if an economically efficient legal norm were to deprive many of the minimum required to live with dignity or if it were so unpopular that it risked democratic overturning, then economic goals would have to be balanced against dignitarian and democratic ones. Finally, fourth, Posner's economic ideology, as all others, is inevitably contestable. Even assuming, for the sake of argument, that the science of economics is objective, why acquiesce to wealth maximization as the prescriptive goal of all economics? As already emphasized, there are many strong arguments against subscribing to the ideology of wealth maximization. From our own perspective, however, a much bigger problem stems from the contestability of all economic ideologies. Does that imply that the quest for the justice essentials will be ultimately reduced to a contest between ideologies? This question certainly deserves further in-depth inquiry which will be deferred to Part III.

V Rereading Marx on Law as a Tool in the Arsenal of a Materialist Political Economy

The crucial differences between Marx and Posner are not merely ideological—Posner being an unabashed cheerleader of capitalism while Marx called for its overthrow in order to usher in communism—but also ontological and phenomenological. For Posner, good law promotes (or mimics) market efficiency and wealth maximization, but law itself remains distinct from economics. Indeed, Posner accepts as valid laws not only those on economically intractable subjects such as the constitutional treatment of abortion but also those that directly bear on the economy without being efficient, such as anticompetitive constitutional or statutory provisions. In contrast, for Marx, as mentioned earlier, the economy is the base and law only one of many superstructures linked to that base. This implies that all laws are, and should be understood as, being through and through instruments of the political economy, and more precisely of the particular mode of production that drives the political economy at a given time in history (Cain & Hunt 1979: 62–8). Feudal law is accordingly attuned to the feudal mode of production, and Western European law in Marx's own time fitted to the capitalist mode of production.[11]

What exactly is the relationship between base and superstructure, mode of production and law, or more generally for our purposes, Marx's conception of law and a present-day inquiry into the justice essentials is far from obvious. Therefore, all this calls for some further clarification and justification which is complicated by the fact that Marx and Engels did not develop any systematic theory of law and that their views on the subject are scattered throughout their voluminous work (*Id.*: xii). On the other hand, there is an abundant and diverse literature on Marxism and law developed both by scholars who labored within the bounds of Soviet communism and by others operating within the intellectual backdrop prevailing in Western democracies (Collins 1982). This literature has generated many controversies, such as the earlier mentioned one regarding whether or not Marx considered capitalism to be unjust, and ideological confrontations between twentieth-century scholars sympathetic to Marxism and others hostile to it to the point of caricaturing Marx as a mere misguided precursor of Soviet excesses (Cain & Hunt 1979: xiii). With this in mind, I will circumscribe the following discussion of Marx by limiting it to the following two concerns: first, the relevance of Marx to present-day major issues in political economy; and second, the articulation of plausible though contested interpretations of the key relationships that Marx envisages as tying laws to the political economy with a view to assessing how these might impact the quest to approximate the justice essentials.

---

[11] See Marx, *Capital I*, 672–93 as reproduced in Cain & Hunt 1979: 70–6.

152   LAW REDUX

Marx has been glorified—and one could add with a touch of irony quasi-deified—by those in power in authoritarian and totalitarian communist regimes while at the same time being vehemently vilified by numerous defenders of capitalism. His views have been at times grossly distorted as no fair reader could plausibly find support within his writings for the horrors or sordid excesses of the so-called Marxist agenda brutally imposed by Stalinism or Maoism. On the other hand, many of those who have summarily dismissed Marx during the Cold War have done so, for the most part, on the basis of his place and image as projected in repressive communist dictatorships without much evidence of familiarity with his writings as a political philosopher. Given that minds have much cooled on all sides in the years that followed the fall of the Berlin Wall in 1989, it now seems propitious to reread Marx (Derrida 1994) and to assess how his writings might shed light on the subjects of discussion within this chapter as well as on certain others addressed elsewhere in this book.

From the outset, a post-Soviet reader of Marx needs to stress a distinction that a pre-Soviet counterpart might well have glossed over. That distinction is the one that separates Marx the critical thinker from Marx the utopian or messianic speculator. In his critical capacity Marx has elaborated a sharp and stinging account of the political economy of capitalism (Marx, *Capital* 1970; 1974; 1972). In his utopian vein, in contrast, Marx imagined a classless, communitarian, thoroughly cooperative society beaming in solidarity in which both the state and the law would become superfluous. This was meant to happen after the successful culmination of the proletarian revolution that would have put an end to the all the evils and contradictions of capitalism (Marx/Bottomore 1984: 155–67). Even if the long and for the most part oppressive imprint left by communist regimes does not irrefutably belie Marx's utopian imaginary, it seems completely unproductive and arbitrary to pin any hope into some transformation of our current predicament into a classless (or some equivalent smoothing out of all friend/enemy dynamics), self-sufficient communitarian society marching in unison propelled by indestructible bonds of solidarity. That Marx's utopia strikes us as irrelevant with respect to forging any conceivably useful path to the future does not, however, deprive it of all theoretical value. Indeed, discarding the utopian value of a classless society or its equivalent does not foreclose ascribing to the latter a critical counterfactual role. In other words, focus on a counterfactually posited classless society may sharpen awareness of the tensions, conflicts, and contradictions within our own societies, thus allowing us to fine-tune our critique as well as to unearth paths toward partial amelioration while remaining aware of the impossibility of full resolution. In this sense, Marx's utopian classless society can be analogized to the ideal of a perfect free market in neoclassical economics. Because all economic markets are actually imperfect, the image of the perfect market can be used either to validate or to bolster a critique of an actually existing imperfect market. Validation would be based on the assertion that the relevant actual imperfect market is the closest possible approximation to the perfect ideal. Critique, on the other hand, would concentrate on the unbridgeable gap between current imperfect markets and the perfect ideal and suggest non-market supplements or replacements. Finally, returning to Marx, what emerges as most salient, for present purposes, is the principle of distributive justice that he believes would prevail in a classless, fully realized communist society, namely "from each according to his ability, to each according to his needs" (Marx "Critique of Gotha," *Selected Works* 2: 24).

Before inquiring into how this latter principle of justice may figure in the context of Marx's critique of capitalism, there are two key preliminary questions that must be briefly addressed. First, is Marx's critique of nineteenth-century industrial capitalism still relevant when attempting to cope with the justice concerns raised by twenty-first-century globalized capitalism? And second, Marx's political economy centers exclusively on the prevailing mode of production accordingly grounding his conception of law as a tributary to the economy. But is the mode of production nearly as prominent in contemporary political economy as it was in Marx's own time? And, if not, would that itself run counter to any plausible conception of law as being ultimately completely encompassed within the economy?

At first glance, there are glaring differences between the nineteenth-century industrial factory-centered capitalist economy in England that occupies a prominent place in Marx's analysis and the globalized capitalism in the twenty-first-century era of automation, the Internet, and increasing reliance on artificial intelligence. Also, whereas certain protections for factory workers, mainly involving limitations on the maximum hours of work, were adopted through various English Factory Acts in the nineteenth century (Marx *Capital I* [1979]: 253–4), in Marx's day there was nothing comparable to the constitutionally or statutorily guaranteed social welfare benefits that, as discussed in Chapter 2, are prevalent in present-day advanced capitalist economies. Accordingly, if we add Bismarck's late nineteenth-century social welfare legislation—which was deliberately undertaken to inoculate Germany from a turn to socialism—to Roosevelt's New Deal and to the firm implantation of the capitalist welfare state that has prevailed for more than a half century throughout Western democracies, then arguably the Marxist call for a proletarian revolution is but a mere relic harking back to a long gone cruel and inhuman era immortalized in Dickens' novels.

Upon further consideration, however, in spite of the just noted great differences, Marx remains relevant to our current predicament and that is because of his dialectical approach. Marx adapted Hegel's idealist dialectical approach—which will be discussed further in connection with the workings of comprehensive pluralism in Chapter 7—and adapted it for the materialist setting of his political economy. Consistent with the dynamic of this materialist dialectic, every mode of production sets in place a political economy that is historically bound to generate conflicts and contradictions that cannot eventually be contained within the prevailing institutional setting. Once the driving internal struggles reach a boiling point, there is no viable solution but to supersede the existing mode of production and its institutional architecture, often through a violent revolution, by replacing it with a new mode of production that settles the previously prevailing conflicts, but which in developing its own dialectical journey is bound to generate new contradictions of its own. Thus, the feudal mode of production—with its aristocracy having become parasitic and its serfs' attachment to the land an impediment to securing a sufficient urban labor force to meet the needs of a growing process of industrialization—became obsolete and counterproductive. That led to the advent of the capitalist mode of production, which solved the contradictions surrounding aristocratic privilege and the immobility of the serfs, but which then generated its own class war between the bourgeois capitalists and the proletariat.

In order to place contemporary global capitalism within the logic of Marx's dialectic, it is important to underscore the key distinction he draws between reform and revolution. Even in his own lifetime, Marx acknowledged that certain reforms, like those driven by the above-mentioned Factory Acts, did somewhat improve the material conditions of the proletariat. Moreover, his account of the conflict between the capitalists and the proletariat is not that of two monolithic blocs in a stand-off, but a much more complex and nuanced one that led to partial alliances, certain splits within classes, and certain incorporations rather than rejection of certain laws devised for a superseded mode of production. Thus, for example, regarding the reduction of the maximum hours of work, large factory owners sided with labor against small factory owners (Marx 1979: 87). That alliance was not out of altruism but because the reduced hours gave large owners a competitive advantage as they could hire more workers who would work in shifts whereas their smaller counterparts lacked the resources to do the same (*Id.*). Also, nineteenth-century English capitalism did not simply repeal all of that country's feudal property laws, but incorporated, adjusted, and reinterpreted some of them (*Id.*: 94–101) in spite of the on its face basic incompatibility between feudal estates property law and absolutely owned and freely alienable private property legal protection attuned to market capitalism. Given these particulars, a distinction must be drawn between the dialectic of the capitalist mode of production as it operates at the macro level as contrasted with its day-to-day fluctuations at the micro level. As Marx saw it, the reforms of his day did not alter the exploitation and alienation of the proletariat even if they led to some material amelioration. Accordingly, he concluded that only a revolution followed by a transitional period of proletarian dictatorship culminating in a classless society could bring about the emancipation of all that no capitalist economy or institutional setting could ever achieve.

The transition from industrial to welfare capitalism and from the latter to global capitalism has unmistakably brought enormous changes. It is nevertheless unclear from a Marxian dialectic standpoint whether the changes involved amount to a revolution or to a series of reforms. Arguably at least, for all the material improvements since Marx's times, the more recent vastly increasing wealth disparities and concentrations of power in the hands of the very few as well as the dislocations due to automation and the much-increased mobility of capital and labor, which were discussed in Part I, have fostered new forms of capitalist exploitation and alienation that may differ in content from those of the industrial era, but not in intensity. Further along these lines, are the contemporary calls for illiberal populism, for retreat from transnational engagement, and for economic protectionism homologous to the calls for a proletarian revolution in Marx's day? Leaving aside the utopian Marx and concentrating on the critical one, a good case can be made that Marx's dialectical appraisal of nineteenth-century capitalism still resonates today. Specifically, from our own perspective, the question is whether contemporary capitalism as circumscribed by a liberal pluralist democratic constitution comprising a generous array of social and economic rights can reduce exploitation and alienation fostered by global capitalism to the point of coming close to achieving the justice essentials. To be sure, contemporary capitalism can succeed without linkage to constitutional democracy as attested by various authoritarian economically successful instances such as those of Franco's Spain and of Xi's China. From the standpoint of recognition- and representation-based justice, however, the presence of constitutional democracy looms as an indispensable prerequisite to contemporary capitalism edging towards (peaceful) revolution as opposed to remaining confined to various reforms with too little impact on widespread perceptions of exploitation or alienation.

Turning to the second question posed earlier, Marx's conception of the economy as the base and of law as part of the superstructure was predicated on the paramount importance of the capitalism he knew as a mode of production. For both the industrial capitalist and the industrial worker the economy was virtually exclusively driven by the process of production. Much has changed, however, in the era of global capitalism. Automation has replaced human labor in many instances and with the further development of artificial intelligence may someday largely supersede human production by the many with human administration of production by the few. This would shift much of the power linked to capitalism from production to distribution. Also, the alienation of under-compensated, undervalued, and unfulfilled factory workers would give way to what we can imagine as a comparably unsettling alienation of the large masses of those who would no longer work while still remaining subject to the powers of the small group in charge of planning and administering wealth and economic output. Also, since Marx's times capitalist corporate ownership has been largely separated from corporate management and, according to some economists, in the twenty-first century, the ever-increasing inequality between the richest top 1 per cent and the rest is more driven by revenue on accumulated wealth than on production-related income (Piketty 2013: 16).

These differences would be transformative, making Marx's concentration on production much less relevant at present, if the economy were viewed as a separate self-standing system. But as Marx's dialectical critique was aimed at a political economy, the transformations of capitalism since the late nineteenth century do not necessarily render his account of class struggle currently irrelevant. Actually, as welfare capitalism and its narrowing of income gaps has given way to global capitalism and its exacerbation of income and wealth disparities, ironically the proportion of gaps between the haves and have nots in advanced capitalist societies is closer to what it was in Marx's days than to what it was in the mid-twentieth century (*Id.*). Moreover, in Marx's context, the concept of political economy implies that politics is inextricably linked to economics. In Marx's own case, it seems fair to conclude that at the deepest level the economy drove politics, thus setting the economy as the base. Global capitalism also has its own political economy that includes open transnational markets, free trade, and free flow of capital and labor across borders. Whether with the relative decline of the centrality of the process of production the current day political economy is somewhat more tilted to politics than it was in Marx's day is an open question beyond the scope of the present inquiry. Be that as it may, the political economy of global capitalism seems largely dictated by those who control its course—no matter how different they may be from the nineteenth-century English factory owner—while the march of global capitalism appears to foster increasing alienation and, if not exploitation, very significant concurrent economic and political disenfranchisement. This is attested by the previously alluded to loss of employment to cheaper labor abroad coupled with the "democratic deficit" typically associated with increasingly intrusive transnational economic policy-making. Accordingly, it is entirely plausible to regard the prevailing tightly knit political economy as persistently hovering over all the contemporary uses of law detailed in Part I, extending even to certain economically prompted abuses of law—such as, already mentioned, those by companies like Google that willingly pay hefty fines for deliberate law-breaking that opens the way to vast increases in profits.

In light of these observations, it is now possible to address how Marx's account of the relation between base and superstructure, and that between mode of production—together, in the present-day context, with administration and distribution—and law can best inform the question of justice both in relation to Marx and to the justice essentials. As many have pointed out, Marx's understanding of the relation between base and superstructure should not be understood in any simple unidimensional mechanical way but instead as an "expression" or "reflection" of the base (Cain & Hunt 1979: 48). Because within Marx's dialectic the political economy that functions as the base is full of conflicts and adjustments centering on the class struggle and on all efforts to salvage and further the capitalist project, the accompanying body of law should be understood as reflective and expressive of the conflictual and dynamic trajectory of the base as well as of its persistent overall objectives. Moreover, law within capitalism not only identifies and affirms its correlate mode of production but sometimes serves the latter through negation. Thus, the principal legal tool for the exploitation of labor by capital, according to Marx, is the law of contract. Under that law, all individuals are free and equal which allows them to bargain for legally binding mutually beneficial agreements. Although formally free and equal, the factory owner and those seeking employment in the factory do not share any material equality in bargaining power, and their eventual contract, whatever its terms in nineteenth-century England, will actually result in the worker having to furnish some unpaid labor power which will yield a surplus value for the employer.[12] Superficially, the law in question may seem to contradict the reality that unfolds at the level of the base. But the very purpose of the law is at once to facilitate and to negate, by concealing through formally neutral legal terms, the exploitation of the worker by the capitalist.

In the latter example, contract law performs an ideological function, misleadingly highlighting freedom and equality, as well as a purely legal one. And both of these functions are integrated as part of the superstructure that sustains the base. More generally, law fuels the political economy by helping it navigate through the conflicts and adjustments, and thrusts it toward the objectives of the capitalist mode of production. Accordingly, though in this perspective law figures as a language game of its own, its ultimate meaning, logic, and validation can only be properly understood as expressions and reflections of the corresponding mode of production. Finally, in this latter respect, the law of global capitalism does not appear to differ in kind from its industrial capitalism counterpart. If anything, the global capitalist has many more legal tools than his industrial counterpart to further his politico-economic objectives. Indeed, the nineteenth-century capitalist operated virtually exclusively within the unified legal system of a single nation-state. Today's global capitalist, in contrast, can often chose among a plurality of nation-state legal regimes, layered and segmented transnational ones, and in many cases, as discussed in Chapter 1, on private legal regimes of her own making which she can entrust to the supervision of like-minded private arbitrators.

As mentioned at the beginning of this section, there is a scholarly dispute concerning whether or not Marx considered capitalism to be unjust.[13] Both sides in this dispute cite to statements by Marx that favor their own respective position. For those who claim that Marx did not consider capitalism unjust, the following passage is key:

> [The] content [of economic transactions] is just whenever it corresponds, is appropriate to the mode of production. It is unjust whenever it contradicts that mode. Slavery on the basis of capitalism is unjust; likewise fraud in the quality of commodities. (Marx, *Capital III* [1979]: 138.)

---

[12] See Marx, letter to Engels of August 24, 1867.
[13] Compare Tucker 1969 and Wood 1980 who argue Marx did not consider capitalism unjust to Husami 1980 who claims that Marx did condemn capitalism as unjust.

158   LAW REDUX

As against this, those who argue that Marx deemed capitalism unjust point to passages such as those noting "the concentration of capital and land in a few hands ... the misery of the proletariat ... the crying inequalities in the distribution of wealth" (Marx & Engels 1848 cited in Husami 1980: 43) or "the capitalist gets rich ... as he squeezes out the labor power of others, and enforces on the laborer abstinence from all life's enjoyments" (Marx *Capital I* cited in *Id.*). One way to try to reconcile these two very different kinds of statements is by linking the first of them to capitalism as a mode of production taken as a whole and the other two to the class struggle within capitalism. Be that as it may, whether consistent with Marx, capitalism is only unjust if more coercive than needed for its preservation or internalized as profoundly unjust by those who may eventually gather together to overthrow it, is largely immaterial for our own purposes. Indeed, in terms of this chapter's focus on how economics and politics impact on the law in general and the constitution in particular, Marx's subjugation of law to political economy in general, and to its capitalist iteration in particular, leaves the question of the justice essentials completely open. In other words, whether it is futile to fight for the justice essentials within capitalism as the emancipation of the majority under its sway depends on revolution, or whether contrary to Marx—who regards not only laws within capitalism but also constitutions as the handmaidens of the bourgeoisie (Marx 1979: 220–1)—reform within global capitalism might suffice, it is clear that his version of the capitalist mode of production would not satisfy any plausibly currently acceptable conception of distributive justice based on redistribution, recognition and representation. Finally, regardless of Marx's ultimate stance on capitalism and justice, his future-looking utopian projection requires examining it retrospectively as superseded by the principle of "from each according to her ability and to each according to her needs."

If we take this latter principle as a critical one rather than a utopian one, then Marx's tying law to the capitalist mode of production aimed at wealth maximization leads from our external perspective to the opposite conclusion to that advanced by Posner. If aiming at satisfying everyone's needs is just, then satisfying those of the capitalists at the expense of those of the much larger proletariat is unjust whether or not overall wealth is maximized. In sum, if law is guided by economics or absorbed into it, then law's justice proves parasitic on that of the economy or, more precisely, justice according to law becomes reducible to justice according to the economy. But as the juxtaposition of Marx and Posner highlights, particular conceptions of economic justice loom as inherently contestable, thus making them poor candidates for purposes of harmonizing the universal, the singular, and the plural.

To conclude, one further look at Marx's utopian principle of justice recast as a critical counterfactual seems warranted. In Marx's utopia, two preconditions seem crucial and implicit. First, each person feels duty bound to contribute to the maximum of her ability because of the all-encompassing commitment to solidarity assumed to be prevalent in the classless post-capitalist society. And second, in such a society it is possible to satisfy every person's needs due to conditions of abundance that guarantee the means to providing for everyone's totality of needs. Although neither of these preconditions is satisfied in present-day actual societies, would setting Marx's utopian principle as a counterfactual critical and aspirational standard usefully contribute to piecing together the justice essentials? Without venturing any definitive answer at this point, two caveats are in order. First, complete solidarity is nonexistent in the age of global capitalism and its approximation both factually and normatively subject to contestation. Indeed, should an individual with the capacity to discover the cure to a widespread lethal disease be compelled to go to medical school when his dream is to become a gourmet chef? Second, there is currently no sufficient abundance to satisfy all the needs of all the people. Accordingly, any counterfactual ideal would lead to the need to prioritize certain needs over others and, under certain circumstances featuring competing needs, to favor the needs of certain persons over those of others. Needless to add that both prioritizing certain needs and favoring certain persons' needs seem inevitably contestable.

Our review of various theories that contemplate that politics and/or economics puncture or subsume law led to the realization that neither law itself nor the politics or economics of law yield criteria of justice that would secure an adequate foundation for the justice essentials. Concentration on the politics and economics of law yields a number of useful caveats and suggests some pointers in the quest toward the justice essentials. It is clear that the latter require some iteration of justice beyond law that transcends mere political or economic justice. In the next chapter, I will explore whether an entirely different approach, proceeding from the top down, from the universal to the singular, and from self-standing morals and justice, is better suited to set us on a viable course toward the justice essentials.

5

Kantian Universalism Reframed for a Post-Totalitarian Age

The Legacy of Rawls, Habermas, and Dworkin

I Introduction

In terms of the quest for the justice essentials, the two preceding chapters lead to two critical insights relating respectively to law itself and to the interface between politics, economics, and law. The first of these is that the systematicity of law yields but a bare minimum of justice that is by and large only procedural in kind coupled with an impulse toward law abidingness based above all on guilt, remorse, and hypnotic infatuation with a charismatic leader and exclusionary identification with fellow followers of the said leader against those who are cast as outsiders. The second insight, in turn, is that politics permeates or supersedes law, that in pluralist ideologically divided societies politics is far more likely to frustrate than to advance justice, and that economics, in contrast, bears directly on matters of material distributive justice but it does so in manifestly contestable and actually vividly contested ways. As outlined in Chapter 1, a legitimate law and a just constitution can be productively envisioned as simultaneously satisfying the two requirements of self-givenness and universalizability. If a law qualifies as self-given, it means that I would have imposed it on myself because I identify with it, regard it as beneficial, or as establishing a fair ratio between the likely benefits and burdens that I expect will result from its implementation. On the other hand, if a law is universalizable (whether worldwide or within the bounds of the relevant constitutional unit) this means that all others subject to it ought to consider it as self-given, either factually, because they will perceive it as benefitting them, or counterfactually, because it would amount to a logical or a performative contradiction for them not to consider the law in question beneficial and fair. Moreover, because citizens have individual as well as group-based interests and attachments, self-givenness and universalizability ought to combine so as to strike a fair balance between the universal, the singular. and the plural.

Law in itself, as well as politics and economics, as we have seen, clearly fail to meet, or obviously to advance, the requirements of self-givenness and universalizability, which suggests that it may be profitable to look elsewhere in the quest to find a solid grounding for the justice essentials. One seemingly highly promising

A Pluralist Theory of Constitutional Justice. Michel Rosenfeld, Oxford University Press. © Michel Rosenfeld 2022.
DOI: 10.1093/oso/9780198862680.003.0006

alternative is to look to Kant's moral theory and to its second half of the twentieth-century adaptations by Rawls and Habermas. The great strength of Kant's approach is that it severs questions of justice and of what is right or wrong from questions of the good. A major problem for those who tie justice to the good is that contemporary pluralist societies typically harbor several competing conceptions of the good. Thus, as discussed earlier, for Posner wealth maximization represents the good and laws that optimize its achievement ought to be deemed just. But to one who regards pursuit of wealth maximization as doing more harm than good, many of the laws that Posner would deem just would actually be unjust. Contrary to Posner's teleological or consequentialist theory, Kant's deontological moral theory opens up the way to finding criteria of justice that stand above or beside all of the contested conceptions of the good in circulation within the relevant polity. If Posner's wealth maximization objective, or for that matter Marx's insisting on from each according to her ability and to each according to her needs, were enshrined within a particular constitution, many of those affected would be likely to regard the inclusion at stake as a setback rather than as an advance in the quest for the justice essentials. On the other hand, if a Kantian formulation of justice and rights that stood on its own above all conflicts over the good were incorporated into the justice essentials, then the contents of the justice essentials could be authoritatively settled in part or whole for all concerned. With this in mind, let us briefly inquire into Kant's deontological theory of morals followed by an examination of its more contemporary adaptations by Rawls and Habermas. Finally, focus will bear on Dworkin's constitutional theory which, though not Kantian in nature, bears close affinity to Rawls' views on justice.

II Kant's Categorical Imperative and the Severing of Justice from the Good

Before exploring how the categorical imperative which figures as the lynchpin of Kant's moral philosophy might pave the way to justice in laws and in constitutions, it is necessary to refer back to references made to Kant in preceding chapters. This is called for to clarify the seeming paradox of appealing to Kant's conception of morals rather than to his views on law in order to assess how his philosophy may shed light on the justice essentials of constitutions. As will be recalled, in Chapter 3 Kelsen's positivist theory of law was characterized as Kantian in nature, but that was in reference to the systematicity of Kelsen's approach to law which substantially replicates the systematicity of Kant's approach to morals. In other words, for Kelsen, law is a self-enclosed comprehensive system (or language game) with its own logic as is morals predicated on the categorical imperative for Kant. As mentioned, Kelsen was critical of Kant's legal theory which he regarded as imbued with some natural law elements that he attributed to Kant being influenced by certain

162 KANTIAN UNIVERSALISM FOR POST-TOTALITARIAN AGE

dominant ideas which prevailed during the late eighteenth century.[1] Furthermore, in Chapter 4 reference was made to Kant's legal theory in comparison to that of CLS. What was remarkable in that respect is the low threshold that Kant sets for law's legitimacy. Indeed, Kant only objects to laws that set or validate unequal status-based privileges among human beings, such as those predicated on the hierarchical estates structure of feudal times[2]—or as a Marxist thinker might put it, for Kant, laws suited for the capitalist mode of production are legitimate, but not those attuned to the feudal mode of production. In short, from the standpoint of justice to Kelsen's bare minimum depending on consistency, Kant adds a requirement of formal equality that must extend to all individuals who can be considered legitimately bound by any given law.

There is a wide dichotomy between morals and law within Kant's philosophy as morals are cast as universal and strictly confined within the bounds of the categorical imperative whereas laws may be legitimate so long as they are pragmatic and within the weak constraints imposed by the just-mentioned formal equality requirement (Kant 1970: 118–19). This dichotomy, which can be explained in terms of the distinction in German philosophy between morals (*Moralitaat*) and ethics (*Sittlichkeit*), does not necessarily bear on any Kantian assessment of the justice essentials as the constitution may conceivably be constrained by moral norms that do not extend to cover ordinary laws that are nonetheless deemed legitimate and not contrary to the minimum of justice imposed by the constitution. As we shall see, this last observation seems to square fully with Rawls' derivation of "constitutional essentials" from his principles of justice.

"Morals," for Kant, and later for Hegel, encompass universally valid rights, duties, and norms of justice that apply to all persons at all times and that transcend all conceptions of the good. "Ethics," in contrast, refers, under this approach, to the mores, the prudential maxims, and normative standards of a historically grounded community with its own (overall) conception of the good.[3] Accordingly, ethics understood in this sense represents the normative convictions as opposed to the identitarian affiliations associated with every particular *ethnos*. Furthermore, for Kant morals rest on the postulation of the equal autonomy of all individuals and on the ability of each of them to rely on the rule of reason. This leads, according to Kant, to self-imposed morals derived from the categorical imperative which prescribes that all human beings should treat one another exclusively as ends in themselves and not as means (Kant 1969: 53–4).

---

[1] See CP3.9–CP3.10.
[2] See pp. 141–42.
[3] These definitions of "morals" and "ethics" run somewhat counter to the understanding of these terms in Anglo-American philosophy. Nevertheless, the definitions in question are particularly useful for our purposes as they not only better account for the views of Kant and Hegel, but also for those of Rawls and Habermas.

The morals based on treating all fellow humans as ends in themselves are universal and they stand above all conceptions of the good that inform the varied iterations of ethics that circulate throughout the globe. Moreover, ethics and conceptions of the good do not only divide along national or constitutional boundaries but also in many instances within the same community of communities. Thus, for example, the United States with its "melting pot" vision carves out an ethic that differs from that of Canada which is committed to thriving as a "multicultural mosaic" (Kymlicka 1995: 14). At the same time within Canada, there are differences in ethics between the Quebeçois and their Anglo compatriots as attested by the former's recent prohibitions against certain wearing of the Muslim veil consistent with French notions of *laïcité*, but at odds with typical English speaking countries' greater openness to public manifestations of cultural and religious diversity.[4]

The universality of Kantian morals and the rights, duties, and principles of justice that derive from the prescription to treat persons as ends in themselves are conceived not only as transcending all conceptions of the good but also as remaining, in principle, neutral as between all of the latter. Because of this, no matter the actual ethics of a particular polity, or for that matter the number of diverse subnational ethics competing within it, the same moral rights, duties, and principles of justice would be equally valid and equally applicable throughout the entire globe. Thus, for instance, freedom of religion, in the sense of tolerating and respecting the religious commitments of every individual, comports with the duty to treat every person as an end in herself. It is therefore a moral duty to adhere to freedom of religion rights and to scrupulously follow the duty to accord them full respect. It is also easy to understand how this moral right can be turned into a constitutional one with legal force that would become part of the justice essentials. Indeed, universal respect of the right to freedom of religion is fully congruent with recognition-based distributive justice. Finally, this example illustrates how incorporation of a Kantian moral right into the justice essentials does not require its extension into ordinary law. As a matter of morals and of essentially just constitutional norms, all adherents to all religions must in principle be accorded equal rights.[5] But that may well lead to adopting different ordinary laws in diverse constitutional units without thereby contradicting the categorical imperative. For example, in a country comprising only Christians and Jews, a law that allows a choice between Saturday and Sunday as a paid weekly day of rest would be consistent with the constitution but not equally applicable to all religions practiced throughout the world. If, on the other hand, the country in question had a sizeable Muslim community, then the

---

[4] See Dan Bilefsky, "Quebec's ban on public religious symbols largely upheld," *NY Times*, April 20, 2021 (Quebec court upholds ban with exception applying to English language schools within the Province).

[5] This is true in principle, but may not be in fact, as for example one religion may trample on others as would be the case when a religion mandates proselytizing the young children of those who adhere to other religions.

164 KANTIAN UNIVERSALISM FOR POST-TOTALITARIAN AGE

law at stake would be unconstitutional as discriminatory and hence in contravention of the justice essentials for not including Friday on the same terms as Saturday and Sunday.

In spite of the logical possibility of converting some norms consistent with the categorical imperative into legal ones incorporated into the justice essentials of constitutions, there remains a wide gap between what Kant deems moral and what he is willing to accept as a legitimate law. Surprisingly, particularly in view of current sensibilities, for Kant himself the only law that appears to strictly conform with the categorical imperative is the imposition of the death penalty for murder. Indeed, murder amounts to the very elimination of another human being as an end in himself, and can only be rectified through ridding the world of the perpetrator who has by his act forfeited any claim to membership in the community of free and equal moral beings (Kant 1980: 102). Kant goes as far as to specify that even if civil society were to be dissolved and all its members about to scatter in all directions, the last murderer lingering in jail would first have to be executed (*Id.*). But what about all other laws that do little more than conform with formal equality among humans thus seeming unjust to many, but nonetheless remaining perfectly legitimate consistent with Kant's views?

One needs to improve one's grasp of the seeming dichotomy between the strict universality of Kant's morals and the wide plurality of laws that a Kantian would accept as satisfying justice according to law (even though they may raise reasonable grounds of disagreement as to whether they meet certain widely shared criteria of justice beyond law). It is useful, in this connection, to distinguish between the positive and the negative implications of Kant's categorical imperative. From a positive standpoint, further reflection reveals that Kant's categorical imperative renders plurality incompatible with morals and morals impossible. This is because the moral duty to treat others only as ends and not as means leaves no room for pursuit of actual interests or for intersubjective dealings among proponents of conflicting conceptions of the good. If, to be moral, a person must treat all others only as ends in themselves, then all market exchanges, employment contracts, professional services, and the like would be immoral because they require treating the other, at least in part, as means. It would therefore make no difference if an employment contract were fair or unfair, exploitative or generous, for both employer and employee would per force have to relate to one another in some significant way as means.

As Hegel emphasized, Kant's morals loom as ultimately purely formal and empty (Hegel 1952: paras. 135, 135A), and that is because they require total suppression of all singularity and all plurality. On the one hand, the individual must set aside all interests and attachments in order to deal only with the other according to the dictates of the categorical imperative. This is vividly illustrated by the oft-mentioned case of the unexceptionable Kantian duty never to lie which prevents an individual from falsely denying to a would-be assassin that her spouse and children are hiding in a concealed space within a few steps from where the murderous intruder has been questioning her. On the other hand, it becomes plain that one's mores, ethics, cultural, or religious beliefs or convictions regarding the good, either shared throughout society as a whole or animating one of the many groups active within the latter, have nothing to do with one's moral duties and must therefore be set aside to the extent that they may interfere with the fulfillment of moral obligations. In short, in order to safeguard its universality, Kantian morals must shred the individual's singularity and transform every person into a purely abstract ego with reasoning powers wholly detached from all interests or affects. At the same time, the plural as embodied in ethics and in identitarian manifestations is to be completely set aside and neutralized.

Even if a norm consistent with the categorical imperative is incorporated into a constitution, such as the freedom of religion right discussed earlier, its inevitable interpretation and enforcement are impossible without considering interests or without making some choices among competing conceptions of the good. Suppose, for example, that a pandemic is likely to result in massive casualties within a country unless 80 per cent of the population is given a readily available fully effective vaccine. Suppose further that 50 per cent of that country's population belongs to a religion that forbids all vaccinations and objects to an infra-constitutional law that requires all to be vaccinated except those who have valid health reasons for refusing. Finally, 20 per cent of those not belonging to the religion that prohibits vaccinations adhere to a religion that commands taking all the life-saving precautions that are humanly possible. It becomes obvious that no court could resolve the constitutional dispute at stake without considering the interests in health of those who are benefitted by the law as well as the competing conceptions of the good advanced respectively by the 50 per cent religion, to the effect that a transcendent God has exclusive authority over human life and death issues, and by the 20 per cent religion, to the effect that a transcendent God has commanded all humans to actively pursue all available life saving measures.

In contrast to the rather limiting positive implications of Kant's morals, the latter's negative implications emerge as more promising from the standpoint of the justice essentials. In essence, Kant's theory boils down to the revolutionary proposition that morals are both indispensable to ground the necessary unity of the universal and impossible in the real world. Moreover, as a consequence of this, it appears that the Kantian universal leaves no room for singularity or plurality. The negative implications of this conclusion, however, do paradoxically open a path towards justice and harmonization of the universal, the singular, and the plural. Explicitly, the negative implications or critical dimensions of Kant's theory amount to the propositions that there can be no perfect or purely transcendent unity that would sustain the universal above all else combined with the impossibility of legitimately deriving morals from any single contested conception of the good or any particular culturally grounded vision of ethics. But whereas these negative implications foreclose the legitimacy of any substantive theory of morals and justice, they open the door to procedural vindications of the latter which can be encompassed within the scope of deontological moral theory.

The procedural approach that meshes with the critical dimension of Kantian morals is that put forth by modern social contract theory—or more precisely by one of its two principal variants, namely pure social contract theory as opposed to its derivative counterpart (Rosenfeld 1985: 857). Pure social contract theory holds in essence that given fair bargaining conditions, just and legitimate norms and institutions are those that are the product of a freely entered into, mutually agreed upon pact among all those who will be subjected to the norms and institutions in question. This approach is meant to be purely procedural; once the would-be contractors are included and granted equal participation within the bargaining process, whatever results will automatically be deemed legitimate and just (self-given and universally valid for all affected). Also, as purely procedural this approach seems to have three important advantages over Kantian morals: it does not set the realm of unity above and beyond that of plurality; it does not require the individual social contractor to shed her interests or conception of the good as a precondition to participating in the bargaining process; and it presumably allows for fair substantive results which would permit (re)integrating morals within the realm of the possible. Finally, in contrast, derivative social contract theory, which incidentally counts Kant as a proponent, uses the bargaining procedure as a heuristic device, and at bottom legitimates the outcome by reference to an independent substantive normative criterion (*Id.*). Indeed, as already noted, for Kant morals depend on abstract reason and the legitimacy of law on abandoning hierarchical status for formal equality. Accordingly, for Kant the outcome of the social contract is predetermined by the strictures of abstract reason and commitment to formal equality (Gough 1957: 18), thus making reference to the process largely rhetorical. The outcome in question is thus only "self-given" in the sense that for Kant no-one can without contradiction reject what reason commands, or without a basic commitment to elementary morals reject the foremost moral principle that all persons are inherently free and equal.

Because his conception of the social contract is ultimately derivative, Kant fails to reconcile universalism with singularity and pluralism. By blending contractarian proceduralism and Kantian universalism, Rawls has attempted to overcome Kant's limitations and to adapt the deontological approach to justice and rights for use under contemporary conditions. Similarly, Habermas has sought to build upon Kant's universalism by combining it with a consensus-based theory of legitimation that is rooted in contractarian proceduralism, but that does in the end exceed the latter's bounds all the while purporting to remain purely procedural in nature (Rosenfeld: 1998a: 33).

III Rawls' Hypothetical Social Contract, His Two Principles of Justice, and the "Constitutional Essentials"

Rawls considers his theory of justice as being purely procedural in nature and that suggests that his hypothetical social contract behind "a veil of ignorance" (Rawls 1971:11) might qualify as an instance of pure social contract theory. Unlike Rawls, the two preceding pure social contract theorists, Hobbes and Rousseau (Rosenfeld 1985: 857), do not rely on a "hypothetical" agreement. To understand why this difference matters, it is useful to draw on the analogy between the pure social contract conception and a typical legal contract within the freedom of contract paradigm (*Id.*). In the case of the latter, provided the requisite background conditions (which determine whether the parties involved are competent to enter into contracts) are met, it is the fact of agreement that renders the contract valid regardless of the content of the actual contractual provisions involved (provided they are not unlawful). Thus, two competent contractors in the absence of any fraud may agree to a valid contract of sale at a price that falls short or that exceeds the market value of the object of exchange. Because of the actual agreement between the contractors, any deviation from market value is irrelevant from the standpoint of the validity or binding nature of the contract. But clearly, in this context, the validity in question could not be extended to any hypothetical contract. Does that doom Rawls' hypothetical social contract from ever qualifying as purely procedural?

Although Hobbes and Rousseau do not conceive their respective social contracts as being hypothetical, these are of course not factual in nature but instead counterfactual. Nevertheless, in Hobbes' and Rousseau's cases, the counterfactual pretty much imitates the factual (as each of these philosophers depicts it), which justifies considering them pure social contract theorists. Indeed, for Hobbes, for example, the question is whether actual human beings in constant fear for their lives would agree to join together to organize a civil society in which their lives would become secure. Given the stark Hobbesian choice, one would have to be highly irrational to prefer constant violence and insecurity to an orderly and secure existence. In contrast, for Locke, who like Kant is a proponent of derivative social contract theory (*Id.*), what is paramount are innate individual natural rights that transcend all social organization, and in this context only a social contract that would promote or improve the securing of such rights would be acceptable. Finally, the difference between counterfactual and Rawlsian hypothetical is that the former purports to take people as they are whereas the latter somewhat re-engineers them to remove unproductive distortions. Thus, for example, if a society were pathologically racist, it may make sense to imagine that all its members could enter a period of racial amnesia so as to consider what their political interaction would be like absent racism. With this in mind, let us now first turn to Rawls' theory of justice and then tackle the question of whether his hypothetical social contract might still be consistent with a purely procedural approach.

Rawls' hypothetical social contract incorporates Kantian universalism but does not exclude the realm of human interests. Each hypothetical contractor knows she has interests and a conception of the good, but the veil of ignorance shields her from knowing which interests and which conception of the good is hers. In addition, the veil deprives the hypothetical contractors of all information concerning their "class position or social status ... fortune in distribution of natural assets and abilities ... [and] special psychological propensities" (Rawls 1971:12). The purpose of these exclusions is to correct for disparities in bargaining power that often arise in actual legal contracts and to overcome the moral arbitrariness of Hobbesian (pure) contractarianism based on each contractor seeking the most advantageous term to optimally further his own arbitrary will. In other words, the veil of ignorance is supposed to shift the concern of the contractors from pursuit of their own interests to searching for principles of justice that will best guarantee fair social cooperation among persons with competing interests and conceptions of the good. From our own perspective, therefore, Rawls' hypothetical contract is supposed to result in a unifying concept of justice that will allow for fair harmonization of the singular, the plural, and the universal—the latter for Rawls being framed by "justice as fairness."

In addition to these limitations, Rawls has his contractors adopting the "maximin" rule according to which alternative conceptions of justice available for adoption through the hypothetical contract are to be assessed from the standpoint of those who would end up worst off under each of the alternatives under consideration. The maximin rule would then compel the choice of the alternative wherein the worse off would fare better than would the worse off in any other available alternative (Rawls 1971: 152–3). Accordingly, Rawls attributes to the hypothetical contractors a key psychological propensity toward prudence and risk averseness. Operating within all their constraints, the Rawlsian contractors end up settling on his two principles of justice. The first of these, which is lexically prior to the second, is the "equal liberty" principle (Id.: 60). The second, the "difference principle," prescribes for its part that inequalities in wealth and social status are only justified if they improve the lot of the worse off and if they adhere to fair equality of opportunity regarding access to positions of wealth and power (Id.: 302).

Rawls' two principles of justice are meant to be universally valid just as Kant's categorical imperative, but unlike the latter they are supposed to provide normative guidance to the basic structure of society. Moreover, if a society's basic structure is just, then it provides, according to Rawls, the optimal setting for harmonious accommodation of individual interests and collectively shared conceptions of the good. In this hierarchic normative setting, which is topped by the two principles of justice, and which proceeds all the way down to actual political and societal institutions as well as to a system of everyday laws, the adoption of a constitution that conforms to the constitutional essentials occupies the next to the highest place in the hierarchy.

The constitution sets the basis for social cooperation within a society built on a just basic structure. To decide on a particular constitution, the Rawlsian hypothetical contractors must recover some of the information previously concealed from them by the veil of ignorance. Indeed, the contractors becoming constituents must have the means to determine the relevant constitutional unit and the history and mores that inform the latter. This is obvious from the flexibility afforded by the first of the two, already briefly mentioned, constitutional essentials that Rawls' principles of justice impose on the hypothetical contractors turned constituents. The features of the first essential pertain to "the general structure of government and the political process; the powers of the legislature, executive and the judiciary; [and] the scope of majority rule" (Rawls 2005: 227). Thus, for example, the particulars relating to structure of government and deployment of democracy differ in France, Germany, and the United States, which results in three distinct elaborations of the contents of the first constitutional essential. This, in turn, presupposes that the constituents must be fully appraised of the *ethnos*, history, mores, and political culture of the political unit for which they are supposed to design a constitution consistent with the first Rawlsian constitutional essential.

The second Rawlsian constitutional essential, as will be recalled, affords much less room for variation. In Rawls' last formulation, it requires "equal basic rights and liberties of citizenship ... the right to vote and participate in politics, liberty of conscience, freedom of thought and association, as well as the protections of the rule of law" (*Id.*). Although arguably this second essential does not require the constituents to have as much information as does the first one—for example, for all their differences regarding structure of government, all three mentioned countries protect freedom of speech—when all is said and done, it seems best to regard both essentials as requiring the constituents to have the same additional information not possessed by the contractors operating fully behind the veil. Indeed, whereas equality rights are essential, their formulation and interpretation may legitimately differ in a polity besieged by a history of racial discrimination as opposed to one torn by persecution of religious minorities.

What is most salient, for our purposes, about Rawls' transition from the principles of justice to the constitutional essentials is that the latter incorporate the equal liberties principle, but leave out the difference principle (*Id.*: 228–9). Rawls' reason for leaving the second principle out of the constitutional essentials and thus relegating it to the realm of ordinary politics and infra-constitutional law is essentially twofold. First, Rawls asserts that there is much more disagreement about what amounts to fair equality of opportunity and to securing the welfare of the worst off than about fundamental rights guaranteeing equal liberties. And second, given their complexity, matters of social and economic justice are less amenable to incorporation within a constitution (*Id.*: 229–30).

In terms of the previous analysis throughout this book, Rawls' conclusions lead to two important observations. First, Rawls, whose discussion of constitutional particulars is almost exclusively based on US constitutional jurisprudence (*Id.*: 334–71), implicitly embraces the proposition that second-generation rights are much less amenable to constitutional ordering than their first-generation counterparts. As detailed in Chapter 2, that proposition is highly contestable and many jurisdictions other than the United States have successfully managed to administer constitutionally enshrined second-generation rights. Moreover, the fundamental rights that Rawls enshrines in his second constitutional essential may generate widespread agreement in the abstract—all liberal constitutional democracies agree on liberty and equality in the most general terms—but they also lead to heated controversies which clearly emerge in their interpretation and application as exemplified by the intense disputes over the scope of freedom of religion rights discussed in Chapter 1. Furthermore, the second observation relates to the contrast between Rawls' transition from justice as fairness to the constitutional essentials and this book's inquiry into the link between the constitution and the justice essentials. Besides Rawls starting with justice and then going to the constitution and this book departing from the constitution and then seeking for a normatively compelling incorporation of a certain minimum of justice within it, there is one more crucial difference. Although for Rawls the first principle of justice is lexically prior to the second, in advanced societies with abundant economic wealth both principles loom as equally worthy of implementation. Accordingly, from our own perspective, both principles, if universally valid as Rawls claims, ought to be proportionately incorporated into the justice essentials of the constitution. Consequently, assuming agreement with Rawls on all other significant points, all that would be required is a manageable adjustment in order to factor in a significant array of second-generation rights. Accordingly, achievement of the essence of Rawls' second principle of justice could also be incorporated into the constitutional essentials. This leads, in turn, to the much more momentous question of whether Rawls' two principles of justice can be relied upon to determine the scope and substance of the justice essentials. As the discussion which follows will seek to explain, the answer to this last question is in the negative. With this in mind, further analysis of Rawls' proceduralism is required, followed by a careful review of the process that leads the hypothetical contractors to the adoption of Rawls' two principles of justice.

Rawls distinguishes pure procedural justice, that he maintains is achieved in the passage from the original position to the two principles of justice, from perfect and imperfect procedural justice (*Id.*: 72ff.). Perfect procedural justice occurs when there is consensus on the desired outcome and the procedure guarantees the latter. An example of that is provided by dividing a pie into equal-size slices with the intent that all who are served it obtain a same-size portion. Imperfect procedural justice results from a procedure that is more likely than not to lead to the desired outcome, but that cannot guarantee it. The most cited example of imperfect procedural justice is the criminal trial procedure designed to sort out the innocent accused from the guilty ones, and which inevitably results in some (hopefully small number of) erroneous results. And finally, pure procedural justice refers to situations where the following of the procedure determines the just result in situations in which there is no agreed upon *ex ante* desired outcome. The standard example is a lottery where the winner is drawn at random. No-one who enters a lottery is entitled to become the winner, but if the latter is not selected by a procedure that gives all entrants an equal opportunity to become the winner of the coveted prize, then the result of the lottery in question would end up being unjust.

The concept of pure procedural justice that Rawls claims for his contractarianism, and that, as will be discussed in the next section, Habermas enlists for his consensus-based normative theory, appears to be independent of all substance. Yet Habermas has characterized Rawls' theory as being ultimately substantive and Rawls has returned the favor by arguing the same about Habermas' proceduralism (*Id.*: 421). As Rawls specifies, proceduralism only makes sense in the context of certain substantive assumptions (*Id.*: 421–33). Thus, in all pure contractarian settings, it is essential to postulate that all would be contractors are inherently free and equal. The fact of agreement makes a legal contract valid where there is equality of bargaining power and no fraud among the parties. Similarly, a social contract justification (or, as we shall see shortly, a consensus-based one) only makes sense if it is assumed that all concerned are free and equal as morally endowed beings. Thus, modern social contract justifications are incompatible with substantive commitments to feudal hierarchies or to any prescriptions of a transcendent divine being that may contravene the free and equal postulate.

That all individuals are free and equal as moral beings is a substantive premise shared by all Enlightenment-grounded liberal constitutions and therefore proceduralism based on this single substantive premise would seem *prima facie* entitled to a presumption of validity. To be clear, many modern constitutions, such as the original 1787 US one that accommodated slavery, or the very many others that denied women equality and many other fundamental rights, fly in the face of the substantive premise in question as a practical matter. Nevertheless, the modern liberal constitutional ideal itself, as often pointed out throughout the preceding discussion, does conform to the relevant substantive premise. Accordingly, in evaluating Rawls' proceduralism, it is necessary to begin by taking a critical look at his substantive premises. Are they, in their context, as uncontestable as the premise relating to free and equal beings, or are they essentially contestable among those who share the ideal of liberal constitutional democracy?

I have criticized Rawls' contractarianism and characterized it as ultimately derivative rather than pure elsewhere (Rosenfeld 1991: 233–7; 1998: 226–8). I will therefore concentrate here on three problems that highlight how the derivation of Rawls' two principles of justice from the original position is only procedural in a heuristic sense and how it patently fails to maintain neutrality among all conceptions of the good that accept the premise that all human beings are free and equal. Also, because of this, Rawls' contractarianism emerges as ill suited to account properly for singularity and plurality.

The first problem is that the veil of ignorance hides so much from the social contractor that all she knows is that persons have interests and a conception of the good, but she has no idea of the particulars in her own case and in that of all her fellow contractors. From this standpoint, contractors have no handle on plurality and how it might affect them and thus there seems to be little difference between Rawls' contactors and Kant's purely abstract egos.

The second problem stems from an important difference in how Rawls and Kant arrive at unity and universality, and that difference creates serious additional problems for Rawls. Unlike Kant, who casts unity as transcendent and otherworldly, Rawls operates within the real world of intersubjective dealings but peels off so many layers of actual identities, differences, and commitments that his contractors are in the end all reduced into interchangeable purely abstract individual units. Most notably, Rawls' process of abstraction is not neutral, however, and it ends up favoring certain perspectives and certain conceptions of the good over others. Is the abstract ego that emerges at the end of the said process man or woman? Neither? Both? Even if one could imagine a completely sexless human being, how could that person account for, or factor in, the various gender-related issues prevalent throughout contemporary societies? Moreover, even if one concedes that Rawlsian contractarianism is not in itself gender biased, the hypothetical social contractor could not operate in a genderless way. He/she could imagine not knowing whether he/she is a man or a woman, but it seems inconceivable that gender-based issues could be handled neutrally from the standpoint of "a view from nowhere" (Nagel 1986). Similarly, in a polity torn by racial divisions, one can imagine a contractor without any specific skin pigmentation, but how would that person perceive the different historically deeply rooted racial conflicts that have besieged the United States, South Africa, or Brazil? In short, whereas Kant's categorical imperative, which provides a critical negative insight, only depends on reason and the conviction that all free and equal human beings should be morally treated exclusively as ends in themselves, Rawls' hypothetical contractors seem bound to inject unacknowledged interest-based and conception-of-the-good-based biases in the course of selecting what are supposed to be universally valid principles of justice.

Finally, the third problem concerns Rawls' adoption of the maximin principle for all his contractors to embrace in the course of adopting principles of justice. Not only is maximin far from neutral but it actually incorporates two key biases that go to the heart of Rawls' proceduralism. First, risk aversion is hardly universally shared and therefore some contractors might very plausibly prefer to assume a greater risk to aspire to a loftier best-off alternative rather than assuring the least painful worst-off possibility. Because of maximin, however, the less risk-averse perspectives would be excluded *ex ante*, thus nullifying the otherwise identical input of less risk-averse contractors. Second, maximin works in contexts in which quantification is relevant, but not in most others. Maximin is certainly geared to social and economic policy as the difference principle attests. But what about contractors who place recognition-based concerns above social and economic ones? For example, what if someone values religious or ethnic integrity above economic well-being? To be sure, the actual contractors would not know whether after removal of the veil of ignorance they will prize identitarian bonds above economic well-being, and the two may not be mutually contradictory, but it is nevertheless plausible to imagine that someone for whom identitarian concerns are paramount would select an alternative wherein she might be materially less well-off but spiritually or ideologically better fulfilled. Maximin, however, appears to distort, if not altogether to exclude, this latter alternative.

Given all this, Rawls' principles of justice squarely fail the pure proceduralist test as a wide range of his substantive incorporations, whether explicit like his maximin premise or implicit like the non-neutral factoring of inevitable attributes such as those pertaining to gender or race, are essentially contestable. Moreover, the very nature of his two principles of justice and of his constitutional essentials, with their emphasis on individual-regarding fundamental rights and on material redistribution-focused justice, tilt Rawls' theory toward binding the individual to the universal without leaving any distinct room for the collective or the plural.

In the end, although Rawls' pure proceduralist aims fall short, his theory does afford us several valuable insights. First, in line with Kant, Rawls highlights the importance and attractiveness of universal criteria of justice that transcend conflicts over the good and over interests. Second, as already emphasized, very notoriously from the standpoint of the present inquiry, Rawls interlinks justice and constitutional ordering and his theory provides one instance in which some of justice, namely his first principle, must be incorporated within the constitution, and some of it, what is required by his second principle, must be pursued in a relatively messier way in the day-to-day dealings that extend beyond the constitution. Finally, although procedurally wanting, substantively Rawls' two principles of justice appear to have much that is attractive in terms of the justice essentials of constitutions and particularly so since constitutionalization of second-generation rights turns out to be much less problematic than he thought it was. Before pursuing this substantive avenue any further through examination of Dworkin's constitutional jurisprudence, however, it is first necessary to turn to the other major pure proceduralist approach to legitimation elaborated by Habermas.

IV Habermas' Dialogical Proceduralism, the Dynamic between System and Lifeworld, and the Call for Constitutional Patriotism

Habermas correctly characterizes Kant's and Rawls' respective approaches as monological (Habermas 1990: 66, 195, 203–4) and proposes to replace them by one that is dialogical and that allows for full access to all interests without any filter or censorship (*Id.*: 122). Kant's and Rawls' approaches are monological because the abstract egos on which they rely all turn out to be identical and interchangeable, with the consequence that any single thoroughly abstract individual is fully equipped to discover universal morality and fair principles of justice. Habermas proposes to overcome monological and social contractarian shortcomings by moving from consent to consensus, by drawing on a nexus between Kant and Rousseau, and by doing away with any veil of ignorance in the dialogical process that is supposed to yield just laws. Like Rawls' hypothetical contractors, Habermas' interlocutors participate in an ideal (and therefore counterfactual) speech situation that is best suited to lead to a consensus. These interlocutors act as free and equal individuals who relate to one another as strangers seeking to live together in a common just and fair legal regime (Habermas 1996: 415–16). Unlike Rawls, however, Habermas allows for each participant in the idealized discourse procedure—in which all participants benefit from an equal opportunity to present their arguments, and all agree to be persuaded exclusively on the basis of the inherent persuasive force of the arguments before them—to bring all his or her interests to the table.

The ideal speech situation forms part of Habermas' discourse-based normative theory and it is to be distinguished from speech occurring in what he calls "strategic action," namely a situation in which the interlocutors "are interested solely in the success, i.e., consequences or outcomes of their actions, [and] they will try to reach their objectives by influencing their opponent's definition of the situation ... through [use of] weapons or goods, threats or enticements" (Habermas 1990: 133). In short, the ideal speech situation greatly resembles a meeting of scientists where rational persuasion is based on adherence to the proven strictures of the institutionalized language game of science, whereas strategic action mimics the ways of the archetypical unscrupulous salesman who uses cajoling, half-truths, and deceit to induce the consumer to purchase something he really does not need. More generally, Habermas' ideal speech situation is supposed to provide a purely procedural means to generate legitimate and valid norms and it sets a clear demarcation between the making of valid intersubjective norms and their use to one's own advantage.

As already referred to in Chapter 1, Habermas considers a law legitimate if it can be justified at once as self-given and as universalizable, thus combining Rousseau and Kant, and doing so through his discourse-based normative theory. Before further examining Habermas' proceduralism, however, two preliminary matters need to be briefly addressed. First, unlike Rawls, Habermas speaks for the most part of legitimacy and of validity rather than of justice. One possible explanation for this is that within Habermas' communicative action setting (Habermas 1984; 1987), it is the constant and ongoing dialogical process that provides legitimacy and validation and that the concept of justice may misleadingly suggest that validation is settled once and for all.[6] Indeed, whereas for Rawls the contract procedure no longer plays any active role after the two principles of justice are set and available for use, for Habermas the dialogical process itself must be invoked on each occasion in which a question of legitimacy or validity is raised. In other words, for Habermas, in the search for normative validation there is no recourse beyond the discursive procedure itself, whereas for Rawls, upon the conclusion of the hypothetical contract the two resulting principles of justice stand on their own.

The second matter concerns the difference between law-making and law use referred to earlier. In one sense, that difference is obvious. As a law-maker I would agree to punish murder severely and consider that warranted for all people at all times. On the other hand, under conditions of great oppression and stress, I may wish I could kill my tormentor with impunity. There is, however, another sense in which the difference in question arises and in which it seems somewhat more problematic. Clearly, democratically adopted infra-constitutional laws are quite often not universalizable and accordingly not in any obvious way "self-given" for those they disadvantage. For example, there are laws that favor landlords at the expense of tenants. Whereas I have tried in Chapter 1 to offer a plausible account for some laws to count as self-given even though they may not factually seem to be so, Habermas' dialogical proceduralism requires a more systematic examination of this seeming paradox.

One possible way to move beyond the paradox in question is by drawing a straight line between Rousseau and Kant. Rousseau's civic republicanism requires that each self-governing individual legislate in accordance with the dictates of the general will which binds the polity as a unified whole (Rousseau 1947). As both part of the governors and of the governed and understanding the general will as yielding the common good of the political unit as a whole, each individual is supposed to engage in law-making that is by definition "self-given." At the same time, in the process of law-making, legitimacy and validity are to be secured discursively by reaching a consensus among all affected, and that consensus would certify the universalizability of the law in question along Kantian lines.

This combination of Rousseauian republicanism and Kantian universalism may have value in a negative or critical sense, but that would be limited as it would require casting the vast majority of actual laws as strategic, partial, and, frequently, for most of those affected, not self-given. There is, however, a seemingly more

---

[6] I thank Rainer Forst for suggesting an understanding of Habermas' theory along these lines.

productive path towards overcoming the paradox under consideration while otherwise remaining within the confines of Habermasian proceduralism. That path consists in separating constitutional law-making from its everyday infra-constitutional counterpart. Thus, at the constitutional level only civic republican and universalizable consensus-based norms would be legitimate whereas at the infra-constitutional level, strategically oriented democratically enacted norms that do not contravene the constitution would be accepted as legitimate. Moreover, to the extent that Habermas' proceduralism prescribes a legal regime that reconciles legal and factual equality (Habermas 1996: 415–16), it appears to coincide with what figures as justice in other contexts. Accordingly, it seems at least *ex ante* plausible that Habermas' proceduralism may lead to outcomes largely congruent with those called for by the justice essentials of the constitution.

Turning now specifically to the relevant components of Habermas' discursive proceduralism, it must first be emphasized that only those views which are amenable to evaluation through the use of reason, and which thus qualify as "post-metaphysical" are admissible for discussion within the ideal speech situation. This leaves out all views based on religious dogma or revelation (Rosenfeld 1998: 136), except to the extent that they may be translatable into post-metaphysical language. An example of the latter is the biblical belief that man was created in the image of God, which Habermas has interpreted as corresponding to the secular belief in human dignity (Habermas 2006: 45). Whereas it bears returning to this exclusion of metaphysical views, for the moment suffice it to note that Habermas has consistently upheld the spirit of the Enlightenment against all postmodern, post-rational, and repoliticized religious attacks (Rosenfeld 2011: 271). Accordingly, the substantive base underlying Habermas' proceduralism is built upon belief in intersubjective communicative exchanges based on reason combined with commitment to respect for the equal liberty of all interlocutors willing to submit to the procedural strictures of the ideal speech situation. At least at first sight, these substantive commitments loom as consistent with the most basic presuppositions of liberal constitutional democracy and thus they leave the door open for a genuine purely procedural normative vindication of the latter. Furthermore, the ideal speech situation not only requires listening to one's interlocutors' interests, beliefs, and aspirations but also to consider them in all seriousness by calling for the complete reversibility of the perspectives embraced by the participants in communicative action (Habermas 1990: 122). In other words, Habermas' proceduralism requires that conflicts presented for discursive resolution be considered by all participants from each and every perspective involved as a prerequisite to reaching a legitimate consensus. And consistent with this, at least initially, Habermas' proceduralism appears well suited to handle the singular and the plural as well as the universal.

Within his normative discourse theory, Habermas distinguishes between morals and law and specifies that the former requires consensus while the latter may, in part, settle on compromise (Habermas 1996: 460). Consensus, as Habermas understands it, means agreement on the same grounds among all those involved as opposed to compromise in relation to which those who agree could each do so on different grounds (*Id.*: 459–60). Consensus requires that all which is being agreed to be universalizable, and that is imperative in the realm of morals that extends to all human beings at all times (*Id.*: 109). Legal regimes, on the other hand, are most often aimed at single polities. Accordingly, morality must generate consensus among proponents of all conceptions of the good whereas law must only do so among proponents of those conceptions of the good present within the relevant polity. Thus, for example, morality must seek consensus equally compatible with all the world's religions whereas a country without a single Buddhist or Muslim need not adopt legal norms that would garner the consensus of adherents to the latter religions. For present purposes, however, the distinction between consensus and compromise can be glossed over to the extent that from the perspective of a constitution committed to the justice essentials, all those affected must, for practical purposes, reach an agreement for the same reasons with all those with whom they join in the same constitutional project.

Habermas maintains that there have been three post-metaphysical paradigms of law that have purported to harmonize legal and factual equality. These are: the liberal-bourgeois paradigm which provides for equal formal rights, but in effect preserves factual inequality; the social welfare paradigm which is meant to remedy the factual inequality of the preceding paradigm, but in so doing reduces welfare recipients into passive clients dependent on state welfare bureaucrats; and, finally, the proceduralist paradigm, which is supposed to overcome the shortcomings of its two predecessors (*Id.*: 418–19). Indeed, under the proceduralist paradigm everyone subjected to a law is in essence both its author and someone who has willingly embraced it as being just, thus satisfying both self-givenness and universalizability.

From the standpoint of distributive justice, Habermas' liberal-bourgeois paradigm is wanting from the stance of material redistribution, and the social welfare paradigm from that of recognition and of representation. Moreover, the liberal-bourgeois paradigm favors the market economy whereas the social welfare paradigm depends on the extensive deployment of a state bureaucracy. In complex contemporary settings, both the economy and the bureaucracy function as self-regulating systems that Habermas contrasts with what he calls the "lifeworld." Thus, as already mentioned in the course of discussing Luhmann earlier, the economy subjects everything to monetarization and transforms all intersubjective dealings into market transactions. Similarly, in the bureaucratic state, problems of social organization are systematically transformed into issues of administrative coordination.

In Habermas' view, competing against these systems is a society's integration pursuant to its commonly shared lifeworld which provides "social integration based on mutual understanding, intersubjectively shared norms, and collective values" (Habermas 2001: 82). Furthermore, as Habermas specifies, the lifeworld is comprehensive, fully internalized, and it provides a confluence of common meaning to all those who happen to partake in it (*Id.*). In terms of our own set of distinctions, Habermas' concept of a society's lifeworld is made up of a combination of *ethnos* and *demos* which unifies the community of communities within the relevant constitutional unit.

As systems naturally expand and risk becoming all encompassing, Habermas asserts that they pose an ever-increasing threat of "colonizing" the lifeworld (Habermas 1992). Thus, in the context of post-Second World War Western Europe, the prevalent lifeworld prompted preserving a decent level of social welfare for everyone while limiting the spread of economic inequalities within the relevant populations. With globalization, however, transnational markets and migrations of capital and people have systematically eroded the guardrails erected consistent with the then-prevailing Western European lifeworld. This, in turn, requires adjusting the relevant lifeworld to cope with the new modalities of colonization spawned by the globalized market economy. In Habermas' estimation the systemic global economy can only be contained by expanding the lifeworld beyond the confines of the nation-state. Habermas considers that to be feasible through adaptation of constitutional democracy for purposes of transnational application through further use of the proceduralist paradigm of law (Habermas 2001: 73–4). This transnational dimension of the lifeworld layered upon the nationally grounded traditional counterparts is propelled, according to Habermas, by the spread of "constitutional patriotism" (Habermas 1996: 465–6, 499–500).

Building on a concept generated in West Germany (Sternberger 1979), Habermas has promoted the thesis that the traditional link between constitutional ordering and the nation-state can be transcended through patriotic embrace of the ideal of constitutionalism. And that this as he sees it, in turn, provides the foundations for a constitutional regime assuring democracy and protection of fundamental rights that is susceptible to successful implementation beyond the confines of particular nations. Habermas' conception of constitutional patriotism has been elaborated in the context of efforts to endow the EU with a constitution of its own. From our perspective, transnational EU-fitted constitutional patriotism requires a major thinning of the ethnocentric grounding of the new constitutional unit combined with a much greater focus on its democentric potential. Ethnocentrically, it would be what the various EU member-states share in common in terms of mores, culture, and tradition that would bind together the then contemplated new transnational constitutional unit. On the other hand, the latter was meant to strengthen EU wide democracy, adherence to the rule of law, and protection of fundamental rights. Furthermore, consistent with Habermas' conception of constitutional patriotism, it seems quite plausible that at least segmented truly global constitutional regimes could eventually emerge and endure. For example, climate change and existential threats to the environment are global issues that affect all of the earth's inhabitants. To deal with these daunting challenges, one can imagine a choice between rallying around a constitution-based approach or operating under a more traditional international relations approach. Assuming adoption of the first option, it would seem that the ethnocentric component would be pretty much restricted to a deeply shared sense of human frailty in the face of worsening environmental conditions and that the bulk of the constitutional approach would depend on unwavering commitment to building and maintaining a common worldwide *demos*—albeit one limited to distinct segments of governance through law.

For our purposes, a critical assessment of Habermas' theory is best divided into two separate inquiries: first, an appraisal of his proceduralism; and second, an accounting of his fierce commitment to Enlightenment values as reflected in his treatment of the relation between system and lifeworld as well as in his deployment of constitutional patriotism.

As I have extensively addressed the difficulties that confront Habermas' proceduralism elsewhere and concluded that it fails to meet the pure proceduralism requirements (Rosenfeld 1998: Ch. 5), I will only deal here with two major problems that confront it. First, Habermas' exclusion of metaphysical viewpoints, including all those connected to religious commitments to transcendent sources of truth or authority, presents a major problem in terms of the procedural viability of his ideal speech situation. This exclusion limits the input into the process, and it therefore skews its output. Moreover, the exclusion in question is even more pervasive given the requirement of reversibility of perspectives alluded to earlier. Thus, for example, a Catholic's commitment to a total prohibition of abortion on the grounds that God-willed personhood starts at conception cannot be given any consideration within the bounds of the ideal speech process. But presumably beyond that, the frustration and sadness a Catholic may experience due to exclusion of one of his most heartfelt religious beliefs and commitments from the arena chosen for legitimation of morals and laws is also to be excluded. And as a consequence, the holders of post-metaphysical views would not have to put themselves in the place of one who has Catholic beliefs or feelings before moving from consideration of various perspectives advanced by fellow interlocutors to articulating a consensus among the post-metaphysically committed participants. More generally, any view that a religious way of life is preferable to a secular one or that ethnocentric nationalism ought to prevail over reason-based overtures to outsiders would also be presumably banned from deliberation and empathic internalization within Habermas' discourse-proceduralist setting.

These latter exclusions are clearly distinguishable from the two earlier discussed substantive commitments that underly Habermas' normative discursive approach. Indeed, equal freedom and commitment to reason in the production of constitutions and laws is uncontestable from an Enlightenment-based liberal constitutional standpoint. But the same cannot be said for the view that religious life is more fulfilling than a secular one and that free and equal persons will find a much better communal life in an ethnically homogeneous constitutional unit. In other words, one can appeal to reason and argue that religious and ethnic commitment lead to a more satisfactory life and the presumable wholesale exclusion of such arguments from the relevant public discourse undoubtedly skews the final procedural outcome. To be clear, whereas equal freedom itself commands respect for a person's choice to live a religious life, the position that religion is better than its absence when it comes to construing valid moral and legal norms for society as a whole would be excluded from consideration in a Habermasian ideal speech situation.

The second major problem is that it is hard to see how consensus and thus universalizability would result from the ideal speech situation, except as a matter of pure contingency. And this even if only post-metaphysical positions are allowed into the discursive arena. Again, equal freedom and reason as the uncontestable substantive premises of the Habermasian dialogical process figure as per se universalizable within the relevant discursive setting. But beyond that, it is hard to imagine that a fair and principled discussion of secular disagreements at the constitution-making level would necessarily lead to a consensus, much less a universalizable one. Consider, for example, the following highly contested questions in numerous contemporary constitutional democracies. Should euthanasia and assisted suicide be constitutionalized? Should genetic engineering be permitted to correct for life-threatening conditions? Should hate speech be unexceptionally constitutionally prohibited? Should equality rights be inclusive or exclusive of any preferential treatment of women or racial minorities? All these constitutional questions are highly contested in various contemporary constitutional democracies and there are significant secular arguments for all sides in the corresponding debates. Accordingly, it is difficult to imagine even in the rarified atmosphere of the ideal speech situation how discussion would inevitably, or even more often than not, lead to agreement on the same grounds by all those involved.

In the end, Habermas' proposed pure proceduralism fails because it is not neutral among all views, perspectives, and conceptions of the good that could be openly discussed consistent with equal freedom and commitment to appeals to reason. This proceduralism also falls short because there seems to be no more than a purely contingent link between the procedural means employed and the sought Kantian ends that Habermas envisions. The limitation to post-metaphysical views makes Habermas' proceduralism deficient as insufficiently pluralistic and by extension it is also lacking from the standpoint of singularity to the extent that the identity and self-realization of many individuals is deeply intertwined with communally shared metaphysical perspectives. Finally, due to its inevitable frequent veering into pure contingency, Habermas' proceduralism seems seriously lacking in securing legitimacy, validity, or justice understood in terms of congruence between factual and legal equality.

Taken separately from his proceduralism, Habermas' most relevant substantive commitments and prescriptions requiring further consideration in the present context include: his unrelenting adherence to Enlightenment values; his aspiration to establish normative validation based on the combined criteria of self-givenness and universalizability; his recourse to the lifeworld to constrain the potentially all encroaching economic and bureaucratic systems; and his adaptation of the concept of constitutional patriotism to provide a solid foundation for transnational constitutionalism. As we shall see, Habermas' substantive positions, while clearly subject to various criticisms, ultimately provide many positive and negative insights that seem bound to prove valuable in the quest for the justice essentials.

Habermas has been a formidable unbending defender of modernism and the project of the Enlightenment against all odds and all foes (Habermas 2001: 130–56). Habermas has also been particularly critical of Derrida and postmodernism, charging the latter's deconstructive approach, which will be further explored in Chapter 6, with reverting to a pre-Enlightenment mystique detrimental to the project of modernity (Habermas 1990: 181–4). Although Habermas and Derrida eventually reconciled and joined hands against global terror in the aftermath of the 9/11 attacks (Borradori 2003: xi), the unshakable persistence of Habermas' commitment to the Enlightenment is perhaps best illustrated by his interpretation of the murder-suicide of the 9/11 perpetrators in the name of Islamic fundamentalism as falling within the bounds of modernism (*Id.*: 18). In the broadest terms, Habermas considers the 9/11 attackers as, in the last analysis, engaging in "distorted communication" about the economic miseries that Western-driven economic globalization has wrought on economically disadvantaged Muslim countries (*Id.*: 32–3, 36). Consistent with this interpretation, the terrorists' appeal to religious fundamentalism results from the frustration stemming from the impotence of Muslim societies subjugated by Western materialism and permissive culture in the face of the relentless spread of globalization across their borders. Both the globalizing profiteer and the jihadist Muslim fundamentalist engage in strategic or distorted communication and if all involved shifted to good-faith Habermasian discursive interaction, they would presumably agree on taming and mitigating the excesses of globalism, thus vindicating the spirit of the Enlightenment.

As I have argued at greater length elsewhere, Habermas' assessment of violent fundamentalist religion is unpersuasive (Rosenfeld 2011: 287–8). Suffice it for now to refer to certain Christian fundamentalists in the United States who are not economically disadvantaged, who are unqualified supporters of US capitalism but who believe that all abortion amounts to murder against defenseless unborn children and accordingly justify the killing of physicians who perform lawful abortions. These fundamentalist beliefs are certainly not "distorted" as they straightforwardly express a shared—albeit by a very small minority of Christians—interpretation of what figures as a transcendent religious truth which justifies as supposedly religiously prescribed certain homicides that clearly amount to murder under prevailing law. Moreover, if by Enlightenment-grounded reason we mean that which can be justified or rejected through use of reason, then not only religious fundamentalism should be regarded as contrary to the Enlightenment but also a large share of what is prescribed by mainstream religion, ardent nationalism, exclusionary ethnic identity, postmodern perspectives, and a large swatch of conceptions of the good circulating within most contemporary polities. For our purposes, therefore, Habermas' conception of Enlightenment-based normative constraints, just as, incidentally, Rawls' conception of "reasonable pluralism" (Rawls 1993: 64), presents a significant problem in relation to recognition-based and representation-based justice. Indeed, whereas from a redistribution-based justice standpoint Habermas' conception seems perfectly compatible, it is inadequate when it comes to consideration as contrasted with vindication of identitarian claims for inclusion within the constitutional bounds required by the justice essentials. Finally, from a representation-based perspective, both the equal-freedom-based and the reason-based requirements promoted by Habermas become somewhat problematic. Whereas within a constitution all individuals and recognized groups ought to be granted equal or proportionate democratic participatory rights, in the framing of constitutions there are inevitable questions of inclusion and exclusion which result in some having the representational rights of citizenship and others not. In some cases, questions of exclusion are obvious, such as the prohibition against a short-term visiting foreign tourist from voting in a country's parliamentary elections. But in other cases, representational questions may be highly contestable. Why should an employed tax-paying legal immigrant be prohibited from voting for parliament in her country of residence? In short, whereas both a dialogical approach and some adapted or modified Enlightenment framework loom as desirable, Habermas' theory falls short in several key respects. I will return to these questions in Part III and argue that a pluralist approach is better suited to provide satisfactory answers.

On achieving self-givenness and universalizability (at least on the scale of the relevant constitutional unit), Habermas does not deliver any ultimately determinative positive insights. His focus on this correlation provides, however, a useful negative referent. Focus on the relevant correlation can help in the determination of what fails on either or both accounts. In addition, relying on the substantive presuppositions underlying any legitimate liberal constitutional order, and on relevant uncontested contextual factors, one can advance, as already alluded to, plausible counterfactual arguments in favor of self-givenness and universalizability that may only be contradicted in violation of reason or logic or else through engaging in a performative contradiction.

Habermas' focus on the interplay between system and lifeworld and his admonition that action must be taken to prevent the former from colonizing the latter strongly resonate in the contemporary constitutional context. As observed by political scientists examining the widespread transition to liberal constitutionalism in the post-Soviet era, the latter requires an economy that stands somewhere between a pure state economy and a pure market one as well as a well-functioning state bureaucracy (Linz & Stepan 1996: 113). Also, as discussed in Chapter 2, constitutionally enshrined and judicially vindicated social welfare rights do limit the domain of both legislative majoritarianism and that of the market economy, thereby lending credence to the plausibility of lifeworld-based constraints. Habermas' assumption of a unified, society-wide, all-encompassing lifeworld does, however, raise two key questions. First, is such unity likely in ideologically and identity-based divided polities? And second, are commonly shared lifeworld bonds likely to spill into transnational and global spheres of interaction?

Habermas himself suggests a positive answer to these questions by casting the lifeworld as society wide and actually and potentially transnational. Moreover, whereas within the traditional Westphalian nation-state the lifeworld seems to trace the relevant society's ethics (as contrasted to morals in a Kantian and Hegelian sense) closely, in the era of globalization the ethics in question seem increasingly reliant on constitutional patriotism. As Habermas portrays it, constitutional patriotism emerges as a transnational and potentially universal ethics that for purposes of constitutional ordering transcends all other ethics, including those that unify nations as well as those that divide them. In Habermas' own words:

> A previous background consensus, constructed on the basis of homogeneity and understood as a catalyzing condition for democracy becomes superfluous to the extent that public, discursively structured processes of opinion-and-will-formation make a reasonable political understanding possible, even among strangers. (Habermas 2001: 73)

In other words, in view of the alternatives—and since Habermas wrote these words the threats of illiberal nationalism and populism seem to have grown exponentially—the only way to overcome the globalizing systemic threats, as well as the ever more divisive balkanizing counterthreats that the latter have given rise to, is through investing the liberal constitutional ideal with the kind of passion traditionally reserved for one's nation or one's most closely revered subnational communal affiliations.

As I have argued at greater length elsewhere, Habermas' linking of the emotions associated with the kind of patriotism that leads some to willingness to die in defense of their nation to the rather abstract ideas that justify commitment to prioritizing constitutional ordering is largely unpersuasive (Rosenfeld: 2010: 258–61). Based on that, my own answer to the two above questions is in the negative. Multinational, multi-cultural, and sharply ideologically divided polities may have a very thin common lifeworld struggling to remain viable above important subnational conflicts of ethics. Furthermore, it seems obvious that the conflicts in question are bound to be more intense at transnational than at national levels. This is confirmed by the current exacerbating tensions between illiberal members of the EU, such as Hungary and Poland, and their more liberal counterparts.[7] More broadly,

---

[7] See Monika Pronczuk, "Europe tightens purse strings to try to pressure Poland and Hungary," *NY Times*, October 8, 2021 ("For the past few years, Hungary and Poland have repeatedly gone up against the long-established rules and values of the European Union, even though they are members.").

Habermas seems to overemphasize the universal at an unwarranted expense of the singular and the plural.

That said, Habermas' arguments in favor of constitutional patriotism do provide helpful insights that are both negative and potentially positive. The negative lesson, in view of the various present-day assaults on liberal constitutional democracy, is that adherence to constitutional ordering and commitment to the justice essentials is crucial in the fight against the various current trajectories towards authoritarianism. From a positive standpoint, on the other hand, whereas constitutional patriotism itself may have limited utility, it can be productively refashioned into two separate concepts. As I have more extensively argued elsewhere, the first of these is human rights patriotism and the second, constitutional necessity (*Id.*: 261).[8] Indeed, although what the precise content of a legitimate human rights regime ought to be is a controverted matter, there is a convergence of passionate advocates, non-governmental organizations (NGOs), dedicated judges, and other committed defenders of human rights that operate at both national and transnational levels. This, in turn, results in a segmented, constitution-like—that is functionally constitutional though most often formally treaty-based—legal regime with an ethos of its own. Human rights patriotism thus cuts across other ethos and *ethnos*-based commitments and provides for networks of integration that can readily extend beyond traditional boundaries. Moreover, from the standpoint of segmented constitutional solidarity—which I find to be a more apt term than "patriotism" to describe the phenomenon at hand—the case of human rights is exemplary rather than unique. Climate change, refugees, world hunger, pandemics, and many other subjects can also bring together various actors who join in solidarity to create and manage a cross-boundary constitution-like regime to make up for what seem to be insurmountable lacunae within traditional legal regimes.

The second positive lesson to be drawn from Habermas' conception of constitutional patriotism derives from the logic that underlies the latter rather than from the solidarity it is supposed to foster. Constitution-like ordering within any large and complex legal setting has become so pervasive as to suggest that it is now a necessity. The ordering in question relates to structuring with a view to generating a viable organizational hierarchy and unity for large units whether public or private. Constitutional necessity thus confronts a worldwide organization such as the World Trade Organization (WTO) as well as any complex multinational corporation or NGO. Furthermore, if layering and segmenting, already discussed in Chapter 1, are taken into proper account, then the pervasiveness of the necessity to institute constitutional logic and structuring should become even more apparent.

---

[8] The following discussion briefly draws on the more comprehensive one provided in Rosenfeld 2010: 261–9.

A prime example of this is provided by the failed attempt to adopt an already crafted treaty-constitution for the EU in 2005 combined with the ongoing decisions by the constitutional courts of EU member-states to the effect that national constitutions trump contradicting EU-wide legal norms, thus seemingly negating a full functioning constitution-like hierarchy and unity within the EU as a whole. Viewed more closely and functionally rather than purely formally, however, as already noted, the EU has pretty much adopted the substance of the rejected treaty-constitution recast as one treaty among many while notably emerging purged of all references to a constitution. In addition, through the layering of EU law and of national constitutions, the two regimes have remained *de facto* compatible without actual significant national constitutional interference with the pervasiveness of EU law, except in the very recent case of illiberal member-states such as Poland (Dorsen 2022: 183–4).

Both the constitutional solidarity and the constitutional necessity that bear some affinity to Habermas' concept of constitutional patriotism raise questions of justice. In the case of solidarity and of its particular ethos, its layered or segmented deployment calls for assessment in relation to the ethos, *ethnos* and *demos* of those whom it significantly impacts. In the case of necessity, on the other hand, the impact is structural rather than substantive, but as already emphasized, constitutional structuring—even if limited by layering or segmentation—does substantially affect both *ethnos* and *demos* and thus raises questions of justice of its own. In short, Habermas' distinction between system and lifeworld and the lessons we can derive from his commitment to constitutional patriotism can be usefully factored into the quest for the justice essentials and will be accordingly further addressed in Part III.

V Dworkin's Substantive Political Philosophy and Liberal Egalitarian Constitutional Jurisprudence: A Path to the Justice Essentials?

Dworkin's constitutional jurisprudence touches upon a number of subjects that have been thus far addressed. First, Dworkin specifically rejects Rawls' contractarian proceduralism (Dworkin 1973) while espousing substantive positions that are very much in line with those of Rawls (Rawls 2005: 211, n. 42). Second, as a jurist, Dworkin engages with, and distances himself from, many of the approaches to law that have been examined above, specifically positivism—though he focuses on Hart rather than Kelsen, a choice that is of no significant consequence from our own perspective—CLS, and law and economics. And third, Dworkin's theory of constitutional justice and fairness addresses the interrelation between constitution-making, constitutional interpretation, and the role of judges in confronting constitutional provisions that are in part or whole contrary to what he considers is required by constitutional justice. As we shall see, focus on

186 KANTIAN UNIVERSALISM FOR POST-TOTALITARIAN AGE

this latter contribution by Dworkin looms as particularly relevant regarding our examination of the quest for the justice essentials in different actual constitutional settings.

Dworkin's objections to Rawls' contractarian proceduralism are similar enough to those detailed above, thus requiring no further discussion here. What is remarkable, in view of Dworkin's rejection of proceduralism, is his adherence to a deontological approach that seems in its broadest outlines to fit within the Kantian tradition (Dworkin 2011: 14). In Dworkin's own words, a liberal society is:

> one where political decisions must be as far as possible independent of any particular conception of the good life, or of what gives value to life. Since the citizens of a society differ in their conception, the government does not treat them as equals if it prefers one conception to another .... (Dworkin 1978: 127)

Moreover, although Dworkin does not explicitly adhere to Rawls' two principles of justice, he nonetheless adopts positions both in his writings on legal theory and in those on constitutional jurisprudence that place him squarely within the liberal egalitarian camp. Specifically, Dworkin embraces a moral and political philosophy that is grounded in the proposition that all persons are equals entitled to be treated with equal concern and equal respect (Dworkin 1978: 180–3). This leads him to insist on "boundaries around acceptable theories of distributive justice" (Dworkin 2011: 2) and to rule out both a pure free-market economy and a redistribution that would aim at equal wealth for all as falling clearly outside the relevant boundaries (*Id.*: 2–3).

Dworkin's jurisprudence is of particular interest in the context of the present chapter in as much as he does with respect to law-making and legal interpretation something analogous to what Rawls has proposed in the realms of moral and political philosophy. They both proceed from what they posit as the universal and work their way to the singular. Rawls, as we have seen, does so through what he presents as contractarian proceduralism but, as I have argued, is better understood as essentially substantive. Dworkin, in contrast, starts from an explicitly substantive position and strictly adheres to it, insisting that he can draw a straight line from his politically and morally premised jurisprudence to the single right answer for every hard judicial case. (Dworkin 1978: Ch. 4; 2003: 660–2). Based on the preceding discussion, Rawls does not ultimately deal in a satisfactory manner with the singular and the plural. What is intriguing about Dworkin's jurisprudence, however, is that even if his moral and political theory raises similar problems as does Rawls', if Dworkin's claims for his jurisprudence hold, the latter might plausibly advance the quest for the justice essentials while leaving questions of justice extending beyond the requisite minimum open to vigorous contestation.

Aimed directly against positivism, CLS, law and economics, and all process-based theories, Dworkin's jurisprudence offers a theory of law's coherence, integrity, and legitimacy that is substantive in nature and that posits that law can be made meaningful, just, and determinate—down to the single right answer for every hard case—only to the extent that it is grounded in the right political philosophy and corresponding morality (Dworkin 1981: 469, 478). Through his criticism of Hart's positivism, Dworkin evokes the core traditional natural-law conviction that legitimate law is inextricably tied to morality (Dworkin 1978: 40–5). But whereas natural law relies on divine prescription or reason as the source of morally grounded legitimate law, Dworkin embraces a political philosophy firmly anchored in the Enlightenment. Accordingly, whereas traditional natural law theory purports to be truly universal, Dworkin's theory is admittedly tied to Enlightenment values, and thus can only count as universal among those who share an Enlightenment based *ethos*—which, as already observed, need not pose a problem for anyone committed to constitutionalism predicated on equal liberty. Also, at least for now, although Dworkin's liberal egalitarian political stance is unquestionably contestable among Enlightenment liberals as it rejects certain conceptions of justice consistent with equal liberty such as the libertarian one, for example, that does not necessarily foreclose a sufficient convergence between Dworkin's jurisprudence and the justice essentials.

Dworkin attacks the mere law approach of positivism and the reduction of law to politics of CLS along similar lines. They are both associated with an undesirable level of judicial discretion and indeterminacy which Dworkin considers to be erosive of justice and fairness. The positivist approach allows too much discretion to judges interpreting laws because in a large percentage of cases it is impossible to handle positive law mechanistically or syllogistically. For its part, CLS, as we have discussed, reduces legal adjudication to an instrument for political manipulation. As far as Dworkin is concerned, however, his integrated and principled approach can remedy the failings of positivism and of CLS while assuring a significant measure of justice and legitimacy. Dworkin builds his case for justice and determinacy through his use of the distinction between principle and policy. As he specifies, "arguments of principle are arguments intended to establish an individual right; arguments of policy are arguments intended to establish a collective goal" (*Id.*: 90). In the broadest terms, for Dworkin law is fundamentally distinct from politics in as much as law unfolds in the realm of principle whereas policy does in that of politics. Furthermore, based on that distinction one may generally conceive of law-making as the pursuit of some collective goal through an allocation of certain rights (and correlative duties), and of adjudication as a matter of principle in as much as it is focused on interpretation of laws in terms of the specific rights and correlative duties which they carve out for the parties before the court (and in common law jurisdictions through the force of precedent for similarly situated parties). In short, assuming a common set of political and moral values and a commonly shared set of objectives, policy-making will involve pursuing these as collective goals, whereas law-making, legal interpretation, and adjudication will consist in turning these into principles and in sorting out the particular individual rights (and duties) that these principles warrant.

Dworkinian principles are supposed to constrain legal rules and to guide collective aims embodied in policies pursued through laws. There is, however, one important question that Dworkin's distinction between principle and policy leaves unanswered: why is his liberal egalitarian political philosophy and moral outlook preferable to any competing one that is consistent with the equal liberty principle? Dworkin does not provide any full or satisfactory answer to this question, but he tellingly asserts that the US Constitution happens to enshrine fundamental liberal rights as legally binding constitutional rights (*Id.*: 184–205).

Leaving aside this last contestable assertion, particularly since the present inquiry is not confined to the US Constitution, the best way to evaluate the potential of Dworkin's jurisprudence is to assess it in light of two important distinctions: that between constitutional and ordinary law; and that between the factual and the counterfactual. Although as a general proposition all laws apportion rights and duties, it is but a mere formality to assert that they do so on the basis of principle, let alone that they in any way imply that the principles involved need be just or fair. As already noted, laws can systematically favor landlords over tenants or employers over employees in ways that any liberal egalitarian would find patently unjust. Moreover, effectively the claim that law relies on principle merely requires consistency and thus results in minimal constraints that mirror those imposed by positivism. If we move from ordinary to constitutional law, however, the role of principle becomes much more substantive and much more meaningful. Indeed, typical liberal constitutional rights to liberty, equality, privacy, or dignity embody principles grounded in substantive values and, to use Dworkin's own term, they "trump" (*Id.*: ix) all majoritarian collective policies embodied in ordinary laws. Accordingly, for our purposes, it suffices if Dworkin's one right answer thesis works at the level of constitutional law, or even more narrowly at that of constitutional rights as distinct from constitutional structure or process.

Even consistent with this narrowing to constitutional rights, it is obvious that certain actual constitutions do or can contain principle-based rights that Dworkin and most other contemporary constitutionalists would find highly unjust. As already mentioned, slavery was lawful in the United States prior to its constitutional abolition in 1865, and thus no judge could credibly or reasonably proclaim in 1800 that a slave owner in a slave-owning state did not have a constitutionally protected private property right in the possession of his slave. Similarly, prior to 1944 there was no credible way to interpret the various extant French constitutions as granting women the right to vote. By drawing on the distinction between the factual and the counterfactual, however, one can avoid situations in which the obvious single right answer is also manifestly morally reprehensible and unmistakably thoroughly unjust. Accordingly, a Dworkinian would turn to the counterfactual whenever the factual left no room for a morally or legally acceptable juridic outcome. Moreover, this recourse to the counterfactual can also prove promising from a critical or perfectionist standpoint. The slavery example is too obvious, but in many other instances it may be unclear that a constitution is inherently unjust before trying to work out its plausible interpretations and applications. And in yet other instances, it may become plain that though the constitution is not necessarily unjust, certain changes or certain interpretive shifts may enhance its potential for justice.

If confined to constitutional law, and adaptable as between the factual and the counterfactual, Dworkin's principled interpretive approach, which will be briefly described shortly, looms as distinctly preferable to those characteristic of positivists or of CLS proponents. Indeed, in contrast to Dworkin's single right answer in every case, these two theories only offer respectively a large measure of pure discretion or virtually unlimited room for manipulation. Law and economics, of which Dworkin is also critical, however, does pose a serious challenge to Dworkin's single right answer claim. And that is because, as discussed in Chapter 4, Posner's theory proposes the criterion of wealth maximization as the measure of optimal constitutional and ordinary law as well as the guiding principle of judicial interpretation. As we have pointed out, Posner's wealth-maximization criterion does not provide a single right answer in all cases, but it does so in the vast majority of them consistent with Posner's conception of economics. Therefore, even assuming the superiority of the single right answer, why would Dworkin's be preferable to Posner's? In short, does not the difference between Dworkin and Posner boil down to a clash among two contestable competing conceptions of the good, namely the liberal egalitarian one against the libertarian one?

Dworkin seeks to differentiate his theory from Posner's, through reliance on the distinction between principle and policy. But does this distinction sufficiently differentiate Dworkin's theory from Posner's to lend support to the conclusion that even if law and economics leads to a single answer in hard cases that answer is illegitimate because it is based on policy rather than principle? Or, in other words, because it completely subordinates individual rights to collective goals? The answer could be in the affirmative if Dworkin's theory of principle and of rights were strictly Kantian or deontological in nature. In that case, the equal concern and respect principle would preclude treating persons as means in their capacities as rights holders. The goal of wealth maximization pursued by law and economics, on the other hand, is teleological as it places its conception of the good above the right, and it arguably always treats the individual as a means (to the greatest possible collective wealth) rather than as an end in him or herself—though Posner himself insists that wealth maximization is itself a means towards optimization of opportunities for individual self-realization. Be that as it may, wealth maximization largely prioritizes policy over principle whereas a rigid categorical version of rights ought to systematically place principle above all policy.

Upon closer examination, Dworkin's argument for the superiority of his own single right answer theory is unpersuasive on two different yet related grounds.

The first, and more general of these, is that typical constitutional rights unlike Kantian moral rights cannot be implemented in a rigid immune-to-policy manner. Contemporary constitutional rights are limited either within the four corners of the constitution[9] or through judicial interpretation,[10] and these limits must be invoked either when conflicting rights are at stake or when vindication of a particular right would undermine a vitally important policy. Thus, for example, there is no readily available categorical answer to a conflict between a right of freedom of the press and an individual's privacy right, or to a clash between the former and a military policy that relies on strict secrecy to ensure the protection of the lives and safety of the citizenry. Constitutional courts resolve many cases according to the proportionality standard (Dorsen 2016: 238) that requires factoring policies in a large number of instances. In short, at the level of constitutional adjudication, Dworkinian principle and policy cannot be neatly disentangled from one another.

The second, more particular ground relates specifically to Dworkin, and arises as a consequence of inconsistencies between his more abstract theoretical pronouncements and the detailed workings of his constitutional jurisprudence. Dworkin does not adhere to a deontological conception of principle or right when focused on constitutional adjudication as he specifies that a "principle might have to yield to ... an urgent policy with which it competes on particular facts" (Dworkin 1978: 92). Accordingly, far from being lexically prior to goods, rights are to be given a weight which is measured by their "power to withstand ... competition" with policy goals (*Id.*). Dworkin insists that "it follows from the definition of a right that it cannot be outweighed by all social goals" (*Id.*).

What this amounts to is that, in Dworkin's view, a right is not simply reducible to a goal or policy so that it would automatically have to yield to a marginally weightier collective objective. This requirement is ultimately very weak. It means that a right can be overridden by important policy considerations, but not by trivial ones. In the absence of any specific quantitative standards, it would seem that consistent adherence to law-making and adjudication of legal disputes in the language of principle and in the form of rights would come a long way toward satisfying Dworkin's minimum requirements. Furthermore, to the extent that Posner promotes his wealth maximization standard within the framework of common law adjudication which inevitably results in an allocation of rights and duties, it is difficult to imagine why it would not be able to satisfy Dworkin's minimum requirements. To be sure, given their diverging conceptions of justice, Dworkin and Posner might well often disagree with respect to *which* policy objectives would be

---

[9] See, e.g., Article 5 of the German Basic Law which provides in Section 1 that "[e]very person shall have the right freely to express and disseminate his opinions in speech" and in Section 2 that this right "shall find its limits ...in provisions for the protection of young persons and in the right to personal honour."

[10] See, e.g., *Schenck v. United States*, 249 US 47 (1919) (speech that poses a "clear and present danger" is not constitutionally protected).

important enough to constrict or expand certain rights. For Posner, wealth maximization would in an overwhelming number of cases be a paramount policy objective whereas for Dworkin it would in most cases standing by itself have to yield to principle as embodied in rights.

In the end, Dworkin's single right answer is only apt to convince liberal egalitarians just as Posner's is likely to do the same for libertarians. Moreover, even in the best of circumstances and assuming ideological congruity, the single right answer for hard-cases thesis seems ultimately unpersuasive (Rosenfeld 2005). As Posner himself acknowledged, wealth maximization gives no guidance in abortion cases while Dworkin's conclusion that the state should stir clear of the abortion issue because it essentially boils down to a religious dispute—which would automatically protect the right to an abortion—is question begging.

In the last analysis, although Dworkin emphasizes substance as against Rawls' reliance on procedure, the two end up with a similar liberal egalitarian conception of justice that is contestable, and hence unfit to be posited as universal throughout the globe or in any political unit wherein it is actually contested. There is also an analogy between Habermas' procedural envisioning of dialogical consensuses and Dworkin's substantively grounded single right answer in hard cases: in both instances, actual conforming outcomes seem more likely to be due to contingency than to necessity. Dworkin, like Kant, Rawls, and Habermas, is right that something above the competing conceptions of the good that divide humanity, or the relevant polity, is needed to ground the requisite universal. But as even within the United States there is no consensus about the precise political and moral philosophy pedigree of the U.S. Constitution, let alone about any relevant criterion of justice, Dworkin's aspiration to universality fails even if confined within the boundaries of his own country.

In spite of these failures, Dworkin's theory provides useful insights in terms of the pursuit of the justice essentials. First, there is a need for a substantive normative grounding that is above all operative contested conceptions of the good in order to bind together any community of communities that is meant to cohere into a constitutional unit. Second, law-making, legal interpretation, and application can be better guided and aimed towards justice within a framework that tracks a cleavage analogous—though not literally equivalent—to that drawn by Dworkin in his dichotomy between principle and policy. From the standpoint of the justice essentials what ought to occupy the place of Dworkinian principle are the measures of redistribution, recognition, and representation necessary to assure the nature and scope of justice prescribed by the justice essentials. The measures in question may in part be akin to Dworkinian principles, but also in part directed towards objectives, but, unlike Dworkinian policies, endowed with what in his terms would amount to principle-like priority. Thus, for example, a principled right to individual and collective dignity would seem mandatory consistent with the basic requirements of recognition-based distributive justice. In contrast, redistribution-based justice through social welfare guarantees may often require, as discussed in Chapter 2, more in the way of constitutionally mandated legislation than in that of judicially secured individual right vindications. And third, whereas Dworkin's single right answer claim is unpersuasive, his insistence that law-making and legal interpretation must draw on moral and political philosophy is worthy of endorsement in the quest to conform the constitution to the justice essentials. Reliance on political and moral norms may only occasionally lead to a single right answer in hard cases, but such reliance can nonetheless provide essential guidance in deciding cases and in narrowing the range of plausible right answers. These insights drawn from Dworkin will be further developed in the course of the discussion in Part III. With this in mind, suffice it for now to conclude our consideration of Dworkin by briefly focusing on his theory of judicial interpretation which he maintains is best suited to advance the quest for constitutional justice and fairness.

Dworkin elaborates a theory of judicial interpretation from within a common law perspective where judges build upon precedents, and he approaches constitutional interpretation virtually exclusively by reference to the US Constitution. Consistent with the common law approach, Dworkin envisages the interpretive enterprise as a reconstructive one seeking to build a bridge between the past, the present, and the future through the use of factual and counterfactual means (Dworkin 1986). At the foundation of this interpretive journey is the moral equal care and equal respect principle and Dworkin goes as far as to specify that judges in a "wicked legal system" have a moral duty to either refuse adjudicating unjust laws or to resign (*Id.*: 219). Fortunately, from Dworkin's perspective, in the United States the Constitution imposes the "abstract egalitarian principle that people must be treated as equals" (*Id.*: 382) Moreover, Dworkin asserts that the U.S. Constitution enshrines the concepts of liberty and equality among others, but specifies that it does not impose any particular *conception* of these *concepts* (*Id.*). Accordingly, the judge must proceed in an interpretive task that Dworkin likens to that of literary interpretation in order to find the best "fit" between the constitutionally enshrined concept, relevant judicial precedents, and future expectations by choosing one among the many prevailing "conceptions" of that concept (*Id.*). As actual judges often fail to find the best fit—due to contextual constraints and frequent failures to integrate fully all relevant complex factors that must be addressed to reach the best fit—Dworkin relies on a counterfactual judge of his creation whom he names "Hercules" and who is meant to rise above all the limitations that afflict real life judges (*Id.*: 265). Dworkin does not endow Hercules with divine or prophetic attributes, but only with enhanced and expanded human capacities that clearly exceed those of any ordinary judge. Accordingly, the contrast between Hercules and an ordinary judge is somewhat analogous to that between a mathematical genius and an ordinary person with mediocre mathematical skills. Hercules is, therefore, capable of discovering the right answers and the unity and coherence within an existing legal system through a process of correction, rational completion, and perfection.

Hercules is supposed to arrive at the right answer for every hard case by reconstructing all the available relevant material into the best possible fit, relying on a combination between the dynamic between concept and conception, that between justice and fairness, and through scrupulous adherence to what Dworkin labels as the principle of integrity. In Dworkin's view:

> Justice ... is a matter of the right outcome of the political system: the right distribution of goods, opportunities and other resources. Fairness is a matter of the right structure for that system, the system that distributes influence over political decisions in the right way. (*Id.*: 404)

In other words, Dworkin aims at the best possible interpretation consistent with the optimal outcome from the standpoint of distributive justice within an institutional setting that facilitates reaching the sought after just outcome.

As Dworkin believes that justice and fairness in his sense of these terms do not always fully mesh (*Id.*: 177–8), he resorts to the concept of integrity to fill in the resulting lacunae. Translated into our own terminology, Dworkin draws attention to the fact that the prevailing institutional setting and the power relations it fosters often inhibit rather than facilitate the advancement of distributive justice in its three constitutionally relevant dimensions. Thus, for example, the current judicially and constitutionally approved, virtually unlimited amount of corporate money that can be spent on elections in the United States[11] is prone to adversely affect justice in all its three dimensions as it definitely skews representation, is likely to lead to inhibiting equitable redistribution, and quite possibly thwarts even-handed recognition. Dworkin maintains that the gap between justice and fairness can be filled through recourse to constitutional and ordinary law-making as well as to adjudication that conforms with the requirements imposed by the principle of integrity. Furthermore, Dworkin also appeals to integrity for guidance in the passage from concept to conception and in the judicial binding of the past to the present and to the future.

As elaborated by Dworkin the principle of integrity is a multifaceted one. It has a positive as well as a negative role, and a legislative as well as a judicial dimension (*Id.*: 176). In a nutshell, integrity requires consistent adherence to moral principle, and accordingly its negative role in counterfactual reconstruction is obvious: unprincipled, purely political—in the sense of advancing narrow partisan political interests—or deceitful handling of legislative or judicial responsibilities evince a lack of integrity and are *ipso facto* illegitimate. This negative role, moreover, is an important one in counterfactual reconstruction as critique, and seems consonant with Habermas' injunction against strategic action in dialogical settings. Also, in

---

[11] See *Citizens United v. Federal Election Commission*, 558 US 310 (2010).

the judicial context, negative integrity fits well within the distinction between judicial philosophy and ordinary politics that, as discussed earlier, is supposed to insulate judges from falling into the vicissitudes of ordinary everyday politics.

The positive role of integrity, however, is much more difficult to grasp. Dworkin asserts that:

> We have two principles of political integrity: a legislative principle, which asks lawmakers to try to make the total set of laws morally coherent, and an adjudicative principle, which instructs that the law be seen as coherent in that way, so far as possible. (*Id.*)

Let us assume that the legislative principle enunciated by Dworkin—particularly as confined to constitution-making in conformity with the justice essentials— is transparent enough to provide a workable positive criterion of integrity. But what about integrity as an adjudicative principle which requires interpreting law as morally coherent "so far as possible?" Is that coherent or determinate enough to endow integrity as a positive force with a sufficiently fixed or commonly accepted workable content? To narrow the inquiry, I will assume that we are dealing with a legal system that generally comports with the equal concern-and-respect principle broadly understood, but that nonetheless encompasses broad ideological disagreements and a wide array of legislation and adjudications that cannot be reconciled under a single conception of the above essentially contested principle. Thus, the legal system in question would not include legalized slavery or apartheid as the US legal system did in the past, but it would include some legislation and adjudications compatible with a libertarian conception of the equal concern-and-respect principle but not with its egalitarian counterpart, and vice versa. The question then becomes whether Hercules can rise above the conflict among conceptions through positive deployment of the principle of adjudicative integrity.

It becomes apparent that the answer to the latter question ought to be in the negative once we link the positive dimension of integrity to the inevitable judicial passage from concept to conception. As already noted, the concept of equality can be particularized either according to a libertarian conception or an egalitarian one (among many others). From a libertarian standpoint, restrictions on freedom of contract, such as those struck down by the US Supreme Court in its 1905 *Lochner* decision,[12] are unjust both from a redistribution and recognition perspective. Indeed, the social welfare legislation struck down in *Lochner* seemingly runs counter to wealth maximization while violating the freedom and autonomy as equals of those it seeks to protect from certain privately bargained contractual

---

[12] See *Lochner v. New York*, 198 US 45 (1905).

arrangements. From an egalitarian standpoint, in contrast, social welfare materially redistributive legislation is not only legitimate but also necessary. And as such, for both justice-in-distribution and justice-in-recognition purposes. In other words, for the egalitarian, wealth maximization must yield to a decent material welfare for all, and freedom of contract must give way when it militates against the equal autonomy of those who suffer from a disproportionate inequality in bargaining power. Accordingly, Hercules cannot secure a better "fit" than ordinary judges among contested conceptions of equality. He can, like his creator Dworkin, prefer egalitarianism over libertarianism, but that does not deprive the contesting libertarian of a legitimate claim that she also fully satisfies the equal concern-and-respect concept.

In view of this analysis, what can be adapted from Dworkin's account of constitutional interpretation for purposes of achieving the justice essentials or unearthing obstacles to their realization boils down to the following: moral and political norms bearing on the three dimensions of distributive justice must be factored into constitution-making and into constitutional interpretation. Universalized accepted concepts may have to be particularized into applicable conceptions, but so long as the latter remain contested there is no justification for granting interpretive preferences to any among them. Dworkin's distinction between principle and policy is not adaptable as such, but it suggests maintaining an interpretive divide between what may be imperative to the justice essentials and what may be trivial or indifferent to the latter. Finally, Dworkin's integrity in its negative dimension is worthy of incorporation whereas the door ought to be left open to integrity in a positive dimension in as much as it may be possible to overcome the limitations of Dworkin's version of the same.

In the end, all theorists discussed in this chapter, firmly steeped as they are in the Enlightenment tradition, proceed from the universal to the individual and display little if any adequate concern toward the plural. Kantian morals and Rawlsian justice are grounded on purely abstract and interchangeable egos, Habermas excludes an important segment of the relevant population from his dialogical process to the extent that they adhere to metaphysically grounded ideologies, and Dworkin engages from a substantive position that embraces a contested conception of a concept of liberal constitutionalism that excludes all other plausible conceptions of the said concept. In all cases, the dynamic that is emphasized above all is that between the universal and the individual, but in none of them does the individual figure as in any meaningful way singular. This is exemplified by Rawls' postulation of the maximin principle which is contrary to fact in that some flesh and blood individuals are risk averse and others not at all. Finally, and this is perhaps the most important lesson to be drawn from the above inquiry, all except Kant in his morals at the highest level of abstraction (which provides a paramount but exclusively negative insight), fail to advance a version of the universal that is, or can be made, compelling for all those affected, whether they be the world's population or that of a typical contemporary constitutional democracy. The quest for the universal must be further examined, as it will be in Part III, and it should aim at discovering something that can equally handle the claims of all relevant competing conceptions of the good while properly accounting for the singular and the plural.

6

Tragic Deconstruction Set Against the Impenetrable Singular and Reconstruction as Spectacle and Administration

From Derrida to Agamben

I Introduction

Whereas Derrida's deconstruction and Agamben's placement of law at the intersection of spectacle and administration are highly dense and *sui generis*, they relate in important ways to the theories discussed in the three preceding chapters. Moreover, Derrida's deconstructive approach to the nexus between law and justice and what I refer to as Agamben's reconstruction, which approaches law in terms of a blending of spectacle and administration, can be paired as complementary. Deconstruction is a methodological and interpretive philosophy which Derrida endowed with an ethical and ontological dimension in his account of the relation between law and justice (Rosenfeld 1998: Ch. 1). The deconstructionist approach to law is in many ways congruent with that deployed by CLS, but with one major difference. Unlike CLS, which is exclusively critical all the way down, as we shall see, Derrida's deconstruction of law and justice embraces an ontology of self and other and prescribes an ethics that requires doing justice to the other taking the latter's singularity into full account (*Id.*). This obligation towards the other, while doomed to fall tragically short, does add, as will be detailed in this chapter, a positive dimension that is lacking in CLS. In broader terms, Derrida frames his critical assessment of the nexus between law and justice in terms of the confrontation between Kantian universalism (Derrida 2003: 167–94) and the irreducible singularity of every individual self and other as it emerges in the philosophical tradition originating in Nietzsche and Heidegger (Derrida 1982: 109–36). As emphasized in the preceding chapter, Kant, Rawls, and Habermas do not provide a satisfactory account of the singularity of each individual, thus overemphasizing the universal. Derrida, in contrast, provides an exhaustive account of the singular which casts the confrontation and desired harmonization between the universal and the singular in a different light. As I shall explain shortly, this Derridean insight into the

A Pluralist Theory of Constitutional Justice. Michel Rosenfeld, Oxford University Press. © Michel Rosenfeld 2022.
DOI: 10.1093/oso/9780198862680.003.0007

irreducibility of the singular raises important questions in relation to the justice essentials. Furthermore, adapting Derrida's deconstructive approach to legal interpretation results in an intertextual grid that yields a relatively limited plurality of plausible outcomes (Rosenfeld 1998: 26–7). This grid thus at once punctures the rigidity of Dworkin's single right answer thesis and the infinite malleability attributed to legal texts by CLS. Moreover, as we shall see, the interpretive plurality at stake bears certain noteworthy implications for the justice essentials.

Derrida's ultimate conclusion regarding the nexus between law and justice is tragic in that he considers everyone as morally obliged to make laws just and never to relent in this quest, but as forever doomed to fail as law can never at once satisfy universalism and singularity (Rosenfeld 1991a: 1267–8). Derrida's tragic vision regarding justice is thus reminiscent of Camus' famous account of the myth of Sisyphus (Camus 1955). As against this, Agamben "reconstructs" law as combining religious allegory, myth, symbolism, spectacle, and acclamation, on the one hand, and administration—to which he refers by the Greek term *oikonomia*—on the other (Agamben 2011). Agamben's theory is most directly related to that of Schmitt and they both draw on theology. They also both focus on the exception, but whereas Schmitt ties the exception to emergencies, Agamben much more radically links the exception to every law, as for him there is an unbridgeable gap between every piece of legislation and its implementation via administration calling for the exercise of bureaucratic discretion (Agamben 2005: 24–31). In addition, Agamben's conjunction of spectacle and administration seems fit to fill the gap between Kelsen's theory of law as a self-enclosed system and Freud's linking law to guilt, remorse, identitarian concerns, and attempts at reinforced self-constraints through external projections of the superego. Agamben's theory also has relevance in relation to Habermas' distinction between system and lifeworld while Agamben also directly engages Habermas by claiming that the latter's conception of dialogical consensus is better understood as amounting to an acclamation of law as an originally divinely inspired spectacle (Agamben 2011: 258–9). Finally, although *oikonomia* is not synonymous with economy, there are worthy insights to be drawn through comparing Posner's law and economics to Agamben's view that law must devolve into administration. As we shall see, Agamben's reconstruction can be configured—though he does not do so himself—as an answer to Derrida's deconstruction. Specifically, Agamben provides a vision of the plural that is totally lacking in Derrida while displacing justice from its Derridean impossibility in the real world onto the symbolic imaginary framed by the imprint of divine ordering. In the last analysis, however, the overriding question is whether Agamben's reconstruction overcomes the Derridean impasse or whether it merely papers over it, thus resulting in a further setback.

In order to tackle this latter question, the chapter proceeds as follows. Section I provides an account of Derrida's deconstructive method and of its impact on the ethical dimensions of the confrontation between law and justice. Section II explores the Nietzschean and Heideggerian origins of Derrida's radical conception of singularity. Section III critically assesses the consequences of the necessary but tragic confrontation between Derridean law and justice. Section IV addresses the mainstays of Agamben's theory and places his contribution in its broader theoretical context. Finally, section V sets Agamben's reconstruction against Derrida's deconstruction and aims at unravelling its implications for the quest of the justice essentials.

II Derrida's Deconstruction of the Nexus between Law and Justice: Confronting Irreducible Fissures in the Context of Interpretation and Ethics

Derrida's deconstructive interpretive method is based on the priority of writing over speech, which leads him to deny that speech is better suited than writing to convey clear, transparent, or true meanings.[1] Derrida considers all writings to be intertextual and intersubjective, thus creating a dichotomy between what a writing is intended to mean and what it is constrained to mean. That dichotomy is due to the fact that every writing embodies a failed attempt at reconciling identity and difference, unity and diversity, and self and other. If a writing appears to have achieved the relevant reconciliation, it can only be because of ideological distortion, suppression of difference, or subordination of the other. Moreover, this applies particularly well to modern legal discourse with universalist aspirations prone to projecting an ideologically slanted unity, suppressing unassimilable differences, and concealing substantive inequalities imposed on the "other" under the veneer of merely formal equality.

Because all writing is intertextual, all meaning must be *deferred*. The meaning of a writing depends on interweaving readings of past and future writings. For example, our understanding of past historical events, even those in the distant past, would have to be revised upon findings of relevant hitherto unknown past writings. This newly discovered body of writings should prompt a rereading and reinterpretation as should future writings that shed further light on past or present ones, thus prompting reinterpretations of past and present historical occurrences. More generally, a present writing is both a completion and an erasure of a past writing and a text that must face future completion and erasure by yet unwritten texts that will be material in establishing the present text's full meaning.

As I have argued elsewhere (Rosenfeld 1998: Ch. 1), deconstruction's intertextual method of interpretation meshes well with common-law judicial interpretation based on reliance and elaboration of precedents. Indeed, most precedents

---

[1] This brief account of Derrida's deconstructive interpretive methodology summarizes the more extensive account provided in Rosenfeld 1998: Ch. 1.

are open-ended and subject to present and future interpretation as well as to re-interpretation of the past. For example, in an attempt to downplay the importance of nineteenth-century, broad-based condemnation of same-sex sodomy in the United States, Justice Kennedy reinterpreted such condemnation as directed to the practice of sodomy itself regardless of whether it occurred in homosexual or heterosexual sex. Based on this rereading, Justice Kennedy concluded that a contemporary Texas law criminalizing homosexual sodomy but not its heterosexual counterpart was unconstitutional.[2]

The main question this analogy raises is whether deconstructive interpretation and precedent-based legal interpretation are completely indeterminate or in some meaningful non-trivial sense constrained so as to allow for a limited number of interpretive options without making for any single definitive answer. If both were to end up being completely indeterminate, Derrida's deconstruction would be equivalent, for interpretive purposes, to CLS. We need not inquire, however, whether the deconstructive method taken alone would rise above sheer indeterminacy. This is because, as I have discussed elsewhere, when such method is paired with Derrida's ethics and ontology it does lead to the combination of certain openings and certain closings of a finite number of plausible paths of interpretation (Rosenfeld 1998: 26–7). In short, given the ontology and ethics involved, every interpretation must be consistent with separation and coexistence between self and other as well as with optimization of opportunities aimed at coming closer to giving its full due to the other's singularity.

Because it postulates that all human beings are in some important sense essentially equal, Derrida's theory must contain in its ontological dimension some relevant conception of the universal and of the individual. It is the individual who is the subject of equality, and the equality that binds all individuals together in law, ethics, and politics must project a universal dimension. Moreover, in as much as particular legal regimes are meant to rule within pluralist-in-fact nation-states with a confluence of multiple competing conceptions of the good (or within supra-national polities that encompass less than all of humanity) and that laws within such polities are the product of democratic majorities, legal theory must also account for the plural. As will become clear in the following discussion of Derrida's account of the relation between law and justice, his theory concentrates almost exclusively on the dynamic between the universal and the singular, thus for the most part ignoring the plural.

For Derrida, justice poses a paradox. As he succinctly puts it:

> To address oneself to the other in the language of the other is, it seems, the condition of all possible justice, but apparently, in all rigor, it is not only

---

[2] See *Lawrence v. Texas*, 539 US 558 (2003).

impossible ... but even excluded by justice as law (*droit*), inasmuch as justice as right seems to imply an element of universality, the appeal to a third party who suspends the unilaterality or singularity of the idioms. (Derrida 1990: 949)

In other words, for Derrida justice through law ought at once to satisfy the universal and the singular, but that is impossible. Absent the inexhaustible ethical duty to reach toward the other to give each person her singular due, this would end up in a tragedy likely to prompt fatalism and paralysis. However, animated by the unbreakable ethical obligation to the other, each manifestation of the impossibility of justice ought to give rise to a new attempt in a continuous never-ending process. The key question raised by this ceaseless pursuit of justice, in turn, is whether although achieving justice is impossible some attempts at doing so might lead to closer approximations to justice than others. If the answer to this question were in the negative, then although the gesture towards the other may enhance solidarity, it would in the end not reasonably lead anywhere beyond resignation. On the other hand, if some attempts at justice resulted in better approximations than others, then some laws and some legal interpretation alternatives would definitely be preferable to others, albeit that they would always leave something to be desired.

Before delving any further into this last question, let us take a closer look at Derrida's claim that justice must satisfy simultaneously both the universal and the singular and that this makes it impossible. Derrida's dichotomy between justice through law and justice as each person's due is reminiscent of Aristotle's distinction between justice as equality and justice as equity (Aristotle 1980: Bk V). For Aristotle, the latter is supposed to supplement the former and equality is embodied in general legal rules whereas equity is achieved through the carving out of discrete exceptions. Thus, for example, if a general rule were to prohibit motor vehicles from entering a public park and provided fines for violators, equity would require making an exception for ambulances coming into the park to provide life-saving help to heart attack victims. Derrida also ties justice to equality and equity, but in sharp contrast to Aristotle, maintains that in every case justice requires simultaneous satisfaction of the rule *and* of the exception. Equality and the general rule require conformity with the universal whereas equity must account for singularity in its full particularity. Even assuming it possible to satisfy the universal and the singular separately, doing so through the same law simultaneously is obviously impossible. Indeed, almost all democratically enacted laws are both over- and under-inclusive which makes them unsuitable for any simultaneous compliance with even the most loosely drawn notions of universal and singular. Given Derrida's Kantian universalism and Nietzschean and Heideggerian conception of singularity, however, the impossibility in question would extend to all laws, including those that most legal observers would consider as being neither over-inclusive nor under-inclusive. Moreover, this Derridean impossibility for any law to be just should become all the more apparent when combining the previous discussion of

202 TRAGIC DECONSTRUCTION SET

the universal as understood by Kant, Rawls, and Habermas with the account of the singular to be provided in the next section.

The unbridgeable gap between law and justice is particularly troubling for Derrida because he conceives of law as being inextricably associated with violence (Derrida 1992: 5–6). In this perspective, all law is violent in that it forces those subject to it to do or to refrain from doing something against their will, convictions, self-image, aspirations, and the like. The violence of laws is wide ranging, from the brutality of the death penalty to the relatively inconsequential inconvenience of a traffic rule mandating yielding to an incoming vehicle. The violence of a law may be legitimate if that law is just. If the relevant universal, singular, and plural are all satisfied by providing for a year in prison for those who are convicted of having committed certain types of burglaries, then temporarily depriving by force the burglar of some of the most basic individual liberties amounts to fully justified, officially sanctioned violence. But since for Derrida no law can be just, whenever a "self" presses a successful claim in the name of justice against another, the latter is bound to suffer from unjustified violence. By the same token, whenever a "self" refrains from pursuing a deemed-just claim against another, that self does some violence to himself. Consistent with this, all laws are unjustly violent, and that leads back to the key question of whether certain laws can be meaningfully characterized as being more or less unjust than others. In order to be in a better position to tackle this last question, however, it is first necessary to examine Derrida's radical concept of singularity in its broader philosophical context.

III The Nietzschean and Heideggerian Roots of Derrida's Radical Conception of Singularity

As already pointed out, a strictly Kantian conception of universalism cannot be approximated in the realm of laws or of constitutions and neither can any conception of singularity that postulates that every person is unique in ways that cannot become intelligible to any other person. Derrida does not dwell upon the Kantian universalist component of his theory of justice, and for convenience we may assume for present purposes that Derrida's turn to the universal could be broadly understood as coming close to Habermas' criterion of universalization. Unlike Habermas, however, Derrida's belief in the impossibility of justice precludes the possibility of any instance of successful universalization. Moreover, whereas Habermas underplays singularity or excludes certain iterations of it, Derrida magnifies it to the point of articulating an ethics of difference (Rosenfeld 2011: 253–4). Because of its importance for Derrida's theory, and because of its uniquely distinct nature, it is imperative to inquire further into the theoretical underpinnings and the surrounding dynamics of Derrida's conception of singularity. In addition, the inquiry in question is needed in its own right given the indispensable place of singularity within the configuration of the justice essentials and given that the theories discussed in the preceding chapters have not adequately accounted for the singular.

In view of the Enlightenment's postulation of the equality of all individuals, of liberal constitutionalism's focus on individual rights, and on representative democracy's dependence on the right of each individual to cast her very own vote, it seems highly ironic that the placing of the individual centerstage has been accompanied by a most dramatic institutional and societal "de-singularization" of each and every living human being. This process of de-singularization is already present in Rousseau's famous distinction between the bourgeois and the citizen, the latter being cut off from the singular desires, aspirations, and interests of the former to ensure concentration on the general will (Rousseau 1947: 14–16). Also, as already noted, the modern individual rights holder is for the most part cast at a high level of abstraction as is the individual who enters a contract as a buyer, a seller, a lender, a borrower, an employer, or an employee. Further alienation and de-singularization is also manifest in mass industrial production, mass consumption, mass transportation, and mass entertainment. In short, from Nietzsche's lifetime in the second half of the nineteenth century to the contemporary world that Derrida inhabited, the individual in liberal constitutional democracies has seemingly incessantly gained in importance while at the same time being treated by society, the bureaucracy, and the political establishment in abstract, reductive, distorted, and partial ways that de-singularize her. All this creates the unsettling paradox of concurrent increasing individualization and ever more pronounced alienation from one's own singularity. Moreover, this trend continues through novel means in the present post-Derridean period as attested by the spread of surveillance capitalism discussed in Chapter 1. Indeed, as will be recalled, through use of the new technologies, the surveillance capitalist does not focus on the individual in any abstract way, but instead by appropriating as many of his singular particularities as possible in order to turn the latter against him. In other words, the surveillance capitalist operates below the individual's zone of awareness and breaks down and appropriates for her own profit discrete tastes, desires, ideological and political predilections of particular individuals in order to create or refashion particular identitarian and consumer needs and objectives of which the targeted individual remains unaware. Accordingly, the surveillance capitalist literally alienates the singular individual from the attributes of her own singularity and then repackages the latter to colonize the targeted individual. In the end, that individual is deprived of mastery over her singular attributes which she could have otherwise enlisted and developed for her own purposes. Instead, that individual becomes largely an unaware colonized person who unwittingly acquiesces to adjust her singular aspirations to conform to the will of her profit-maximizing economic colonizer.

Nietzsche and Heidegger embraced individualism and considered the world in their respective lifetimes to be in a profound state of crisis (Megill 1987: 107). Both these philosophers were very influential on Derrida, and in particular on the latter's confrontation with the quandaries surrounding what he regarded as the irreducible singularity of every human being. Accordingly, a brief inquiry into aspects of these two philosophers' views relevant to the topic of singularity is warranted, but before proceeding any further it is important to keep in mind the following caveats. Both Nietzsche and Heidegger are complex and dense thinkers who are not always internally consistent and who have given rise to multiple, often contradictory, interpretations. Some have divided Nietzsche's thought as falling into three distinct periods (Strong 2009: xvi) and noted a wide variety of diverging interpretations of his works (*Id.*: xiv–xv). As for Heidegger, there also are numerous, often inconsistent, interpretations as well as a division of his works into those of the "early" and those of the "late" Heidegger (Megill 1987: 105, 127). With this in mind, in what follows I will limit myself to widely accepted generalities regarding their respective philosophies, specific statements made by these philosophers, and plausible, though contested, interpretations of their theories, all with the aim of shedding light on their generally converging, yet in part diverging, conceptions of singularity. Moreover, my focus on the contributions of these two philosophers will be further narrowed down to their direct relevance to Derrida's understanding of the concept of singularity, and to the latter's potential contribution to a better grasp of the justice essentials.

For both Nietzsche and Heidegger, the profound crisis that besets the world as they see it leaves individuals starkly alone and cut off from the religious, moral, and traditional social bonds that once contributed to their finding meaning during the course of their lives on earth. For Nietzsche, the crisis itself is embodied in his famous dictum that "God is dead" (Nietzsche 1924: sec. 125), thus leaving human beings isolated and without shelter to fend for themselves in an inhospitable world. And this must be done not only without transcendent faith-based guidance, but also without any other reliable earthly normative directives. Just as religion, morals for Nietzsche have been used to enslave and to deprive those under their yoke of their individuality and of its true potential (Nietzsche 1966: secs 4, 32). The imprint of religion and morality leads to ignorance (Nietzsche 2006: VI, 1) and to a herd-like passivity (Nietzsche 1966: secs 201–203). To extricate oneself from what is but a stark depiction of nihilism, and to strive to find or construct meaning, the individual must start with a "transvaluation of values" that will allow her to reach a promising point of departure toward self-realization somewhere "beyond good and evil" (Nietzsche 1966). In other words, consistent with Nietzsche's views, religion, and morals as well as other social movements and ideologies, including socialism (*Id.*: sec. 202), de-singularize the individual. Moreover, the de-singularization in question not only alienates and renders the individual passive but it also subjugates him to a set of false and disempowering, albeit at times seemingly reassuring, normative beliefs and edicts. Accordingly, it is only by first ridding herself of these fabricated and oppressive constraints that the individual can rediscover her singularity. And not before that is done, can the individual embark on a quest for a meaningful life through fulfillment of the full potential of her unique attributes and abilities.

For Heidegger, the relevant crisis is the one he actually lived through in Germany between the two world wars. Heidegger, who was influenced by Nietzsche, asserted that he took the latter "seriously as a thinker,"[3] and the two of them shared a sense of profound crisis that they linked to nihilism. Unlike Nietzsche, however, Heidegger embarked on a systematic questioning of the modern Western rational philosophical tradition from Descartes to Kant, and of its account of human society in terms of the natural science paradigm and the division into subject and object (Megill 1987: 11). As against this, Heidegger launched into an ontology severed from metaphysics originating in "Being-in-the world" (Id) or "Being there" (*Dasein*) (Heidegger 1962: 116–17) which connotes presence as well as existence. As Heidegger specifies, "man's '*substance*' is not spirit as a synthesis of soul and body; it is rather '*existence*'" (*Id.*: 153).[4] In essence, what Heidegger conveys is that at the deepest level, one's consciousness of being is revealed as mere presence or existence in a world which turns out to be purely contingent—there happens to be humans who exist, but the contrary could have just as easily been the case—and in-and-of-itself meaningless. Rationalism, history, traditional philosophy, religion, social mores, and the like which have been invoked to account for the place, role, and purpose of human beings prove ultimately inauthentic and without meaning (and this conclusion must have seemed particularly resonant in Heidegger's defeated inter-war Germany which was beset by one crisis after another). That leaves human beings with nothing but their existence—"where existence is understood (via etymological considerations) as *ek-sistence*, that is, as a standing out"[5]—to muster any authentic quest toward meaning. All that separates the individual from her bare "being there" can be said to de-singularize her in that it wraps her in layers of inauthentic false images of herself and of her world that prevent her from taking charge of her own existence and thus stand out (authentically in accordance with her singular potential).

There is one important qualification that bears mentioning in reference to Heidegger's prioritizing existence and that distinguishes it from its subsequent adaptation by Sartre. Based on his famous dictum, derived from Heidegger's language quoted earlier, that "existence precedes essence" (Sartre 1948: 13), Sartre predicates singularity on ridding oneself of all inauthentic baggage in order to use one's freedom to engage in the invention and pursuit of one's own authentic trajectory within the world. For Heidegger, however, as made plain in *Being and Time*,

---

[3] Heidegger cited in Megill 1987: 105.
[4] Emphasis in the original.
[5] Michael Wheeler, "Martin Heidegger," *The Stanford Encyclopedia of Philosophy* (2020 edition); Edward N. Zalta (ed), <https://plato.stanford.edu/archives/fall2020/entries/heidegger/>, visited April 3, 2022.

authenticity is linked to nostalgia and to a return to an idealized version of the ancient Greece of pre-Socratic philosophy (Megill 1987: 115). This longing for this imagined lost way of being that supposedly preceded Plato's lifetime does add an essence-based backward-looking ideal that seemingly qualifies the scope of priority Heidegger reserves for existence. This may have political implications in as much as it opposes the crisis-prone complexities of the contemporary world to the supposedly much more simple and serene life attributed to a very distant past. Moreover, whereas this nostalgia may be plausibly loosely linked to Heidegger's Nazi inclinations, its main salience for our purposes is its suggestion that the quest for singularity can be at once both backward and forward looking. And that is certainly the case for Derrida in view of his commitment to intertextuality which requires constant concurrent engagement with both past and future.

Before considering how Nietzsche and Heidegger envisage the recovery of singularity upon full recognition of the state of crisis and its entailment of nihilism, it is useful briefly to address claims linking their respective philosophies to Nazism. Some have characterized Nietzsche as a "pre-fascist" thinker (Megill 1987: 17), whereas Heidegger unambiguously publicly endorsed Hitler in 1933 (*Id.*: 131). This led one post-war commentator to state that "Heidegger's listeners were never quite sure whether they should take up the study of the pre-Socratics or join the Storm Troopers" (*Id.*: 130). Regardless of any Nazi drawing on Nietzsche's writings for support or of Heidegger's incontestable allegiance to the Nazis, the key question for present purposes is whether their respective views on how best to vindicate singularity can be fairly regarded as standing on their own without any inherent implications that would lend support to either Nazi or fascist perspectives. As will become obvious, the answer to this question is clearly in the affirmative as the individualism, existentialism, and devotion to artistic creativity, which they both enlisted to cope with the crises they confronted, give rise to plausible interpretations consistent with outright rejection of any Nazi or fascist tendencies.[6] In this respect, Heidegger's legacy—and certainly his influence on Derrida—is akin to that of Schmitt which was discussed in Chapter 4. Both men had despicable Nazi

---

[6] Some may argue that the mere rejection of the philosophical tradition established through the trajectory that led from Descartes to Kant and abandonment of the priority of reason and of the natural sciences paradigm opens the door to the combined evils of nihilism, irrationalism, and relativism that eventually pave the way to authoritarianism of all stripes, including fascism and Nazism. This type of argument, which has a slippery slope quality to it, is however largely unpersuasive. Indeed, many proponents of individualism, existentialism, and of various different versions of postmodernism—including Derrida—are strong supporters of democracy. More importantly, from the perspective of the justice essentials, the relevant question is whether radical individualism or existentialism must be considered inherently incompatible with the requisite minimum of constitutional justice. Whereas the answer to this last question is ultimately context dependent, an excess of individualism seems more prone to favor libertarianism than fascism, and existentialism seems much more likely to thrive in a constitutional regime that affords ample room for individual liberty in sharp contrast to the inevitably oppressive ways associated with authoritarian rule, whether fascist or not.

allegiances, but their respective theories can be fairly read in ways that do not raise fascist or Nazi implications.

Nietzsche and Heidegger embarked on a positive project to overcome nihilism and to unleash the potential in humans to achieve authentic singularity by combining individualism, existentialism, and esthetic activity that emulates the process of creation in literature, music, and the plastic arts. For Nietzsche, the existentialist component is implicit and animated by the "will to power" (Nietzsche 1968) being deployed "beyond good and evil." For Heidegger, on the other hand, the turn to art that emerges as a supplement or a substitute to nostalgia occurs around 1930 (Megill 1987: 127, 143), a few years after the publication of *Being and Time*. As of 1940, Heidegger regarded art as a counterweight against technology. As one commentator put it:

> If technology is the destroying power, one that turns man into an object even as he seeks to make himself master of objects, then art stands ... as the saving power. In a totally degraded, totally alienated world, a world of pure manipulation, a light gleams out: hope is not entirely lost. (*Id.*: 143)

Nietzsche and Heidegger are committed to individualism, but theirs is an elitist anti-democratic type of individualism only open to the few who are enterprising and creative enough (Kateb 2009: 377). This individualism, moreover, is radical but anti-social as the philosopher-poet with access to singularity rises in solitude above the passively conforming social masses (*Id.*: 383). As one commentator observed, building on Nietzsche's statement in *the Gay Science*, that existence is only bearable as an esthetic experience:

> only if we imagine ourselves and everything else as necessary elements in the composition of a great artist, and adopt that artist's point of view, can we justify existence. (*Id.*: 392).

In other words, it is only if one recreates oneself and one's world as does a great artist who composes a masterpiece that one can arrive at a meaningful existence. From the standpoint of singularity, the artistic creation itself requires both an element of negation and of affirmative creation. In Nietzsche's vision, the type of individual who can carry out this double feat, of ridding herself of oppressively imposed commonplaces and of redesigning her world through creating (the equivalent of) an esthetic masterpiece, is *Übermensch*—translated by some as "overman" (Danto 1970: 197). Overman stands in contrast with what Nietzsche calls the "last man" whom he regards as typifying the late nineteenth-century herdsman (*Id.*). Furthermore, overman seeks to achieve his unique potential through exercise of his "will to power" (Nietzsche 1968). As Nietzsche conceives it, the will to power propels humans to higher achievements: the slave towards freedom; and the outstandingly gifted individual to positions of leadership (*Id.*: 407). Accordingly, the slave must work to remove the impediments that prevent him from giving expression to his singularity while the leader must muster her unique capacities and vision to shepherd those under her guidance to a better future.[7]

Nietzsche's path to singularity may strike us as purely forward looking, if it were not for what has been characterized as his "most exotic doctrine," namely that of "Eternal Recurrence" (Danto 1970: 2001). What Nietzsche means by this doctrine remains mysterious and some have even characterized it as "ultimately unintelligible" (Megill 1987: 19). Nevertheless, there are two plausible derivations from the idea of eternal return that seem particularly helpful in terms of reconciling Derrida's view of singularity with Nietzsche's. The first of these is phenomenological: the future paths toward meaning bear strong similarities to past ones, thus counseling simultaneous backward- and forward-looking references to advance the quest towards (i.e., the advance and recovery of) singularity. The second derivation is, in contrast, ontological: eternal recurrence signifies that there is no path to transcendence. After the death of God, all meaning remains immanent, and pursuit of the esthetic does not lead beyond the momentary and existential enjoyment of the creative burst.

The above understanding of Nietzsche's eternal return allows for a bridge to Heidegger's reliance on nostalgia. When combined with the later Heidegger's already mentioned esthetic turn, the two philosophers end up in a pretty similar position regarding their past- and future-looking path to recovery and to further deployment of singularity. Heidegger is only more radical than Nietzsche in two respects that are of particular relevance to the question of singularity. The first of these concerns the absolute contradiction he perceives between crisis and technology, on the one hand, and art, on the other. Accordingly, as one interpreter summarized it, "[t]he complete degradation of the extant world ... prepares the ground for an aesthetic creation *ex nihilo*" (Megill 1987: 143). The second respect, in turn, concerns Heidegger's insistence on Being's contingency which provides the key to its meaning while being kept in mind and reaffirmed through existence (*Id.*: 156). Because art stands on its own for Heidegger, its pursuit constitutes an affirmation of the contingency of our being wherever we happen to be. Also, as Heidegger believes that art reached its ideal expression with the Greeks (*Id.*: 150), nostalgia becomes key to recovery of the present and to rising above nihilism in the future. Thus, singularity for the elite individuals who are capable of esthetic creation consists of a combination of recovery and reinvention. Finally, and this is important in relation to Derrida, Heidegger increasingly conflated language and art and saw both as vehicles whereby the gifted individual could combine philosophy and the

---

[7] Nietzsche was a great admirer of extraordinary political leaders, such as Julius Cesar and Napoleon (Danto 1970: 198).

arts in order to project an "imaginary" that could encapsulate her own lived singular truth (*Id.*: 162–70).

Derrida does conflate language, philosophy, and art in the tradition of Nietzsche and Heidegger (*Id.*: 17), but he differs sharply from these predecessors when it comes to individualism. Because of his Kantian universalist commitment, Derrida's individualism is egalitarian. Accordingly, Derrida extends singularity to all as opposed to a particularly gifted elite dwelling in the midst of a de-singularized passive herd. Moreover, the combination of Derrida's embrace of the Kantian universalist imperative and of a universally expanded democratic Nietzschean/Heideggerian conception of singularity leads to a dual failure in the pursuit of justice. As already noted in discussing Kant's categorical imperative, the latter can only provide negative input in the quest for justice through law, and consistent with this whatever iteration of the universal may be invoked in any initiative to dispense justice would be bound to fall short. Logically, this conclusion follows from the fact that it is impossible within the realm of law to treat everyone exclusively as an end in herself, and phenomenologically, from the fact that given the singularity that differentiates every individual from everyone else, it is foreclosed that all concerned would agree that any universally applicable legal rule is equally fair and just to all those it affects. This first failure at the level of the universal is compounded by a second one at that of the singular. In Derrida's universe of democratized singularity, every individual is different and no law—by the mere fact of having to be general—can capture all the differences of any single individual, let alone the universe of differences that account for the singularity of each and everyone. In other words, in Derrida's intertextual universe, each author/reader has a unique standpoint from which she engages with past, present, and future texts. To be sure, important commonalities among authors and readers must be present, lest intersubjective communication would be impossible. Nevertheless, certain gaps, aporias, and contradictions are insurmountable, and that for Derrida makes singularity irreducible and justice unreachable as no determinate meaning can be plausibly attributed to it (Derrida 1990: 949).

Paradoxically, this double impossibility to do justice does not exempt the ethical duty to strive for it but instead reinforces it consistent with Derrida's account. The Kantian impossibility revealed through practical reason should be understood as a stern reminder that whereas we are always bound to fail in fully meeting the categorical imperative, we should persistently strive to approximate it as much as possible and to condemn those who refuse to do so. The Nietzschean/Heideggerian impossibility, on the other hand, does not foreclose constantly striving to better account for the other's singularity and thus aiming at factoring in differences without ever being able to give them their full due. Derrida's insistence that the double inevitable failures involved inexorably mandate an ongoing ethical obligation to strive for the impossible thus prevail in terms of both the universal and the singular. Moreover, this is evidenced not only in relation to Derrida's views on law and justice, but also by his analysis of the dynamic between self-regarding and other-regarding friendship (Derrida 1994a) and of that between conditional and unconditional forgiveness (Derrida 2001). Also, perhaps the most salient example of Derrida's comprehensive ethical approach, for present purposes, is his insistence on the dichotomy between majoritarian democracy and the "democracy to come" (*la démocratie a venir*) (Borradori 2003: 120). Rationally pursuing the will of the majority seems certainly preferable to non-democratic forms of government, but it remains insufficient as it does not allow for full respect for the irreducible singularity of each person and with leaving sufficient room for such singularity to flourish (*Id.*: 130). In other words, democracy is ultimately impossible for Derrida because self-rule through majority-based decisions cannot ever culminate in "the democracy to come," which requires self-rule for every person according to what his irreducible singularity requires. In sum, for Derrida, justice and democracy are ultimately impossible, but we are not only ethically bound permanently to acknowledge that, but also continuously to muster our best efforts to strive for closer approximations that will nevertheless always fall short. This, in turn, directly raises the key question already identified: are actual approximations to justice and democracy possible within Derrida's theory, and does the latter provide actual criteria to determine what amounts to a meaningful approximation and whether one possible alternative would lead to a better approximation than others?

IV Derrida's Insurmountable Gap between Law and Justice: A Pure or Merely Relative Tragedy?

It is certainly preferable to recognize and acknowledge injustice than to ignore or deny it. But if nothing can be done about it, or if attempts to mitigate it cannot be measured or meaningfully compared, then the justice essentials could only figure as negative reminders that constitutions cannot advance justice. Common sense suggests that some laws are more unjust than others and thus, consistent with Derrida's insight, more unjustifiably violent. For example, creating an apartheid legal system is highly unjust and inflicts constant profound violence against those who belong to the disenfranchised race. In comparison, a law that commands restitution of stolen property may be regarded as imposing little unjustified violence and as far closer to justice than any apartheid legal norm—albeit that restitution may be deemed unacceptably violent and arguably downright unjust in some cases, such as when the parent of starving children steals a loaf of bread from a wealthy and politically influential bakery owner who financially supports politicians who oppose all social welfare legislation.

There is no question that Derrida and his ethics of difference embrace the proposition that some injustices are greater than others and that laws that remove a greater injustice to replace them with lesser ones are worthy of pursuit. This is made manifest by Derrida's implacable opposition to the death penalty (Derrida 2013), his pleas for legally sanctioned hospitality towards immigrants and refugees (Derrida 2001), and his forceful wholesale condemnation of global terrorism (Borradori 2003). All these positions are consistent with Derrida's ethics of care and the obligation to recognize and vindicate the singularity of the other. The important remaining question, however, is whether Derrida's deconstructive method and his philosophical appraisal of the impossibility of justice and of democracy can be cogently theoretically paired with criteria-making for reliable comparisons concerning degrees of injustice. To be sure, some injustices are so grossly disproportionate in comparison to others that the differences between them would be obvious to all. But what about less obvious, yet important cases, such as whether preferential hiring of women to remedy past systematic discrimination against them is preferable to instituting strict equality of opportunity for purposes of better approximating justice among the sexes?

In Derrida's intertextual universe, impossibility entails complete lack of means of expression or of representation. There is no possible account of justice at once fully compliant with the universal and the singular. Because of this, from a systemic theoretical perspective there is always an infinite gap between attempted justice through law and actual justice. And the infinite cannot be logically captured in any comparative endeavor. That leaves Derrida with an intuitive existential approach in his quest to opt for lesser injustices in all cases where there is no unanimous accord. This approach bears some significant resemblance to Sartre's existential philosophy relying on authenticity as the means to avert "bad faith" and conformity with injustice and oppression (Sartre 1966: 86, n. 10). Derrida acknowledged having been influenced by Sartre (Derrida 1996: 7–54). What approximates Derrida's commitment to singularity to Sartre's existential leap is the need to act solely on intuition and good faith, as no guidance from pre-existing established norms can be counted on in an ever-changing, endlessly diverse normative setting. What separates Derrida from Sartre, on the other hand, is Derrida's commitment to Kantian universalism.

Derrida's Kantian conception of the universal combined with what approximates an existential thrust toward the singular make his reliance on authenticity and good faith insufficient. This is not only the case where no guidance is available to decide among plausible alternative options in order to approximate justice. It is also more important in the case where individuals are engaged in seemingly irresolvable conflicts against one another. In such situations, accommodating the singularity of one of the antagonists seems bound automatically to detract from the singularity of others. This latter problem is perhaps best illustrated by Derrida's reaction to global terrorism as exemplified by the attacks on September 11, 2001 (Borradori 2003: 147). As noted in Chapter 2, Derrida condemns the 9/11 terrorist attackers as perpetrating what amounts to an act of pure violence without meaning or future and thus remaining outside the ambit of intertextual exchange, which is indispensable in the ethical quest to further vindicate the singularity of the other (*Id.*). Particularly, in as much as Derrida acknowledges that traditional terrorism at the level of the nation-state—such as ETA (the Basque Euskadi Ta Askatasuna (Basque Homeland and Liberty)) in Spain or the IRA (Irish Republican Army) in the United Kingdom—is meaningful (even if subject to condemnation; *id.*: 103), his conclusion regarding global terrorism is altogether unconvincing. Indeed, global terrorists certainly have a message, an ideology, and objectives. Moreover, viewed retrospectively, the 9/11 attackers certainly had a "future," as evinced by the various changes involving increased security, decreased liberty, and ever more onerous restrictions affecting air travel as well as many other costly measures that have been adopted in numerous countries hit or threatened by terrorist violence.

Derrida strongly condemns global terrorism, but his condemnation appears squarely inconsistent with his ethics of difference and its requirement to honor singularity all the way down. Although the global terrorists' acts are extremely violent and certainly worthy of the strongest condemnation, they are not meaningless. Accordingly, these acts ought to be factored within the relevant intertextual streams instead of being altogether excluded from any consideration. In sum, Derrida's ethics is superior to its existentialist counterpart because of his Kantian universalism. However, because he allows for an unbridgeable gap between the universal and the singular, Derrida's ethical commitment to honor all singularity opens him up to the same criticisms that afflict the existential leap. The gesture may be authentic, but it may be as likely to advance justice somewhat as to set it back somehow. Finally, as already mentioned, Derrida's ethics of difference and its fixation on singularity does not leave much room for the plural. And that leaves his deconstructive ethics at a loss when it comes to filling the gap between the universal and the individual.

V Agamben's Reconstruction: Law's Split into the Glow of Divine Glory and the Minutiae of Administration

As already noted, Agamben engages directly with Schmitt concerning the relationship or, more precisely, the disjunction between law and the exception. Beyond that, however, Agamben is difficult to place within the ambit of the political philosophies and jurisprudences that bear on the relationship between, law, legitimacy, justice, and the justice essentials. This is in great part due to Agamben's grounding his jurisprudence within the religious confines of Christendom and its sociocultural by-products which defies any neat placement alongside theories that are in various important ways tied to the Enlightenment. With this in mind, I proceed with a counterfactual reconstruction: if we had to find a place for Agamben in the unfolding history of contemporary theories bearing on law and justice and the interplay between the universal, the singular, and the plural, where would that place be? The most fruitful hypothesis, as I have already suggested and will attempt to buttress below, is that Agamben is best regarded as providing a reconstruction that replaces or supplements Derrida's deconstruction. Admittedly, upon initial impression, casting Agamben as providing a reconstruction that complements and/or transcends Derrida's deconstruction of law might well seem oddly paradoxical. Indeed, Agamben's theory rests in a crucial sense on an immovable disjunction, namely, that between law and *oikonomia* or administration. Is it not, accordingly, better to characterize Agamben's gap between law and administration as a displacement of Derrida's gap between law and justice, with both of these gaps bearing a strong analogy from a deconstructive standpoint? To dispel this apparent paradox, it is first necessary to try to unravel Agamben's linking of Christendom, human affairs, and *oikonomia*.

Although both Agamben and Schmitt rely on the exception to link law to disjunction, in Schmitt's case the disjunction is much more fluid than in that of Agamben. This is because for Schmitt the exception which "interrupts" law and dissolves it into politics occurs only intermittently in cases of emergency. In contrast, for Agamben, the disjunction is radical and systematic as all laws require independent discretionary administration which amounts to an exception (Agamben 2005). In both cases, the disjunction involved requires legitimation and justification as well as means to safeguard or foster solidarity within the affected constitutional unit. Remarkably, both Agamben and Schmitt turn to theology to fill the legitimacy and solidarity gaps exacerbated by their respective recourses to disjunction (Schmitt 2005; Agamben 2011). Moreover, both of them turn to Christian theology, but whereas Schmitt's reliance on the latter is rather generic, Agamben relies on intricacies relating to the Holy Trinity. As will be remembered from the discussion in Chapter 4, Schmitt relies on Catholicism's claim to universality and on the transition from the divine empowerment of kings to the charismatic leadership of modern secular political leaders. For his part, Agamben locates the origin of contemporary politics in Christian theology's account of the mystery bound up in the relationship between the immutable unity of God and the plurality of the Holy Trinity resulting in the unfolding in historical time of divine providence and grace as it pertains to human beings (Agamben 2011: 109–43). Originating in the theology in question and still taken to be in full force at present is what Agamben posits as an immutable political–constitutional–legal matrix that separates the sovereign from those who govern and the legislator's law from the actual conduct of the affairs of the polity through an *oikonomia* (*Id.*). Strikingly, although historically moored in Christian theology, the matrix unveiled by Agamben is apparently so hardwired as to become impervious to the abandonment of Christianity or the repudiation of all religion (*Id.*: 286–7).

Agamben's disjunction can only be properly understood if viewed in terms of what is for him the crucial juxtaposition between the realm of theology and that of the orderly conduct of human affairs. What emerges as central for Agamben is the role of Christian theology as determinant in shaping the deep structure of legal/administrative systems, including contemporary ones notwithstanding the latter's self-understanding as being purely secular (*Id.*: 284–5). Before tackling the particulars of Agamben's theological paradigm and evaluating how it may advance the quest for legitimacy of contemporary legal regimes, it is necessary briefly to highlight his direct criticism of Schmitt. Beyond their differences concerning the state of the exception discussed earlier, Agamben objects to Schmitt's political theology as failing to account for Christian theology's division between God's sovereign power and the government (administration) of the economy as delineating two separate paradigms that frame a "bipolar" system (*Id.*: 66–7). As Agamben sees it, by refusing to separate the sovereign from government, Schmitt eliminates all non-political elements in governance and law, thus privileging peoplehood, race, culture, and religion and confining legitimacy to the friend–foe spectrum (*Id.*: 74–7).

Among the most notable consequences that follow from Schmitt's brand of political theology is the rejection of pluralism alluded to earlier as well as that of liberal democracy's separation of powers. Accordingly, the broad friend–foe political framework embraced by Schmitt (at least in its secularized iteration) excludes not only pluralism but also universalism to the extent that he reduces all legitimate *demos* to the *ethnos* (that figures as the relevant community of friends). Consistent with this, the source of Schmittian legitimacy is the collective singular and the legitimacy involved looms as circular in that the law of a people emerges as legitimate to the extent to which it is that people's law.

Christianity is a universal religion in its scope and self-understanding. Schmittian Christian political theology may thus be considered to comport a universal dimension that disappears upon its secularization. Agamben's theological theory, steeped in Christianity, also projects a universal dimension, and one of the important questions that this raises is whether unlike in the case of Schmitt, in Agamben secularization does not have to precipitate a fall from universalism. At least, upon first impression, it is quite plausible that in Agamben's case secularism need not displace universalism. Indeed, whereas for Schmitt the source of legitimacy of the divinely anointed monarch is the universal God and in that of the modern polity, a particular nation, ethnic group, or other community of friends, for Agamben the relation between the Christian Deity and the *oikonomia* is structural and systemic, as is its counterpart in the secularized polity.

The key to Agamben's conception of legitimation is the dynamic between theological conjunction of the relationship between God and humans and the disjunction between the sphere of the transcendent and that of the immanent wherein government and *oikonomia* unfold. Within the Christian vision that Agamben lays out, legitimation, the universal, the singular, and the plural all neatly align into a coherent whole. Moreover, the guarantor of this legitimate order is God (even if he remains absent within the realm of the *oikonomia*) and true religion. Accordingly, the key question that secularization raises in terms of legitimacy, on the assumption that the structural and systemic interplay between law and administration remains the same, is whether the relationship between the universal, the singular, and the plural can be meaningfully harmonized, with each among these receiving its due. In other words, can the kind of legitimacy regarding law and administration guaranteed by Christianity endure the latter's demotion from *the* true religion to one contested conception of the good among many?

To be in a position to consider this last question properly, it is imperative to mark a sharp distinction between structural ordering, systemic functioning, acquiescence, and acclamation, on the one hand, and legitimation and persuasive normative justification, on the other. Even if we were fully to agree with Agamben's account of the workings of the relationship between law and administration from medieval Christianity to the present, the kind of legitimation that has been available in the context of Christian hegemony is no longer available in our contemporary religiously and ideologically diverse political environment. Because of this, either Agamben's factual account is equally compelling whether one can count on a God absent from administration or no God at all, in which case, Agamben's legal theory comes close to Luhmann's autopoietic one (discussed in Chapter 4) from the standpoint of legitimation: functionally and systemically, modern society requires the operation of a complex legal regime that cannot be further legitimated in terms of justice or of broader normative commitments. Or else, in view of the lapse of its Christian source of legitimation, Agamben's theory must be paired with a contemporary persuasive equivalent or, in the absence of the latter, be cast as standing for the proposition that the necessary nexus between law and administration present in every contemporary polity is beyond legitimation. In the latter eventuality, Agamben's gap between law and administration would bear, after all, an uncanny resemblance to Derrida's gulf between law and justice.

Agamben's legal theory derives from his assertion that Christianity separates God from his government of the world (*Id.*: 54). For the world to be well governed, it is necessary that God remain disempowered (*Id.*: 106), thus separating the transcendent order of the Kingdom of God from the immanent order of the government of human bodies (including the body politic) and souls (*Id.*: 46, 82). Although God the Father and God the Son are one (together with the Holy Spirit) ontologically, it is the passion of Jesus that manages the *oikonomia* in pursuit of salvation through providence (*Id.*: 47). It is through history that Jesus as his Father's vicar acts and governs in the latter's name (*Id.*: 138) to bring about divine grace upon the governed humans (*Id.*: 137). Providence, however, must confront the "nature of things," which are contingent and inhere within the immanent economy, thus making what appears marginal the very core of what is subjected to the act of governing (*Id.*: 118–19). In short, even divinely inspired governance must be carried out by (from a practical standpoint) an agent who must administer the contingent in his deployment of providence in the pursuit of salvation, and all that for the glory of God, the Father (*Id.*: 202). As Agamben puts it, the economy of salvation

216 TRAGIC DECONSTRUCTION SET

that Jesus institutes on earth is undertaken for the glorification of the Father and is hence an economy of glory (*Id.*).

In this account, God is omnipresent but remains completely inactive in the administration of human bodies and souls. Agamben specifies that the machine of government functions as a theodicy wherein the sovereign presence is symbolized by a supervising eye, the government, by a hand that leads and corrects, and the judgment (or judicial power) by the word that judges and condemns (*Id.*: 130). Notably, this theodicy is structured and functions like the modern state built on the rule of law (*Id.*: 142–3). The secular legislator thus becomes the vehicle of the transcendent, whereas the executive power becomes the administrator that gives life to the law by adapting it to creating order amid the unmanaged particularities and contingencies that happen to inhere within the polity. Moreover, Agamben insists that even glory has not disappeared from the modern rule-of-law state. Glory in that state may no longer be proclaimed in relation to God, but it is nonetheless directed to the people as sovereign. This secular form of glory is an acclamation expressed through public opinion, and it is to be understood as the manifestation of the people's consensus in relation to the *oikonomia* that brings them order and that furthers their destiny (*Id.*: 170). Modernity may push the transcendent divine pole of the bipolar theological government and administration model completely out of the picture, but Agamben insists it does not thereby eliminate the theological model itself (*Id.*: 284–5). On the contrary, in some important sense, atheism completes the theological model in question by taking it to its logical conclusion. In Agamben's words, "God has made the world just as if it were without God and governs it as though it governed itself" (*Id.*: 286).

Before I examine Agamben's account from the standpoint of legitimation and justice, two additional points are in order. First, Agamben observes that the theological idea of a natural order of things is also present in modern economic theory, as dramatically illustrated by Adam Smith's postulation that the economic market's functioning is guaranteed by the workings of an "invisible hand" (*Id.*: 282–4). And second, Agamben suggests that glory is best understood in terms of the void, given that the key conjunction between the king's majesty and his necessary idleness for purposes of governance is the image of an empty throne (*Id.*: 242–5). This suggests that both the expression of glory and the targeted object of one's glorification are completely open-ended, as presumably anything may suffice to overcome a pure void.

One plausible way to account for Agamben's theory involves interpreting his Christian model as figuring as an exemplary allegory of the structure and function of all legal systems and their inevitable devolution into administration. In that case, from the standpoint of legitimation, Agamben would be highly reminiscent of Luhmann. All societies require an administered *oikonomia*, and as long as order is preserved and the citizenry maintains its acclamation by glorifying some contingent being or entity, it is pointless to search for any further source of justice or legitimacy. On the other hand, one can also read Agamben's account of the Christian paradigm in its own context wherein it is inextricably linked to the acceptance of Christianity as the true religion. The main virtue of this latter reading is that it yields a rich and illustrative counterfactual that allows for a deeper and more thorough critical understanding of the problem of legitimation and the question of justice in secular contemporary rule-of-law polities.

From within Christianity, legitimation of the Christian *oikonomia* with Jesus as the vicar of God the Father is self-referential and self-explanatory. The creation is, after all, God's design, and he is the source of all truth and justice throughout the world.[8] Moreover, the bipolarity of the Christian *oikonomia* may owe to certain peculiarities of the Christian narrative (as presented by Agamben), such as the concern with reconciling providence, grace, and human free will, but does not detract from its truth and justice. What is more interesting from the present standpoint, however, is how the Christian *oikonomia* exemplifies how the universal, the singular, and the plural can be harmonized. Ontologically, the Holy Trinity is unified and embodies the universal. On the other hand, as incarnated, Jesus becomes an individual with a history, and he stands as a bridge between the individual and the universal, of which he ontologically forms a part. He also partakes in the plural in a variety of ways. Indeed, Jesus in his historical dimension is a Jew who lives in the land of Judea. Also, as a vicar of God the Father charged with the governance of human bodies and souls, Jesus confronts plurality framed by the contingent immanent factors that make up the "nature of things" that must be managed in each realm and for each generation.

Jesus as one with God and the Holy Spirit, as a Jew, and as an individual who was crucified incarnates at once the universal, the singular, and the plural. But what happens to the universal, the singular, and the plural and to the quest for their harmonization and legitimation once Jesus and Christianity have been rendered inoperative within the bounds of the secular rule-of-law state and of its godless *oikonomia*?

What remains in the secular context, consistent with Agamben's account, is the separation between sovereignty and governance and the need for acclamation in recognition and affirmation of glory. Without the reassuring presence of a universally shared religion, however, it seems that acclamation and glory become most problematic. This, as Agamben underscores, is attested by the glorification of Mussolini and fascism in Italy during the 1930s and by the rift between Il Duce and Pope Pius XI, as praise and acclamation shifted from the Christian faithful

---

[8] For present purposes, justice within the perspective of any given religion based on a transcendent divine being and claiming sole possession of the truth is ultimately either axiomatic or merely superfluous. Either the divinely prescribed is inherently just or justice plays no role in the moral/religious submission to the divine and to her godly edicts. To be sure, by divine decree humans may have free will and the choice to behave justly or unjustly. But in all cases, the relevant *criterion* of justice would exclusively be the one decreed by God.

218   TRAGIC DECONSTRUCTION SET

to fascist militants (*Id.*: 192–3). Moreover, what about the *oikonomia* without Christian providence, grace, or salvation? As already underscored by Habermas' contrast between system and lifeworld, neither the economy as a system nor bureaucratic administration standing alone can guarantee *good* governance. Likewise, the sole realization of order over the "nature of things" in a polity by no means suffices to ensure justice or legitimacy.

What Agamben's model calls for once Christianity or any other equally sweeping conception of the good fails to garner widespread consensus within a polity is first, a basis for acclamation that may be subject to legitimation consistent with the coexistence of a plurality of conceptions of the good; and second, the means to differentiate between good and bad administrative governance in light of the unbridgeable gap between law and administration.

In the end, Agamben's invocation of acclamation and administration can be interpreted as providing a path toward reconstruction when set against Derrida's deconstructive engagement with the insurmountable gap between law and justice. Moreover, as Agamben's model fails to offer a satisfactory solution to the contemporary challenges posed by the quest for justice, Agamben's reconstruction is best posited as a complement to, rather than as a replacement of, Derrida's deconstruction. Tellingly, both Derrida's and Agamben's respective theories suffer from the same crucial lack. In Derrida's case, there is no cogent criterion for distinguishing more relatively unjust laws from relatively less just ones. This bears a striking resemblance to Agamben's lack of criteria to distinguish normatively acceptable acclamations and glorifications from pernicious ones and relatively better administrative governance from relatively worse ones.

Derrida's deconstructive model, with its insurmountable gap between law and justice, makes room for the interplay between the universal and the singular, but leaves no viable space for the plural. Agamben's reconstructive model, on the other hand, once detached (ontologically as opposed to structurally or systematically) from its Christian matrix, is in the abstract ambiguous, though arguably able to integrate in its own peculiar way the universal (mostly as an empty vessel to be filled by something or someone meant to symbolize the citizenry as a whole), the singular, and the plural. More concretely and more tellingly for our purposes, however, the secular version of Agamben's account seems poised to make room for the plural and the individual, but not the universal (except in some putative populist polity completely bereft of any internal others or enemies). Indeed, those who acclaim and who glorify always constitute a collective unit that is distinguishable from others, whereas the inevitable presence of the contingent and of the particular in any unit to be administered by an *oikonomia* presupposes an interaction between distinct individualities and pluralities of interests. At the same time, as God the Father is replaced as the one to be glorified by a king, president, dictator, or other personifier of the sovereign, the polity involved seems bound to retreat from the universal to a flawed figure who seeks to become a personal symbol of the whole, but who cannot avoid fostering division and opposition from within (whether latent or manifest depending on how authoritarian a particular regime may happen to be). In other words, glory and acclamation itself seems insufficient to provide the necessary glue to hold together the requisite community of communities. Thus, for example, a Roosevelt or a Churchill may be glorified in the context of their Second World War leadership, but that would be very different from the glorification of a Hitler, a Mussolini, or a Stalin. In the case of the former two leaders, acclaim is embedded in the context of a constitutional tradition, an established rule-of-law regime, and guaranteed democratic institutions. In contrast, in the case of the latter three leaders, it is the person involved standing alone that garners glory and acclamation, but that is far from unanimous as many of those under his implacable tyrannical rule only relate to him with a mixture of terror and revulsion.

VI Assessing the Coupling of Derrida's Deconstruction and Agamben's Reconstruction from the Standpoint of the Justice Essentials

Derrida's lack of room for plurality and Agamben's seemingly purely contingent emotional collective acclamation and glorification coupled with a necessary systemic administration impervious to normative justification definitely amount to serious obstacles in the quest for justice or the justice essentials. Derrida's account of the singular and his stress on its importance without losing sight of the demands of the universal provides both an important caveat and a daunting challenge. The caveat is against de-singularization of the individual or the citizen to whom the promise of justice is addressed. The challenge is whether, in spite of the impossibility of justice, it would nevertheless be possible to find a cogent and consistent way, going beyond existential leaps made in good faith, to rank laws according to whether they are more or less unjust. Derrida himself does not furnish any guidance relating to this last quest, which is due to a large extent to his failure to address the plural. In terms of the dimension of constitutional justice that depends on harmonization between the *ethnos* and the *demos*, Derrida fiercely zeroes in on the latter, through his focus on the impossible to achieve ideal of the democracy-to-come, while nearly completely leaving out the concept of the *ethnos*.

Agamben's reconstruction does supplement Derrida's deconstruction in as much as he not only accounts for the *ethnos* but also places it squarely in the forefront. Within the Christian Holy Trinity, which Agamben argues is imprinted into every Western legal system, the universal, the singular, and the plural are all, as indicated earlier, perfectly unified, differentiated, and harmonized. But with the "fall" into secularism, the *ethnos*, which can be apparently filled in at will in the space carved out by the absent king's empty throne, becomes the main glue that holds the administrative polity together. This *ethnos* based on Agamben's vision is certainly fit to embody the plural—either one nation as distinct from others or the "insiders" within a nation as against the "outsiders" in their midst—but it may be purely arbitrary or contingent. Indeed, a charismatic leader, or an ethnic or ideological idealized projection that does not become incorporated into an appropriate national and constitutional identity may well be bereft of any connection to a workable *demos* as well as incompatible with any polity wide legitimation or justice. What Agamben adds to Derrida's account in particular, and to the search for the justice essential, in general, is focus on the indispensability of the *ethnos* and on the place of symbolism, myth, allegory, and imaginary narrative in the configuration of the ethnocentric axis of legitimation. Where Agamben fails, on the other hand, is in advancing no substitute for Christian truth and justice once his Trinitarian model of law and *oikonomia* is secularized and unmoored from its transcendent origins. In spite of this failure, however, Agamben's reference to the empty throne should serve as a reminder, which will be further pursued in Part III, that to move closer to legitimation and justice it is necessary to construct or refit both *ethnos* and *demos* in order to maximize accommodation of a plausible harmonization of the universal, the singular, and the plural.

In the end, the complementarity between Derrida's deconstruction and Agamben's reconstruction can be interpreted in two diametrically opposed ways, one negative, the other positive. The negative interpretation is that Derrida's impossibility of justice can be covered up or cast away into the background by a pure spectacle that artificially and arbitrarily alludes to glory and orchestrates acclamation. In this case, the quest for justice would fade away under a soothing illusion of glory reinforced by choruses of fervent and mutually encouraging acclamations. This scenario is most disheartening as in this interpretation Agamben's glory and acclamation bears a strong affinity to Freud's allusion to the hypnotic attachment to a leader. And consistent with this, a Hitler would fit the acclaimed and glorified leader bill as well as a Gandhi or a Mandela would.

The positive interpretation, on the other hand, seems much more encouraging. Derrida's tragic impossibility of justice does not render recourse to constitutions superfluous from the standpoint of legitimation or justice. In this interpretation, Agamben's pointing to the need for a unifying referent worthy of glorification and acclamation can be enlisted for the construction or refitting of common narratives that open paths towards cogent differentiation of lesser injustices from greater ones. Under this interpretation, construction or refitting of an appropriate *ethnos* and *demos* is an ongoing dynamic process that is never completed and always subject to revision and improvement. Moreover, within this scenario the impossibility of justice is not inconsistent with achieving the justice essentials. As emphasized from the outset, constitutions are only meant to guarantee the minimum of justice called for by the justice essentials, and therefore the assumption that full justice can never be achieved does not foreclose the possibility that some more just or lesser unjust constitutions may satisfy the justice essentials and others not. In this positive interpretation, Agamben's reconstruction adds to Derrida's deconstruction and opens the door for a sufficiently just constitution for polities that inevitably will fail to achieve anything approaching full justice no matter how hard they may try. In the last analysis, whether the promise suggested by this interpretation may actually ever come close to realization raises many difficult questions that defy any ready-made answers. These questions will be explored in Part III in the course of laying out the thesis that starting the quest for the justice essentials from the standpoint of the plural is more likely to prove fruitful than approaching the task from either the standpoint of the universal or that of the singular.

More generally, the inquiry into Derrida and Agamben and to plausible theoretical links between the two both completes the theoretical journey undertaken in this part of the book and sheds further light on some of the insights laid out in the course of the preceding chapters. Turning to certain key particulars, Agamben's disjunction between law and administration can be invoked to accentuate still further the seemingly unbridgeable gap between Kelsen's account of the systematicity and formal self-enclosure of law and Freud's psychological account of the emotional motivations for submission to law. As will be remembered, for Freud these motivations stem from guilt and remorse, on the one hand, and hypnotic attachment to a leader figure, on the other. To Kelsen's law corresponds Agamben's administration, and the two are analogous in their supposed systematicity and inherent independence from morals or politics. As against Freud's guilt and hypnotic dependence, Agamben offers glory and acclamation, which on a negative interpretation ends up being pretty equivalent, but on a positive interpretation, a possibly notable improvement. Indeed, if that which evokes glory and acclamation could be stirred towards greater legitimation, justice, and solidarity, it would exalt adherence to law as self-given for one's betterment—which is especially important in the realm of constitutional law. And this would be clearly preferable to affectively relating to law because external repression of the antisocial drives of one's Freudian id provides relief against constant fears of failure in the exercise of societally requisite self-control.

Focus on Agamben also sheds further light on the vicissitudes associated with attempts to absorb or reduce law into politics or economics. Besides his direct criticism of Schmitt briefly discussed earlier, Agamben's *oikonomia* can be profitably paired with Posner's economy as he envisions it in relation to law. To be sure, "economy" is not synonymous with *oikonomia*, but the parallels between the two in the respective hands of Agamben and of Posner are quite striking. In its early historical understanding, *oikonomia* meant the prudent ordering or management of the household; in the modern prescriptive sense invoked by Posner, the economy is the prudent-stirring management, preservation, and increase of a polity's resources with a view to maximizing wealth in order for the society involved to achieve the best possible order and harmony. In the modern context, *oikonomia*, in Agamben's view, connotes administration rather than economy. But, consistent with Habermas' distinction between system and lifeworld, both the contemporary economy and bureaucratic administration function as self-enclosed and self-sufficient systems that remain distinct from the particular lifeworlds with which they share a common social space.

If the systemic aspects of economics and administration are brought to the fore, then Posnerian law ideally would tend to dissolve into economics, whereas law in Agamben's account would become reduced to administration. Accordingly, within a law and economics ideal, reducing law to economics would be coherent and self-justified as fitting within the overall objective of achieving wealth maximization. Similarly, within Agamben's conception, recourse to administration is necessary and inherently justified as contingent human affairs require systemic management. But as we have seen, Posner's commitment to wealth maximization is inextricably linked to an embrace of a highly contestable libertarian conception of justice rejected by many in any typical contemporary constitutional democracy. Similarly, in the case of administrative bureaucratic governance, what amounts to good governance is inevitably contestable, both in terms of the internal functioning of the bureaucracy and of the lifeworld-based constraints on the deployment of the administrative system. As already alluded to, while some maintain that the administrative state veers to professional expertise, thus being largely apolitical; others, consider administration thoroughly political and "expertise," in fact, oriented toward certain (usually powerful) particular interests to the detriment of others (Rosenfeld 2011a: 2048–51). In short, what consideration of Posner and Agamben reveals from the standpoint of the justice essentials is that both the economic and administrative systems must be properly factored into the constitutional order, but that their legitimacy lies somewhere beyond wealth maximization or autonomous systemic administrative rule.

Derrida's ethics of difference and dogged emphasis on the singular highlight the shortcomings of attempting to derive the justice essentials by privileging the universal as do the theorists discussed in Chapter 5. First, except for Kant, the remaining theorists considered in that chapter put forth contestable iterations of the universal. As will be remembered, both Rawls and Habermas posit as universal actual configurations determined by contestable inclusions and exclusions, such as the exclusion of holders of metaphysical views for Habermas and of those who do not fit within reasonable pluralism for Rawls. In addition, Dworkin's universal is a contestable account of the US Constitution's community of communities from a liberal egalitarian standpoint. As against this, Kant does put forth an uncontestable account of the universal, but it is a purely formal and axiomatic one based on moral equality and the categorical imperative that only offers a negative critical tool in the pursuit of justice. All of these theories, as consideration of Derrida's insights underscores, variously de-singularize the individual and, besides Kant who completely de-singularizes her, do so in ways that reinforce their own contestable vision of the universal. Moreover, as already mentioned, Derrida's deconstructive approach to intertextuality strongly militates against Dworkin's single right-answer-in-hard-cases thesis. And on further thought, Dworkin's positing the contestable as a manifestation of something that takes the place of the universal within the US polity can be plausibly interpreted as bearing a significant affinity to Agamben's appeal to glory and acclamation as complementing the administrative characteristics of *oikonomia*. Dworkin does draw on one ideology among the many deriving from the Enlightenment and then ties it to the US Constitution, which happens to be widely acclaimed and at the very center of US glory. Also, arguably Dworkin's Hercules magically ensures the right ordering and alignment of law and justice through the guarantee of infallible interpretation. Is this comparable to Agamben's reliance on the Holy Trinity for purposes of endowing *oikonomia* with providence and grace? Are Dworkin and Agamben equally resorting to artifice to cover up, respectively, the contradictions and limitations of the Enlightenment and the mirage of a purely self-standing administrative system of governance?

In the last analysis, none of the approaches examined thus far rise above the contestable, except in ways that remain purely formal and hence lacking in positive orientation towards the justice essentials. Proponents of different contested universals, of irreducible singularity, or of various degrees of de-singularization, as well as those who entertain competing conceptions of the good that do not dwell on the universal or the singular, are all bound to foster disagreement over what constitutes legitimate law, true justice, or valid morality. Accordingly, both on the level of theory and on that of the practical embrace of religion, morality, political agendas, or ideology, there is no consensus in contemporary polities that adhere to constitutional democracy. Notably, this lack of consensus opens the way to two plausible alternatives: a struggle among competing contested normative outlooks with no reasonable basis for a consensus on legitimate law or justice, or a quest for accommodation of the relevant competing conceptions of the good within a more broadly encompassing normative framework that would make room for some workable harmonization of the universal, the singular, and the plural. Starting from the universal or the singular has not been encouraging in relation to this second alternative. In what follows, I endeavor to make the case that starting from the middle, and anchoring the quest on the plural, makes it possible to bring this second alternative to fruition and to uncover a path towards the justice essentials that may equilibrate the *ethnos* and the *demos* and allow for genuine harmonization of the universal, the singular, and the plural.

PART III

BUILDING A COMMONLY SHARED BASIS TOWARD A PLURALIST INCLUSIVIST CONSTITUTION

The analysis undertaken in Part II leads to the conclusion that neither theories starting from the top, namely from the universal, nor from the bottom, namely from the singular, can satisfactorily carve out a persuasive common ground that ought to garner consensus regarding the justice essentials. Part III starts from the middle, namely from the plural, to claim that it affords the best means to secure the justice essentials in contemporary contexts in which there are widespread disagreements on the substantive requirements issuing from distributive justice. Specifically, Part III draws on comprehensive pluralism, a theory that is pluralist all the way up and all the way down and is thus distinguishable from the limited pluralism linked to philosophical liberalism and from the value pluralism articulated by Isaiah Berlin. Comprehensive pluralism is dialectical in nature, and it emerges in sharp contrast to both philosophical monism and relativism. Comprehensive pluralism is a teleological theory that rejects the proposition that justice can be properly conceived as being independent from the good. For comprehensive pluralism, justice is a good committed to the greatest possible accommodation of competing conceptions of the good—including competing conceptions of distributive justice. In order to be maximally inclusive, comprehensive pluralism must call for a minima of fixed core prescriptions which give shape to the contours of the justice essentials.

7

The Dialectics of Comprehensive Pluralism

Approaching the Justice Essentials from the Middle

I Introduction

The critical analysis of theories relevant to the philosophical grounding of constitutional justice undertaken in Part II of this book has revealed the many difficulties inherent in finding a suitable criterion to determine what the justice essentials require in the context of liberal democratic constitutions. Law's systematicity, as articulated by Kelsen, yields a bare minimum of justice through consistent rule through law, but that falls far short of what the justice essentials may plausibly call for. Similarly, internally motivated attachment to law, through guilt or remorse as Freud sees it or through glory and acclamation as Agamben suggests, seems inherently purely contingent as far as the justice essentials are concerned. Furthermore, reducing law to politics appears largely indifferent in terms of advancing the justice essentials while subsuming law to economics has a direct impact on law's justice, but only gives rise to contested conceptions of justice that cannot garner consensus within contemporary pluralistic constitutional units. Shifting the theoretical focus and starting from the universal has also proved wanting. As we have seen, this latter approach either yields a purely negative grounding that ought to be beyond cogent contestation as is the case with Kant, or contestable non-neutral procedural constructs that inevitably skew in favor of some competing conceptions of the good against others as became apparent in the course of our discussion of Rawls and Habermas. Finally, as Derrida has underscored, law cannot at once satisfy both the universal and the singular, hence suggesting that justice is impossible. And whereas this last conclusion is by no means fatal to the quest of the justice essentials—which by definition are meant to provide substantially less than full justice—the challenge of harmonizing the universal and the singular looms as daunting. Indeed, whereas both the Enlightenment economic and democratic theory as well as the philosophies that start from the universal equate singularity with the individual, they all end up variously conceiving the latter in such abstract terms as to in effect very significantly de-singularizing her.

In the end, all the theories examined in Part II fail in important respects along the two axes that pave the way to the justice essentials: the proper harmonization of the *ethnos* and the *demos*; and the right balance between the universal, the singular, and the plural. Neither the approach from the top, through the universal,

---

A Pluralist Theory of Constitutional Justice. Michel Rosenfeld, Oxford University Press. © Michel Rosenfeld 2022.
DOI: 10.1093/oso/9780198862680.003.0008

228 DIALECTICS OF COMPREHENSIVE PLURALISM

nor that from the bottom, through the singular—understood in its irreducible particularized differentiation as made manifest in the Nietzschean, Heideggerian, and
Derridean tradition—have yielded a satisfactory outcome. In Part III of this book,
I pursue an alternative that starts from the middle, namely from the plural, and
I endeavor to make the case that pluralism is better suited than its rivals to provide
an adequate grounding and a sufficient delimitation of the justice essentials that
ought to be incorporated into liberal constitutions. In this chapter, I inquire into
the kind of pluralism that seems best suited for the task at hand, namely what I have
referred to in previous work as "comprehensive pluralism" (Rosenfeld 1998: Chs
7 & 8; 2011: Ch. 1), and which is characterized by a normative commitment to
pluralism all the way up and all the way down. Based on the normative implications
flowing from comprehensive pluralism, Chapter 8 addresses what would amount
to a suitable combination of a minimum of justice, of common identity, of individual, group, and overall autonomy, and of solidarity both among those within the
relevant constitutional unit and toward the institutional order set within the latter
for purposes of paving the way toward realization of the justice essentials. Next,
the chapter explores the dialectical consequences of comprehensive pluralism with
a view to unearthing the key constitutional particulars best suited to advance the
quest toward the justice essentials. As will be explained, comprehensive pluralism
requires the establishment of what considered separately emerges as a seemingly
anti-pluralist fixed minimum designed to yield an open-ended pluralist maximum. In other words, as a conception of the good in its own right, comprehensive
pluralism prescribes a set of fixed norms that are not susceptible of compromise.
But as a unique conception of the good that seeks to accommodate as many other
conceptions of the good as possible—and that would, in fact, be rendered meaningless if no plurality of such conceptions were in play—comprehensive pluralism
commands as extensive as possible a flexibility toward, and openness to, alternative conceptions of the good; that is, so long as the latter prove *compatible* though
not necessarily *consistent* with comprehensive pluralism by not materially trampling on its bare minimum. The interplay between the said minimum and maximum, in turn, suggests certain constitutional orderings, certain constitutional
self-understandings, certain constitutional processes, principles, and standards,
that will be briefly explored in the context of optimizing the means to the justice
essentials.

The logic behind starting from the middle is predicated on the hope that the proponents of clashing and competing conceptions of justice—and for our purposes,
primarily of distributive justice—could find sufficient common ground to agree to
a mutually acceptable constitution compliant with some suitable negotiated justice
essentials. Beyond the minimum required by the justice essentials, all remaining
contested facets of justice could then be relegated to appropriate realms of extra-
constitutional and infra-constitutional interaction. Moreover, what is essential
is for proponents of competing conceptions of justice to settle on a single set of

justice essentials for their particular constitutional unit. And this can be achieved by adhering, either factually or counterfactually, to the normative constraints imposed by comprehensive pluralism. As we have seen, there is no common ground that would prompt a wealth maximizer, a Marxist, a Schmittian, a Rawlsian, and a Derridean to reach a principled agreement on the justice essentials. Accordingly, what adherence to comprehensive pluralism is meant to achieve, as will be detailed in what follows, is either to convince the above-mentioned antagonists of the need for pluralist accommodation at the constitutional level or to impose on intransigent anti-pluralists, such as militant Schmittians, the minimums necessary to allow for the fair pursuit of as extensive as possible a measure of pluralist inclusion within the relevant constitutional ambit.

II Comprehensive Pluralism's Negative and Positive Dialectical Moments and Their Hegelian Origins

As I have laid out the tenets of comprehensive pluralism extensively elsewhere, I will concentrate here on those of its principal features best suited to highlight its potential in the context of constitutional justice. To begin with, it is important to underscore that philosophically comprehensive pluralism is distinguishable from both monism and relativism (Rosenfeld 2011: 26), and that it also differs significantly from value pluralism as articulated by Isaiah Berlin (*Id.*: 37–42). Monism, whether deontological or teleological, primes unity and the universal at the expense of the plural. In deontological theories within the Kantian tradition, justice transcends all competing conceptions of the good and is hence conceived as being truly universal. In teleological theories, such as utilitarianism or wealth maximization, the underlying conception of the good—the greatest happiness of the greatest number, or the greatest possible total wealth to help enable each individual to realize her lifelong objectives—is cast as universally valid and as superior to all competing ones. More generally, all monistic normative theories—whether a religion, such as Christianity,[1] an ideology, such as Marxism, or a moral and political philosophy, such as libertarianism or liberal egalitarianism—proceed on the assumption that they are the possessors of a monopoly on the truth, on right and wrong, on justice, and on the good.

Philosophical liberalism (as contrasted to political liberalism) may seem at first not to fit within the monistic mold in as much as it does call for pluralism. But upon further consideration, the pluralism in question is limited rather than

---

[1] Even if under certain interpretations of Christianity allowance is made for other Abrahamic religions as partaking in the beliefs and dictates of true religion, in the end for Christians the full truth only belongs to one religion, namely their own. As noted in Chapter 1, Pope Benedict XVI has asserted that Catholicism is the sole possessor of *the* truth, including in morals and law, and that the truth in question can either be revealed through faith or deduced through reason (Cartabia & Simoncini 2015: 3–9).

comprehensive in nature. For example, as emphasized by its great nineteenth-century proponent, John Stuart Mill, liberalism accords outright priority to the individual over the group and to liberty over all other values except (individual) physical integrity and life (Mill: 1961). In other words, within liberalism, liberal norms and values are hierarchically entrenched as true, right, good, and just, but leave room for, and even encourage, some limited deployment of pluralism. Thus, liberalism fosters freedom of religion and provides for coexistence of a wide array of religious and non-religious conceptions of the good. Nevertheless, the core liberal precepts that are monistically justified impose constraints upon the free exercise of religion and thus prime individual liberty over any conflicting religion-based moral or legal imperative. In sharp contrast to this limited pluralism fostered by liberalism, comprehensive pluralism, as will become clear shortly, does not grant any *prima facie* priority to any norm, value, or conception of the good—such as the individual over the group, or liberty over plausible competing values—that is not inextricably tied to pluralism itself.

Relativism stands as the philosophical opposite of monism, and in strict logic provides that norms, values, truth, and justice can only legitimated from within the conception of the good from which they issue. Thus, Catholic truth is only persuasive to Catholics, Marxism to Marxists, liberalism to liberals, and fascism to fascists. Strictly understood, relativism is dangerous in that it places all conceptions of the good on a par and allows for no cogent comparison among them. Consequently, Nazi justice is as good under Nazism as is pacifist justice under pacifism or environmental justice under environmentalism. Needless to add, systematic adherence to relativism precludes any plausible balance among the universal, the singular, and the plural in any polity that is not exclusively made up of a citizenry that unanimously embraces the very same conception of justice.

Because it is a conception of the good among others—as it primes maximizing accommodation of the greatest possible plurality of perspectives—comprehensive pluralism has been accused of ultimately being monistic (Michelman 2020: 1962–70). Moreover, because of its predisposition to being inclusive of a wide array of distinct and often clashing conceptions of the good, without chasing away many clearly anti-pluralist ones, comprehensive pluralism has also been criticized as being in the end relativistic (*Id.*). If these criticisms are warranted and it is either monistic or relativistic, or worse some combination of the two, then comprehensive pluralism would figure as least apt to lead the way to the justice essentials. Indeed, as a conception of the good in its own right comprehensive pluralism would be one among the many competing contested ones vying for primacy, but as already noted, no contested conception of the good is fit to yield norms of justice that may be vindicated as legitimate for all those encompassed within the same constitutional unit. On the other hand, if it accommodates conceptions of the good that contradict its own, such as a religion which has no tolerance for those who do not share its vision of the truth and which discourages its adherents from having contact with those who do not belong to their religious community, then comprehensive pluralism may well appear to be veering towards relativism. In the worst-case scenario, the comprehensive pluralist is bent on advancing his own ideology against those of others while at the same time affording protection to anti-pluralist and anti-liberal ideologies with the consequence of accommodating a wide range of conflicting ideologies regardless of their anti-pluralist convictions or agendas.

These criticisms can be refuted, and comprehensive pluralism defended as neither monistic nor relativistic—though in its own special way partially incorporating aspects of the two—if the process the latter sets in motion is understood dialectically. Moreover, in order to situate the dialectic in question in context, it is helpful first to briefly distinguish comprehensive pluralism from Berlin's value pluralism. Berlin attacks monism on two fronts: first, it is hard and artificial to establish a hierarchy of values to preserve unity (Berlin 2002: 12); and second, monism tends to be all-encompassing which facilitates subjugation of large numbers of people as exemplified by certain forms of nationalism, Marxism, and fascism (Berlin 1997: 20–48). Thus, instead of tying oneself in knots to try to find a cogent hierarchical order involving liberty and equality, one ought to recognize that both liberty and equality are morally compelling, that their demands are sometimes contradictory, and that we ought to adjust to this plurality. By accepting a plurality of values, Berlin believes that human cruelty and oppression can be considerably reduced (Berlin 2002: 13). In other words, as Berlin sees it, monism risks turning unity into an instrument of oppression while pluralism not only makes us aware of human vulnerability but also makes us more accepting of human diversity. Thus, for example, those who prefer liberty should be accepting of those who prefer equality as both are equally worthy values and neither ranks above the other. Berlin is ultimately a proponent of limited pluralism because aware of the dangers of falling into the moral abyss of relativism, he specifies that there are many different morally worthy values, but not too many (*Id.*: 11). Whereas Berlin is unclear as to whether one can articulate a cogent and consistent criterion to distinguish between worthy and unworthy values—and he allows for worthy values to depend, at least in part, on time and place (Berlin 2001: 157)—his unmistakable exclusion of a large number of values clearly prevents him from falling into relativism while leaving open the question of whether he is in the last analysis a monist. Berlin himself has expressed an unbending preference for political liberalism (Berlin 2002: 47–8) and a predilection for negative liberty over positive liberty (Berlin 1970: 171). For present purposes, the best way to understand Berlin is to regard him as embracing a mid-level limited pluralism leaving open at a deep level whether or not there is a monist principle to sort out unworthy values. Although limited, Berlin's pluralism is distinguishable from that of liberalism in that, unlike in the latter pluralism, value pluralism is not circumscribed and thus limited by a hierarchal unified monist vision.

In contrast to Berlin's pluralist theory, comprehensive pluralism is, as already mentioned, pluralist all the way up and all the way down, and its dialectic is all

232 DIALECTICS OF COMPREHENSIVE PLURALISM

encompassing thus extending to law, morals, politics, and all domains of justice. The dialectic involved draws on Hegel's, but with one major difference relating to Hegel's conception of a historical progression culminating in the end of history. Hegel's dialectic, as encapsulated in the struggle for recognition between the lord and the bondsman (Hegel 1977: paras 178–196), is one that pits a self against (an) other in a series of conflicts that can only be resolved through shifts in perspectives and a reordering of priorities that in turn reposition or transform selves and others in ways that provoke new conflicts that also call for resolution. In the case of the lord and the bondsman, the antagonists are transformed through a series of dialectical reversals. The lord first seeks recognition without having to reciprocate, by enslaving the bondsman. But by forcing the bondsman to work for him, the lord becomes dependent on the labor of the bondsman, and accordingly their relationship becomes transformed. As a consequence of this dialectical reversal, in the words of Jean Hyppolite, the slave becomes the master of the master, while the master becomes the slave of the slave (Hyppolite 1946: 166). Furthermore, this reversal makes it plain that the desired recognition, which led the lord to subordinate the bondsman, cannot be realized so long as the antagonists remain unequal. To resolve the struggle for recognition another dialectical reversal must take place, in order to put the antagonists in a position mutually to recognize one another as equals.

Hegel envisions his dialectic as carving out a progression throughout history and culminating at the end of history with a complete alignment between reason and reality in Absolute Spirit. This progression and its culmination have been characterized as highly implausible by contemporary critics, such as Charles Taylor (Taylor 1975: 547, 551). Comprehensive pluralism shares Taylor's conclusion and approaches each conflict with a view to its dialectical resolution without any presumption regarding any systemic progression, and much less any expectation of some kind of final culmination. What is crucial for comprehensive pluralism is the dialectical process that Hegel proposes to resolve conflicts that pit those who conceive themselves as selves against those whom they conceive as others. In such a conflict, self and other operate as separate parts that lack connection into a commonly shared whole. For Hegel, the dialectical process leads to the incorporation of the contending parts into a whole that transcends them in a way that results in both a cancellation and a preservation of the parts involved. Hegel refers to this process as *Aufhebung*, and specifies:

> What transcends (*Aufheben*) itself does not thereby become [n]othing ... It ... retains the determinateness whence it started. To transcend (*Aufheben*) has this double meaning, that it signifies to keep or to preserve and also to make to cease, to finish ... Thus, what is transcended is also preserved; it has only lost its immediacy and is not on that account annihilated. (Hegel 1999: 119–20)

Adapting this Hegelian approach to the constitutional context, it bears emphasizing that at all levels, constitution-making, constitutional interpretation, and constitutional reform or overhaul, there is at the base some conflict between what can be characterized as a self or selves and (an) other or others. This relates, moreover, to the universal as well as to the singular and the plural. Thus, for example, at the making of the US 1787 Constitution, slaves and women were for the most part left out from the carving out of the constitutional community of communities as well as from some of the most coveted benefits that the said constitution imparted. Similarly, during the same period, the French revolutionary constitutions made the Third Estate into the whole while excluding women and privileging the bourgeois middle class as against the more impoverished strata of the people. More generally, in the course of the life of all liberal constitutions, some can complain of suffering from inegalitarian constitutional designs or consequences while others benefit from the same. Furthermore, these constitutions seem bound to be to some extent inegalitarian with respect to all three dimensions of constitutionally relevant distributive justice. If a constitution as a whole favors the entrepreneurial class and disadvantages those who must join the labor force, then the latter can complain that their constitutional community of communities causes them to incur material redistribution injustices. Similarly, a gay person or a member of a religious minority can complain of identitarian or recognition-based injustice in the absence of constitutional protection based on sexual orientation and in the presence of a constitutional preference afforded to the religious majority to the detriment of religious minorities. Finally, there have been glaring injustices in representation wherever women were denied the right to vote, and perhaps somewhat more subtle ones at present in cases in which, within the same polity, some ethnic groups enjoy greater self-determination than others due to an existing imbalance in the carving out of electoral districts.

Drawing on an analogy to Hegel's lord/bondsman dialectic, those who wittingly or unwittingly benefit to the detriment of others under a particular constitutional status quo stand in the shoes of the lord. Furthermore, comprehensive pluralism starts from the position that in the first (dialectical) moment[2] all conceptions of the good at play—whether relating to material welfare, recognition, or representation—are considered to be *prima facie* entitled to equal treatment and equal recognition. And accordingly, in its first dialectical moment—the negative moment—comprehensive pluralism requires the negation of all lord-like constitutional inegalitarian designs or consequences to level the playing field so all contending relevant selves and others can be placed on an equal footing. Moreover,

---

[2] Comprehensive pluralism's dialectic is made up of a logical succession starting with a negative moment followed by a positive one and culminating in a dialectical resolution that eliminates the original conflict while leaving the door open to new ones. The logical sequence involved may correspond to a historical one, but there is no necessary temporal correlation between the two.

234　DIALECTICS OF COMPREHENSIVE PLURALISM

this negative levelling of all inegalitarian advantages is likely to extend to all among the *ethnos* (constitutional identity being distinct from national or transnational identity), the *demos* (who is or not included and how are distinct relevant groups faring under proportional representation), the universal (who is the people, and who is integrated better or worse into it), the singular (are certain classes of individuals or certain attributes of singularity favored to the detriment of others?), and the plural (are certain relevant groups unacknowledged, unrepresented, or underrepresented?).

Completion of the first dialectical moment of comprehensive pluralism, which in Hegelian terms consists in the negation—through eradication or exposure—of all prevailing inequalities among proponents of distinct competing conceptions of the good, seems bound to result in an actual or counterfactually imagined levelled field that proves constitutionally unmanageable. Indeed, if religious fanatics bent on converting or killing the infidel are to be as equally accommodated as Marxists, libertarians, atheist nationalists, and populists, and many others with a wide range of conflicting values and objectives, then institutional peace, order, or justice would seem utterly impossible. Accordingly, the first dialectical logical moment and its levelled field must be (logically) followed by a second positive dialectical moment—the negation of negation in Hegelian terms—in order to provide a factual or counterfactually cogent and plausible constitutional construct susceptible of advancing the quest toward the justice essentials. The aim of this second positive moment is the restructuring of the now levelled (but immobilized) playing field according to comprehensive pluralism's *ethos* which prescribes the greatest possible inclusion and accommodation of the greatest possible number of diverse conceptions of the good that happen to have adherents within the relevant constitutional unit. Furthermore, deployment of this second dialectical moment could well lead to the total exclusion of some of the now equalized conceptions of the good—if no aspects or aims of the above-mentioned fanaticized religion can be disentangled from its convert or kill the infidel mandate, then it ought to be altogether excluded from the pluralist constitutional order—and partial inclusion to various degrees of the remaining conceptions of the good. Although *how much* of *which* conceptions ought to be accommodated in this second dialectical moment is context- as well as content-dependent, no perspective other than that of comprehensive pluralism is to be fully accommodated on its own terms and according to its own truth.

To illustrate the two moments of the comprehensive pluralist dialectic and their journey towards a Hegelian *Aufhebung* resulting in a redeployment of conflicting parts into a new whole, one can refer to how the European wars of religion between Catholics and Protestants led to secularism which, as mentioned in Chapter 1, became a mainstay of liberal constitutionalism. Let us assume that in a Catholic majority country where Catholicism is the official state religion that dominates all public life, a civil war erupts between Catholics and Protestants, who constitute a significant minority. Institutionally in that setting, there are glaring inequalities that favor Catholics over Protestants. Furthermore, assuming that the religious civil war looms as endless as neither side is strong enough to secure a total victory, what we confront is a mutually destructive and apparently insoluble all-out war over imposing two incompatible conceptions of religious truth. Although both sides may be seeking victory in order to impose their own theological truth to all within the realm, it becomes apparent that no theologically framed outcome is likely to occur. Applying the pluralist dialectic to this situation, in the first negative moment, all Catholic state privileges would be eradicated. That would make Catholics and Protestants institutional equals but would not in any way alter their theological-based impasse. Accordingly, in the pluralist dialectic's second moment the state would become decoupled from religion through the introduction of institutional secularism. This would presumably allow for a truce between the religious antagonists by creating a public space within which they would both be excluded and a private space allowing each of them freely to organize their own communal life. This would entail a reordering in which each of the warring religion's claim to exclusivity would be negated in exchange for peace and a somewhat constrained pursuit of their respective objectives. In particular, each of the two religions involved would be precluded from pursuing the imposition of its truth beyond its own confined communal boundaries. In other words, if each of these religions believes that it has a divine mission to impose its truth universally within the polity and to do so through the powers of the state, the implantation of institutional secularism will equally limit and frustrate them. Finally, as alluded to in Chapter 1, once deployed, institutional secularism gives rise to new contradictions and new claims of inequities—such as that secularism is anti-religious rather than neutral and that it (at least implicitly) favors some religions over others. Accordingly, the contradictions of institutional secularism will also end up calling for a redeployment of the two moments of the pluralist dialectic in the quest for a more inclusionary and more equitable integration of the relevant contending parties experiencing increasing frustrations within the confines of institutional secularism.

The dialectical logic of comprehensive pluralism and of its two distinct moments engender a division of norms, values, and the good into two separate categories. All norms associated with all conceptions of the good *other than* comprehensive pluralism figure as *first-order norms*. On the other hand, the norms issuing from comprehensive pluralism itself constitute *second-order norms*. In the first negative moment of the dialectic, the second-order norms require a complete levelling of differences and resulting equalization of all competing conceptions of the good and all the first-order norms which the latter (jointly or severally) promote within the relevant constitutional unit, *regardless of the content* of any of the first-order norms involved. In contrast, in the dialectic's second positive moment, all now levelled but immobilized first-order norms vying for inclusion within the confines of a working constitutional order must be considered for (re)admission and accommodation pursuant to the dictates of comprehensive pluralism's second-order norms.

236 DIALECTICS OF COMPREHENSIVE PLURALISM

In this positive moment, any conflict between first-order norms and second-order norms must be resolved in favor of the latter, thus ascribing second-order norms a lexical priority over their first-order counterparts. For example, if a religious, fascist, Marxist, or nationalist conception of the good depends for its very survival on the total suppression of all possible rivals, then any activation[3] of the project of the conception at stake would have to be altogether banned within the relevant constitutional unit consistent with the second-order norms imposed by comprehensive pluralism. In other words, militant, aggressive, uncompromisingly prone to violence anti-pluralism has no place in a constitutional unit that incorporates comprehensive pluralism's second-order norms.

Banning completely militantly and aggressively anti-pluralist ideological deployments represents an easy case under the second-order norms operating in the course of the positive moment within comprehensive pluralism's dialectic. Much more difficult cases arise when sets of conflicting first-order norms that are not incompatible with second-order norms cannot be all equally accommodated within pluralist constitutional confines. Suppose that a country is 60 per cent Christian, 30 per cent Muslim, and 10 per cent Jewish, and that the common welfare of the polity as a whole requires preservation of a six-day work week, but that giving each of the concerned religions its own day of rest would result in unacceptable economic hardships. Since the three religions involved require respectively Sunday, Friday, and Saturday as the normatively mandated day of rest, one way to preserve (at least formal) equality among them would be to designate some other day, say Tuesday, as the country's official day of rest. That would, of course, be an unacceptable solution from the standpoint of comprehensive pluralism's standpoint as it would amount to a total denial of pluralist accommodation (pursuant to the second moment of the dialectic's imperative) for purposes of preserving (first moment acquired) equality, resulting in total frustration of all involved. One default solution under these circumstances would be to choose Sunday as that would accommodate 60 per cent of the citizenry as opposed to only accommodating 30 per cent or 10 per cent. But that default solution would not be justified if comparing the place and role of the day of rest in each of the three religions, we found out that it was much more important in one of them than in the other two. Let us imagine (and this is pure hypothetical speculation as I claim no expertise on the subject) that Judaism requires total abstention from work on the Sabbath whereas Christianity allows working on Sunday so long as one attends Church and Islam similarly requires Mosque prayers but no work ban on Fridays. In that case, within the hierarchy of first-order norms inherent within Judaism complete abstention from work on the

---

[3] I distinguish "activation" from "advocacy" for reasonable minds and different constitutional democracies differ over whether advocacy of fascism as opposed to action in pursuit of its institutionalization ought to be protected speech or punishable anti-democratic incitement. See Rosenfeld 2012 (contrasting the legality of pro-Nazi speech in the United States with its prohibition under criminal law in Germany).

Sabbath would rank much higher that it would within its counterparts in either Christianity or Islam. And accordingly, based on a comparison of the import of abstention from work on the day of rest within each of the three religions' cluster of first-order norms, the best pluralist accommodation may be to choose Saturday as the official day of rest while prescribing affording Christians and Muslims enough time on their respective days of rest to fulfill their collective religious obligations.[4]

In the preceding example, all three religions could be satisfied as far as their essential requirements were concerned, although two of them would have preferred another outcome. In many cases, however, accommodation of one conception of the good can only come at the expense of another. In the latter context, comprehensive pluralism requires an inter-communal comparison of the respective importance of the sought after scarce good within each of the contending bundles of first-order norms, with a view to awarding the latter to the group for which it turns out to be more important. For example, suppose a small village's last bottle of wine is sought by two groups, a religious one which uses wine as part of a sacred ritual and another group which uses wine to make a toast in celebration of a successful fundraising campaign in the pursuit of environmental protection objectives. On the surface, both claims involved appear to be on an equal footing. But on further examination under comprehensive pluralism's criterion of "justice as reversible reciprocity" (Rosenfeld 1998: 214, 245–50), proponents of the religious group should trade places with those of the environmentalist group so that both sets of proponents can grasp the importance of the wine from *within* each of the perspectives involved. After those in each group imagine themselves as adhering to the bundle of first-order norms of the other group, they may well conclude in our example that drinking the wine is more important within one of the two perspectives involved. For example, the drinking of wine might be part of an important traditional religious ritual whereas the environmentalist group might just as well achieve its celebratory objective by switching to beer.

To recapitulate: the second positive moment of the pluralist dialectic conditions accommodation within the constitutional order on *compatibility*—not conformity—with pluralism's second-order norms, and with resolution of conflicts among perspectives involving different sets of first-order norms by submission to the dictates of justice as reversible reciprocity—to be contrasted with "mere reciprocity" which only requires acknowledging that the other has a perspective without any obligation to try to understand or imagine any conflict with the other from within the latter's perspective. Furthermore, it should be clear by now how relativism and monism figure in the dynamic of the pluralist dialectic. The negative moment is relativistic in that it takes every conception of the good it encounters on

---

[4] I leave aside, for present purposes, whether at some point the number of adherents of each religion ought to be factored in so as to change the result. What if there were only 1,000 Jews in a country of 30 million?

its own terms. The positive moment, on the other hand, is monistic as it subjects all the equalized conceptions of the good it confronts to its own set of normative constraints. Within this dynamic, however, the relativist moment only preconditions passage through a monistic process which itself only figures as a necessary step towards the best possible deployment of the comprehensive pluralist *ethos.* In Hegelian terms, the relativism in the dialectic fuels the initial deployment of negation which is countered by a monistically driven negation of the negation to result in an *Aufhebung* that yields an end-state that is at once both pluralist all the way up and down and inevitably bound to lead to new conflicts and contradictions calling for a new round of the pluralist dialectic's levelling and (re)accommodation.

Adapting the pluralist dialectic to a constitution aspiring to the justice essentials requires constitutionalizing pluralism's second-order norms and instituting constitutionally grounded processes that allow for adhering to the requirements of justice as reversible reciprocity. The fixed second-order norms and associated processes can be regarded as establishing a (seemingly anti-pluralist) fixed minimum apt to guaranteeing a pluralist maximum predicated on inclusion and accommodation. An inquiry into this minimum and maximum and into its adaptation into the constitutional order in the pursuit of the justice essentials will be postponed until Chapter 8. What is essential at this point, given the preceding focus on the contours of the pluralist dialectic, is to address the question of *why* turn to comprehensive pluralism now that we have a better idea on *how* to proceed should we be morally and constitutionally impelled to doing so.

III The Normative Case for Comprehensive Pluralism

Liberal constitutionalism is inextricably committed, albeit sometimes implicitly, to some measure of (limited) pluralism. Moreover, the minimum of pluralism which must be incorporated within any liberal constitutional order implicates at least two of the three relevant dimensions of distributive justice that we have discussed throughout. Indeed, whereas plurality may be plausibly deemed normatively irrelevant with respect to material redistribution consistent with the justice essentials, the same cannot be said with respect to recognition or representation. All contemporary constitutional units at the national or transnational level comprise a plurality of ethnic, ideological, religious, cultural, philosophical, linguistic, or national identities adhering to competing and at times conflicting bundles of first-order norms. Even if group identity were rendered completely constitutionally irrelevant, as has largely been the case in the French secular republican tradition, the mere differences in singularity among the individuals concerned would require plurality sustaining and promoting constitutional norms. Thus, for example, freedom of speech and freedom of religion rights both assume and encourage pursuit of different views and conceptions of the good through which various individuals manifest an identity of their own which is distinct from that of many, if not all, others. Similarly, the right to vote and equality in representation would be largely meaningless in the absence of a plurality of group and/or individual views of the common (universal), individual (singular), and group-based (plural) good. In short, all relevant constitutional units are pluralist in fact and the very concepts of liberal constitutionalism and of the justice essentials associated with the latter require some degree of normatively prescribed and constitutionally enshrined pluralism.

Consistent with this, liberal constitutionalism and the justice essentials call for the limited pluralism of philosophical liberalism or even perhaps for value pluralism. But that itself does not provide any persuasive reason to justify moving from qualified to comprehensive pluralism. Accordingly, it is necessary to make a positive case for comprehensive pluralism, to specify how it might better serve the ideal of liberal constitutionalism, and how it might optimize the justice essentials destined for incorporation within the constitution.

Comprehensive pluralism is a conception of the good in its own right and it is teleological in nature. Just as utilitarianism proclaims that the good consists in maximizing utilities, comprehensive pluralism posits the good as the greatest possible accommodation of plurality within the constraints imposed through the deployment of its two-pronged dialectic. All societies confront plurality at the level of individual singularity, of collective allegiance, of the community of the whole, and of interactions between the society at stake and others beyond. As mentioned, liberal constitutionalism requires adherence to at least limited pluralism and can thus be satisfactorily integrated within liberalism in its many deontological and teleological guises. Moreover, although this will not be addressed any further in what follows, liberal constitutionalism can also be paired with republicanism or with communitarianism, provided these leave adequate room for diversity comparable to that assured by limited pluralism (Rosenfeld 1998: 217–24). Given all this, the burden that confronts proponents of comprehensive pluralism is to provide persuasive arguments concerning why and how their conception of the good furnishes a preferable normative grounding to both liberal constitutionalism and to its justice essentials.

The case for comprehensive pluralism as the best means to the good and to the promotion of justice—which can made generally, but which will be largely limited here to the constitution and to its justice essentials—is essentially threefold. Comprehensive pluralism best promotes and sustains enrichment of the self; it is uniquely positioned to foster what I have termed "a superior normative aesthetics"; and it provides for the best possible mutual accommodation among proponents of different perspectives and conceptions of the good (Rosenfeld 2011: 43). These three goods, moreover, are complementary and mutually reinforcing.

The self, whether individual or collective, cannot prosper or thrive without mutual recognition as highlighted in Hegel's dialectic of the lord and the

240 DIALECTICS OF COMPREHENSIVE PLURALISM

bondsman. More specifically, at all levels of the individual, the universal as embodied in constitutional units, and the various groups coexisting and often competing within the polity, human beings interact as selves confronting others and must forge a destiny for themselves and with others by successfully negotiating the tensions resulting from confrontations among poles of identity and poles of difference or diversity. As illustrated by the example of the German woman who is a Catholic and a feminist discussed in the Introduction, the very singularity of the typical contemporary individual living in a constitutional democracy is drawn from, and oriented towards, a plurality of perspectives and of bundles of first-order norms. Accordingly, the widest possible pluralist exposure affords the greatest challenge and opportunity to find the best suited expression of one's singularity while entering into the most promising allegiances to forge a successful path to self-enrichment and self-realization from both an individual and a collective standpoint. To be sure, everyone is born and raised in particular settings that imbue her with singularities and allegiances that she cannot, or does not want to, discard and which limit her choices among the plurality of available alternatives within the ambit of the constitutional unit to which she belongs. However, even for the most exclusionary and self-enclosed groups who are nonetheless deserving of accommodation consistent with the applicable second-order norms, pluralism looms as the preferable alternative. Take the example of a virtually hermetically self-enclosed religious community that wants to remain apart from the rest of the citizenry whom it morally abhors for what it regards as its ungodly ways, but that behaves peacefully, within the rule of law, and without any attempt to proselytize any non-believer. Arguably, such a community is better off under a pluralist vision that is likely to be more accepting and accommodating than its competitors. Indeed, whereas the prevalent tendency may well be to treat the community in question as a hostile "other" that ought to be criticized for rejecting the values that are dear to most, ignored, or at best barely tolerated, comprehensive pluralism counsels approaching the religious community involved as fellow citizens devoted to self-enrichment and self-realization just as the rest of us are. Furthermore, if we follow the pluralist *ethos* thoroughly, we ought to try to empathize with the group in question by imagining how we would wish to conduct our own lives if we shared their religious commitments. In sum, pluralist accommodation may end up adding little to mere tolerance from the perspective of a separate hermetically self-enclosed group, but it looms as clearly better from that of outsiders and of the constitutional unit as a whole. Also, in contemporary polities even the most self-contained groups cannot avoid contact with outsiders, whether because they need hospitals, welfare assistance, or other limited interactions with actors within the state or civil society. And in the latter case, members of the group in question would visibly and directly benefit from the attitude of others committed to pluralist accommodation.

What I have labelled as comprehensive pluralism's "superior normative aesthetics" stands as a corollary to pluralist self-enrichment. Based on the premise that plurality and diversity enrich the arts and ought to be therefore variously pursued and encouraged, comprehensive pluralism counsels an analogous openness, accommodation and promotion of exposure to as many perspectives and conceptions of the good as can be productively integrated within the polity. From the standpoint of self-enrichment through exposure, interaction, and creative involvement in art, it seems optimal to have access to museums that collectively house a wide variety of styles, schools, ideologies, and plastic visions. Indeed, the diversity in question is likely to enhance the opportunities for one who seeks inspiration in art for purposes of self-definition and self-enrichment as well as for one who endeavors to embrace the language game of art to pursue self-expression and self-realization. Moreover, these engagements with the plastic arts, literature, or music in all their diversity are poised to benefit those interested both in their singular individuality and in their collective allegiances. Analogously, exposure to different religions and various secular conceptions of good, diverse political ideologies, and multiple ethical outlooks, may contribute to mapping out multiple constructive paths to intersubjective cooperation and individual self-realization.

In this latter respect, the embrace of pluralism against monistic universalism issuing from religion or from the Enlightenment-based secularism by Jonathan Sacks, a contemporary Orthodox rabbi and philosopher in Isaiah Berlin's tradition (Sacks 2003), is particularly instructive. As a leading religious leader and once Chief Rabbi of the United Kingdom, Sacks largely confines his pluralism to the realm of religion in all its manifest diversity, but the logic of his moral argument can be easily extended to encompass secular as well as religious conceptions of the good. The central thesis advanced by Sacks is:

> that *difference* is the source of value, and indeed of society itself. It is precisely because we are not the same as individuals, nations or civilizations that our exchanges are non-zero-sum encounters. Because each of us has something someone else lacks, and we each lack something someone else has, we gain by interaction. (*Id.*: 14–15)

Sacks exhorts us to forsake both tribalism and monistic universalism in order to embrace the "dignity of difference" (*Id.*: 21). Moreover, whereas he provides an answer to the question left open by Berlin's value pluralism by asserting that the monotheistic God of the Abrahamic religions is the ultimate guarantor of normative validity, he insists that the purpose of divine creation was to promote the sanctity of human life and the blessing of freedom through the flourishing of diversity (*Id.*: 19). Sacks drives home this essential insight through a powerful recasting of the one the most widespread religious creeds, namely that God created man and woman in his own image:

242 DIALECTICS OF COMPREHENSIVE PLURALISM

> God makes every person in the same image—His image—and each is different. The
> challenge to the religious imagination is to see God's image in one who is not in our
> image. That is the converse of tribalism. But it is also something other than univer-
> salism. It takes difference seriously (*Id.*: 60).

Although accused by some within his own religious community of betraying Jewish
beliefs (*Id.*: vii), Sacks at once asserts seemingly paradoxically that he adheres to *the*
truth of Orthodox Judaism, but that humanity is richer and normatively better off because of the contributions of other religions, including non-Abrahamic ones such as
Buddhism and Hinduism (*Id.*: 18).

Comprehensive pluralism's normative esthetics can both account for the seeming
paradox in Sacks' position and extend the scope of the dignity of difference by being
as inclusive of non-religious conceptions of the good as of religious ones. Starting
with greater inclusivity, from a comprehensive pluralist standpoint there is no normatively significant difference between those who aim to eradicate poverty because
of their faith in Christ and atheists who are just as committed to the same objective
because they regard mitigation of human suffering as their moral, ethical, and political duty and as an indispensable component of their journey toward self-realization
as individuals and as members of certain historically situated collective units. More
generally, both those who reject religion to make the most of their stay on earth and
those who embrace contemplative religion oriented towards a transcendent afterlife
are equally poised to contributing to an enrichment of human expression and self-
fulfillment and to an enhancement of the dignity of diversity. Thus, consistent with
comprehensive pluralism, everyone is encouraged to find or preserve *her own truth*
so long as the latter does not prompt her to act in ways that are *incompatible* with its
second-order norms.

Turning to Sacks' seeming paradox, the pluralist normative esthetic is in no way
meant to undermine anyone's commitment to his own conception of the good or
belief in the truth of his own religious, areligious, or irreligious outlook. It is not the
aim of the pluralist esthetic to relativize everyone's convictions and propagate self-
doubt, but instead to encourage recasting the differences demarcating the others
from the self in ways that promote better understanding and mutual accommodation. Instead of treating those who adhere to religions other than mine as enemies of the truth, the esthetic approach counsels that I learn to focus on the latter
as persons who seek the same type of spiritual goods and avenues to fulfillment
as I do. And accordingly, Sacks is perfectly consistent when he says that he absolutely adheres to *his* truth, namely that of Orthodox Judaism, which for him is in
no way equivalent to that of Hinduism. Indeed, Sacks can welcome the latter, for
even if for him it is in error, it still enriches humankind as it allows a larger segment of humanity to expand the good faith search for truth and the quest for divine

inspiration.[5] In short, instead of veering toward mutual destruction in the name of the truth, the world will be better off if we all acknowledge that most others work toward the truth as we do, but (from our firmly anchored perspective) only succeed in part.

At a deeper level, Sacks' insight—namely, that absolute fidelity to one's own truth is enhanced, not diminished, by witnessing others' very different searches for truth that will result in partial, if any, success from one's own perspective—is systemically vindicated by the normative esthetics of comprehensive pluralism. Indeed, even if one adheres to the latter systematically, one would still have to be in some important ways non-pluralistic and that would have to extend to some of one's normative choices. Assuming that one embraces comprehensive pluralism's second-order norms as paramount and treats all constitutional, legal, institutional, and society-wide issues accordingly, the norms involved would become pretty superfluous if everyone relied on them exclusively in all aspects of life. If all humanity became nothing more than comprehensive pluralists, the latter's second-order norms would become transformed into the only valid set of universally embraced first-order norms. But for comprehensive pluralism to make sense, even its most ardent proponents must, as indicated earlier, have legitimate non-pluralist convictions and objectives so long as these are not incompatible with pluralism. In the context of esthetics, as a city's only museum's director, pluralism would require me to assemble a collection that is as inclusive as possible of diverse schools and styles. But as a private collector who displays art at home, it would be perfectly appropriate that I collect surrealist art to the exclusion of all other types of works. As long as I do not treat those who prefer abstract expressionism as esthetic pariahs who lack taste but as people who seek, as I do, enrichment through art, then I serve the dignity of diversity better than if I were to preach suppression of purely personal preferences. Similarly, in the realm of pluralism's normative esthetics, it is preferable to choose or follow a religion or non-religious conception of the good than to abstain in order to preserve neutrality among all first-order norms. Accordingly, an orthodox Jew like Sacks, a Christian, a Muslim, or an ardent proponent of the truth of any other religion or non-religious ideology—except for those which are squarely incompatible with pluralism, such as crusading Christianity, Jihadist Islam, or Nazism—is certainly better poised to serve the normative aims of comprehensive pluralism than one who equates *ethos* with abstention and exhaustive self-restraint.

---

[5] It bears pointing out, as Sacks himself does, that Judaism is the religion of a people and as such is inherently compatible with the coexistence of a plurality of religions—as Jews accept that non-Jews observe other religions so long as they abide by Noachide norms prescribed by God for humanity after the biblical flood (Sacks 2003: 57). Nevertheless, even a universalist religion such as Christianity is susceptible of more or less pluralistic interpretations for those who firmly adhere to its truth. At one end of the spectrum are crusaders bent on converting or killing the infidel; at the other, those who preach tolerance of Judaism and Islam as sharing many, though not all, of the truths of Christianity and who believe that the moral and legal imperatives issuing from Christian faith can also be derived from reason.

244 DIALECTICS OF COMPREHENSIVE PLURALISM

The third essential prong of comprehensive pluralism, namely aiming for the best possible mutual accommodation among proponents of different perspectives and conceptions of the good, becomes nearly self-explanatory when considered in terms of the two other prongs considered earlier. If greater diversity multiplies opportunities for self-enrichment and affords a greater number of paths towards self and other regarding legitimate normative fulfillment, then maximizing the potential for diversity is poised to better serve those who wish to be vindicated for who they are as well as those others who seek to expand their horizons to shape whom they aspire to become. Accordingly, as a teleological conception of the good, comprehensive pluralism bears some analogy to utilitarianism. Keeping in mind that these two conceptions differ in their respective assessments of what constitutes the good, they nevertheless bear one striking resemblance. Just as utilitarianism counsels maximizing utilities to optimize the greater happiness of the greatest number, so too comprehensive pluralism prescribes maximizing diversity within the bounds of mutual dignity to optimize individual and collective opportunities for self-enrichment and self-fulfillment.

How the three-pronged essentials of comprehensive pluralism impact on questions of distributive justice will be for the most part addressed in Chapter 8, but a few preliminaries are in order here. As already alluded to, the pluralist *ethos* bears significantly on determining recognition-based and representation-based justice. Moreover, although on first impression material redistribution-based justice— particularly as regards minimums and the justice essentials—may seem impervious to plurality or diversity, further inquiry partially belies this conclusion. To be sure, some material justice questions admit of a single right answer, such as would be the case if all medical experts agreed on the minimum calorie intake necessary to ensure the health of a young child.[6] But at least in two key respects material justice bears on plurality and diversity that the pluralist *ethos* admonishes must be taken into proper account. The first of these, already touched upon, is that material justice is often linked to recognition-based and representation-based justice. Thus, for example, recognition-related education and health care benefits necessarily have material justice implications. Furthermore, the second respect in which plurality is intertwined with material justice stems from the fact amply illustrated in the preceding chapters that there are a great number of competing and conflicting theories of (material) distributive justice that bear on devising a constitutional order and in determining what ought to count as the justice essentials. Whereas comprehensive pluralism may in the end lead to a preference of some such theories over others, all these deserve consideration in the process towards optimizing

---

[6] While it is conceivable that a young child's parents would embrace a conception of the good that prioritizes something that could result in relegating their child's healthy nourishment concerns to a lesser plane, comprehensive pluralism and its interpretation of the justice essentials would nonetheless allow the state to impose the requisite minimum. Otherwise, the child's future ability to carve out and pursue a conception of the good of his own might be seriously compromised.

plurality, and all the more so given that such optimization is to some significant degree context dependent and thus likely to vary among polities. Finally, the nexus between material justice and plurality not only impacts the balance between the universal, the singular, and the plural but also harmonization between the *ethnos and* the *demos*. This is well illustrated by conditions in Iraq, one of the world's richest countries in oil reserves. Iraq has three distinct ethnic groups, the Sunnis, the Shiites, and the Kurds, but its oil reserves are highly disproportionately located in areas populated by the Shiites.[7] Given historical differences between the three ethnic groups involved, it would have been fair to consider, at least at certain times, whether all concerned would be better off from an identitarian and representational standpoint by breaking up the country into three separate, ethnic-based constitutional democracies. It would be impossible to answer this last question from a pluralist perspective, however, without factoring in the very substantial material gains benefitting Shiites and corresponding material losses plaguing Sunnis were any partition along ethnic lines to be undertaken.

IV Comprehensive Pluralism's Responses to Critics

Before proceeding further, it is necessary to address certain actual or potential salient objections to important components of the normative case I have here advanced in support of comprehensive justice. Some of these have been already partially broached but can now be placed in sharper relief and more fully met. One objection that needs to be revisited is the one that casts pluralism as either monistic or relativistic or worse, an unruly combination of the two. My initial response zeroed in on the dialectical nature of the ceaselessly dynamic deployment of the comprehensive pluralist ethos, but Sacks' reliance on an omnipotent God who secures the universal without imposing hermetically monistic assertions of it on earth, who designates the dignity of diversity as His normative design for humans, and who by definition forecloses relativism dramatically reveals the depth of the conundrum that confronts pluralists. Absent explanatory recourse to a transcendent divine norm setter, can the key question left unanswered by Berlin be given a truly satisfactory answer? On further inquiry, comprehensive pluralism relies on both process and substantive norms and values derived from a contested conception of the good. Can these be harmonized, or do they collapse into one or the other as Habermas suggested when he wrote: "comprehensive pluralism is not substantive theory, but rather proceduralism in substantive garb" (Habermas 1998: 405)? Consistent with Habermas, one could argue that the first moment of the pluralist dialectic amounts to an instance of pure proceduralism whereas the

---

[7] See "*27 maps that explain the crisis in Iraq*," <http://www.vox.com>. Archived from the original on June 1, 2016. Retrieved April 26, 2018.

246 DIALECTICS OF COMPREHENSIVE PLURALISM

second does not depend on the good but on a set of rights and duties that figure much like those that inhere in Rawls' two principles of justice. Conversely, one could insist that comprehensive pluralism is ultimately purely substantive and that its process-based aspirations prove hollow. For example, for practical purposes is it not obvious that Nazism ought to be excluded *ex ante*, thus making its requisite provisional inclusion pursuant to the first moment of the pluralist dialectic a mere, rather meaningless, formal contrivance? Finally, does not pluralism all the way up and down in the end foreclose any cogent iteration of the universal, thus countering Rawls' and Habermas' failures to account properly for the plural with an alternative that is equally deficient because it unduly favors the plural at the expense of the universal?

In reply, it is important to begin by stressing that the dialectic of comprehensive pluralism requires the combination of a process-based and a substantively driven approach. Drawing on the distinction between pluralism-in-fact and normative pluralism, at the societal, constitutional, legal, and political levels normatively required plural accommodation is inescapably context-dependent. A society and constitutional unit made up of ethnic Serbs, Croats, and (Muslim) Bosniaks, such as Bosnia, raises different concrete issues of plural accommodation, universal confluence, and acknowledgment and deployment of singularities than counterparts divided along language and culture, such as Canada or Belgium. More generally, differences in material conditions, identity-based perceptions and antagonisms as well as representational aspirations and perceived imbalances differ from one constitutional setting to the next. Thus, whereas certain normative prescriptions may be implanted in a universal context-free setting—such as the categorical prohibition against torture that extends to all human beings regardless of any contextual differences—those relating to constitutions and the justice essentials do not. Accommodating the interface between Hindus and Muslims is a paramount concern in India that need not be given any constitutional consideration in any Western European country so far as none of the latter confronts religious tensions among these two religions. Moreover, from comprehensive pluralism's perspective, all contextual issues require procedural processing which is incorporated in both moments of its dialectic. In the first negative moment, the process is close to the purely procedural paradigm as it requires equalization—in fact or counterfactually to lend normative support to calls for recalibration or redeployment—regardless of the substantive merit of the ideologies advantaged or disadvantaged by the process of negation in play. In the second positive moment, on the other hand, process is still indispensable as workable peaceful coexistence among the competing ideologies that vie for vindication within a particular polity depends to a substantial degree on the actual bundles of first-order norms that happen to stack up against one another. A polity that needs to accommodate Catholics and Protestants does not confront the precise same balancing issues as one that seeks to bring peace and harmony to long-feuding multiple ethnic antagonists or as one that pits former colonizers against long-unjustly treated indigenous groups. Unlike process in its first moment, however, the one in the second moment of the dialectic is manifestly substantively driven as pluralism's second-order norms provide criteria of admission into, or rejection from, the various relevant intersubjective dealings within the affected constitutional unit. Accordingly, the procedural dimension of the second moment is akin to what Rawls refers to as imperfect procedural justice. Because comprehensive pluralism's conception of the good supplies criteria of admission and rejection, the procedural steps in pursuit of accommodation have a set goal, but that goal is never fully realized. Indeed, as emphasized earlier, the dialectic unleashed by comprehensive pluralism yields more equitable resolutions of conflicts, but these are never perfect, and they inevitably give rise to institutional rearrangements that result in new inequities of their own.

Against those who would consider inclusion of Nazism in the first moment of the pluralist dialectic as a pure contrivance, the proponents of comprehensive pluralism would draw attention to those who have embraced Nazism within the relevant historical and institutional setting. In Hitler's time, Germans may have been, at least in part, attracted to Nazi ideology because of the humiliations their country endured after the end of the First World War and of the dire economic conditions that instilled them with fear and insecurity. Likewise, contemporary neo-Nazism may be attractive to those uprooted and rendered vulnerable and insecure as a consequence of the rapid and seemingly unstoppable upheavals fueled by globalization. Whereas these burdens and hardships in no way justify embracing Nazism, understanding the grievances that motivate the turn to what Nazism purports to offer and empathizing with the suffering that Nazism proposes to alleviate are certainly of use in revolutionizing, reforming, or adapting the relevant constitutional unit so as to make it more pluralistically equitable and inclusive. If Nazism and Nazis were exclusively and single-mindedly obsessed with the extermination of Jews, then it would be pointless to afford them any recognition in the first moment of the pluralist dialectic. But to the extent that those oriented towards Nazism have concerns and aspirations that differ in nature or intensity from those of others within the polity, taking these into account could aid both in pinpointing existing injustices and in fashioning a pluralist path towards greater justice.

Concerning grounding comprehensive pluralism all the way up and down without recourse to Sacks' God or another comparable guarantor, there is one key factor that must be underscored in addition to the dialectical dynamic that constantly pits monism against relativism without allowing either of the two to settle in. That factor stems from the very nature of comprehensive pluralism as a conception of the good. Utilitarianism and Rawlsian liberal egalitarianism need no recourse to any transcendent source to systematically justify their conceptions of justice or of the good.[8] And neither does comprehensive pluralism which relies on

---

[8] To the extent that Rawls' deontological approach severs justice from *the* good, suffice it to assume for present purposes that he considers the achievement of justice to also constitute *a* good.

the dignity of diversity as a hierarchically superior unifying normative imperative. As we have seen, however, both Rawls and utilitarians advance contested conceptions of justice and of the good as admittedly does comprehensive pluralism. With this in mind, there is one crucial difference between comprehensive pluralism and these other contested conceptions. Because the very substantive content of comprehensive pluralism is to be inclusive of as many other contested such conceptions as possible, the pluralist approach is poised to foment anti-pluralist perspectives as well as partially pluralistic ones. Accordingly, comprehensive pluralism can be regarded as combining a monistic overriding commitment to the contested normative dictates of the dignity of diversity with a relativistic process opening the door to the competition for admission to the pluralist polity to proponents of all existing conceptions of the good no matter how repulsive any of these may be, and with a teleological mission that is pluralistic through and through. In short, comprehensive pluralism is thoroughly systematic and self-contained because of its dialectic and because of how it structures the interaction between its normative imperatives, the (process-based) means by which it seeks to implement them and the purposes which it seeks to realize.

Finally, appearances to the contrary notwithstanding, comprehensive pluralism does not have to undermine the universal in the course of prioritizing the plural. In some cases, as in the already alluded one of torture, the constitution and the justice essentials require uniformity *regardless* of context. In such cases, comprehensive pluralism consistent with a wide array of other conceptions of the good imposes an absolute unqualified worldwide universal prohibition. In other cases, comprehensive pluralism furthers the universal as fitted for a particular relevant context, such as the constitutional community of communities that has been referred to throughout this book. Thus, for example a fair and legitimate pluralist constitutional arrangement for a political unit made of Catholics and Protestants would necessarily satisfy the relevant universal framed within the bounds of the conjunction between Catholics and Protestants. That particular iteration of the universal would exclude the needs and aspirations of Jews and Muslims, but that would be irrelevant if none were present or expected within the political unit at stake. More generally, the claim made on behalf of comprehensive pluralism, which will be further detailed in Chapter 8, is that starting from the middle, or the plural, frames the constitutionally enshrined universal and its singular counterpart in ways that are most likely to optimize the balance among the three.

8

Justice Essentials Minima and Comprehensive Pluralism's Fixed-core Minimum Set Against its Plural Maximum

I The Justice Minima under Comprehensive Pluralism: Linking Justice to Identity, Autonomy, and Solidarity

To determine what the justice essentials would require, consistent with comprehensive pluralism in any particular constitutional setting, it would be necessary to weave together content and context, process, and substance, and the requisite minimum of fixed normative prescriptions that would allow for an optimal accommodation of diverse conceptions of the good. Before proceeding any further, however, it is important to set a baseline as without certain minimums, in hand or within reasonable reach, constitutional ordering could not plausibly yield any meaningful iteration of the justice essentials. The minimums involved are all linked and mutually re-enforcing, and they include: the bare bones of justice fit for pluralists; minimal identity as mediating between inward retreat and outward lurch; minimum autonomy at the combined levels of the individual, the group, and the community of the whole; and minimum solidarity as a means to manage care and concern without trampling on dignity in order to differentiate—without trespassing on any person's right to equal dignity—between insiders and outsiders within the polity and beyond.

(a) The bare bones of pluralist justice

As noted earlier, pluralism confronts two major challenges in relation to settling on principles of distributive justice for any constitutional unit: different conceptions of the good may have different justice requirements, and different relevant actors may embrace conflicting theories of justice. Thus, for example, on the one hand, libertarians and egalitarians disagree on how to achieve justice whereas on the other, Christians who broadly share the same religious outlook and values may well be divided, with some embracing libertarianism and some others egalitarianism. These divisions call for resolutions and open an inquiry into whether the

A Pluralist Theory of Constitutional Justice. Michel Rosenfeld, Oxford University Press. © Michel Rosenfeld 2022.
DOI: 10.1093/oso/9780198862680.003.0009

latter ought to be context-dependent through and through or whether they ought to be grounded on some immutable baseline of justice aligned with comprehensive pluralism. If the justice essentials were confined to material redistribution concerns, then the needs of the individual citizen would loom as paramount. And in that case, the discussion of social welfare rights in Chapter 2 would provide a fair and thorough account of what the justice essentials ought to encompass. However, since comprehensive pluralism requires coordination between material redistributive justice, recognition-based justice, and representation-based justice, this opens the door for tensions and conflicts among two or more of these. Suppose, for instance, that a polity is equally divided between a religious community (resembling in outlook the small Amish community in the United States) that rejects the use of important mainstays of contemporary technology in the economy and a secular community that is firmly in favor of maximizing reliance on available technology with a view to optimizing the economic welfare of all. Suppose further that the religious community involved adheres to a prohibition against using technology in economic production as well as against consuming any product generated or transformed through application of such technology. Whether or not the religious community's prohibition against using technology is only meant intra-communally or inter-communally as well—by regarding the prohibition in question as applying to all whether believers or not—it is clear in this example that the identitarian self-fulfillment of half the population would be clashing against the material welfare objectives of the other half. If the clash in question resulted in widespread malnutrition within the polity, then pluralism aligning with liberalism and many other conceptions of the good would call for overriding the identitarian objections to technology for purposes of satisfying the most basic material welfare needs of all. But what about a case in which honoring the identitarian imperatives would significantly adversely affect overall material welfare, but with much less dire consequences than those culminating in malnutrition?

The case involving the prospect of malnutrition indicates that there is a minimum of material justice that comprehensive pluralists would impose and incorporate in the constitution as mandated by the justice essentials, even if that minimum appears to de-singularize the individual, ignore the plural, and trample on recognition and representation within the universal as delimited by the relevant constitutional unit. Beyond that, however, two main concerns emerge: the justice essentials require more than the bare-bones minimum in all societies with considerable economic means, and material requirements do not *necessarily* override identitarian and representational ones. At the bare minimum level, material justice concerns become paramount because below a certain baseline level of material welfare it would be impossible to carry out identarian or representational pursuits meaningfully. But once the minimum is achieved, the justice essentials, in the most general terms, would require wealthy countries to assure a higher level of material welfare while properly factoring in recognition-based and representation-based aspirations. Because the justice essentials fall short of full justice, many difficult and contested line-drawing questions can be postponed for subsequent infra-constitutional resolution. Moreover, within the bounds of the justice essentials it seems fair to assume that, up to some point, material justice concerns ought to be given priority over its counterparts, and that all remaining justice issues ought to be resolved by equally factoring in all three prongs of constitutional justice.

The criterion for whether or not to prioritize material welfare beyond bare minimum conditions follows from comprehensive pluralism's commitment to afford full and fair opportunities for everyone to choose, change, or adjust her allegiances, values, and commitments in pursuit of self-enrichment, of a normative esthetic path of her own, and of widening the horizons of self-realization. To the extent that choices of allegiances and commitments would be unduly limited without further prioritization of material welfare, comprehensive pluralism would justify setting aside competing recognition and representation concerns. This is well illustrated by the circumstances surrounding the US Supreme Court 1972 decision in the *Yoder* case.[1] In that case, the Court sided with the Amish parents of a fourteen-year-old who claimed that a Wisconsin law that required twelve years of education violated their freedom of religion rights, and held that the child in question could leave school after eight years as his parents had requested. The Amish, a very small Christian denomination that is largely self-contained and economically self-sufficient in the United States, did not cause any adverse effect on the US economy, and the fourteen-year-old about to be taken out of school was deemed by the Court to have been adequately educated to partake fully in his own isolated community's life. From a pluralist standpoint, however, the Court's decision was wanting as it deprived the boy involved of many individual- and group-related choices he might have otherwise had upon reaching adulthood. Because of the combination of the size and isolation of the Amish community in the United States, *Yoder* lacked significant society-wide implications. But what if the Amish had represented a third of the US population? In that case—even assuming that they remained economically self-sufficient and that they had no adverse effect on the economic fate of their fellow citizens—exempting Amish children from otherwise mandatory secondary school education and accordingly reducing the public education budget for such education by a third to align material welfare and identitarian priorities would be uncalled for from a pluralist standpoint. Indeed, compelling secondary education and funding it would enhance pluralism in the relevant context with the consequence of correspondingly requiring some prioritizing of material welfare benefits over accommodation of competing identitarian-related priorities.[2]

---

[1] *Wisconsin v. Yoder*, 406 US 205 (1972).

[2] I assume, based on my reading of the *Yoder* case, that the Amish parents were not opposed on religious grounds to secular education as such, and that they only objected to not having their fourteen-year-old as a full participant in their communal religiously prescribed endeavors. Accordingly, I do not address here the more vexing question of a religion that opposes all secular education or that prohibits the education of girls and women.

That material justice requires a minimum of welfare which increases, for purposes of the justice essentials, with the level of wealth of a constitutional unit, and that it must be pursued up to a point above recognition and representation related justice concerns, fully conforms to the dialectic and the logic of comprehensive pluralism. Although the dynamic between the factually (but not normatively) non-plural baseline and the normative goal of maximizing the room for plurality within constitutional units will be more fully laid out in section II of this chapter, it is important for both theoretical and practical purposes to keep in mind, from now on, that deployment of comprehensive pluralism second-order norms, such as in the above instance of certain prioritizations of material justice, ought not be mistaken for retreats into limited pluralism. The test to determine whether a factually seemingly non-pluralist prescription derives or does not derive from comprehensive pluralism consists in following the dialectical logic of comprehensive pluralism and assessing whether what appears non-pluralist flows directly from the deployment of the logic in question. Accordingly, the limited predominance of material justice emphasized in the preceding discussion has been justified entirely in terms of comprehensive pluralism's teleological aspirations. In contrast, the boundaries of liberalism's limited pluralism are not internal to any pluralist "ought" but instead imposed by overriding values external to pluralism, such as those commanded by the hierarchical normative priority of individual liberty.

Turning now to the question posed by conflicts among proponents of competing theories of justice within the polity, a distinction must be drawn between those that arise at the level of "is," or of political and economic science, and those that emerge at the level of "ought" and that emanate from clashes among divergent conceptions of the good. The first of these ought to be cast as pluralist-in-fact challenges that must be tackled from the standpoint of comprehensive pluralism's norms and objectives. Thus, if a Marxist and a Posnerian wealth-maximization champion propose different means to optimize the political and economic path towards satisfaction of the social welfare needs of the citizenry, the task of the comprehensive pluralist would be to determine which of the two proposals would best serve the demands of material justice—assuming all else would remain the same. And, if different political and economic policies would affect not only material welfare but also recognition- and representation-based justice, then the policies in question would have to be comparatively assessed from the standpoint of comprehensive pluralism's aim to accommodate all three relevant prongs of distributive justice in the best way possible, as they relate to the justice essentials. Thus, for example, assuming that a free-market economy would optimize the means to satisfy the demands of material justice, the comprehensive pluralist may still have to opt for constitutionally enshrined constraints on the market so as to avoid serious threats to representational justice due to the disproportionate influx of money into politics typical in some societies that experience large increases in inequalities in wealth.

The above example distinguishing between Christian libertarians and Christian egalitarians was meant to evoke reference to persons who share the same conception of the good, but who disagree on how best to (factually) implement the Christian command of social justice for all. But as against that, and as an instance of the second type of conflict at the level of "ought" among theories of justice, one can imagine a conflict opposing Catholics who believe in the necessity of contemporary state intervention to secure the welfare of the poor (as charity alone would be completely inadequate in any large present-day political setting) to members of certain Protestant denominations that equate free-market success with the dispensation of divine grace and view interferences with the market as contrary to divine prescription. In this latter case, the disagreement over justice reflects a normative disagreement stemming from the confrontation between two (relatively) divergent (religiously grounded) conceptions of justice. Moreover, a similar normative split can also occur when the conceptions of the good involved are purely secular and principally concentrated on matters of justice. Thus, Robert Nozick's libertarian theory alluded to earlier is ultimately predicated not on wealth maximization designs but on an absolute normative prioritization of liberty and private property rights. In contrast, Rawls' egalitarianism is grounded in his conviction that his two principles of justice are normatively mandated as they are necessary preconditions to the advancement of all legitimate conceptions of the good—the latter being encompassed within his understanding of "reasonable pluralism."

In sum, theories of justice can be oriented to questions of "is" or of "ought," or even, in some cases, of both—as would be the case of those who believe that the free-market economy actually maximizes wealth while at the same time vindicating the normative priority of liberty and private property rights which is meant to prevail regardless of actual economic consequences. In cases involving "is," the comprehensive pluralist's concern is *advancement* of the pluralist minimum from the standpoint of the justice essentials. Accordingly, as already pointed out in Chapter 2, Nozickian and Posnerian libertarianism are unsuited to sustain the minimum under contemporary globalized economic conditions given the institutional market advantages enjoyed by operators who can choose, fashion, or evade the law, coupled with the vertiginous speed with which vast disparities in wealth are becoming exacerbated. In sharp contrast, however, in cases involving an "ought," the pluralist's focus is on *accommodation* of diverse normative outlooks, with conflicting visions of justice competing for inclusion with all other conceptions of the good within the polity under the criteria set by comprehensive pluralism's second-order norms. At first glance, it may seem that differences in conceptions of justice are distinguishable from other kinds of conceptions of the good. If libertarian ideology thoroughly frustrates rather than advances the minimum of justice envisioned by comprehensive justice, how can it be accommodated on normative grounds? The answer may well be that it cannot, but that would hardly differ from the case of a purely religious ideology requiring conversion or

254 JUSTICE MINIMA AND COMPREHENSIVE PLURALISM

killing of the infidel. More generally, whereas there is a conceptual, and sometimes factual, meaningful difference between advancing pluralism outright and doing so through accommodation of non-pluralist perspectives, in the context of achieving a minimum of justice, advancement and accommodation may at times be squarely at odds with one another.

(b) Minimal identity as mediation between inward retreat and outward lurch

A minimum of common identity, both in the sense of shared similarities and of a commonly partaken sense of collective selfhood, is necessary to sustain any society-wide political project, let alone one that is normatively grounded in a constitutional order in pursuit of the justice essentials. Also, given the three distinct facets of constitutional justice, the requisite minimum of identity must be fairly and plausibly apportioned among the singular, the plural, and the universal while allowing for a workable balance between *ethnos* and *demos*. It should be hence obvious that a Schmittian stand-off between immovably entrenched friends and enemies, a Freudian group psychology-based hypnotic attachment to a leader, and a Nietzschean or Heideggerian retreat into an inexhaustible singularity, would all fail the comprehensive pluralist test for minimal identity. At the other end of the spectrum, an overriding Habermasian "constitutional patriotism" purporting to bring identity to a transnational constitutional project at the scale of the EU or eventually of the entire globe would also equally fail the pluralist minimum. And this because such constitutional patriotism, even if workable at all,[3] would operate at a purely universal level without allowing for adjustments to accommodate the singular or the plural while at the same time requiring a complete subordination of the *ethnos* to the *demos*—or even an abandonment of both, if read in strictly Kantian terms as requiring a categorical embrace of universally valid constitutional norms.

All identity formation or preservation must negotiate, apportion, and configure in a workable and meaningful way clusters of similarities and of differences into series of complementary relationships between self and other. From a constitutional standpoint, since the Enlightenment, at the level of the singular every individual is entitled to assert her identity as a self and to treat the remainder of humanity as others. At the level of the plural, collective groups can self-constitute on the basis of certain similarities and differences. Thus, for example, in Belgium, language but not religion serves to differentiate the French-speaking community from its Flemish counterpart whereas in Northern Ireland it is religion and not language that serves to set apart the historically antagonistic Catholic and

---

[3] For an argument that Habermas' conception of constitutional patriotism seems unsuited to assume a positive role in transnational constitutional identity building, see Rosenfeld 2010: 258–60.

Protestant communities. Finally, I have equated the universal (self) with the relevant constitutional community of communities while recognizing that what is literally universal—throughout the whole world or throughout what philosophers refer to as all possible worlds—applies to all constitutional orderings. With this in mind, what comprehensive pluralism requires at a minimum is that at all three levels there be a recognition of entitlement to selfhood and that there be some significant openness among selves and others both within each of the three levels and among them.

Identity-based recognition and the minimum it requires consistent with comprehensive pluralism should be clearly set apart from what is currently pejoratively characterized in some quarters as "identity politics"—namely, tribalism based on race, religion, or ethnicity, combined with demands for preferences based on claims of victimhood, and accompanied by disregard or disdain for the good of society as a whole.[4] Even what may superficially seem to come closest to identity politics within the dialectic of comprehensive pluralism, the process of equalization in its first moment relates to claims regarding conceptions of the good and not focus on attributes that nurture assertions of victimhood. That said, historical experience of racial discrimination or colonial oppression may well entirely legitimately inform certain conceptions of the good, but would be subjected to comprehensive pluralism's second-order norms during the second moment of its dialectic. Although redressing past mistreatment and victimization is primarily a matter of corrective justice, past injustices may also have a present distributive impact on all three facets of justice. Thus, an undereducated and impoverished ethnic minority, as a consequence of having been long reviled by a country's majority, may indeed require some material redistribution; identity-boosting measures—such as encouragement to enter certain professions for which past stereotypes characterized them as being unworthy, and affirmative representational support to achieve proportional parity within the polity.

Although as an individual I am uniquely singular—even identical twins have some different experiences and lifelong points of divergence—I cannot build or maintain an identity of my own without sharing certain clusters of identity with others while, at the same time, rejecting some tokens of identity which yet others promote on their own behalf. All identity-based pursuits at all levels thus require certain inclusions and exclusions. In cases where the nation-state is the relevant constitutional unit, the citizenry is supposed to rally around a narrative that binds together the imaginary community into a common national identity. It is obvious that different national identities must be to a significant degree mutually exclusive. Paris has thus named one of its main train stations "Austerlitz," the place of one of Napoleon's greatest military victories, while London, confronted with a

---

[4] See, e.g., Fukuyama 2018.

similar naming task, settled on "Waterloo," the place of Napoleon's final and definitive military defeat. Whereas this last example reflects differences in appreciation of the same past historical events, identity-related conflicts regarding inclusion and exclusion can turn into matters of life and death as nation-states have proven when they go to war over a disputed territory. Also important, from our perspective, are relations of inclusion and exclusion that mark boundaries between the same polity's national and constitutional identities. These two identities are ideally meant to apply to the same community but they are imagined somewhat differently, and often to some extent as in conflict with one another. Thus, a nation-state marked by active competition and some tension among a plurality of different ethnic groups may give full expression to its multi-ethnic configuration in its national narrative while forbidding ethnic-based political parties in its constitution.[5] In that case, the prevailing constitutional identity would have to negate the ethnic-based national identity narrative and either displace it or repress it in its own narrative. Furthermore, the inclusions and exclusions operative at the national and constitutional levels would also impact identity formation and preservation for the various groups that are, or ought to be, constitutionally recognized within the polity, and finally for individuals who undertake their singular journey within, among, or beyond, the aforementioned groups.

Some instances or patterns of identity-related interactions between inclusions and exclusions have no justice or pluralist implications. It is thus difficult to imagine how creation of a jazz music club devoted to all things jazz and open to all interested in jazz could be unjust or anti-pluralist for excluding those who are exclusively interested in other types of music or who intend to join only to advocate for the club's inclusion of other types of music. Conversely, some other handlings of the nexus between inclusion and exclusion are flatly unacceptable from both a justice and a pluralist standpoint. Thus, if in a Catholic majority country all children whose parents belonged to other religions were legally obliged to go to daily mass and this violated the fundamental tenets of their parents' religion, this would amount to forced (identity-denying) submission to what is strictly to be excluded from the relevant identity-bearers' perspective.

These two examples represent easy cases, but what about religiously based opposition to state-sanctioned abortion or same-sex marriage relating to those who do not share the same religious beliefs? And what about criminalizing refusal to perform mandatory military service without exemptions for those who have an absolute religious obligation to refrain from all military activity? It is cases like these and many others that cannot be readily open and shut, and that therefore

---

[5] See, e.g., Constitution of the Republic of Ghana, December 16, 1996, art. 55(4) ("Every political party shall have a national character and membership shall not be based on ethnic, religious, regional, or other sectional divisions").

require further inquiry into identity-relating minimums consistent with the norms of comprehensive pluralism.

In terms of managing self-chosen inclusions and exclusions, retreating inward appears prone to maximize self-control whereas, at the other end of the spectrum, upon mounting frustration and repeated failures to achieve a satisfactory mix of inclusions and exclusions the best option may be a lurch outward. Retreat inward is best achievable in the context of unlimited freedom of belief and freedom of conscience rights and somewhat less so in that of largely intra-communally homogeneous groups with very limited inter-communal dealings. Outward lurch or exit, on the other hand, is called for at the level of the whole where constitutional divorce is best for the self-identity of all as it apparently was when Czechoslovakia broke into the Czech Republic and Slovakia. Such a constitutional divorce may be problematic in other cases of identity-based conflict, such as that of Quebec, where sizeable minorities of non-French speakers appear to identify more with a Canadian than a conceivable fully developed Quebeçois constitutional identity.[6] Similarly, at the level of groups that coexist within a constitutional unit, whether constitutionally recognized as is the case in identity-based (as opposed to distributive-based) federalism (Dorsen 2016: 427–8) or constitutionally indifferent, members ought to be entitled to a right of exit whenever their self-identity can no longer be harmonized with that which happens to prevail throughout their group.

Some degree of retreating inward and of lurching outward ought to be guaranteed as an identity-based minimum. That would ensure some freedom to attend to singularity as well as to partake in collective projects one identifies with while withdrawing from those that one no longer considers compatible with one's self-fulfilling objectives. Inevitably, the right to retreat or to lurch outward would be subject to limitations within any pluralist-in-fact contemporary constitutional unit. One can imagine a very small, distinct, and ideologically and societally tightly knit self-sufficient group living completely separately from the rest of the polity and thus in peace with the rest of the population, without contributing to or interfering with the intersubjective dealings within the community of the whole. But that scenario is likely to be exceedingly rare since, as observed already, the group in question might need municipal services, police protection, or specialized medical services not available intra-communally. Once retreats inward have consequent externalities for one's own or other groups or the constitutional unit as a whole, however, rights to be left alone or to having one's group remain isolated would have to be assessed in accordance with the norms issuing from comprehensive pluralism. Thus, in the case of conscientious objection to military service, if the effect were trivial on justice and security grounds (say the group of objectors is tiny and the increased risk of harm to those going to war infinitesimally small)

---

[6] See *Reference Re Secession of Quebec*, [1998] 2 SCR 17 (Canada).

then the exemption could readily be granted. Otherwise, accommodation could be provided where possible (say objectors could be obligated to do civilian service that would contribute to the national defense alongside military service). But in yet other cases, only a right of exit may exempt the conscientious objector as security and justice concerns would strongly militate against remaining within the polity but refusing to defend it against military threats.

If we assume that a polity is made up of a large series of disparate and mutually isolated groupings with virtually nothing in common, then either the polity would be largely dysfunctional as there would be no significant points of convergence for society-wide undertakings, or the need for polity-wide initiatives would massively trample on identitarian interests. Fortunately, in most working contemporary constitutional democracies these two extremes are easily avoided. The reasons for that are mainly twofold: identity formation tends to draw from a plurality of available sources, and a sufficiently agreed-upon commonly shared *ethnos* makes for a sufficient commonality of interests and aspirations to lay the ground for a shared basis for society-wide decision-making. The plurality of sources of identity formation and development are exemplified by readily available amalgamations of religious commitments, gender-based aspirations, environmental concerns, cultural associations, social justice objectives, and the like. The commonly shared *ethnos*, on the other hand, may vary in depth and breath, but its unifying force seems best encapsulated in the interplay between the polity's national identity and constitutional identity narratives. These commonalities combined with the frequently plural sources drawn upon for self-identity purposes seem likely to create a sufficient degree of harmonization in relation to important patterns of inclusion and exclusion to align the singular, the plural, and the universal sufficiently to guarantee the requisite minimums of identity consistent with achievement of the justice essentials. Finally, regarding the identitarian bonds emanating from the *ethnos*, these may contribute to the minimums associated with the justice essentials notwithstanding significant variations in depth and breadth depending on the relevant circumstances.

Identity building itself requires a dynamic of inclusion and exclusion that operates at all relevant levels, including that of constitutional association in pluralist-in-fact settings. All just constitutional configurations must equitably manage nodes of identification (involving commonly shared notions of inclusion and exclusion) and nodes of alienation (resulting from unwelcome impositions of unwanted inclusions and exclusions). At the nation-state level, the *ethnos* imprinted in the national and constitutional identities is supposed to provide a rallying locus of common identification for all those affected. In terms of minimums, however, the depth of the ethnocentric bond may vary. Thus, in a federal republic, federated state nodes of common identity may well be significantly more intense than their federal or national counterparts. Citizens of Alabama may share with one another much more intensive and extensive bundles of particular inclusions tied to correlated exclusions than they have in common with their out-of-state compatriots. The apportionment of ethnocentric identification does not necessarily matter in and of itself, however, provided the relevant aggregations satisfy the requisite minimums. Thus, if the intensity of the sum of ethnocentric identifications which is split within a federal republic matches that which is manifest in an undivided unitary republic, then presumably in both cases the identitarian minima could be equally met. On further thought, apportionment of ethnocentric allegiance among clusters of greater and lesser identitarian intensity may, under certain circumstances, result in more than a zero-sum outcome. Thus, if a country is made up of two traditionally antagonistic religious groups, each geographically concentrated in its own distinct region, then the combination of intensely religiously unified federated entities with a much less intense alliance devoted to a limited number of subject matters, such as foreign affairs, at the national level would seem better suited to maximize identification and to minimize alienation than any plausible unitary alternative. Furthermore, this latter insight may be transposed to the transnational context, where layered and segmented legal regimes could be matched with corresponding (partial) constitutional systems. For example, even a little intense relatively shallow EU-level constitutional identity may mitigate tensions and bursts of alienation that periodically flare up within member states with sharp identitarian divisions, such as Belgium or Spain. Indeed, some of the tensions at stake may well be better managed or defused through interaction among subnational spokespeople within EU institutional settings than through direct confrontations within national borders (Rosenfeld 2010: 237). Finally, as all constitutional identity requires projection of a self and hence depends on credibly positing a real or imaginary other, global constitutional identity appears least suited to yield the minimum identitarian requisite. The EU can define itself in contrast to the United States, Russia, or China, but where could the requisite other be found if humanity as a whole is bundled together into a single constitutional self? With layering and segmenting available, and with the usefulness of relatively shallow identitarian links in mind, global constitutional identity need not be foreclosed (Rosenfeld 2014). One area in which one could imagine an eventual segmented constitutional approach satisfying the identitarian minimum is that of climate control. In that context, the constitutional subject would be humanity as a whole confronting extinction due to climate related catastrophic deterioration; and the "other" would be those within the global polity who counter or ignore the mortal threat that is rapidly spreading throughout the earth.

We are accustomed to confronting deeply rooted *ethnos*-based identitarian bonding at the levels of the nation-state and at those of subnational units that may be even more tightly knit together, but *ethnos*-based identitarian convergences at the supranational level seem problematic. The common identity of the twenty-seven member states of the EU seems bound inevitably to be shallower in nature than those of nation-states or of subnational ethno-centric regions. And shallower identitarian bonds seem problematic in two principal respects. First, the closer the identitarian glue comes to dissolving, the less likely it would seem that equitable integration of the singular, the plural, and the universal could be maintained, or that alienation could be held sufficiently at bay for coherent and unified projects dependent on identitarian convergence to thrive. Assuming, for the sake of argument, that France were unanimously *laique* and Poland unanimously devoted to Catholicism, then EU policy that would divide the secular from the religious would inevitably appear to be unjust from a recognition-based identitarian perspective either to the French or to the Poles. Moreover, such schism could also have adverse representational consequences. If all the French are secular, then keeping that country's public schools strictly secular would be arguably representationally just and legitimate regardless of whether or not the issue were put up for a vote. Suppose, however, that the EU imposed a secular education requirement, and did so subject to a referendum of all its citizens, with the Poles and all others who shared their opposition to such education comprising but a small minority within the EU In that case, even after full participation in the referendum, Poles could quite plausibly assert that the resulting secularism is representationally unjust as far as it concerns them. Indeed, the situation of the Poles in our example would be analogous to that of a racial minority subjected to apartheid conditions in their country of citizenship. In that case, recognitional and representational injustice would go hand in hand. Voting on issues of apartheid would seem meaningless, if not downright insulting, if the minority in question is in all instances assured of defeat as the majority routinely and expectedly nearly unanimously votes in favor of racial segregation.

The second respect in which shallow identitarian links are problematic concerns the boundary between identity-based and interests-based undertakings. This problem is compounded, moreover, by the fact that constitutional arrangements tend to be portrayed as interest based as attested by the prevalence of the social contract metaphor. Family and tribal relations are heavily laden with deeply rooted identitarian bonds whereas nation-state constitutions project imagined communities constructed to unify sets of strangers commonly joined through a (hypothetical or counterfactual) social contract. Actual legal contracts are motivated by interests whereas intense family relations are non-contractual in nature; as is often said, it is only when marital love wanes and that a couple edges toward divorce that the spouses will regard their relationship as largely contractual in nature. Constitutions, similarly, can be regarded as being launched contractually but as not truly able to function or endure without attaching to an *ethnos* which in the nation-state case is encapsulated in the imagined community carved out by the interplay between national and constitutional identity. In the transnational setting, in contrast, the working constitution's necessary identarian profile stacks against the thoroughly contractually grounded interest-driven treaty which has traditionally figured as the staple of constructive international relations. Two countries entering into a treaty mutually to exempt their respective products from tariffs, which would otherwise be levied upon importation, are each acting out of self-interest and joining hands for the limited purpose of advancing a circumscribed project delimited by a discrete overlapping joint interest ultimately legitimated severally by each of their separate self-interests. Such contractual treaty-based joint interests are often hard to sort out from shallow identarian bonds. Instructive, in this respect, is the EU's failed attempt to give itself a constitution through enactment of a "treaty-constitution" which was agreed upon by all its then member states in 2004 but rejected in referenda by the Dutch and the French in 2005 (Rosenfeld 2010: 1–2).

Conceptually, a working constitution casts the community of communities over which it presides as a single self (manifested at least at the level of the universal) whereas international treaties are between self and other, if bilateral, and self and others, if multinational. This difference is crucial from the standpoint of constitutional justice as by definition that justice in all its three facets pertains to a single unified order. There is no US constitutional material distributive obligation to Brazil's poor, or recognition-based obligation to German-speaking ethnic minorities in Italy, or else any representational duty toward (at least out of the United States) citizens of Nigeria. Although interests and identities are bundled up together in real-life situations, and although even conceptually the line between the two is often hard to draw, the distinction remains very important in addressing questions of constitutional justice. Furthermore, for purposes of distinguishing between identity concerning and interest concerning legal ordering, matters of form ought to be subordinated to those of substance. Thus, for instance, after the failure of the 2004 EU Treaty-Constitution, as already recounted, its content was virtually completely reincorporated into the 2007 EU Lisbon Treaty with a systematic removal of all references to the word "constitution" (Dorsen 2016: 112). Arguably, the EU had enough of a common identity to sustain a (layered) constitution in 2004 (Rosenfeld 2010: 274) and the same could be said as of 2007.[7]

As already noted, the possibility of constitutional justice making sense at the global level seems most problematic as it is difficult to imagine a common identity sticking in the absence of a delimited other. In a science fiction scenario with dealings between humans and extraplanetary aliens, there may well be a sufficiently enduring common human identity to allow for a constitutionally enshrined, as contrasted with a treaty-based or each-polity-for-itself approach, to possible cooperation with, or warding off threats from, extraterrestrial political actors. As suggested earlier, however, at least a limited segmented constitutional ordering with justice essentials implications seems possible if only humans are involved on a

---

[7] I do not address here events subsequent to 2010, such as the economic crisis, Brexit, or Hungary's and Poland's disputes with the EU over the rule of law, all of which may be relevant in determining whether the EU retains a sufficiently distinct constitutional identity at present.

global scale. Returning to the threat of extinction due to climate change, there seem to be three different approaches to the problem: power politics with each player on the international scene trying to muscle its way as much as possible; limited contractual-like cooperation through treaty agreements; and limited segmented constitutional-like coordination based on a common identitarian commitment to set aside differences in order to save the human race from imminent extinction.

Although transition from one to another of these approaches is not likely to be neat or linear, once identitarian commonalities loom as coherent and not merely as very short lived (such as the momentary waves of empathy that surge in the aftermath of a devastating earthquake), they become susceptible of management and criticism under the aegis of constitutional justice. And this is important as is particularly well illustrated by the consequences of the globalization of the economy. From the standpoint of distributive justice in general, it makes no difference whether the great disparities of wealth generated by the free movement of capital and labor can or cannot be encompassed within any single constitutional regime. From that of constitutional justice within the confines of a nation-state, in contrast, the flight of capital and the associated impoverishment and increased unemployment of local workers may well remain beyond reach. Indeed, short of insulating national capital by prohibiting its export and assuring the well-being of the nation's workers, raising high tariffs on more cheaply produced foreign-made goods among other restrictive measures—all of which may end up unduly impoverishing a nation-state that opts for thoroughgoing protectionism in pursuit of greater distributive justice within its boundaries—the nation-state seems deprived of sufficient tools to counter mounting inequities. Treaty-based international agreements can improve the situation as evinced by the recent commitment by more than 130 countries to levy a minimum worldwide corporate tax rate of 15 per cent.[8] But it would seem better if the inequities in question could plausibly be dealt with within the single set of justice essentials arising under a worldwide narrowly layered or segmented unified constitutional regime.[9] Whether or not such a constitutional scenario will ever materialize, from an identitarian perspective, the possibility of a thin globally shared *ethnos* should by no means be categorically discarded. In the climate context, the bond of identity would extend to humanity as a whole; in that of globalization, to *homo economicus* wherever found throughout the world.

---

[8] See Alan Rapperport & Liz Alderman, "Global deal to end tax havens moves ahead as nations back 15% rate," *NY Times*, October 8, 2021, <https://www.nytimes.com/2021/10/08/business/oecd-global-minimum-tax.html>, visited April 3, 2022; "Organization for Economic Cooperation and Development (OECD), international community strikes a ground-breaking tax deal for the digital age," *OECD*, October 8, 2021, <https://www.oecd.org/tax/international-community-strikes-a-ground-breaking-tax-deal-for-the-digital-age.html>, visited April 3, 2022.

[9] A thin-layered or segmented, worldwide, and constitutional regulation of global economic matters would not in all likelihood suffice to achieve the requisite equities. Accordingly, the global constitutional regime would have to supplement rather than replace other regimes already in place.

(c) The combined minimum of autonomy and solidarity within a just constitutional order: care and concern for insiders without demeaning the dignity of outsiders

Autonomy and solidarity are necessarily intertwined with identity, and they relate to one another in a dynamic that ranges from mutual alignment to mutual opposition. Those who share a common identity, particularly if the latter has to compete with others in its quest for self-preservation and self-fulfillment, are quite naturally drawn together by bonds of solidarity. Moreover, these bonds can either be defensive, such as when a common identity is under threat, or constructive, when enlisted to strengthen the resolve to advance a common agenda. Thus, for example, Jews as a religious minority within a polity where they encounter significant instances of hostility may unite (defensively) in solidarity to combat antisemitism, and to do so in spite of profound intra-communal divisions, such as those which otherwise split the ultra-Orthodox from those who are vehemently secular but strongly identify with Jewish culture and history. On the other hand, there is a sizeable portion of the US citizenry that strongly believes in US exceptionalism and is likely disposed to join in (constructive) solidarity to advance the latter domestically, and at times, to flout it even beyond the country's borders.

Bonds of solidarity tend to be strongest where relations of identity are most intense, as attested by the frequency with which family concerns and objectives take priority for its members over those relating to larger groupings. As a general rule, parents are much more interested in their own children's welfare and education than in those of their neighbors or of strangers. And because of these strong identity and solidarity bonds within the family, it seems for the most part best to entrust the care of children to their parents even if that would assure inequalities given material and other disparities among family households. From the standpoint of institutional design, and assuming all involved families possess the means to provide for the essential material and educational needs of their children, it seems far preferable to entrust children to their parents than to adopt any alternative scheme that would improve the chances of equalizing the situation of all children within the relevant constitutional unit. In the relevant respect here, the common identity of the family unit is largely unquestioned and the strong bonds of solidarity in the vast majority of cases sufficient to ensure an adequate fulfillment of the material welfare and educational needs of the child.

A strong enough combination of common identity and mutual solidarity frames or in some cases even resolves certain salient questions of justice. Consistent with this example regarding children, if the matter were constitutionalized, identity and solidarity factors would dictate both the relevant rights and obligations within the family and the nature of the appropriate justice essentials under the circumstances—namely, parent autonomy if all households have adequate means or state subsidies to ensure that all parents end up with the requisite minimum.

This example admittedly idealizes the case of the family in contemporary polities, but does so with the purpose of highlighting the much more challenging task of finding a productive link between identity and solidarity at the level of the constitutional unit, be it national or transnational. In a typical nuclear family, it is usually fairly obvious who belongs and who does not, but that may be a much less obvious or more contested matter in relation to a constitutional unit. Moreover, these difficulties can arise not only with respect to identity but also with respect to solidarity. Concerning identity, can an otherwise qualified attorney at law who is a legal immigrant but not a citizen be barred from the practice of law in his country of residence on the basis that she does not share enough in common with members of her profession that happen to be citizens?[10] And concerning solidarity, both Quebeçois and Catalans are clearly meant to be included as equal citizens within the respective constitutional orders of Canada and Spain. But given their respective frequent calls for greater autonomy, and periodically for secession, it seems fair to conclude that both these subnational units suffer from a solidarity deficit when compared to most others within their respective larger national and constitutional units.

Solidarity may vary in intensity as it would appear that family or small ethnic- or religious minority-associated solidarity would very likely exceed in intensity its counterpart at the national level in a vast federal republic or at a transnational level such as that of the EU. What is essential to retain in this context, however, is that whether links of solidarity are deep and seemingly firmly entrenched in the long run or more superficial and channeled into a circumscribed common purpose such as countering the existential threats posed by climate change, such links would seem in principle sufficient to sustain a common *ethnos* making for constitutional as opposed to contractual or merely peacefully competitive and collective interaction. To this must be added two additional critical factors. First, solidarity may be embraced in an aspirational way or sought to be prompted or reinforced in repressive ways. And second, in contemporary settings it is more accurate to refer to *solidarities* in the plural rather than to *solidarity* in the singular. Moreover, as will be detailed in what follows, consideration the two factors in question underscores the importance of the dynamic between solidarity and autonomy.

Aspirational solidarity is at work when one volunteers to risk one's life in the military with the purpose of defending one's country against foreign attacks. Conversely, one may experience great pressure to join the military and to risk one's life for the good of the country with the implication that any objection or hesitation would be a sign of disloyalty and of lack of solidarity. And in this latter case, expressions of solidarity to dispel suspicions of disloyalty could very likely be primarily motivated by feelings of guilt or fear of repressive consequences. More generally, and particularly from the perspective of justice, the legitimacy of a group's

---

[10] See *Andrews v. Law Society of British Columbia*, [1989] 1 SCR 143 (Canada).

demands of solidarity from its members depends to a significant extent on whether or not the members in question enjoy sufficient autonomy to make a significant choice. Where such autonomy is lacking, the singular would become disproportionately subsumed under the universal or the plural, and that itself would frustrate the search for balance called for by the justice essentials.

The importance of linking autonomy to solidarity and both of these to identity is further enhanced by the multiple and sometimes competing calls for loyal adherence and commitment that typically abound within contemporary polities. To return to our oft-used example of the German Catholic feminist woman who is a loyal citizen of the EU, it is plain that all these allegiances combine to shape her identity and that all the collective entities involved elicit from her sentiments of solidarity. It is also conceivable that some of her allegiances may come into conflict with one another and it is therefore crucial for her to have the autonomy to decide for herself whether to live with tensions and perhaps even contradictions or whether to exit, hence withdrawing her solidarity from one group with which she has increasing trouble identifying.

Recognition-based justice—if not also redistribution-based and representational justice—requires acknowledgment of settled identity profiles and corresponding solidarity commitments as well as facilitation and encouragement of choices or changes among available identitarian options coupled with correlated switches in solidarity-based allegiances. Solidarity among those who share a common identity entail relationships of mutual care and concern and divides the world between insiders linked by intra-communal bonds and outsiders from whom one differentiates and with whom one entertains inter-communal relations. In other words, correlations of identity and solidarity divide those engaged in social interaction within the relevant political unit into insiders and outsiders. Furthermore, from the standpoint of justice under comprehensive pluralism, this raises the question of what kind of relationships and corresponding bundles of rights and duties between insiders and outsiders would fall within the range between an acceptable minimum and a desirable optimum. A Schmittian friend/ enemy dynamic would of course be unacceptable as inherently anti-pluralist, but what about, as a minimum, a collection of purely internally focused communal units coexisting in peace side by side without any significant interaction?

If all individuals within that scenario autonomously satisfied their identity- and solidarity-related objectives within their own communal unit, then mere non-interference among the various communal units involved would seem reasonably compatible with achieving an acceptable minimum of justice at the level of the singular and at that of the plural. But what about justice at the level of the universal understood here as corresponding to a constitutional unit that would encompass all the communal units involved? If all communal units were completely self-sufficient then constitutionalization at the level of what would figure as the universal in this context would seem completely superfluous. The same would not be the case, however, if the communal units involved required some very limited cooperation of a bureaucratic nature—such as management and distributions of energy throughout the commonly shared territory, or guarding the borders that separate their own inter-communal expanse from neighboring political units made up of purely external outsiders—and limited cooperation would in no way impinge on intra-communal identity, autonomy, and solidarity. In the latter situation, the optimal constitutional model would be that of a confederation, and particularly one that would delegate a very minimal set of powers to the confederation and leave everything else to the confederated units. This arrangement would result from the standpoint of the universal in something at the very border between a contractual and a constitutional scheme of cooperation.

Such a confederate arrangement, which would allow for a type of "peaceful" inward-looking balkanization without fear of, or hostility toward, neighboring similarly self-isolated communal units, does provide a purely abstract conceptual minimum that seems consistent with notions of justice espoused by comprehensive pluralism. This minimum, however, plainly looms as wholly inadequate in view of the prevailing conditions present throughout contemporary constitutionally ruled polities. Indeed, not only are different groups within such polities bound to interact and to confront certain inter-communal tensions and conflicts, but also intra-communally it seems inevitable that a certain amount of discord will seep into relations between the singular and the plural. Thus, even within the confines of tightly knit families, it is not unheard off to have children break away from parents upon approaching adulthood due to contentious splits regarding religion, lifestyle, or political ideology. Also, it is completely unrealistic to assume that adoption of a minimum watchman state barely binding together the thinnest conceivable community of communities would suffice for purposes of assuring a just or equitable mediation among the singular, the plural, and the universal extending to all relevant intra-communal and inter-communal dealings.

It is impossible to establish a purely categorical test to determine what the justice essentials prescribe concerning the interplay between identity, solidarity, and autonomy at all levels of constitutional interaction. This is because the determination at stake must take into proper account contextual factors that tend to vary from one setting to the next. Assume, for example, that two polities are equally divided down the middle among the same two antagonistic religious groups, but in one of these each of the religions is concentrated in its own region whereas in the other, the two religions are geographically intermingled throughout the polity's territory. Consistent with this difference, a religion- (identity-) based federal constitutional ordering would seem highly likely to advance the justice essentials in the first of these polities, but not in the second.

Keeping in mind the contextual dimension of the inquiry, it is nevertheless instructive to lay out the conceptually optimal scenario for realization of the justice essentials under what would be best from the normative perspective of comprehensive pluralism. This optimal construct would be as counterfactual as its minimum acceptable counterpart, but their juxtaposition should prove helpful in determining in a principled manner what the justice essentials ought to require concerning the subject under consideration once the relevant contextual particulars are factored in.

As discussed earlier, a committed comprehensive pluralist not only wishes to accommodate plurality as he finds it but also to facilitate and promote aspirations toward further and novel iterations of plurality as he regards diversification and multiplication of paths towards self-fulfillment as a paramount good. Ideally, this would require maintaining a balance between established identities and clusters of solidarity, on the one hand, and the affording of opportunities to preserve, change, grow, diversify, and extend identities as well as solidifying, expanding, and shifting links of solidarity, on the other. Consistent with this, autonomy would require harmonizing freedoms and rights to develop and express one's singularity and to secure or forge paths towards self-realization. At the same time, however, autonomy would also require assuming obligations and exercising self-restraint toward others to allow the latter an equal opportunity to cultivate identity-based pursuits and to maintain, switch, or expand bonds of solidarity. Moreover, when pursuits of freedoms and exercises of rights by one clash with obligations and self-restraint towards (an) other, then both self and other ought to revert to the dictates of justice as reversible reciprocity to reach a proper mutual accommodation under the second-order norms propagated by comprehensive pluralism.

This interlinked equalization and maximization of opportunities combined with promotion of mutual self-restraint ought to prevail within all three spheres of the singular, the plural, and the universal as well as in dealings that extend across these three spheres. If everyone strictly adhered to maintaining relations of care and concern towards insiders while consistently affording full respect to the dignity of all outsiders, then recognition-based justice would become fully realized. Accordingly, the justice essentials would become superfluous to the extent that all concerned would fully cooperate to achieve all facets of justice in all their plenitude. Also, in this ideal pluralist setting the dynamic between insiders and outsiders would be fluid and evolving, with everyone enjoying a virtually unrestricted freedom to associate and dissociate so long as the freedom in question did not impinge on that of others. Furthermore, in such a pluralist utopia the *ethnos* would dissolve into comprehensive pluralism's *ethos*, thus allowing the relevant community of communities to occupy any contingent terrain of interaction among all those who actively deal with one another in a dynamic of insiders and outsiders within both the sphere of the singular and that of the plural. Consistent with this, conceptually the community of communities taking the place of the universal could span from the city-state to the entire globe. Finally, under these utopic conditions, the *demos* would approximate Derrida's *democracy to come* discussed in Chapter 6, with one important difference: everyone would be able to engage in

268 JUSTICE MINIMA AND COMPREHENSIVE PLURALISM

self-determination not only at the level of the singular but also at those of the plural and the universal. Indeed, everyone would be free to choose who she wishes to be and what course she ought to follow towards self-realization, whom she should associate with as insiders among a plurality of options, and with whom and how she should associate to maximize her options at the level of the singular and the plural. Ironically, in this best of imaginable pluralist worlds, given the nature of the all-encompassing *ethos* and the fullness of the perfectly attuned *demos*, the constitution would ultimately become as superfluous as the justice essentials. Indeed, the all-encompassing force of the pluralist *ethos* would presumably allow strict wholly voluntary adherence to morals which would obviate the need for law, whether constitutional or infra-constitutional.

It may seem that in this best of all pluralist worlds, pluralism itself would become superfluous or self-contradictory. As already noted, comprehensive pluralism is parasitic on there being other conceptions of the good susceptible of being accommodated. If adherence to comprehensive pluralism's *ethos* is universally embraced, does that not inevitably result in the end of pluralism? Upon careful consideration, the answer to this last question is in the negative. Indeed, if everyone strictly adhered to the pluralist *ethos*, that would not eliminate diversity but instead would create optimal conditions for every person to pursue singularly and collectively her self-chosen (normative) esthetic project. Like Rousseau's individual who, as already noted, is split into a citizen who must pursue the republican common good of the polity and into a bourgeois who attends to his private interests, in the ideal pluralist utopia every individual would embrace the same morality, but each of them would be an artist unto herself with the freedom to choose her own (normative) esthetic project which she can pursue individually or collectively with others with whom she agrees to collaborate. Like for Nietzsche and for Heidegger, the pluralist ideal would elevate the metaphor of the creative artist to the apex of human potential and achievement. Unlike these two philosophers, however, the ideal pluralist's artist is not elitist. In sharp contrast to Nietzsche's overman, the pluralist exalts everyman and everywoman in pursuit of his or her own (normative) esthetic path, regardless of whether the latter leads to the creation of a masterpiece or to self-enhancement through exposure to, and inspiration from, the esthetic output of others.

Back in the real world, the comprehensive pluralist is bound to encounter many who are not willing to embrace her *ethos*, many who wish to restrict entry into or exit from the groups they belong to, and even many who fail implicitly or explicitly to give their due to the dignity of both insiders and outsiders. Under such circumstances, various degrees of frustration and impediment are bound to interfere with smooth and equitable harmonization of identity, solidarity, and autonomy. These inevitable imperfections make it necessary to ground every viable constitutional order in a commonly shared *ethnos*. This *ethnos* is to be made up of a composite of imagined community images, and of traditional and aspirational convictions and orientations, and is meant to carve out a basis of common identity as well as to supply the props needed to mount an inspiring spectacle. The identity in question should circumscribe the *who*, the *what*, and the *range of options* that ought to be entrusted to the *demos*. Accordingly, the *ethnos* both sets the table for a particular working constitutional democracy and sets aside that which ought to be left off that table. The constitutional subject (the who) thus starts from a particular albeit evolving self-image, carves out the subject of the constitution (the what), and links the two through the *demos*. Moreover, the *demos* in question breaks into an imagined ethno-related consensus at the level of constitutional politics combined with an actual democratic process at the level of everyday ordinary politics. To sustain or reinforce the *ethnos*-based groundswell of solidarity in any complex pluralistic polity it is necessary to supplement commonly shared positive imaginaries with negations or repressions of commonly shared and potentially disruptive or destructive ethno-related traumas through the use of "gag rules" (Holmes 1988: 19). Thus, for example, in a country that has long experienced convulsive religious wars, the constitution may prohibit all references to religion in the public sphere while guaranteeing to each of the previously warring religions freedom of religion within the private sphere. Finally, solidarity enhancement may well depend on recourse to spectacle much as Agamben proposes, but without any necessary connection to the Christian trinity. The right kinds of spectacles can inspire and motivate in ways that boost solidarities and reinforce identities. For instance, the pomp and ceremony surrounding certain contemporary constitutional monarchs can unify and motivate the citizenry by stirring evocations of positive common traditions and by strengthening commitment to the unified destiny of the polity as a whole.

Notably, the *ethnos* of any particular constitutionally ordered polity is bound to fall short from the standpoint of comprehensive justice. This is because in constructing the narrative meant to hold together all those who are portrayed as accepting the relevant constitution as self-given, recourse must be had to the three interpretive tools that carve out constitutional identity—namely, negation, metaphor, and metonymy. When assessed in terms of criteria of overall distributive justice in all its three dimensions, all instances of negation, metaphor, and metonymy are bound to create or exacerbate actual inequalities among those affected. For example, French *laïcité* negates religion in the public sphere, but has nevertheless been characterized as blending better with Catholicism than with other religions (Troper 2009: 2568-9). The dictum that the US Constitution is "color blind," on the other hand, is built on the metaphoric assertion that all human beings are equivalent regardless of racial differences.[11] But whereas this metaphor is powerful

---

[11] Color blindness may also be understood as an instance of negation. However, given the importance and the history of race relations in the United States, the metaphoric interpretation looms as more persuasive. We are not dealing here with a Rawlsian veil of ignorance but instead with a plea to look beyond racial differences to acknowledge that all human beings are equal as moral agents and as deserving to be treated with equal dignity.

against racial segregation, it has also been invoked to deny claims of corrective and of distributive justice in the context of affirmative action policies favoring African-Americans (Rosenfeld 1991: 143). Finally, metonymy underlies the reconciliation of Italian secularism with displays of the crucifix in public school classrooms mentioned in Chapter 1, by displacing the crucifix from its position as a central religious symbol for purposes of reframing it as a primarily cultural symbol embedded in the country's national identity.

Though never static, the *ethnos* generates narratives and spectacles that temporarily suspend the trajectory toward full justice. The suspensions in question are warranted to the extent necessary to bolster the common identity and shared solidarity that prove indispensable to the well-functioning of the concerned constitutional unit. Although these suspensions thwart full justice, they may nonetheless fully comply with the partial overall justice called for by the justice essentials. To be clear, a populist *ethnos* that altogether leaves out a country's ethnic minorities clearly fails to meet the minimum called for by the justice essentials and ought to be therefore rejected as a legitimate referent for constitutional ordering regardless of the identitarian or solidarity-based intensities it may arouse among those it designates as insiders. In contrast, French *laïcité* may favor non-believers and Catholics to the detriment of the *full* equal justice owed fellow citizens with different religious affiliations without thereby running afoul the justice essentials—albeit that this latter conclusion is hardly incontestable as attested to by controversies regarding the banning of the Islamic veil in French public schools (Mancini 2009).

Because of its dependence on bonds of identity correlated to bonds of solidarity with room left for iterations of autonomy at the singular, plural, and universal levels, constitutional justice not only falls short of full justice but can also at times stand as a daunting obstacle in the path toward the latter. Returning to the example of French *laïcité*, assuming it to be profoundly imprinted within the French citizenry, and assuming that it inherently disfavors French Jews, Muslims, and Protestants in the same proportion as it favors Catholics, then it would stand against achieving full distributive justice among all the religions at stake. Now, if *laïcité* could not be modified to become more just, and if it could not be replaced without irreparably damaging the French *ethnos*, then preservation of the current French constitutional order would preclude the achievement of full justice. In other words, under these circumstances, whereas a philosopher king might be able to impose full justice among all prevailing religions in France, the current French constitutional predicament would stand as a firm obstacle against this happening.

In sum, the dynamic between identity, solidarity, and autonomy establishes categorical and contextual preconditions to the achievement of the justice essentials. The dynamic in question leaves it to extra-constitutional and infra-constitutional means to pursue justice above that constitutionalized as essential. Whereas a working constitution need not logically become an obstacle to the realization of full justice, in many cases it is. This shortcoming, while real, may not be, however, as serious at it may seem. And this is because once we move away from the likes of philosopher kings or of Dworkin's Hercules, ordinary humans have never come close to approaching full justice even if contra to Derrida they believe that such an undertaking is not conceptually impossible.

II Comprehensive Pluralism's Approach to the Justice Essentials: The Dialectic between the Fixed-core Minimum and the Plural Maximum

It may seem paradoxical, if not contradictory, that in order to maximize plurality within a constitutionally ordered polity it would be necessary to lay down a set of fixed set of core norms that function in ways that appear anti-pluralistic. To be more precise, as noted earlier, there are norms that comprehensive pluralism deems to be literally universal, such as the prohibition against torture, in that *regardless of context* there can be no justification whatsoever for torturing a fellow human. The same is not the case, however, with respect to the comprehensive pluralist requirement to teach the virtues of pluralism and tolerance to all children with no exception. In the latter case, context does matter, and a completely self-contained fundamentalist religious group that believes it possesses the absolute truth and chooses to live peacefully while shunning all inter-communal contact could certainly be *accommodated* within a polity without forcing on the latter any ideas or normative dictates that the group in question would find abhorrent. Imposing on school-age children within that fundamentalist group exposure to civic virtue lessons advocating acceptance and tolerance of outsiders whom their parents consider mortal sinners does indeed seem at first sight unwarranted. Whereas the teaching at stake can be easily defended within liberalism or republicanism, impositions that could lead to erosion of group intra-communal autonomy or solidarity would appear anti-pluralistic unless they amounted to a justified precondition to accommodation.

On further reflection and given the dialectics of comprehensive pluralism, the teaching of rudiments of civic virtue to fundamentalist children is justified even where a proper contextual analysis suggests that it is *prima facie* anti-pluralist. This and other fixed requirements that emerge at first as seemingly illegitimate because of their apparent disregard of relevant contextual factors underscore what can be designated as the "paradox of pluralism" which bears some affinity to Karl Popper's "paradox of tolerance" (Popper 1966: 265, n. 4) and to the principle of "militant democracy" enshrined in certain contemporary constitutions (Muller 2012: 1258–9). Before exploring this further, it is important to emphasize from the outset that the paradox of pluralism in no way implies that because it relies on certain fixed seemingly acontextual norms, comprehensive pluralism amounts in the end to just another version of limited pluralism.

The paradox of tolerance is based on the claim that tolerance of the intolerant eventually results in the very abolition of tolerance. Similarly, the principle of militant democracy rests on the assumption that treating extremist anti-democratic political parties as lawful dangerously increases their chances of coming into power and abolishing democracy. The paradigmatic example highlighting both cases is Hitler's accession to power in Germany both legally and democratically, followed by his Nazi regime's total abolition of both tolerance and democracy. More generally, there is an analogy between systematic hate speech aimed at vilifying and demeaning a particular minority group resulting eventually in widespread intolerance against it throughout the polity and use of democratic means for undemocratic ends (Roach 2004: 171, 183). To avoid the dehumanization and potential violence associated with systematic hate speech, some jurisdictions such as Germany prohibit it with a view to preserving a requisite minimum of tolerance and respect for the dignity of those within the polity who have been all too frequently cast as reviled outsiders.[12] Along similar lines, whereas in ordinary democracies all political parties which adhere to democratic means are allowed to compete for power, in militant democracies parties devoted to undemocratic ends, such as Nazism or Soviet style communism, can be constitutionally banned (Rosenfeld 2006: 47).[13]

In both the cases of tolerance and of democracy, the absence of constraining limitations is thus thought by many to become eventually self-defeating. Much in the same way, and to stick with the example of the fundamentalist children, comprehensive pluralism's concerns with singularity, autonomy, choice among plural alternatives, and need to engage in minimum social and political cooperation with outsiders within the same polity regardless of the latter's conception of the good necessitates a minimum of instruction on the rudiments of pluralist civic virtue. The instruction in question ought to be tailored so as to be the least offensive possible against the fundamentalists' absolutist anti-pluralist stance, but it would unavoidably run counter to their conception of the good. At a minimum, the fundamentalist children would have to be taught about the need for basic respect for the infidels with whom one is bound to interact inter-communally, the need to treat others one encounters in the public place not as enemies (of the truth), but as honest searchers of and believers in their own truth (as erroneous as it may be), and recognition that within society at large every adult ought to be protected in his freedom to carry on the traditions of his family and community but also to decide to choose a different course and to be protected by public authorities from harassment and retribution upon exiting the community into which he was born. Without question, the above instruction limits accommodation of our putative fundamentalist religious community at least somewhat, and possibly severely, if it

---

[12] See BVerfGE 90, Decision of April 13, 1994 (*Auschwitz Lie* Case).
[13] See *Privacy of Communications Case* (*The Klass* Case), 30 BVerfGE 1 (1970).

deems mere exposure to any of the ideas at stake a very serious breach of key divine commands. Notwithstanding this palpable limitation of acceptance of the plural, it is not in the end anti-pluralist, but a necessary step in the deployment of comprehensive pluralism's greatest possible accommodation of plurality. In this sense, pluralist limitations on accommodation prove the equivalent of the intolerances required to safeguard tolerance and of the restrictions against certain democratically sought anti-democratic ends needed for the very protection of democracy.

Even if from a purely philosophical perspective, one may quibble about where to draw the line on full accommodation of exclusively inward-focused, peaceful, and vehemently anti-pluralist conceptions of the good, in the context of a constitution concerned with the justice essentials, mandatory instruction on the basics of civic virtue still looms as indispensable. Moreover, within a typical contemporary constitutional democracy harboring some conceptions of the good that are to varying degrees anti-pluralist, and others for the most part consistent with pluralism but in frequent conflict among one another, there are several other fixed-core minimums that figure as preconditions to securing a maximum of plurality. One of these, already discussed, is prioritizing the constitutional guarantee of the minimum of material welfare necessary to allow each person to have access to obtaining her due under the three facets of constitutional justice. The bundle of material goods subject to redistribution for purposes of securing the said minimum may vary depending on the actual wealth of the polity involved, but the right to such minimum itself ought to be categorically mandated and given lexical priority over conflicting recognition-based and representation-based justice claims.

As also already mentioned, both recognition-based and representation-based constitutional justice require certain material resources, such as those that would assure an adequate education for all. The provision of these resources ought to be included in the constitutionally mandated minimum though, once again, quantitative differences may be warranted depending on the level of overall wealth of the relevant polity. Furthermore, recognition-based and representation-based justice each require additional fixed minimum justice constitutional protections. In order to secure an adequate opportunity to pursue and protect singularity, a certain number of classical liberal rights, such as freedom of speech, of assembly, of conscience, and of religion; the right to privacy and of protection of private life without prejudice because of sexual orientation or of lifestyle; and a broadly understood individual-equality right oriented towards equalization of essential resources and vindication of an equal opportunity for each individual to pursue, shape, preserve, and enjoy her own singularity. Although the rights in question may be, for the most part, formulated in exactly the same terms as they have long been in constitutions firmly anchored in (philosophical) liberalism or republicanism, they would have to differ in their interpretation whenever that would be called for in order to satisfy the pluralist understanding of the justice essentials. For example, whereas hate speech is widely protected under the understanding of free speech in the United

States (Rosenfeld 2012) inspired by ultra-liberal John Stuart Mill, a pluralist interpretation would legitimate restrictions or prohibitions of such speech. Accordingly, the US marketplace of ideas criterion would be replaced or supplemented by one centered on substantive recognition-based injury likely to deprive the victim of hate speech of basic dignity or of an acceptable minimum of respect from others.

Recognition-based justice also requires settling on a minimum of certain fixed-core rights at the level of the plural. The concern here is sufficient equalization of protection of (relevant) group identity, solidarity, and autonomy coupled with adequate protection of rights of entry into, and exit from, particular groups. In this context, there are inescapable threshold issues that vary from one constitutional setting to another. Chief among these is which groups ought to be entitled to constitutional recognition and what would amount to sufficient equalization among recognized groups pursuant to the justice essentials. These key issues can be resolved or subjected to critical appraisal by reference to the particular relationship between the *ethnos* and *the demos* in play in the polity under consideration. Thus, in the case of a highly democentric constitutional tradition, such as that of France, group rights can be minimized provided that collective units can relatively equally thrive within the private sphere. As mentioned earlier, even if *laïcité* somewhat favors Catholics, that itself would not negate compliance with the justice essentials so long as other religions and non-religious ideologies can pursue self-expression and self-realization without undue impediments. If, however, as some have claimed, *laïcité* has a significant adverse effect on the free practice of their religion by French Muslims,[14] then some constitutional adjustments or reforms would be called for in order to meet the fixed minimum of required equalization. At the other end of the spectrum, in an ethnocentric constitutional tradition, group rights figure prominently and ought to be constitutionally enshrined. In this context, the question of *which* groups are entitled to constitutionally enshrined rights, freedoms, and subsidies becomes crucial. Moreover, in this tradition recognition-based equities often go hand in hand with representation-based ones. In Canada, for example, English and French are the official languages, and their respective speakers enjoy constitutionally guaranteed collective language rights[15] that entitle them, *inter alia*, to public school instruction in their native language in areas of the country where they constitute a linguistic minority.[16] In addition, with respect to representation, three of the nine justices on the Canadian Supreme Court must be from Quebec and all of them must be bilingual.[17] This latter requirement has been recently criticized as it has operated as an impediment to the appointment of an indigenous

---

[14] See *S.A.S. v. France*, App. No. 43835/11 EU.Ct.H.R. (2014); Hakeem Yusuf, 2014, "*S.A.S. v. France: Supporting 'Living Together'' or Forced Assimilation?*'" Int'l Hum. Rts. L. Rev., vol. 3, 227.

[15] See Canadian Charter of Rights and Freedoms, 1982, Sec. 23.

[16] See *Mahe v. Alberta*, [1990] 1 SCR 342 (Canada).

[17] See Supreme Court Act, RSC 1985 c. S-26.

Canadian to the Court due to lack of sufficient mastery of French.[18] As there are many other languages other than English and French spoken in Canada, is the limitation of group rights to these two languages contrary to the justice essentials? And, is the grant of linguistic group rights, but not of religious or ethnic-based ones—except for the ones granted to indigenous peoples—objectionable as constitutionally inequitable?

The favoring of English and French as the national languages of Canada is based on historical reasons deeply imprinted in the country's *ethnos*. To the extent that there is no clamoring for adding other languages to the official ones, the constitutional linguistic landscape in Canada seems consistent with meeting the justice essentials. Likewise, the lack of comparable constitutional recognition of religious or (non-indigenous) ethnic group rights remains consistent with the justice essentials given that religious and ethnic differences do not figure as key lines of demarcation within the Canadian *ethnos*. Finally, the linguistic impediments that prevent members from Canada's indigenous population to occupy a seat on the Supreme Court could well be counter to the justice essentials.[19]

Other constitutional democracies in which language figures prominently in the national and constitutional *ethnos*, such as Belgium and Switzerland, have opted for territorially based collective language rights. Thus, French-speaking students are not entitled to a public education in their own language in a German-speaking Swiss canton[20] or a Flemish-speaking region in Belgium (Adams 2014). From an overall justice standpoint, this latter handling of the collective right at stake may be wanting, but given the additional costs and administrative requirements that a Canadian type of arrangement would require, the territorial-based system seems poised to meeting the justice essentials.[21] As this last example further underscores, the contextual variables may be numerous, but the relevant core minimum group rights remain throughout. Moreover, reference to the core minimum is useful both to set up and interpret constitutional rights in ways that further the justice essentials, and as a counterfactual to assess whether a particular constitution is deficient in its dealing with collective rights issues in ways that thwart the justice essentials.

Just as recognition-based concerns call for certain core minimums so do representation-based ones. Representation-based justice is essentially two pronged: it relates, on the one hand, to provisions enshrined in the constitution

---

[18] See Alexandra Nasager, 2020, "The Supreme Court, functional bilingualism, and the indigenous candidate: reconciling the bench," *Alberta L. Rev. Soc.*, vol. 57, 797, <https://www.canlii.org/en/commentary/doc/2020CanLIIDocs500#!fragment/zoupio-_Toc3Page1/BQCwhgziBcwMYgK4DsDWs zIQewE4BUBTADwBdoAvbRABwEtsBaAfX2zgGYAFMAc0ICMASgA0ybKUIQAiokK4AntADky kREJhcCWfKWr1m7SADKeUgCElAJQCiAGVsA1AIIA5AMK2RpMACNoUnYhISA visited April 11, 2022.

[19] See *MacDonald v. City of Montreal*, [1986] 1 SCR 460 (Canada).

[20] See <https://www.internations.org/go/moving-to-switzerland/education> visited April 5, 2022 (education available in the "dominate" language of the canton).

[21] See Case "*Relating to Certain Aspects of the Laws on the Use of Languages in Education in Belgium*," ECtHR 1 EHRR 252 (1968).

to secure the justice essentials, and, on the other, to the process designed to enable effective democratic decision-making for matters falling beyond the purview of the justice essentials. For example, if the constitution guarantees to everyone full state coverage of expenses in medical emergencies but not beyond, that may be deemed to satisfy the justice essentials provided that the citizenry can then decide democratically whether or not the state should pay for ordinary medical services. Accordingly, the democratic process required to yield legitimate resolutions of questions of justice beyond what is within the essentials as well as other policies must itself be constitutionalized consistent with the pluralist dictates relating to the singular, the plural, and the universal. In other words, whereas democratic process *outcomes* are themselves infra-constitutional and any increment of justice which they might produce above and beyond the essentials, the *process itself* must satisfy the representation-based justice essentials. Consistent with this, for a citizen to have a full-fledged equal vote on a referendum concerning a proposal requiring the state to assume the cost of all medical services she will need to enjoy both certain antimajoritarian rights, such as that to free speech, to become sufficiently informed to cast an intelligent vote, and a constitutionally enshrined voting process that guarantees each voter an equal voice in reaching a democratic resolution.

Pluralist justice in representation requires a fixed, for the most part well-worn, core minimum at the level of the singular. This includes an equal vote for each citizen, an equal opportunity to affect the outcome of the election—through, among other things, the designing of proportionate voting districts and through restriction of corrosion and corruption by limiting the influx of private interest money into elections and politics, and through assuring the "representativeness" of parliamentary members through various means, including gender-based affirmative action to assure parity between the sexes in political party candidate lists (Dorsen 2016: 952–3).

Establishing the core fixed minimum at the level of the plural, in contrast, seems to be much more challenging. Indeed, it is clear for a pluralist that all relevant groups within the polity ought to have an equal or proportionate representation relating to their collective objectives and interests, but there is no readily available "one-size-fits-all" way to accomplish this. Here again, a crucial role is played by the particular relationship between *ethnos* and *demos* that happens to prevail in any given polity. In a thoroughly democentric polity—a more systematically secular republic than France—it may be sufficient to guarantee a full panoply of individual rights constitutionally, including generous social welfare ones, to allow for private sphere organizational viability of various religious communities as well as comparable non-religious ones. Based primarily on freedom of religion and freedom of assembly rights, particular religions could organize, build, and maintain houses of worship, provide religious education, and provide many other pertinent religious services. To be sure, in such a setting, there would be inevitable inequalities among religious communities due to various contingent factors, such as differences in size, in wealth, in costs associated with provisions of essential religious services, and the like. Nevertheless, in spite of these differences, as long as each group could function adequately the justice essentials might well be satisfied. As against this, in a heavily ethnocentric polity, in which the constitution provides for the state first to recognize religions officially in order then to subsidize them, it would be the responsibility of the state to sufficiently equalize its affirmative support of the relevant groups in order to meet the justice essentials. In this latter situation, inequalities would undoubtedly persist, but the state would have a constitutional duty to keep them relatively proportionate in order not to infringe against the justice essentials. In short, in both these cases and all others in between, pluralism requires that the constitution provide or protect the means necessary to allow for all relevant religious and non-religious equivalent groups to be able to conduct and sustain their basic collective endeavors. And in all cases, in order to achieve this, certain fixed-core constitutional norms would have to be in place, with the consequence of some greater accommodation of certain collective pursuits at the expense of others, with a view to maintaining a sufficient measure of equalization consistent with the pluralist understanding of the justice essentials.

The necessary interplay between a fixed-core minimum and contextual variables in order to maximize the plural also extends to the universal. At that level, fixed-core constitutional provisions and standards need to address the three facets of justice as they concern the community of the whole as well as on how they impact the relationship between the latter and the singular and plural. At a very minimum, fixed constitutional norms must determine who belongs as an insider and who does not as an outsider within the relevant constitutional unit. Moreover, without dwelling on any details, fixed rules for various essential functions taking place at the level of the universal in typical contemporary polities, such as (at least some significant) regulation of the economy, national defense, and foreign affairs, loom as necessary for purposes of achieving justice essentials that comport with the comprehensive pluralist conception of the good. Thus, for example, whereas a healthy economy and a beneficial monetary policy require some degree of fixed constitutional guideposts in any complex contemporary setting, the pluralist will aim to make sure that these align with her conception of redistributive material justice, and to the extent relevant with her recognition- and representation-based one. As in the case of hate speech mentioned earlier, the relevant fixed constitutional provisions may very much resemble traditional liberal ones, but they would have to be modified in their design or interpretation to align with pluralist aims.

The pluralist handling of the relations between the community of the whole and individuals as well as constitutionally relevant groups also requires certain fixed constitutional rules or standards. In cases of emergency, such as a foreign military invasion, for instance, emergency powers provisions are appropriate and their pluralist justification fully aligns with liberal, republican, or communitarian ones. Survival in the face of foreign aggression trumps all distributive justice concerns.

More specifically within the pluralist *ethos*, solidarity and unity at the level of the universal justify whatever necessary and proportionate temporary correlative sacrifice which may be required concerning autonomy to pursue the singular and autonomy or solidarity to advance the plural. Furthermore, this illustrates how even pluralism all the way up and all the way down can cease to call for plurality in conditions pitting friends at actual war against implacable belligerent enemies. If the conditions involved are temporary, then emergency powers imposing serious constraints on the singular and the plural are fully consistent with pluralism just as intolerance of the intolerant are with tolerance. However, if actual war pitting friends against enemies were to become a permanent state of affairs, then pluralism would end up proving altogether impossible.

Where pluralism requires a fixed-core minimum but may part company with liberalism, republicanism, and communitarianism is in settings associated with conditions of stress such as those discussed in Chapter 2. In situations where enduring conditions of stress prevail, such as those that arose in the aftermath of the 9/11 attacks, there are two principal developments that pose significant challenges to maintaining the justice essentials. The first of these is readjustment of the boundary between liberty and security. Although such readjustment is also required under emergency conditions, the proper response in conditions of stress is more problematic for two important reasons. First, as already noted, the threat posed in times of stress is not as existential as it is in times of emergency, and second, typically the duration of times of stress is generally much longer and much more indeterminate. As a consequence of this, establishing the proper balance between liberty and security, and thus avoiding undue trampling of singular and plural recognition- and representation-based justice, tends to become more difficult and more controversial (Rosenfeld 2006a). In addition, as global terror was conducted in the name of an extreme jihadist interpretation of Islam, in the aftermath of 9/11 and various other attacks in Western countries this resulted in great increases in discrimination against Muslims. From a pluralist standpoint, both the likely imbalances in the relationship between liberty and security and the increased dangers of discrimination against certain minorities in times of stress are most likely to (seemingly counterintuitively) call for greater rather than lesser protection of fundamental rights to avoid unwarranted departures from acceptable levels of equalization in relation to recognition- and representation-based justice.

The other instance of conditions of stress broached in Chapter 2, that relating to the COVID-19 pandemic, has presented a series of unique thorny challenges to the justice essentials and to pluralism itself. The primary challenge that reaction to the pandemic has brought to the fore is, as already underscored, the upending of settled notions of proportionality—and for pluralists, of proportionality as circumscribed by comprehensive pluralism's *ethos*. Whereas the latter will be further addressed shortly, the disproportionate exacerbations surrounding the COVID-19 pandemic have been manifold. The health dangers caused by the pandemic are global and their solution or mitigation seemingly only realizable through vaccination of the vast majority of people throughout the world.[22] At this writing, in the one year since vaccines have become available, and the two years since the conditions of stress due to the pandemic have prevailed on a worldwide scale, the controversies surrounding COVID-19 have provided a vivid microcosm of the threats that confront both liberal constitutionalism itself and the project set out by comprehensive pluralism. As noted in Chapter 2, although the pandemic is by definition global in scale, countries have retrenched within their borders. In addition, the pandemic has dramatically highlighted the huge wealth gap between rich and poor countries,[23] and between rich and poor within some countries, such as the United States, where billionaires profited enormously while the least well-off (because of pandemic-caused deprivations) had to wait in long lines to collect privately organized food donations.[24] The pandemic has also underscored the inequities within the health care system in certain countries, such as the United States,[25] thus vividly illustrating failures to meet the justice essentials from a redistribution-based justice perspective.

On an entirely separate register, the pandemic has exacerbated confrontations between demagogues and populists, led by Trump while he was president of the United States, on the one hand, and those committed to science and liberal constitutional democracy, on the other.[26] Such confrontations also took place in other countries, such as Bolsonaro's Brazil,[27] and in many additional ones not under populist or demagogic rule,[28] pitting supporters of vaccine requirements policies against those with militantly anti-vaccine stances.[29] What is remarkable about

[22] World Health Organization, *Covid-19 Advice for the Public: Getting Vaccinated*, w.h.o. (November 15, 2021), <https://www.who.int/emergencies/diseases/novel-coronavirus-2019/covid-19-vaccines/advice>, visited April 5, 2022.

[23] Francisco H.G. Ferreira, "Inequality in the time of Covid-19," *International Monetary Fund* (June 2021) <https://www.imf.org/external/pubs/ft/fandd/2021/06/inequality-and-covid-19-ferreira.html>, visited April 5, 2022.

[24] Max Fisher & Emma Bubola, "As coronavirus deepens inequality, inequality worsens its spread," *NY Times* (March 15, 2020) <https://www.nytimes.com/2020/03/15/world/europe/coronavirus-inequality.html>, visited April 5, 2022.

[25] Isaac Chotiner, "The interwoven threads of inequality and health," *The New Yorker* (April 14, 2020) <https://www.newyorker.com/news/q-and-a/the-coronavirus-and-the-interwoven-threads-of-inequality-and-health>, visited April 5, 2022.

[26] Sheryl Gay Stolberg & Noah Weiland, "Study finds 'single largest driver' of coronavirus misinformation: Trump," *NY Times* (September 30, 2020) <https://www.nytimes.com/2020/09/30/us/politics/trump-coronavirus-misinformation.html>; Jeneen Interlandi, "When science is pushed aside," *NY Times* (October 16, 2020) <https://www.nytimes.com/2020/10/16/opinion/trump-covid-public-health.html>, visited April 5, 2022.

[27] Jaclyn Diaz, "Brazil's Jair Bolsonaro remains defiant on COVID-19 and the environment at the U.N.," *NPR* (September 22, 2021) <https://www.npr.org/2021/09/22/1039540502/brazils-bolsonaro-on-covid-environment-at-the-un, visited April 5, 2022.

[28] Katrin Bennhold, "Vaccinated vs. unvaccinated: Europe's covid culture war," *NY Times* (November 17, 2021) <https://www.nytimes.com/2021/11/17/world/europe/covid-vaccine-germany-europe.html>, visited April 5, 2022.

[29] Neil MacFarquhar, "Far-right extremists move from 'stop the steal' to stop the vaccine," *NY Times* (March 26, 2021) <https://www.nytimes.com/2021/03/26/us/far-right-extremism-anti-vaccine.html>, visited April 5, 2022; Ryan Broderick, "Italy's anti-vaccination movement is militant and dangerous,"

these confrontations, for present purposes, is the animosity between the two sides, which seems better captured by Schmitt's friend/enemy dichotomy than by reference to ordinary political struggles within an ultimately unified community of the whole. Whereas within the language game of medicine there are many uncertainties and reversals, as empirical testing and corroboration as well as the gathering of statistics are key in the case of a new virus, such as the one known as COVID-19, these have been exaggerated, taken out of context, and exploited by those who have flouted anti-science stances and conducted on social media and elsewhere a sustained campaign of disinformation and misinformation.[30] In addition, whereas coping with the pandemic and the conditions of stress it has foisted upon society poses genuine policy choices over which reasonable minds can differ—such as to what extent should lockdowns be imposed to slow down the spread of the virus— the actual political and societal divisions over the matter turned into virulent manifestations of the culture wars.[31] From a pluralist standpoint, the pandemic ought to have produced greater empathy within the polity, greater consensus regarding the science involved—notably, the opponents of vaccines and masks have experienced much higher rates of serious disease and death[32]—and a sense of balance that would have belied untenable individual liberty claims that amount to a license to spread the disease by willfully refusing to adhere to proven preventive measures. In the end, whether the COVID-19 experience will prove unique or a harbinger of a long-term exacerbation of the culture wars, the societal and political tears that it has laid open loom as a serious threat against both pluralism and liberal constitutional democracy.

Conditions of emergency and of stress are prone to creating or increasing injustices to the extent that they foment disproportionate official and societal reactions. To mitigate these tendencies, it is particularly important in those circumstances to adhere to the principle of proportionality. More generally, this latter principle ought to figure as part of the fixed-core minimum constitutional prescriptions consistent with comprehensive pluralism. As already stressed, on a theoretical level, proportionality is essential to manage the reconciliation between the respective demands

---

Foreign Policy (November 13, 2021) <https://foreignpolicy.com/2021/11/13/italy-anti-vaccination-movement-militant-dangerous/>, visited April 5, 2022.

[30] Tiffany Hsu & Marc Tracy, "On podcasts and radio, misleading Covid-19 talk goes unchecked," *NY Times* (November 12, 2021) <https://www.nytimes.com/2021/11/12/business/media/coronavirus-misinformation-radio-podcasts.html>, visited April 5, 2022.

[31] Bennhold, see note 28; Bari Weiss, "The coronavirus makes our old culture wars seem quaint," *NY Times* (April 22, 2020) <https://www.nytimes.com/2020/04/22/opinion/coronavirus-culture-war.html>, visited April 5, 2022; Rick Rojas, "Masks become a flash point in the virus culture wars," *NY Times* (May 3, 2020) <https://www.nytimes.com/2020/05/03/us/coronavirus-masks-protests.html>, visited April 5, 2022.

[32] Deidre McPhillips, "CNN analysis: risk of dying from Covid-19 is higher in red states," *CNN* (December 2, 2020), <https://www.cnn.com/world/live-news/omicron-covid-19-variant-12-02-21/index.html>, visited April 5, 2022.

of the universal, the singular, and the plural, and for the requisite harmonization of the *ethnos* and the *demos*. At the constitutional level, on the other hand, the pursuit of proportionality—as well as other fixed-core minimums—is crucial in the quest of the pluralist understanding of the justice essentials. And this pursuit ought to permeate all the facets of constitutional ordering: constitution making; constitutional interpretation; constitutional amendment, reform, and transformation; and constitutional dissolution through mutually consented upon secession. Finally, although recourse to the standard of proportionality is highly ubiquitous throughout liberal constitutional democracies (Dorsen 2016: 238), the pluralist *ethos* is bound to leave a distinct imprint in the course of its quest for proportionate outcomes. To cite but one example, there is a clear difference in approach between liberalism and pluralism in cases involving conflicts between freedom of religion claims to exemption from generally applicable laws or to priority over competing rights, such as equality between the sexes. Liberalism has difficulty with such conflicts as there is no generally agreed liberal common denominator between claims drawn on transcendent religious truths and secular counterparts. Where there is such a common dominator, for example in a conflict between freedom of the press and the privacy rights of a private citizen, both parties involved and the adjudicator of the conflict presumably share the same liberal constitutional frame of reference. For instance, if a journalist's intent to publish a highly embarrassing story about a non-celebrity private family matter is challenged by that family, a judge would have to balance the public interest in the proposed journalist's story and the privacy interests of the concerned family. Both of the rights involved are secular constitutional ones issuing from the same shared constitutional order. Although judges may somewhat differ over where to draw the line in balancing the two rights involved, the reasonable range of possible variations is highly likely to be narrow enough to have little, if any effect, on the justice essentials. Contrast that with a religious claim grounded in a metaphysical transcendent truth in confrontation against a secular constitutional right or against public policy. In such a case, the liberal constitution, the religious claimant, the judge, and the party opposing the religious claim most probably lack any common denominator that would yield a plausible consensus on a proportionate resolution. Accordingly, the tendency has been to either treat religious claims much like secular ones or to defer to them virtually completely. The US Supreme Court did the former in a case in which it refused to grant an exemption from a criminal law prohibiting the use of peyote to those who used it in a collective ritual mandated by their native-American religion.[33] The same court later seemingly completely deferred to a religious assertion stacked against a weighty secular constitutional interest when, in a 5–4 decision, it granted an exemption to a devout Christian owner of a business corporation employing 11,000 employees

---

[33] See *Employment Division, Department of Human Resources of Oregon v. Smith*, 494 US 872 (1990).

from complying with a federal law mandating coverage of contraceptives for use by its women employees[34]—in spite of precedents establishing that the use of contraceptives is constitutionally protected.[35] Both these decisions can be fairly criticized as disproportionate and as militating against the justice essentials. In both these cases and others, a pluralist approach based on mutual accommodation as best as possible of diverse conceptions of the good and on recourse to justice as reversible reciprocity to handle conflicting claims grounded on clashing first-order norms, would both provide a common denominator for proportionate resolution of the kinds of conflicts at stake and in all likelihood prove better suited to advance the justice essentials. Moreover, whereas it is beyond the scope of the present inquiry to explore how the pluralist *ethos* may actually be adapted to fit within the language game of constitutional doctrine, it seems plain that any workable approximation would yield a more principled criterion of proportionality than those based on counterparts reliant on the *ethos* of liberalism.

III Challenges and Pathologies Confronting Comprehensive Pluralism's Quest to Meet the Justice Essentials

Constitutional justice, in general, and the justice essentials, in particular, confront major challenges because of the apparent lack of fit between liberal constitutions molded for Westphalian nation-states and the global nature of many of the most important contemporary phenomena that have a profound impact on distributive justice issues. As repeatedly illustrated throughout the preceding discussion, the global dimensions of the economy, of pandemics, of certain terrorist agendas, of migration, and of cultural interpenetration through the Internet and social media, pose distributive justice challenges that might be best handled, as a whole or in part, on a worldwide scale. The COVID-19 pandemic provides perhaps the most dramatic example as it has been mired in worldwide needless deaths and suffering for lack of a coordinated global vaccination program benefitting poor countries as much as rich ones in a context in which transmission of the disease and complications due to new variants cannot be controlled so long as vast swathes of humanity remain unvaccinated.[36] Similarly, given the massive discrepancies in

---

[34] See *Burwell, Secretary of Health and Human Services et al. v. Hobby Lobby Stores, Inc. et al.*, 573 US 682 (2014).

[35] See *Griswold v. Connecticut*, 381 US 479 (1965); *Eisenstadt v. Baird*, 405 US 438 (1972).

[36] See Rob Pichetta, "The world has the tools to end the coronavirus pandemic. They're not being used properly," *CNN* (December 6, 2021) <https://www.cnn.com/2021/12/05/health/covid-pandemic-global-solutions-toolkit-cmd-intl/index.html>, visited April 5, 2022. (Several scientists raised parallels with the push to fight climate change—an effort which, even at this critical hour, is being slowed by competing national interests. According to Andrea Taylor of the Duke Global Health Institute: "Some kind of binding legal agreement that countries sign onto could give us something of a coordinated global plan, which is what we're lacking now ... We're never going to make a successful case on altruism ... But

wealth between countries under a global economy, guaranteeing a minimum of material redistributive justice to all human beings would require mandated transfers of wealth—through taxation or legally required subsidies—from the richest to the poorest countries. Also, the large migrations of labor require vast expansions of the right of citizenship consistent with all three facets of distributive justice as migrant workers are *functionally* equivalent to native ones with full rights of citizenship (Rosenfeld 2010: 221–3). These are but some of the salient developments in relation to which it would seem entirely plausible to conceptually devise a worldwide distributive justice system consistent with the pluralist *ethos*, but which could not be adapted for handling within currently workable constitutional frameworks. In some wealthy countries, such as the United States and other Western democracies, this impediment need not compromise the pursuit of the justice essentials since, as discussed in Chapter 2, amply sufficient resources remain in hand regardless of sizeable flights of capital and significant exports of labor opportunities. Beyond that, although as already argued, transnational and global constitutional ordering—particularly of the layered and segmented type—seem entirely possible from a conceptual standpoint, it is at best a messy work in progress at this writing. That creates a major, though not fatal, obstacle to approaching the justice essentials in polities with limited material resources. Indeed, what cannot be achieved through the relevant nation-state constitutional ordering may be at least partially realized through international (contract-like) treaty-making or even purely interest-based interaction. An example of the former is the above mentioned widely spread international agreement to impose a worldwide minimum 15 per cent corporate tax. An example, of the latter, on the other hand, could be imagined if all nations could rise above the culture wars and realize that controlling COVID-19 at home remains seemingly impossible unless resources to fight the virus are directed to polities unable to fend for themselves due to their inadequate material resources.

A much more daunting challenge, and from the respective perspectives of liberal constitutional democracy and of comprehensive pluralism a downright pathology, is the entrenchment of clashing ideologies and the ensuing breakdown of dialogue due to what can be broadly referred to as the culture wars. Whether the transformation of political adversaries and competitors into downright enemies is due to a hardening of intransigence due to the repoliticization of a dominant religion as recounted in Chapter 1, to exacerbation of nationalist or ethnic divides in retreats into manifestations of balkanization to counter the actual or projected evils of globalization, to the embrace of exclusionary populism, or to reversion to authoritarianism out of desperation due to the flaws and messiness of democracy, the result appears, for the most part, the same. Specifically, whichever of the above

with a fresh outbreak anywhere in the world threatening every country, you can make a nationalistic case for the need to do things in a coordinated, global way.")

reasons—or yet others—may be driving former members of a single community of the whole to becoming implacable enemies who speak past one another, liberal constitutional democracy risks fatal erosion of its foundational reliance on dialogue and genuine discussion. By the same token, and perhaps even more ominously, comprehensive pluralism would be deprived of essential means needed to undertake meaningful accommodation, let alone of any plausible path to tackling any conflicting claims under any criterion resembling justice as reversible reciprocity.

What makes matters even worse, is that all the above-mentioned types of attacks on liberal constitutional democracies aim directly or indirectly at what are cast as failures or refusals to advance the cause of justice. Moreover, the perceived failures at stake concern all three facets of distributive justice. Populists can point to the pairing of liberal constitutional democracy with globalization as a convenient means of enabling and legitimating the ever more disproportionate enrichment of economically dominant elites at the expense of their ever more marginalized compatriots.[37] The religiously uncompromising as well as the national and ethnic exclusivists can reproach liberal constitutional democracy for systematically ignoring or flattening out all identitarian claims, thus abdicating all obligations in the realm of recognition-based justice. Finally, all of these implacable critics can equally charge liberal constitutional democracy with blatantly violating representation-based justice for a variety of separate or cumulative reasons. Either democracy is implanted but leaves those accorded the vote with no meaningful voice as is the case in situations, detailed in Chapter 1, in which the wealthiest few can escape their country's laws, write their own regardless of those on the books and officially meant for all, or simply refuse to abide by applicable laws and pay fines that are for them entirely trivial given their inexhaustible financial resources. Or many of the most important decisions in the life of the citizenry are made in far-removed foreign settings without meaningful input or recourse by those who feel unjustly impacted by the resulting policies, as attested by the oft lamented "democratic deficit" prevalent within the EU. In short, if all these critiques were to be accepted at face value, then the confrontation between liberal constitutional democracy and its above-mentioned detractors would appear to set a dialectical standoff along the lines of the one that in Marx's assessment pitted the industrialist capitalist class against the proletariat. And if that were corroborated, far from liberal constitutional democracy proving compatible with any credible progress toward the justice essentials, it would be instead seem bound to eventually seal an inexorable fate culminating in the latter's irreversible failure.

---

[37] See, e.g., Col. N Bhatnagar, "Failing democracies. India as I see it: A soldier's view," *Times of India* (May 14, 2021) <https://timesofindia.indiatimes.com/blogs/india-as-i-see-it-a-soldiers-view/failing-democracies>, visited April 5, 2022. ("The way things stand today, democracy instead of becoming our strength has become a weakness resulting in inefficiency and indifference. It may help the influential but is bringing misery to the poor, deprived, and the common man.")

Assuming provisionally, for the sake of argument, that liberal constitutional democracy fails in terms of possibly meeting the justice essentials consistent with the pluralist *ethos*, what alternatives, if any, lurk on the horizon? From a pluralist perspective, all the positions on the other side of liberal constitutional democracy in the culture wars—with one narrow exception—are to be categorically discarded for they are inherently anti-pluralist and irremediably incapable of advancing the cause of justice. Indeed, dominance by an intolerant majority religion or non-religious ideology, exclusionary national or ethnic group, exclusionary populism transforming part of the citizenry into the whole, and authoritarianism, are obviously bound to fail the minima required by recognition- and representation-based justice. Whereas it is conceivable that particular iterations of all the above would choose to secure the material redistributive essentials of all those within their jurisdiction, they would inevitably treat significant portions of the latter as second-class citizens—and in the case of authoritarians, arguably more as subjects than as citizens, particularly since in authoritarian regimes the benefits of democracy typically become systematically hollowed out.

The narrow exception concerns the already alluded to special kind of populism briefly considered in Chapter 4. The populism in question would pit the people as a whole against the economic and political elites that appear to have commandeered certain liberal constitutional democracies for their own purposes, and would be intent on neutralizing these elites for purposes of returning the affairs of the polity to the people. Factually, such a populist undertaking seems highly unlikely given that actual populist regimes depend on the charismatic rule of an idolized leader and on "sacralized politics" (Zuquete 2017: 451–2). Counterfactually, however, this very unique brand of populism might conceivably aspire to the justice essentials, provided it disempowered elites without vilifying them, and that it replaced checks and balances through separation of powers by frequent fair elections and by prolific consultations of the people by means of referenda.

As against this idealized narrow slice of populism, liberal constitutional democracy still emerges as a clearly superior alternative counterfactually even if not factually. In other words, even if one were to concede that currently liberal constitutional democracy fails the justice essentials, that would not settle the crucial question of whether the deficiency in question could be overcome through adaptations and reforms or whether any realistic hope for the justice essentials would have to await a full-fledged revolution. Although the recent national, transnational, and global failures regarding the handling of the COVID-19 pandemic by liberal constitutional democracies provide ammunition for those who are pessimistic about the latter's future potential for justice, it is by no means clear yet what course of action would be called for to overcome present shortcomings and future threats. Would tinkering and reinforcements suffice, or would recourse to radical changes amounting to a Hegelian *Aufhebung* become necessary to transform or discard constitutions in future pursuits of the justice essentials?

Whatever the eventual answer to this last question may turn out to be, for now two arguments, one counterfactual and the other factual, can be advanced in favor of liberal constitutional democracy respectively against the kind of pluralism under present consideration and against all other alternatives discussed earlier. Counterfactually, liberal constitutional democracy is superior to even the most benign kind of populism imaginable on two salient grounds: singularity and plurality. If the people were inclusive of all within the polity—including the newly less wealthy and less politically powerful former elites—populism's exclusive focus on peoplehood could only be realized at the expense of ignoring or very significantly downplaying the singularity of the individual citizen and the plurality of collective allegiances and pursuits of those who are to be treated as an undifferentiated unitary block when standing as the all-encompassing designated or imagined people. Factually, on the other hand, as already amply indicated, liberal constitutional democracy is not *less likely* than any of its any of its alternatives on the other side in the culture wars to advance the cause of the justice essentials. To paraphrase Winston Churchill, liberal constitutional democracy may appear often inept, untidy, and fairly unreliable for purposes of securing the justice essentials, except when compared to all other alternatives.

Conclusion

Projecting the Nexus between Liberal Constitutionalism and the Justice Essentials into Its Conceivable Futures

Liberal constitutional democracy is conceptually fit and ought to achieve and sustain the justice essentials. By the same token, populism, illiberalism, and authoritarianism are unfit for the task, and are most definitely so when it comes to recognition- and representation-based distributive justice. That said, however, the present conditions of turmoil, and the dramatic retreat from the widespread confidence in the imminence of a definitive triumph of liberal constitutionalism which prevailed through the optimistic 1990s urge for a good measure of caution and reserve. It is therefore particularly appropriate at this juncture to refer to Hegel's famous dictum in the Preface to the *Philosophy of Right*: "when philosophy paints its grey in grey, then has a shape of life grown old. The owl of Minerva spreads its wings only with the coming of the dusk." Has the time of liberal constitutionalism passed and its aptitude to secure the justice essentials become a mere has-, or could-have, been?

It is impossible to answer this last question with any confidence at this point in time, given the current-day challenges to liberal constitutionalism and democracy in countries where they were long thought unassailable, such as the United States and several Western European democracies. Nevertheless, on the working assumption that the core of liberal constitutionalism will eventually prove resilient through adaptation, expansion, reform, or reconfiguration falling short of revolution, then the allure of comprehensive pluralism ought to become even more compelling. What seems particularly threatening at present is that dialogue, discussion, and disputation among proponents of different conceptions of the good, political adversaries, and ideological antagonists have largely devolved into tribalism, *Kulturkampf*, and competing belligerent slogans shouted across enemy battle lines. In this bellicose atmosphere, liberalism is but one entrenched camp against illiberalism, secularism but one truth claiming religion against others including fundamentalist ones, and democracy but one means—and a pretty inefficient one at that—to political ends that proponents deem imperative and opponents catastrophic. If anything is better suited to break up these deadlocks and impasses it is comprehensive pluralism, with its exhortation to engage in dialogue, to make every effort to understand the other from within the latter's perspective, and to

A Pluralist Theory of Constitutional Justice. Michel Rosenfeld, Oxford University Press. © Michel Rosenfeld 2022.
DOI: 10.1093/oso/9780198862680.003.0010

288   CONCLUSION

accommodate as many antagonists as possible—so long as they are willing to re-nounce their outright enmity.

Comprehensive pluralism is also best suited to lead to an optimal equilibrium among the universal, the singular, and the plural because it approaches all three of them in a thoroughly relational manner. I have distinguished throughout between what is literally universal and what qualifies as universal from within the perspective of a working constitutional unit. Ironically, what proves truly universal without relying on any distortion of the singular or the plural, such as Kant's categorical imperative, extends to all human beings at all times in a crucial but essentially negative and admonitory fashion. In contrast, the universal as the constitutional unit's community of the whole is dependent on an actual *ethnos* which per force must incorporate elements of singularity and of plurality. The singular in contemporary polities must selectively draw from the plural in order to particularize intersubjectively circulating tropes of meanings and allegiances. Moreover, by focusing initially on the plural, one can shed light on the concurrent dynamic between particularization to sustain the singular and abstraction (in the etymological sense of "drawing away from") to produce and nourish the common glue that sustains the unity of the relevant constitutional whole. Indeed, everyone is born into one of the many communities that coexist in the typical contemporary liberal constitutional democracy and those communities and the individuals within them (or circulating among them) must aim to construct a common narrative allowing them all to partake equitably in an orderly life together. Within the perspective of comprehensive pluralism, Rousseau's dual division into bourgeois and citizen is replaced by a tripartite one apportioned among the singular individual; the member of one or more of the many identitarian, ideological, religious, cultural, and political groups that are active within the polity; and the citizen belonging to the democratically organized constitutional community of the whole.

This tripartite division finds expression both within each of the three levels of the universal, the singular, and the plural, and among them. Whereas the truly universal will be for the most part unattainable, as will be the singular in all its depth and particularity, and the plural in its full expanse, comprehensive pluralism seems best poised to secure the best possible equitable compromise among all three. This, in turn, can be accomplished through adherence to pluralism's second-order norms and through deployment of the process of reversal of perspectives—for example, how should I juggle my projects as a singular individual to partake in solidarity towards the well-being of my local, regional, or national community—mandated by justice as reversible reciprocity. Where the precise lines in this process are to be drawn will vary depending on relevant contextual factors. Thus, it would be entirely fair to require major sacrifices at the levels of the singular and the plural in a situation such as that of the United Kingdom in 1941 when singlehandedly it had to confront militarily the relentless assault launched by Hitler's armed forces. The same would of course not be in any way justified in the present-day United

Kingdom in spite of its post-Brexit growing pains or its serious difficulties with the COVID-19 pandemic. More generally, reliance on justice as reversible reciprocity ought to much reduce the chance of distorted universalization or disproportionate de-singularization of the individual.

What is currently particularly challenging for comprehensive pluralism and for liberal constitutionalism itself is that the universalization that goes hand in hand with globalization and the systematic and increasing particularized singularization fostered by surveillance capitalism seem to combine in a seemingly ever-growing exacerbation of injustice and alienation. Besides its accelerating the production of disparities in wealth and its enabling dilution of responsibilities under the rule of law among the most powerful who can disperse their belongings and their influence throughout the world, globalization has thrust those it has rattled more towards balkanization than towards aiming at establishing a workable constitutional layer on a worldwide scale. For its part, surveillance capitalism has particularized the singularity of every individual to a much greater extent than ever before, but has done so on the whole not to empower the latter but to colonize him, and to turn his increasingly fragmented attributes as sources of profits for others. Accordingly, the surveillant capitalist alienates those it targets as it turns their ever more particularized singularity against them, thus thwarting their potential for genuine self-realization. Needless to add, balkanization and hyper-singularization of increasingly acutely defined parts against the whole pose existential threats to the viability of liberal constitutionalism, let alone to any plausible prospect of advancing distributive justice in any of its three dimensions.

Conceptually, neither globalization nor surveillance capitalism deal a fatal blow against liberal constitutionalism or against the latter's potential for achieving the justice essentials. As detailed earlier, development of a worldwide thin *ethnos* in the context of layered and segmented constitutional ordering is certainly logically possible, although thus far not firmly anchored in practice. As the nexus between the universal, the singular, and the plural is relational, it seems entirely plausible that a global layered or segmented constitutional ordering will figure as the universal as against the nation-state constitutional order, which will then stack up as the plural in the transnational context while remaining the universal within the national one. Furthermore, as the justice essentials themselves require equilibrium among all relevant universals, singulars, and plurals, there is no logical impediment to their vindication ultimately extending to the sphere of the transnational or even to that of the global. In short, thus far liberal constitutionalism has worked on the scale of the nation-state and has left a functional imprint at a transnational level. Practically, therefore, it remains an open question whether liberal constitutionalism and the justice essentials associated with it could be successfully implanted transnationally or globally.

The problems raised by the type of hyper-singularization deployed by surveillance capitalism, on the other hand, pose seemingly more intractable challenges against the constitutional vindication of the singular and any approximation of recognition- or representation-based distributive justice. On further thought, the de-singularization of the individual noted by Marx and decried by Nietzsche and Heidegger bears much in common, from the standpoint of individual justice, with the present-day hyper-singularization that fragments the particulars belonging to singular individuals with the consequence of removing them from any potential management or control by their individual bearer. This fosters pathologies affecting recognition, self-determination, and representation while exacerbating economic disparities due to the unprecedented pace and size of accumulations of wealth characteristically reaped by the leading surveillance capitalists. Notwithstanding these difficulties, however, hyper-singularization need not be destructive of liberal constitutionalism or of the justice essentials, provided it could become constrained within appropriate constitutional guardrails. Indeed, in some ways, hyper-singularization bears some analogies to the uses of nuclear power, with some of the latter having the capacity to end human life on earth while others being apt to fill considerable energy needs while reducing levels of pollution. Similarly, hyper-singularization can at once be enlisted to collect myriad relevant particular medical details about entire populations and to put them to good use in the mitigation of disease and death in the course of a pandemic, and be deployed so as to rob singular individuals of their particulars with a view to colonizing them for the benefit of the surveillance capitalist and of all those with whom the latter shares the extracted information for mutual profit. This new form of information-based colonization is in one respect even more pernicious than its nineteenth-century counterpart which was carried out by European colonizers in Africa and Asia. Whereas those colonized by the latter could easily be fully aware of their newly imposed subordinate status, the victims of hyper-singularization typically remain largely unaware of the manipulations and misappropriations of their singularities in ways that seriously obstruct their path toward self-realization.

It is certainly conceivable that the benefits of hyper-singularization may be preserved while constitutionally constraining the latter's evils. This could be done through appropriate adjustments of fundamental constitutional rights, such as those to free speech, privacy, and private property combined with a readjustment of appropriate checks and balances to defuse the tendencies toward monopolization thus far set in place by current surveillance capitalist magnates such as Google and Facebook. In sum, the constitutional tools to mitigate the evils of hyper-singularization plainly appear to be within reach. What remains in serious question, however, is whether polities will be willing or able to muster the requisite will power to implement the constitutional changes necessary to redirect the path to liberal constitutionalism and to reset conditions that would reinvigorate the pursuit of the justice essentials.

Globalization of the economy and harvesting of increasingly particular minute bits of personal information for profit-making purposes largely at the expense of those from whom the said information is extracted loom as self-referential, self-sustaining, and self-contained systemic processes. The reactions against these processes (or their outgrowths) in the form of retreats towards balkanization, tribalism, xenophobia, and many other hardenings towards full-fledged friend/enemy Schmittian dynamics may represent mere passing bumps in an inexorable march to a complete worldwide systemic takeover. Or perhaps, these reactions will consolidate into a pole of negation that will eventuate into a new dialectical struggle with a largely unpredictable outcome from the standpoint of where we stand at present. In any event, if, in reference to Habermas, it were possible to prevent these new systemic waves from unduly colonizing the world's seemingly eroding life-worlds, then it would seem that constitutions appropriately linked to a workable *ethnos* and *demos* and with a firm commitment to the justice essentials would become indispensable tools in the quest to reach a new workable equilibrium.

In the last analysis, even in the best of contemporary possible worlds, the constitution would only be able to secure an essential but limited part of distributive justice. As we have seen, the constitution's seemingly inevitable limitations in this respect are due, on the one hand, to the fact that competing theories of distributive justice tend to remain too contested to allow for full inclusion within any sufficiently consensus-based working constitution. These limitations are also due, on the other hand, to the constitution's necessary reliance on an *ethnos* that garners a sufficient measure of identification and of solidarity. Such an *ethnos*, as already stressed, inevitably restricts the constitution from leaping far beyond the justice essentials and securing total justice. This is because the *ethnos* has to reconcile past narratives with present and future ones, to harmonize national (or transnational) and constitutional identity, and to do its best to encompass both conservative and transformative tendencies seamlessly through deployment of the interpretive tools carved out by the combination of negation, metaphor, and metonymy. Indeed, to the extent that total justice would require wholesale rejection of the past, complete reimagination of national identity, or laying bare the interpretive arsenal while eliminating rallying spectacles needed to maintain sufficient solidarity producing acclamations; the pursuit of such justice would culminate in the unraveling of any working constitutional order. Thus, to preserve constitutional order requires some sacrifice in the pursuit of justice just as does leaving the raising of children to their parents which entails sacrificing the full equalization of all children's upbringing.

The inevitable gap between the justice essentials and total justice gives rise to two momentous questions. First, does the constitution facilitate or hinder the quest for justice beyond its essentials? And second, would the overall quest for distributive justice have a better chance of success if the constitution were left out of the process as much as possible or, in other words, if the constitution were disentangled from any justice essentials?

Concerning the first of these questions, as already indicated, there is no logical impediment to working beyond the justice essentials to come closer to total justice through extra- and infra-constitutional means. Whether that would be politically likely or whether the relevant actors within the polity would be psychologically motivated to fight for additional justice once its essentials had been constitutionally secured depends on several contextual variables and hence lies beyond the scope of the present undertaking.

Concerning the second question, however, upon reflection the answer clearly seems to be in the negative. To be sure, the future of liberal constitutionalism is itself uncertain and it is therefore conceivable that constitutions will sever their links to justice. But on the assumption of the continuing viability of liberal constitutions in our currently evolving word, the constitutional route does seem to remain unrivaled in assuring the justice essentials and in leaving the door open to further gains toward total justice. This perhaps best illustrated by a counterfactual evaluation of options available at some future date when the climate crisis will have become much more acute than what is currently perceived by the world's population. As detailed earlier, three different options seem plausible under such circumstances: competition, contract, and constitution. Factually, one can surmise that even if the constitutional form were adopted, the most powerful nations and interests would for the most part impose their will on their weaker counterparts, thus making their newly minted constitutional arrangement the substantive equivalent of a project at the borderline between competition and contract. Counterfactually, however, assuming a search for a veritable consensus among the powerful and the less powerful, the greatest polluters and those who are most victimized by pollution—all realizing that without drastic changes, humanity as a whole will end up perishing—it seems fairly obvious that any common accord reached within the framework of liberal constitutionalism would further the objectives of distributive justice better than any of the available alternatives. In sum, so long as liberal constitutionalism remains viable it emerges as the optimal potential guarantor of the justice essentials while, at worst, remaining neutral with respect to the extra- and infra-constitutional quest for further advances toward total justice.

Bibliography

Adams, Maurice 2014. "Disabling constitutionalism. Can the politics of the Belgian constitution be explained?" *International Journal of International Law (I.CON)*, vol. 212, no. 79.

Agamben, Giorgio 2005. *State of exception*, trans. Kevin Attell, University of Chicago Press, Chicago.

——2011. *The kingdom and the glory: For a theological genealogy of economy and government*, trans. Lorenzo Chiesa & Matteo Mandarini, Stanford University Press, Stanford.

Alvaredo, Facundo, Chancel, Lucas, Piketty, Thomas, Saez, Emmanuel, & Zucman Gabriel 2018. *World inequality report*, World Inequality Lab, Paris.

Anderson, Benedict 1991. *Imagined communities: reflections on the origin and spread of nationalism*, Verso, New York.

Araujo, Robert J 1994–95. "Political theory liberation and theology: the intersection of Unger and Gutiérrez," *Journal of Law and Religion*, vol. 11, pp. 63.

Aristotle. 1946. *Politics*, trans. E. Barker, Clarendon Press, Oxford.

——1980. *The Nicomachean ethics*, trans. Martin Oswald, Oxford University Press, Oxford.

Autor, David H, Katz, Lawrence F, & Kearney, Melissa S 2008. "Trends in U.S. wage inequality: revising the revisionists," *Review of Economics and Statistics*, vol. 90, pp. 300.

Balibar, Etienne 2011. *Citoyen sujet et autres essais d'anthropologie philosophique*, Presses Universitaires de France, Paris.

Beard, Charles 1913. *An economic interpretation of the constitution of the United States*, MacMillan Co., New York.

Benjamin, Jessica 1988. *The bonds of love: psychoanalysis, feminism and the problem of domination*, Pantheon, New York.

Berglund, Jenny 2015. *Publicly funded Islamic education in Europe and the United States*, Center for Middle East Policy at Brookings, Washington, DC.

Berlin, Isaiah 1970. *Four essays on liberty*, Oxford University Press, Oxford.

——1997. *The crooked timber of humanity*, ed. Henry Hardy, Princeton University Press, Princeton.

——2001. *Against the current*, ed. Henry Hardy, Princeton University Press, Princeton.

——2002. *The power of ideas*, ed. Henry Hardy, Princeton University Press, Princeton.

Beydoun, Khaled A 2016. "Islamophobia: toward a legal definition and framework," *Columbia Law Review*, vol. 116, pp. 108.

Birkmeyer, John D, Barnato, Amber, Birkmeyer, Nancy, Bessler, Robert, & Skinner, Jonathan 2020. "The impact of the COVID-19 pandemic on hospital admissions in the United States," *Health Affair*, vol. 39, pp. 2010.

Birnbaum, Pierre 1988. *Un mythe politique: "La République Juvie,"* Fayard, Paris.

Borradori, Giovanna 2003. *Philosophy in a time of terror: dialogues with Jurgen Habermas and Jacques Derrida*, Chicago University Press, Chicago.

Boushey, Heather 2019. *Unbound: how inequality constricts our economy and what we can do about it*, Harvard University Press, Cambridge.

Britton, Joanne 2015. "Muslims, racism and violence after the Paris attacks," *Sociological Research Online*, vol. 20, pp. 3.

294 BIBLIOGRAPHY

Buchanan, Allen 2003. "The Quebec secession issue: democracy, minority rights, and the rule of law," *NOMOS: American Society for Political and Legal Philosophy*, vol. 45, pp. 238.

Cain, Maureen & Hunt, Alan 1979. *Marx and Engels on law*, Academic Press, London.

Camus, Albert 1955. *The myth of Sisyphus*, trans. Justin O'Brien, Alfred A. Knopf, New York.

Cartabia, Marta & Simoncini, Andrea 2015. *Pope Benedict XVI's legal thought*, Cambridge University Press, Cambridge.

Casanova, Jose 1994. *Public religions in the modern world*, University of Chicago Press, Chicago.

Chehabi, H.E. 2001. "The political regime of the Islamic Republic of Iran in comparative perspective," *Government and Opposition*, vol. 36, pp. 48.

Chemerinsky, Erwin & McDonald, Barry P 2019. "Eviscerating a healthy church–state separation," *Washington University Law Review*, vol. 96, pp. 1009.

Cohen, Nicholas & Viswanathan, Manjol 2020. Corporate behavior and the Tax Cuts and Jobs Act. *University of Chicago Law Review Online*, vol. 2020, pp. 1.

Collins, Hugh 1982. *Marxism and law*, Clarendon Press, Oxford.

Craig, Paul 2010. *The Lisbon Treaty: law, politics and treaty reform*, Oxford University Press, Oxford.

Cranston, Maurice 1973. *What are human rights?* 2nd edition, Taplinger Publishing Company, New York.

Crenshaw, Kimberle 1988. "Race, reform and retrenchment: transformation and legitimation in antidiscrimination law," *Harvard Law Review*, vol. 101, pp. 1331.

Cullen, Richard 1990. "Adaptive federalism in Belgium," *University of New South Wales Law Journal*, vol. 13, pp. 347.

Da Silva, Michael 2020. "Correlativity and the case against a common presumption about the structure of rights," *Journal of Value Inquiry*, vol. 54, pp. 289.

Daly, Eoin 2012. "The ambiguous reach of constitutional secularism in republican France: revisiting the idea of laïcité and political liberalism as alternatives," *Oxford Journal of Legal Studies*, vol. 32, pp. 538.

Danto, Arthur C 1970. *Nietzsche as Philosopher*. MacMillan Co, New York.

De Gouges, Olympe 1791. *The declaration of the rights of woman and the female citizen.*

Derrida, Jacques 1982. *Margins of philosophy*, trans. Alan Bass, University of Chicago Press, Chicago.

——1992. "Force of law: the 'mystical foundations of authority," in Drucilla Cornell, Michel Rosenfeld, & David Carlson (eds), *Deconstruction and the possibility of justice*, Routledge, London.

—— 1994. *Specters of Marx: The state of the debt, the work of mourning and the New International*, trans. Peggy Kamuf, Routledge, London.

——1994a. *The politics of friendship*, trans. George Collins, Verso, London.

——1996. "Il courrait mort: salut, salut," *Les Temps Modernes*, vol. 7, pp. 587.

——2001. *On Cosmopolitanism and forgiveness*, trans. M. Dooley & M. Hughes, Routledge, London.

——2003. *Voyous*, Galilée, Paris.

——2013. *The death penalty*, Vol. I, trans. Peggy Kamuf, University of Chicago Press, Chicago.

Dorsen, Norman, Rosenfeld, Michel, Sajo, Andras, Baer, Susanne, & Mancini, Susanna 2016. 2022. *Comparative constitutionalism: cases and materials*, West Group, Minneapolis.

Downs, Gregory P 2019. *The second American revolution: the Civil War-era struggle over Cuba and the rebirth of the American Republic*, University of North Carolina Press, Chapel Hill, NC.

Dumont, Louis 1977. *From Mandeville to Marx*, University of Chicago Press, Chicago.

Dworkin, Ronald 1973. "The original position," *University of Chicago Law Review*, vol. 40, pp. 500.

———1978. *Taking rights seriously*, Harvard University Press, Cambridge.

———1981. "The forum of principle," *New York University Law Review*, vol. 56, pp. 469.

———1986. *Law's empire*, Belknap Press, Cambridge.

———2003. "Response to overseas commentators," *International Journal of Constitutional Law (I.CON)*, vol. 1, pp. 651.

———2011. *Justice for hedgehogs*, Harvard University Press, Cambridge.

Dyer, Owen 2020. "Covid-19: many poor countries will see almost no vaccine next year, aid groups warn," *British Medical Journal*, vol. 371, m4890.

Epstein, Richard 1995. *Simple rules for a complex world*, Harvard University Press, Cambridge.

Fassbender, Bardo 2009. *The United Nations Charter as the constitution of the international community*, Martinus Nijhoff Publishers, Leiden.

Feinberg, Joel & Naverson, Jan 1970. "The nature and value of rights," *Journal of Value Inquiry*, vol. 4, pp. 234.

Fiss, Owen 1986. "The death of law?" *Cornell Law Review*, vol. 72, pp. 1.

Fraser, Nancy 2009. *Scales of justice: reimagining political space in a globalizing world*, Columbia University Press, New York.

Fraser, Nancy & Honneth, Alex 2003. *Redistribution or recognition? A political-philosophical exchange*, Verso, London.

Freud, Sigmund 1950. *Totem and taboo*, ed. & trans. James Strachey, W.W. Norton & Co., New York.

———1959. *Group psychology and the analysis of the ego*, ed. & trans. James Strachey, W.W. Norton & Co., New York.

———1960. *The ego and the id*, ed. & trans. James Strachey, W.W. Norton & Co., New York.

———1965. *The interpretation of dreams*, ed. & trans. James Strachey, Avon, New York.

Frieden, Jeffry 2019. "The political economy of the globalization backlash: sources and implications," in Luís A. Catão & Maurice Obstfeld (eds), *Meeting globalization's challenges*, Princeton University Press, Princeton.

Fukuyama, Francis 2003. *The end of history and the last man*, Free Press, New York.

———2018. "Against identity politics: the new tribalism and the crisis of democracy," *Foreign Affairs*, vol. 97, pp. 90.

Garapon, Antoine & Michel Rosenfeld 2016. *Démocraties sous stress: les défis du terrorisme global*, Presses Universitaires de France, Paris.

García-López, Gustavo A 2018. "The multiple layers of environmental injustice in contexts of (un)natural disasters: the case of Puerto Rico post-Hurricane Maria," *Environmental Justice*, vol. 11, pp. 101.

Glendon, Mary Ann 1993. *Rights talk: the impoverishment of political discourse*, Free Press, New York.

Goklany, Indur M 2007. *The improving state of the world: why we're living longer, healthier, more comfortable lives on a cleaner planet*, Cato Institute, Washington, DC.

Goodrich, Peter 1992. "Critical legal studies in England: prospective histories," *Oxford Journal of Legal Studies*, vol. 12, pp. 195.

Gough, J.W 1957. *The social contract*, Clarendon Press, Oxford.

Gould, Stephen Jay 1977. *Ontogeny and phylogeny*, Harvard University Press, Cambridge.

Grimm, Dieter 1995. "Does Europe need a constitution?" *European Law Journal*, vol. 1, pp. 282.

296 BIBLIOGRAPHY

Gunn, Jeremy T 2004. "Religious freedom and laicite: a comparison of the United States and France," *Brigham Young University Law Review*, vol. 2014, pp. 419.

Habermas, Jürgen. 1984. *The theory of communicative action: reason and the rationalization of society*, trans. Thomas McCarthy, Beacon Press, Boston.

——1987. *The theory of communicative action: lifeworld and system*, trans. Thomas McCarthy, Beacon Press, Boston.

——1990. *The philosophical discourse of modernity*, trans. F. Lawrence, MIT Press, Cambridge.

——1992. "Further reflections on the public sphere," in Craig Calhoun (ed.), *Habermas and the public sphere*, MIT Press, Cambridge.

——1996. *Between facts and norms: contributions to a discourse theory of law and democracy*, trans. William Rehg, MIT Press, Cambridge.

——1998. "Reply to symposium participants," in Michel Rosenfeld & Andrew Arato (eds), *Habermas on law and democracy: critical exchanges*, University of California Press, Berkeley.

——1999. *The inclusion of the other: studies in political theory*, Ciaran P. Cronin & Pablo De Grief, eds, Polity Press, Cambridge.

——2001. *The postnational constellation: political essays*, ed. & trans. Max Pensky, Polity Press, Cambridge.

——2006. *The dialectics of secularization: on reason and religion*, (with Joseph Ratzinger), San Francisco: Ignatius Press.

Halmai, Gabor 2018. "A coup against constitutional democracy: the case of Hungary," in Mark A. Graber, Sanford, & Mark Tushnet (eds), *Constitutional democracy*, Oxford University Press, New York.

Harding, Susan Friend 2000. *The book of Jerry Falwell: fundamentalist language and politics*, Princeton University Press, Princeton.

Hegel, Georg W.F. 1952. *Philosophy of right*, trans. T.M. Knox, Oxford University Press, Oxford.

——1977. *Phenomenology of spirit*, trans. A.V. Miller, Oxford University Press, Oxford.

——1999. *Hegel's science of logic*, trans. A.V. Miller, Humanity Books, Amherst.

Heidegger, Martin 1962. *Being and time*, trans. John Macquarrie & Edward Robinson, Harper and Row, New York.

Hirschl, Ran 2004. *Towards juristocracy: the origins and consequences of the new constitutionalism*, Harvard University Press, Cambridge.

Holmes, Stephen 1998. "Gag rules or the politics of omission," in Jon Elster & Rune Slagstad (eds), *Constitutionalism and democracy*, Cambridge University Press, Cambridge.

Hobbes, Thomas 1973. *Leviathan*, Every Man's Library, New York.

——1978. *Man and citizen*, ed. B. Gert, Humanities Press, Atlantic Highlands.

Horney, Karen 1973. *Feminine psychology*, W.W. Norton & Co., New York.

Horwitz, Morton 1981. "Law and economics: science or politics," *Hofstra Law Review*, vol. 8, pp. 905.

Hume, David 1907, reprinted from 1777 edition. *An inquiry concerning the principles of morals*, The Open Court Publishing Company, Chicago.

Husami, Ziyad 1980. "Marx on distributive justice," in Marshall Cohen, Thomas Nagel, & Thomas Scanlon (eds), *Marx, justice, and history*, Princeton University Press, Princeton.

Hunt, Paul 1993. "Reclaiming economic, social and cultural rights," *Waikato Law Review*, vol. 1, pp. 141.

Hyppolite, Jean 1946. *Genèse et structure de la Phénoménologie de l'esprit de Hegel*, Aubier, Paris.

Ingiyimbere, Fidèle 202. "Bridging the Europe–Africa divide on and through human rights," in Marco Zoppi (ed.), *A tight embrace: narratives and dynamics of Euro-African relations*, Rowman & Littlefield, Lanham.

Joseph, Sarah 2011. *Blame it on the WTO? A human rights critique*, Oxford University Press, Oxford.

Jung, Courtney, Hirschl, Ran, & Rosevear, Evan 2014. "Economic and social rights in national constitutions," *American Journal of Comparative Law*, vol. 62, pp. 1043.

Kateb, George 2009. "Thinking about human extinction: Nietzsche and Heidegger," in Racy B. Strong (ed.), *Nietzsche and politics*, Ashgate, Oxford.

Kant, Immanuel 1969. *Foundations of the metaphysics of morals*, ed. Robert P. Wolff, trans. Lewis W. Beck, Bobbs-Merrill, Indianapolis.

———1991. *Political Writings*, ed. Hans Reiss, Cambridge University Press, Cambridge.

———1980. *The metaphysical elements of justice*, trans. John Ladd, Bobbs-Merril, Indianapolis.

Kearney, M 1995. "The local and the global: the anthropology of globalization and transnationalism," *Annual Review of Anthropology*, vol. 24, pp. 547.

Kelman, Mark 1984. "Thrashing," *Stanford Law Review*, vol. 36, pp. 293.

Kelsen, Hans 1924. "The conception of the state and social psychology—with special reference to Freud's group theory," *International Journal of Psycho-Analysis*, vol. 5, pp. 1.

———1945. *General theory of law and state*, trans. Anders Wedberg, Harvard University Press, Cambridge.

———1967. *Pure theory of law*, trans. Max Knight (from 2nd revised & enlarged German edition), University of California Press, Berkeley.

Keyssar, Alexander 2020. *Why do we still have the Electoral College?* Harvard University Press, Cambridge.

Kiewiet, J 2018. "Legal unity as political unity: Carl Schmitt and Hugo Krabbe on the Catalonian constitutional crisis," *Utrecht Journal of International and European Law*, vol. 34, no. 1, pp. 56–72.

Kymlicka, Will 1995. *Multicultural citizenship: A liberal theory of minority rights*. Oxford: Oxford University Press.

Koenig, Matthias 2015. "Incorporating Muslim migrants in western nations states—a comparison of the United Kingdom, France, and Germany," in Marian Burchardt & Ines Michalowski (eds), *After integration: Islam, conviviality and contentious politics in Europe*, Springer VS, Wiesbaden.

Kommers, Donald P. & Miller, Russell A. 2012. *The constitutional jurisprudence of the Federal Republic of Germany*, Duke University Press, Durham.

Konnoth, Craig 2020. "Narrowly tailoring the COVID-19 response," *California Law Review Online*, vol. 11, pp. 193.

Korioth, Stefan & Ino Augsberg 2015. "Religion and the secular state in Germany," in Javier Martínez-Torrón & W. Cole Durham (eds), *Religion and the secular state: interim reports*, The International Center for Law and Religion, Brigham Young University, Provo.

Lacan, Jacques 1966. *Écrits*, Editions du Seuil, Paris.

Lal, Arush, Erondu, Ngozi A, Heymann, David L, Githai, Githinji, & Yates, Robert 2021. "Fragmented health systems in COVID-19: rectifying the misalignment between global health security and universal health coverage," *The Lancet*, vol. 397, pp. 61.

Landes, William & Posner, Richard *The economic structure of tort law*, Harvard University Press, Cambridge.

298 BIBLIOGRAPHY

Lang, Iris Goldnger 2021. "'Laws of fear; in the EU: the precautionary principle and public health restrictions to free movement of persons in the time of COVID-19," *European Journal of Risk Regulation*, vol. 0, pp. 1.

Le Breton, Mirelle 2007. "Laïcité in the French public school system: an exception française?" *Paroles gelées*, vol. 23, pp. 93.

Lee, David S 1999. "Wage inequality in the United States during the 1980s: rising dispersion or falling minimum wage?" *Quarterly Journal of Economics*, vol. 144, pp. 977.

Lemaitre, Julieta 2012. "By reason alone: Catholicism, constitutions, and sex in the Americas," *International Journal of Constitutional Law*, vol. 10, pp. 493.

Levitsky, Steven & Daniel Ziblatt 2018. *How democracies die*, Broadway Books, New York.

Linz, Juan and Alfred Stepan. 1996. *Problems of democratic transition and consolidation: southern Europe, South America and post-communist Europe*. Baltimore, Johns Hopkins University Press.

Luhmann, Niklas 1987. "The unity of the legal system," in Gunther Teubner (ed.), *Autopoietic law: A new approach to law and society*, W. de Gruyter, Berlin.

——1990. *Essays on self-reference*, Columbia University Press, New York.

——1992. "Operational closure and structural coupling: the differentiation of the legal system," *Cardozo Law Review*, vol. 13, pp. 1419.

Lukes, Steven 1973. *Individualism*, Basil Blackwell, Oxford.

Mancini, Susanna 2009. "The power of symbols and symbols as power: secularism and religion as guarantors of cultural convergence," *Cardozo Law Review*, vol. 30, pp. 2629.

——2012. "Secession and self-determination," in Michel Rosenfeld & András Sajó (eds), *Oxford handbook of comparative constitutional law*, Oxford University Press, Oxford.

——2014. "The tempting of Europe, the political seduction of the Cross. A Schmittian reading of Christianity and Islam in European constitutionalism," in Susanna Mancini & Michel Rosenfeld (eds), *Constitutional secularism in an age of religious revival*, Oxford University Press, Oxford.

Mancini, Susanna & Michel Rosenfeld 2014. *Constitutional secularism in an age of religious revival*, Oxford University Press, Oxford.

——2021. "Nationalism, populism, religion, and the quest to reframe fundamental rights," *Cardozo Law Review*, vol. 42, pp. 464.

Marquand, David 1979. *Parliament for Europe*, Jonathan Cape, London.

Marx, Karl 1846. "The German ideology," in Marx & Engels, *Collected works*. Lawrence & Wishart, Chadwell Heath.

——1859. "A contribution to the critique of political economy," in Marx & Engels, *Collected W=works*, Lawrence & Wishart, Chadwell Heath.

——1964. *Early writings*, ed. & trans. T.B. Bottomore, McGraw Hill, New York.

——1968. *Selected works*, Vol 2, Progress Publishers, Moscow.

——1970, 1974, 1972. *Capital Vols I, II, III*, Lawrence & Wishart, Chadwell Heath.

McAlister, Elizabeth 2012. "Soundscapes of disaster and humanitarianism: survival singing, relief telethons, and the Haiti earthquake," *Small Axe*, vol. 16, pp. 22.

McCrudden, Christopher 2015. "Benedict's legacy: human rights, human dignity, and the possibility of dialogue," in Marta Cartabia & Andrea Simoncini (eds), *Pope Benedict XVI's legal thought*, Cambridge University Press, Cambridge.

Megill, Alan 1987. *Prophets of extremity: Nietzsche, Heidegger, Foucault, Derrida*, University of California Press, Berkeley.

Metzger, Gillian E 2003. "Privatization as delegation," *Columbia Law Review*, vol. 103, pp. 1367.

—— 2017. "Foreword: 1930s redux: the administrative state under siege," *Harvard Law Review*, vol. 131, pp. 1.

Michelman, Frank 2000. "Modus vivendi postmodernus? On just interpretations and thinning of justice," *Cardozo Law Review*, vol. 21, pp. 1945.

Mill, John Stuart 1961. "On liberty," in M. Cohen (ed.), *The philosophy of John Stuart Mill*, Hackett, Indianapolis.

Müller, Jan-Werner 20012. "Militant democracy," in Michel Rosenfeld & András Sajó (eds), *Oxford handbook of comparative constitutional law*, Oxford University Press, Oxford.

——2013. *Safeguarding democracy inside the EU: Brussels and the future of liberal order*, The German Marshall Fund of the United States, Washington, D.C.

——2016. *What is populism?* University of Pennsylvania Press, Philadelphia.

Nietzsche, Friedrich 1924. *The joyful science*, trans. Thomas Common, Macmillan Co., New York.

——1966. *Beyond good and evil*, trans. Walter Kaufmann, Vintage Books, New York.

——1968. *The will to power*, trans. Walter Kaufmann & R.J. Hollingdale, Vintage Books, New York.

——2006. *On the genealogy of morality*, ed. Keith Ansell-Pearson, trans. Carol Diethe, Cambridge University Press, Cambridge.

Nozick, Robert 1974. *Anarchy, state, and utopia*, Basic Books, New York.

Öberg, Marko Divac 2012. "The legal effects of resolutions of the UN Security Council and General Assembly in the jurisprudence of the ICJ," *European Journal of International Law*, vol. 16, pp. 879.

Parry, D.L.L. & Pierre, Girard. *France since 1800: squaring the hexagon*, Oxford University Press, Oxford.

Pateman, Carol 1980. "'The disorder of women': women, love, and the sense of justice," *Ethics*, vol. 91, pp. 20.

——1988. *The sexual contract*, Stanford University Press, Stanford.

Perelman, Chaïm 1980. *Justice, law and argument: essays on moral and legal reasoning*, Jakko Hintikka, Donald Davidson, Gabriël Nuchelmans, & Welsey C. Salmon (eds), Holland: D. Reidel Publishing Co., Dordrecht.

Perry, Ronen 2009. "Correlativity," *Law and Philosophy*, vol. 28, pp. 537.

Piketty, Thomas 2013. *Le Capital au XXIe siècle*, Éditions du Seuil, Paris.

Pistor, Katharina 2019. *The code of capital: how the law creates wealth and inequality*, Princeton University Press, Princeton.

Popper, Karl 1966. *The open society and its enemies: The spell of Plato*, Princeton University Press, Princeton.

Posner, Richard 1973. *Economic analysis of law*, 1st edition, Little Brown, Boston.

——1987. "The constitution as an economic document," *George Washington Law Review*, vol. 56, pp. 4.

——1990. *The problems of jurisprudence*, Harvard University Press, Cambridge.

——1995. *Overcoming law*, Harvard University Press, Cambridge.

Preuss, Ulrich K. 1994. "Constitutional power making for the new polity: some deliberations on the relations between constituent power and the constitution," in Michel Rosenfeld (ed.), *Constitutionalism, identity, difference and legitimacy: theoretical perspectives*, Duke University Press, Durham.

Rawls, John 1971. *A theory of justice*, Belknap Press, Cambridge.

——2005. *Political liberalism: expanded edition*, Columbia University Press, New York.

Richards, David 1994. "Revolution and constitutionalism in America," in Michel Rosenfeld (ed.), *Constitutionalism, identity, difference and legitimacy: theoretical perspectives*, Duke University Press, Durham.

300 BIBLIOGRAPHY

Ricoeur, Paul. 1990. *Soi-même comme un autre*. Paris, Éditions du Seuil.

Roach, Kent 2004. "Anti-terrorism and militant democracy: some western and Eastern responses," in Andras Sajo (ed.), *Militant democracy*, Eleven International Publishing, Amsterdam.

Robinson, George 2001. *Essential Judaism: a complete guide to beliefs, customs and rituals*, Atria Publishing Group, New York.

Rose-Ackerman, Susan & Lindseth, Peter L 2010. *Comparative administrative law*, Edward Elgar, Cheltenham.

Rosenfeld, Michel 1985. "Contract and justice: the relation between classical contract law and social contract theory," *Iowa Law Review*, vol. 70, pp. 769.

———1991. *Affirmative action and justice: a philosophical and constitutional inquiry*, Yale University Press, New Haven.

———1991a. "Derrida, law, violence and the paradox of justice," *Cardozo Law Review*, vol. 13, pp. 1267.

———1998. *Just interpretations: law between ethics and politics*, University of California Press, Berkeley.

———1998a. "A pluralist critique of contractarian proceduralism," *Ratio Juris*, vol. 11, pp. 291.

———2001. "The Rule of law and the legitimacy of constitutional democracy," *Southern California Law Review*, vol. 74: 1307.

———2005. "Dworkin and the one law principle: a pluralist critique," *Revue Internationale de Philosophie*, vol. 59, pp. 363–92.

———2006. "Judicial balancing in the times of stress: comparing the American, British, and Israeli approaches to the war on terror," *Cardozo Law Review*, vol. 27, pp. 2079.

———2006a. "A theory of political rights in times of stress," in Wojciech Sadurski (ed.), *Political rights under stress in 21st century Europe*, Oxford University Press, Oxford.

———2008. "Rethinking constitutional ordering in an era of legal and ideological pluralism," *International Journal of Constitutional Law (I.CON)*, vol. 6, pp. 415.

———2010. *The identity of the constitutional subject: selfhood, citizenship, culture and community*, Routledge, New York.

———2010a. "Should constitutional democracies redefine emergencies and the legal regimes suitable for them?" in Austin Sarat (ed.), *Sovereignty, emergency, legality*, Cambridge University Press, Cambridge.

———2011. *Law, justice, democracy and the clash of cultures: a pluralistic account*, Cambridge University Press, Cambridge.

———2011a. "Constitutional versus administrative ordering in an era of globalization and privatization: reflections on sources of legitimation in the post-Westphalian polity," *Cardozo Law Review*, vol. 32, 2339.

——— 2012. "Hate speech in constitutional jurisprudence," in Michael Herz & Peter Molnar (eds),*The content and context of hate speech: rethinking regulation and responses*, Cambridge University Press, Cambridge.

——— 2014. "Is global constitutionalism meaningful or desirable?" *European Journal of International Law (EJIL)*, vol. 25, pp. 177.

———2014a. "Recasting secularism as once conception of the good among the many," in Susanna Mancini & Michel Rosenfeld (eds), *Constitutional secularism in an age of religious revival*, Oxford University Press, Oxford.

———2019. "Judicial politics versus ordinary politics: is the constitutional judge caught in the middle?" in Christine Landfried (ed.), *Judicial power: how constitutional courts affect political transformations*, Cambridge University Press, Cambridge.

————2020. "Constitution and secularism: a Western account," in Susanna Mancini (ed.), *Handbook on constitutions and religion*, Edward Elgar Publishers, Cheltenham.

———— 2021. "The role of justice in the Constitution: the case for social and economic rights in comparative perspective," *Cardozo Law Review*, vol. 42, pp. 763.

Ross, Tara 2012. *Enlightened democracy: the case for the Electoral College*, Colonial Press, Dallas.

Rousseau, Jean-Jacques 1947. *The social contract*, C. Frankel ed., Hafner Press, Riverside.

Sacks, Jonathan 2003. *The dignity of difference: how to avoid the clash of civilizations*, Bloomsbury, London.

Sadurski, Wojciech 2019. *Poland's constitutional breakdown*, Oxford University Press, Oxford.

Sajo, Andras 2021. *Ruling by cheating: governance in illiberal democracy*, Cambridge University Press, Cambridge.

Sartre, Jean-Paul. 1948. *Existentialism and humanism*. trans. Philip Mairet, Methuen, London.

————1966. *Being and nothingness*, trans. Hazel E. Barnes, The Philosophical Library, New York.

Schill, Stephan W 2015. "Conceptions of legitimacy of international arbitration," in David D. Caron, Stephan W. Schill, Abby Cohen Smutny, & Epaminotas E. Triantafilou (eds), *Practising virtue: inside international arbitration*, Oxford University Press, Oxford.

Schmitt, Carl 1928. *Verfassungslehre*, Duncker & Humbolt, Berlin.

————2005. *Political theology*, trans. George Schwab, University of Chicago Press, Chicago.

————2006. *The nomos of the earth in the international law of the Jus Publicum Europaeum*, Telos Press, New York.

————2007. *The concept of the political*, trans. George Schwab, University of Chicago Press, Chicago.

Shane, Peter 2016. *Madison's nightmare: how executive power threatens American democracy*, University of Chicago Press, Chicago.

Simko, Christina 2015. *The politics of consolation: memory and the meaning of September 11*, Oxford University Press, Oxford.

Singer, Joseph William 1984. "The player and the cards: nihilism and legal theory," *Yale Law Journal*, vol. 94, pp. 1.

Smith, Adam 1776. *An inquiry into the nature and causes of the wealth of nations*, ed. E. Cannan 1976, Chicago University Press, Chicago.

Smith, Anthony D 1981. *The ethnic revival in the modern world*, Cambridge University Press, Cambridge.

Sternberger, Dolf 1979. *Verfassungspatriotismus*, Insel Verlag, Frankfurt.

Stewart Richard & Ratton Sanchez Badin, Michelle 2011. "The World Trade Organization: multiple dimensions of global administrative law," *The International Journal of Constitutional Law (I.CON)*, vol. 9, pp. 556.

Stewart, Terence P 2018. *The broken multilateral trade dispute system*, Asia Society Policy Institute, New York.

Strauss, Leo 2007. "Notes on Carl Schmitt's the concept of the political," in Carl Schmitt (ed.), trans. George Schwab, *The concept of the political*, University of Chicago Press, Chicago.

Strong, Tracy B 2005. "Foreword," in Carl Schmitt (ed.), trans. George Schwab, *Political theology*, University of Chicago Press, Chicago.

————2009. "Introduction," in Tracy B. Strong (ed.), *Nietzsche and politics*, Ashgate, Oxford.

Taylor, Charles 1975. *Hegel*, Cambridge University Press, Cambridge.

————2007. *A secular age*, Harvard University Press, Cambridge.

302 BIBLIOGRAPHY

Troper, Michel 2009. "Sovereignty and laïcité," *Cardozo Law Review*, vol. 30, pp. 2561.

Tucker, Robert 1969. *The Marxian revolutionary idea*, Norton, New York.

Tushnet, Mark 1988. *Red, white and blue: A critical analysis of constitutional law*, Harvard University Press, Cambridge.

——1991. "Critical legal studies: A political history," *Yale Law* Journal, vol. 100, pp. 1515.

——2008. *Weak courts, strong rights: judicial review and social welfare rights in comparative constitutional law*, Princeton University Press, Princeton.

2018. "Comparing right-wing and left-wing populism," in Mark A. Graber, Sanford, & Mark Tushnet (eds), *Constitutional democracy*, Oxford University Press, New York.

Unger, Roberto Mangabeira 1976. *Knowledge and politics*, The Free Press, New York.

—— 1983. "The critical legal studies movement," *Harvard Law Review*, vol. 96, pp. 561.

Vara, Juan Santos 2011. "The consequences of *Kadi*: where the divergence of opinions between EU and international lawyers lies?" *European Law Journal*, vol, 17, pp. 252.

Vijanen, Jukka 2003. *The European Court of Human Rights as a developer of the general doctrines of human rights law*, Tampereen University, Tampere.

Von Bogdandy, Armin 2005. "The European constitution and European identity: text and subtext of the Treaty establishing a Constitution for Europe," *The International Journal of Constitutional Law (I.CON)*, vol. 3, pp. 295.

Walker, Neil 2008. "Beyond boundary disputes and basic grids: mapping the global disorder of normative orders," *International Journal of Constitutional Law (I.CON)*, vol. 6, pp. 373.

Wegman, Jesse 2020. *Let the people pick the president: the case for abolishing the Electoral College*, St. Martin's Publishing Group, New York.

Williams, Daniel K 2020. "Religion and American politics," in Paula Baker & Donald T. Critchlow (eds), *The Oxford handbook of American political history*, Oxford University Press, Oxford.

Williams, Patricia 1987. "Alchemical notes: reconstructing ideals from deconstructed rights," *Harvard Civil Rights Civil Law Review*, vol. 22, pp. 401.

Wittgenstein, Ludwig 1968. *Philosophical investigations*, trans. G.E.M. Anscombe, Basil Blackwell Ltd., Oxford.

Wood, Allen 1980. "The Marxian critique of justice," in Marshall Cohen, Thomas Nagel & Thomas Scanlon (eds), *Marx, justice, and history*, Princeton University Press, Princeton.

Zakaria, Fareed 2020. *Ten lessons for a post-pandemic world*, W.W. Norton & Company, Inc., New York.

Zeidler, Wolfgang 2016. "The Federal Constitutional Court of the Federal Republic of Germany: decisions on the constitutionality of legal norms," in Normal Dorsen et al. (eds), *Comparative constitutionalism: cases and materials*, West Group, Minneapolis.

Zuboff, Shoshana 2019. *The age of surveillance capitalism: the fight for a human future at the new frontier of power*, Hachette Book Group, New York.

Zuquete, Pedro 2017. "Populism and religion," in Cristobal Rovira Kalwasser, Paul Taggart, Paulina Ochoa Espejo & Pierre Ostiguy (eds), *Oxford handbook of populism*, Oxford University Press, Oxford.

Index

For the benefit of digital users, indexed terms that span two pages (e.g., 52–53) may, on occasion, appear on only one of those pages.

A(FC) et al. v. Secretary of State for the Home Department [2004] UKHL56 (House of Lords) 93
Agamben, Giorgio 25–26, 198, 213–18
Alvaredo, Facundo, Chancel, Lucas, Piketty, Thomas, Saez, Emmanuel, & Zucman Gabriel 73
Anderson, Benedict 10–11
Araujo, Robert J. 55–56
Aristotle 129–30, 201–2
Autor, David H., Katz, Lawrence F., & Kearney, Melissa S. 72

Benjamin, Jessica 113–14
Berglund, Jenny 41
Berlin, Isaiah 26–27, 231
Bickel, Alexander 37–38
Birkmeyer, John D, Barnato, Amber, Birkmeyer, Nancy, Bessler, Robert, & Skinner, Jonathan 99–100
Borradori, Giovanna 94–95, 97–98, 181, 210–12
Britton, Joanne 92
Brown v. Board of Education (U.S.) 86
Buchanan, Allen 46–47
BVerfGE 60 (F.R.G.) ("Minimum Livelihood" case) 83–84
BVerfGE 108 (F.R.G.) ("Children Allowance" case) 83–84

Cain, Maureen & Hunt, Alan 151, 156–57
Camus, Albert 198
Cartabia, Marta & Simoncini, Andrea 58
Casanova, Jose 56–57
Chehabi, H.E. 55–56
"Children Allowance" case *see* BVerfGE 108 (F.R.G.)
Cohen, Nicholas & Viswanathan, Manjol 70
Collins, Hugh 151
Comprehensive Pluralism (philosophy) 26–27, 195–96, 227
  critical response to 230–31, 245–48, 282–86
  dialectics of 229–38
    first- and second-order norms 235–36

fixed-core minimum and plural maximum, the 271–82
  principle of proportionality, utility of 280–82
Hegelian origins 229–38
justice essentials, approach to 249–71
justice minima under 249–71
  autonomy & solidarity, combined minimum of 263–71
  identity, autonomy, and solidarity, linking justice to 254–62
  pluralist justice, bare bones of 249–54
liberal constitutions' justice essentials, grounding & outline of 227–29
normative case for 238–45
constitutional rights, challenges to 31–40
disembodied law and 40–53
  alienation 40
  "disembodied" as metaphor for normative disorders 43–44
  "internal" & "external" causative factors 41–43
fragmented & complex administrative regulations 48–50
  legal regime selection by private interests 48–49
layering & segmentation 44–48
  CJEU layering 45
  ECtHR layering 42
  solidarity, potential for 46–48
  WTO segmentation 45
private arbitration 50
religion 53–61
  instrumentalization of reason 55
  repoliticization of 55–61
surveillance capitalism 50–53
  strategic law violations 52
  surplus information, legal extraction of 51–52
tribal politics 61–64
Cranston, Maurice 75–76
Crenshaw, Kimberle 143–44

304   INDEX

Daly, Eoin 36
Danto, Arthur C. 207–8
De Gouges, Olympe 4–5
Derrida, Jacques 25–26, 31–32, 152, 197–98, 200–1, 202, 209–12
Derrida's deconstruction and Agamben's reconstruction (philosophy) 218–19
  attempted & actual justice, infinite gap between 210–12
  coupling of and justice essentials 197–98, 219–23
  deconstruction's interpretation, intertextual method of 199–202
  individual, the, liberalism's "de-singularization" of 202–10
  legal/administrative deep-structure shape, theology's role in 212–19
  singularity of each individual, interpretive plurality and 197–99
distributive justice 130–31
Dorsen, Norman 18–19, 81, 184–85, 189–90, 257, 276, 280–82
Downs, Gregory P. 90–92
Dworkin, Ronald 24–25, 185–88, 190, 192–94
Dyer, Owen 98–99

economic framing of law 129–31, 145–50
  CLS, law and 23–24, 130–31, 140–45, 197–98
    ideology positioned as neutrality 140–41
    indeterminacies'-potential-justice rebuttal 144–45
    judicial philosophy and partisan politics 142–43
    Kantian formal universality, negative implications 141
    law-as-frozen-politics and positive-outcomes rebuttals 143–44
    legislators' bias presumed 141–42
  justice beyond law, Aristotle & Rousseau and 129–30
  law's absorption into economics 23–24, 130–31, 145–50
    justice essentials and distributive-justice, challenge to 145–46
  Luhmann's legal autopoiesis analogized to economic monetarization 132–33
  Marx's relevance to modern capitalism & justice 151–59
    Hegelian dialectic and Marx's economic history 153–54
    income-disparity, automation & interest-wealth 155
    justice-essentials baseline, the 152–53
    power relationship after reforms 154

prioritizing needs & people, justice essentials and 158–59
recognition- & representation-based justice 154–55
Posner and law-and-economics movement 146–47
  contestability-of-all-economic-ideologies, the, 149–50
  efficiency and market-sustainability 147
  nonmarket dignitarian- & recognition-based justice-issues 148–49
  transaction costs, pollution, & unjust distribution 147–48
Schmitt's challenge to liberalism & pluralism 133–34, 138, 198
  animosities, exacerbation of 135–37
  anti-pluralism 139
  crisis-emergencies, president as dictator-pope in 134–35
  liberal deflation of conflicts, existential disdain for 137–38
  secular theology (philosophy) 132–40
  transnational-global ordering, impossibility of 139–40
Epstein, Richard 146

Fassbender, Bardo 18
Feinberg, Joel & Naverson, Jan 75
Fraser, Nancy 4
Fraser, Nancy & Honneth, Alex 66
Freud, Sigmund 113–16, 118–20, 121
Frieden, Jeffry 88–89
Fukuyama, Francis 65–66

Garapon, Antoine & Michel Rosenfeld 95–96
García-López, Gustavo A. 90–91
Glendon, Mary Ann 84–85
global (concept) 65–67
Goklany, Indur M., 65–66
Goodrich, Peter 140
Gough, J.W. 166
Grootboom, 2001 (1) SALR 46 (CC) (South Africa) 82
Gunn, Jeremy T. 36

Habermas, Jürgen 24–25, 31–32, 174–78, 181, 183
Hegel, Georg W.F. 231–32
Heidegger, Martin 205
Hirschl, Ran 38
Hobbes, Thomas 120–21
Holmes, Stephen 268–69
Horney, Karen 113–14
Horwitz, Morton 146

Hume, David 85
Hunt, Paul 75
Hyppolite, Jean 231–32

illiberal constitutional democracy 16–17
  Hungary's Orban and 2, 16–17, 62–64
  populism 88–89, 100, 136–37
    justice, potential for 136–37, 138
Ingiyimbere Fidèle 47

Joseph, Sarah 42–43
Jung, Courtney, Hirschl, Ran, & Rosevear,
    Evan 78–79
justice essentials 1, 4, 20–21, 65–67
  economic inequalities, global economic
    exacerbation of 68–75
  economic inequalities, redistribution &
    recognition strategies 67–68
    American Rescue Plan Act 70
    US Tax Cuts and Jobs Act of 2017, 70

Kant, Immanuel 24–25, 141, 162
Kantian universalism reframed 160–61
  Dworkin's political philosophy and
    constitutional jurisprudence 190
  Enlightenment values 186–87
  evaluation of 188–96
  justice essentials, path to 185–96
  policy considerations and rights 190–91
  principle, adjudication as matter of 186–88
  provisions contrary to justice, judicial
    decisions regarding 185–86
  Habermas' dialogical proceduralism 174–
    85, 198
    "Constitutional Patriotism," call for 178–
      79, 184–85
    discourse-based normative theory 174
    distributive-justice shortcomings 177
    open-ended justice concept 174–75
    "self-given" paradox and constitutional
      law-making 175–76
    "System" and "Lifeworld," dynamic
      between 177–78, 185
  Kant's Categorical Imperative
    (philosophy) 123–24, 161–66
    derivative social contract theory, Kant
      and 166
    morals & categorical imperative, ethics
      and 162–63
    recognition-based distributive
      justice 163–64
    severing of justice from the good, 164–65
    singularity & pluralism, universalism
      disconnected from 166

Rawls' "Constitutional Essentials," 167–73
  first- & second-generation rights 170
  hierarchical placement of 168–69
  hypothetical social contract and human
    interests 167–68
  "maximin" rule and "difference
    principle," 168, 169
  proceduralism, substantive premises
    of 171–72
  process of abstraction, biases of 172–73
Kateb, George 207
Kearney, M. 65
Kelman, Mark 140
Kelsen, Hans 107–8, 109–10, 111–13, 118, 122,
    123–24, 132
Kelsen and Freud (philosophy), 23, 122–24
  broader implications of 124–28
    justice essentials, potential bridge
      to 124–25
    nation-state behavior & identity,
      psychoanalysis and 125–28
  ethnos and demos 105–6, 107–13
    group psychology 107, 118–20
    Kelsen's positivism, Kantian categorical
      imperative and 107–10
  Freudian insights 113–22
    id-ego-superego dynamic 114–15
    guilt, dream-interpretation dynamic
      and 117
    socialization, ontogeny-
      recapitulates-phylogeny dynamic and 115–17
  Freud's phylogenetic transcendence, Kelsen's
    rejection of 122–24
  state, the, as law (Rechtsstaat), 110–12
    Hobbes' political state, "leader"
      (psychology) similar to 120–21
    non-democratic "bare minimum of
      justice," 110–11
    rights & democracy-maintenance, silence
      on 110, 121–22
Keyssar, Alexander 33
Kiewiet, J. 40
Koenig, Matthias 36
Kommers, Donald P. & Miller, Russell A. 14
Korioth, Stefan & Ino Augsberg 41
Kymlicka, Will 163

Lacan, Jacques 117
Lal, Arush, Erondu, Ngozi A, Heymann, David L,
    Githai, Githinji, & Yates, Robert 99
Landes, William & Posner, Richard 148
Lee, David S. 72
Lemaitre, Julieta 58
Levitsky, Steven & Daniel Ziblatt 62–63

306 INDEX

liberal constitutional democracy 31–40, 105–7
  ideal of justice, philosophical grounding of 23
  morals, ethics, politics, & economics, law
    and 107
  universal, singular, plural, the 105–6
    proportionately mediated by law 107
Linz, J. & Stepan A. 182–83
local (concept), 65–67
Lochner v. New York (U.S.), 194–95
Luhmann, Niklas 25–26, 132–33

Mancini, Susanna 17–18, 58–59
Mancini, Susanna & Michel Rosenfeld 53–54,
    55–56, 125–26, 136
Marquand, David 18
Marx, Karl 23–24, 130–31, 152–54, 157–58
McAlister, Elizabeth 90–91
Megill, Alan 203–4, 205–7, 208–9
Metzger, Gillian E. 42–43, 48
Michelman, Frank 230–31
Mill, John Stuart 229–30
"Minimum Livelihood" case *see* BVerfGE 60
  (F.R.G.)
minimum of justice 21, 68–69, 73–87
  budgetary & policy-based implications
    of 84–87
    positive state action, dependence
      upon 85–87
  correlation between rights and duties,
    philosophy of 75–77
    strict correlation theory, contextual
      approach preferable to 77
  legal regimes, transnational plurality of 87–89
    International Covenant on Economic,
      Social and Cultural Rights
      (ICESCR) 88–89
    World Trade Organization (WTO) 88n.71
  social and economic rights in 78–84
    analysis, comparative constitutional
      law 79–84
    aspirational, justiciable, & justiciable-
      aspirational categories 78–79
  stress (condition), effects on 90–94
    global terrorism 94–98
    worldwide pandemics 98–102
Müller, Jan-Werner 2, 136, 271

Nietzsche, Friedrich 204–5, 207–8
Nozick, Robert 27, 72–73

Pateman, Carol 113–14, 116–17
Patriot Act (U.S.) 93–94, 95, 96
People's Union for Civil Liberties v. Union of India
    and Others (PUCL), Writ Petition (Civil)

No. 196 of 2001 (India) ("Right to Food"
  case) 81
Piketty, Thomas 66, 155–56
Pistor, Katharina 43, 49–50
Pluralism *see* Comprehensive Pluralism
Popper, Karl 271
Posner, Richard 23–24, 146–47, 148–50
Prakash Mani Sharma v. Government of
  Nepal 82–83
Preuss, Ulrich K., 8–9, 37

Rawls, John 4, 20–21, 24–25, 34–35, 37, 65–66,
  167, 168, 169–71, 185–86
Richards, David 125–26
"Right to Food" case see *People's Union for Civil*
  Liberties v. Union of India and Others
  (PUCL), Writ Petition (Civil) No. 196 of
  2001 (India)
Roach, Kent 272
Rose-Ackerman, Susan & Lindseth,
  Peter L. 48
Rosenfeld, Michel 1, 3–4, 18–19, 26–27, 33,
  35, 37–38, 39–40, 43, 45, 47, 53–54,
  55, 60–61, 93–94, 108–9, 110, 120–21,
  127–28, 142–43, 144–45, 166–68,
  171–72, 179, 181–82, 183–84, 191,
  197–98, 199–200, 202–3, 222, 227–28,
  237, 239, 258–59, 260–61, 269–70, 272,
  273–74, 278, 282–83
Ross, Tara 33
Rousseau, Jean-Jacques 117, 129–30, 175, 203

Sacks, Jonathan 241–42
Sajo, Andras 2
Sartre, Jean-Paul 205–6, 211
Schill, Stephan W. 42
Schmitt, Carl 8–9, 23–24, 25–26, 37, 130–31,
  132, 133–38, 139–40, 213
Shane, Peter 42–43
Simko, Christina 94–95
Smith, Adam 5–6, 125–26
social rights 125–26
Soobramoney v. Minister of Health (Kwazulu-
  Natal), 1998 (1) SALR 765 (C.C.) (South
  Africa) 80–81
Sternberger, Dolf 178–79
Strauss, Leo 139–40
Strong, Tracy B. 130–31, 133–34, 203–4

Taylor, Charles 53, 232
Troper, Michel 269–70
Tushnet, Mark 140, 142–43

Unger, Roberto Mangabeira 140–41, 142–43

Vara, Juan Santos 45
Viljanen, Jukka 88–89

Walker, Neil 43–44
Wegman, Jesse 33
Williams, Daniel K. 55–56
Williams, Patricia 143–44

Wittgenstein, Ludwig 108–9

Zakaria, Fareed 96, 98–101
Zeidler, Wolfgang 86–87
Zuboff, Shoshana 43, 50–52
Zuquete, Pedro 285